IN THE SHADOW OF THE SHTETL

Jessamyn Ward
Sing Unburied Song

IN THE SHADOW OF THE SHTETL

*Small-Town Jewish Life
in Soviet Ukraine*

JEFFREY VEIDLINGER

INDIANA UNIVERSITY PRESS

BLOOMINGTON & INDIANAPOLIS

This book is a publication of

Indiana University Press
Office of Scholarly Publishing
Herman B Wells Library 350
1320 East 10th Street
Bloomington, Indiana 47405 USA

iupress.indiana.edu

First paperback edition 2016
© 2013 by Jeffrey Veidlinger

Manufactured in the United States of America

The Library of Congress has cataloged the original edition as follows:

Veidlinger, Jeffrey, 1971– author.
  In the shadow of the shtetl: small-town Jewish life in Soviet Ukraine / Jeffrey Veidlinger.
  pages ; cm
  Includes bibliographical references and index.
  ISBN 978-0-253-01151-0 (cloth : alk. paper) — ISBN 978-0-253-01152-7 (ebook) 1.
Shtetls—Ukraine—History—20th century. 2. Shtetls—Ukraine—Vinnyts'ka oblast'—
  History—20th century. 3. Jews—Ukraine—Social life and customs—20th century. 4.
Jews—Ukraine—Vinnyts'ka oblast'—Social life and customs—20th century. I. Title.
  DS135.U4V45 2013
  305.892'404778—dc23

                                                        2013014359

ISBN 978-0-253-02297-4 (pbk.)

2 3 4 5   21 20 19 18 17 16

For those who shared their stories with us.

געדענקשאַפט

די בענקשאַפט
האָט פיל פנימער,
פיל פנימער און בליקן
וואָס יעדערער קען יעדעמען
דערשטוינען און דערשטיקן
נאָר דו,
דו זאַמלסט פנימער,
היטסט זייער טאָן און ניגון,
אַז ס'זאָל שוין קיינער
קיין מאָל מער
זיך ווידער ניט צעקריגן
מיט געדענקשאַפט.

באָריס קאַרלאָוו

Memory

Longing
Has many faces
Many faces and expressions
And each and every one of them
Surprises and suppresses.
But you,
You collect faces,
Safekeeping their tone and timbre,
So that nobody
Will ever
Quarrel again
With memory.

BORIS KARLOFF

CONTENTS

*Publication of this book
is supported by a grant from*

JEWISH FEDERATION OF GREATER HARTFORD

INTRODUCTION

When I first started searching for Jewish life in the small towns of Eastern Europe, the shtetls of Yiddish lore, I thought I would find only cemeteries and dilapidated homes, lifeless remnants of a vanished community. Instead, over the last decade, in dozens of shtetls throughout Eastern Europe, I have taken part in oral history interviews with nearly four hundred Yiddish-speakers, who have shared their memories of Jewish life in the prewar shtetl, their stories of survival during the Holocaust, and their experiences of living as Jews under communism. This book recounts some of their stories.

The story of how the Holocaust decimated Jewish life in the small towns, the shtetls, of Eastern Europe is well known. But it is a story that has been told exclusively by those who left—for America, Israel, or the major cities of the Russian interior—during or immediately after the war. These writers long assumed that nothing remained of the shtetls they abandoned; they variously portray their hometowns as "lost," "vanished" or "erased."[1] The shtetl has always been presented as an erstwhile space, an ur-homeland from which the Jewish people emerged. Sometimes this emergence is presented as a physical migration, as in "from the shtetl to the suburbs," and sometimes as an ideological awakening, as in "from the shtetl to socialism," and often as both.[2] It is a tragic reality that the Nazis destroyed most of small-town Jewish life in Eastern Europe, murdering millions of Jews in the process, and leaving only vestigial remnants of what had once been vibrant market towns. Yet tens of thousands of small-town Jews survived the war—in hiding, in evacuation, or in ghettos and camps—and then returned to rebuild their hometowns. Living in the shadows of the shtetl, they rebuilt their lives, reconstructed their communities, and refashioned their memories. These small-town communities, which survived mostly in Soviet Ukraine, were completely unknown to the outside world until the fall of the Iron Curtain.[3] Their continued existence, and the way their residents remember the last century, complicates the traditional narrative of twentieth-century Jewish history.

The assimilated Soviet Jewish intelligentsia based primarily in Moscow and St. Petersburg, and occasionally in Odessa or Kiev, has come to define Soviet Jewry for the world.[4] Memoirs and biographies of Soviet Jewish *refusniks,* dissidents, scientists, engineers, teachers, and commissars give the impression that they represented the extent of the Soviet Jewish community, and help perpetuate the image of the Soviet Jew as a dissident intellectual.[5] Scholarly writings on the Jewish experience in the twentieth-century Soviet Union also focus overwhelmingly on big-city life in general and on the elite in particular.[6] This trend culminated with Yuri Slezkine's *The Jewish Century,* an influential and provocative text that frames the twentieth-century Jewish experience as one of movement from the peripheral shtetls to the very center of cultural, economic, and political life.[7] Historians have privileged upwardly mobile Jews who reached the pinnacles of power; those who remained in their ancestral lands, often languishing in poverty, have been left out of the historical record.[8] Jewish collective memory has imagined the shtetl as a foil, or simply a wellspring from which Jewish modernity emerged. The Jewish cobblers, market-stall proprietors, barbers, and collective farmers who remained in the small towns and rural areas of Eastern Europe until the dawn of the twenty-first century were conveniently forgotten; they did not conform to the nostalgic image of "the shtetl" with its "simple and pious way of life" that inspired numerous works of literary fiction, Broadway plays, Hollywood films, and academic scholarship.

This study follows the lives of a cohort of individuals, all of whom were reared in the shtetls during the early years of the Soviet Union and were just starting out their adult lives when the world as they knew it was shaken and eventually destroyed with the Nazi invasion. The oldest were born in the midst of the First World War and the violence of the

Russian Revolution and Civil War. Many lived with traumatic memories of those early childhood moments their entire lives. Once the fighting subsided in 1921, they witnessed a period of intense change and material shortage as a new communist government overturned the social fabric of the community and sought to revolutionize daily life. Many of them enrolled in the newly established Yiddish-language schools only to switch schools—and languages—halfway through their education. They survived the forcible collectivization of agriculture that devastated the village economy and food distribution system, and witnessed the deportation and arrests of some 300,000 villagers, who were sent to so-called special settlements in Siberia, Kazakhstan, and elsewhere in Russia. The turmoil that collectivization wrought, combined with a deliberate policy of starvation to subjugate the restless region, led to the Great Famine of 1932–1933, in which at least 3.3 million people starved to death in Ukraine, the breadbasket of Europe.[9] Just as the economy began to recover from the famine and life seemed to be returning to a new normal, Stalin unleashed his Great Terror of 1937–1938, during which officials from the People's Commissariat of Internal Affairs (NKVD) arrested some 300,000 people in Ukraine. Nearly half of those arrested were eventually executed.[10] Many of Stalin's victims were members of the Jewish intelligentsia and spiritual leadership. In the city of Vinnytsya alone, some 9,000 people were massacred and buried in eighty-seven mass graves around the city.[11] However, the high percentage of individual Jews in the ranks of the NKVD meant that Jews were visible both as victims and perpetrators of the terror. The country had not yet recovered when the German Wehrmacht invaded in June 1941. Approximately 2 million Jews were killed in Ukraine alone over the course of the war, constituting about one-third of the total Jewish victims of the Holocaust. Few families survived intact; German executioners and local collaborators murdered entire communities. The survivors also suffered unimaginable misery in their struggle to stay alive under occupation or to escape the Nazi onslaught. When the horror finally subsided with the Soviet victory in Berlin, the war-weary survivors expected a new era of peace and prosperity. Instead, the Jews of Ukraine found that they were no longer welcome in a landscape that had been ethnically cleansed. Many of the remaining Jews were treated as ghosts who no longer belonged in the new ethnically Ukrainian republic. Those who had fought to victory were derided as cowards and were accused of having fought "on the Tashkent front," where many had fled in evacuation. Some Jews turned toward their religion for solace and comfort, but found that a new state policy of antisemitism discriminated against them professionally and against Judaism spiritually. Most married, had children, and later grandchildren, which brought joy and love into their lives. But today the Jews who remained tend to live far away from their beloved progeny, many of whom emigrated to Israel, America, Germany, or the large cities of Russia. The postwar era in general gave Jews few rewards for the sufferings they had endured. It is no wonder, then, that when asked to pinpoint the best times of their lives, many of the people we interviewed simply cried and shook their heads.

This book explores the experiences of some of the last Jewish residents of Eastern European shtetls, those who reside in the small towns of Vinnytsya Province, which includes, in addition to the regional capital Vinnytsya, the towns of Bershad, Bratslav, Mohyliv-Podilskyy (Mogilev Podolsk), Sharhorod (Shargorod), Teplyk (Teplik), Tomashpil (Tomashpol), and Tulchyn (Tulchin), as well as several smaller communities.[12] The province (*oblast*) of Vinnytsya came into being in 1932, when various districts (*okrugi*) of what had been the province (*guberniia*) of Podolia were consolidated. The new Vinnytsya Province drew from what had been Vinnytsya District, including the city of Vinnytsya (Vinnitsa) and the towns of Zhmerynka (Zhmerinka), Lipovets, Nemyriv (Nemirov), Khmelnytskyy (Proskurov), and Voronovitsa. From Berdichev District, the province drew the towns of Pogrebishche and Kazatin; from Mogilev District, the towns of Bar, Mohyliv-Podylskyy, Murafa, Sharhorod, and Yampil (Yampol); all of Tulchyn District, including the towns of Bershad, Bratslav, Haysyn (Gaysin), Kryzhopil (Kryzhopol), Tomashpil, and Tulchyn; and from Uman District, the town of Teplyk. The region is in the heart of the vast territory that the historian Timothy Snyder recently dubbed "The Bloodlands," where Hitler and Stalin's rule overlapped, and where 14 million people were murdered between 1933 and 1945.[13] Located far from the Soviet metropolises, this region was also slow to become fully "Sovietized" before the war. As Amir Weiner has argued in his study of wartime Vinnytsya, the province's chief city served as "the ultimate testing ground for the evolution of Soviet mythology and the quest for purity or a laboratory for social engineering for every political

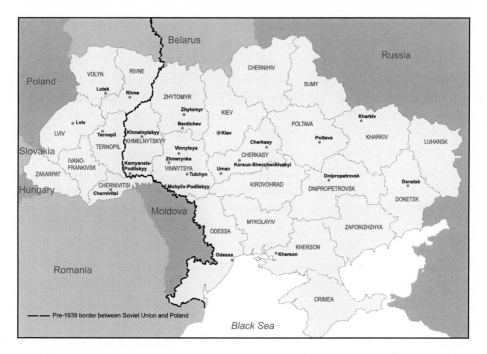

Ukraine

movement that gained the upper hand there."[14] At the same time, local party officials were forced to reckon with deep-held religious beliefs, Zionist aspirations, and endemic poverty in the surrounding towns before they could remake society in the image of Marx and Lenin. The Revolution here moved at the speed of evolution.

Although the focus of this book is on the shtetls of Vinnytsya Province, I also draw from several larger cities, such as Berdichev and Uman, which are neither shtetls nor within the borders of Vinnytsya Province. Uman is situated across the current eastern border of Vinnytsya in Cherkasy Province and was located in Kiev Province under the tsars. Berdichev, in contrast, is just across the current northern border of Vinnytsya in Zhytomyr Province. It too fell within Kiev Province in tsarist times. These cities figured very much within the real world of the Jews of that region, the boundaries of which extended beyond the hills and rivers immediately surrounding their own shtetls. Jews from Vinnytsya Province travelled to these larger cities for multiple purposes—work, trade, school, family visits, and religious pilgrimages. These larger urban centers also had significant Jewish populations, and continue to host sizable Jewish communities.

During the tsarist era, most of what is now Vinnytsya Province was part of Podolia Province, and it is as Podolia that the region has greatest resonance in Jewish popular memory.[15] It is here that pre-Soviet and Soviet collectors of Jewish folklore, like S. An-sky, Moisei Beregovsky, and others, concentrated many of their efforts, believing that the region, deep in the Pale of Jewish Settlement, was somehow "prototypically Jewish" and "authentic."[16] The Hasidic pietist movement began here in the eighteenth century, in towns like Sharhorod, Bratslav, and Nemyriv, as well as in neighboring towns like Miedzyboz (Khmelnytskyy Province) and Berdichev; the movement reached its apogee in the nineteenth century as rebbes held court in virtually every town. Hasidic doctrine declared that holiness could be found in even the basest of material objects. It shunned what it regarded as the gloomy and stagnant lifestyle of the rabbinate, and instead encouraged a life of fervent joy. Although the Hasidic movement encountered stiff opposition when it spread northward into Lithuanian territory, its successes in Podolia were largely uncontested. Its spread here was aided by the political discord that accompanied the disappearance of the Polish state in the late eighteenth century, and the region's incorporation into the vastly expanding Russian Empire.[17] Still today the area regularly welcomes Hasidic tourists and pilgrims, who travel through its cemeteries to pay homage to the graves of their deceased leaders, their *tsadiks* (righteous ones).

The province also includes an area that was known during the Second World War as Transnistria (not to be confused with the post-1990 breakaway republic, currently known as the Transnistrian Moldavian Republic). Transnistria was located along the plains that lie between the Dniester and the Southern Bug Rivers and came under Romanian control during the Second World War. Since survival rates were higher under Romanian rule than under direct German rule, Jewish communities in this territory remained more intact in the postwar period. Vinnytsya Province—along with the neighboring Republic of Moldova, and parts of the Transcarpathian Province—is unusual in that it retained a significant Jewish and Yiddish-speaking population into the postwar period. Other cities, like Chernivtsi (Czernowitz), Dnepropetrovsk, and Kiev, had (and have) much larger Jewish populations, but they tend to be transplants, immigrants to the city, rather than hometown folks. In towns like Tulchyn, Bershad, and Sharhorod, functioning Jewish communities continued to exist with elements of their prewar structure into the twenty-first century.

The primary sources for this book come from the Archives of Historical and Ethnographic Yiddish Memories Project (AHEYM; the acronym means "homeward" in Yiddish), which I co-direct. The archive, which is now held at Indiana University's Archives of Traditional Music, includes nearly four hundred Yiddish-language interviews, mostly with individuals born between 1900 and 1930, conducted in their homes or elsewhere in their Eastern European communities. In order to collect the interviews, I participated in numerous fieldwork expeditions throughout Eastern Europe with an international team led by the linguist Dov-Ber Kerler of Indiana University, and with the participation at various times of Dovid Katz of the University of Vilnius in Lithuania and Moyshe Lemster of the Hebrew University in Jerusalem. All three have deep commitments to the Yiddish language and to the people of the region, and particular expertise in the Yiddish of Ukraine, Lithuania, and Bessarabia respectively. We also traveled with a Belarussian administrative assistant and a Ukrainian driver, and alternated our expeditions between two professional cameramen—Artur Frątczak and Pawel Figurski—both graduates of Poland's famed National Film School of Łódź, who recorded all of the interviews. In later years, we brought along with us two graduate students: Anya Quilitzsch and Margot Valles.

We were able to find our interview subjects with the help of Jewish communal organizations that put us in touch with local Yiddish speakers, and through word of mouth, as those we interviewed directed us to their friends and acquaintances. Sometimes we just pulled into the center of town and asked if there were any elderly Jews in town. Oddly enough, nobody seemed particularly surprised by this question; some just pointed or gave us an address, and others hopped in the van with us and showed us exactly where to go. The most helpful would insist on staying with us until the interview was complete. I remember one young, lanky, and energetic fellow we picked up in the town square, who remembered that a "Jewess," a *Yevreika* in Russian, lived in the old Jewish quarter. He traveled with us from the broad downtown avenues lined with banks, cell-phone stores, and a statue of Lenin, to an area of town on a hill with narrow, meandering, cobblestone streets and dilapidated houses with tin roofs. He jumped out of the car and started hollering "Jewess, where are you?" An elderly neighbor man emerged from his house and shouted, "If you're looking for the Jewess, she lives over there!" Our guide vaulted over the fence, made his way past a kennel of barking dogs, and rapped on the woman's window, yelling "Jewess, come out!" An elderly woman wearing a colorful headscarf and flowered dress opened her door smiling, clearly thrilled to be the center of attention.

At other times we were less successful. In 2008 we took most of the afternoon to travel to a small village off the main roads, where we heard that a ninety-four-year-old woman was living, who spoke Yiddish fluently and had an acute memory. Through an acquaintance we had arranged to meet with a local man who would take us to her. We were delayed on route by a herd of cows that decided to graze in the middle of the road, perhaps munching on the grass that was growing through the gravel. When we arrived at the village center, identified by only a garage and junkyard, a burly chain-smoking man met us and took us to our would-be informant's son. But the son adamantly refused to allow us to meet with his mother: "I simply cannot," he kept insisting in Ukrainian. He explained that he had already lost his job once when people discovered that his mother was Jewish. He could not risk reminding the locals of this part of his past again. I felt sorry for his mother, imagining her sitting alone in her apartment while a group of young visitors waited outside aching to speak with her in her native tongue about her childhood and her life. But the Ukrainian son would not be budged. He wanted nothing to do with these Jews.

We initially designed the interviews with the primary goal of soliciting linguistic data: they were structured around a dialectological questionnaire, asking informants to translate phrases given to them in Russian into Yiddish. An important part of the interview process, though, entailed encouraging free speech by asking the subjects to speak extemporaneously about their lives and experiences. The questionnaire prompted them with specific queries about Jewish life cycles, family structure, religious observance, community organization, cultural activities, education, health, recreation, cuisine, and folklore, but each interview was unique and often deviated from the prompts. We talked about life, sometimes over food and drink. Personal narratives were punctuated with anecdotes, songs, and chitchat. Often we sauntered around town with our interviewees, asking them to show us Jewish sites of memory, such as the former synagogue building, market square, and mass grave from the Holocaust era. The team also photographed private archival collections, including legal documents, letters, photos, and war medals. We visited many interviewees on multiple occasions over more than a decade of research. As I sat in on these interviews, which were led by Dov-Ber Kerler and occasionally Dovid Katz or Moyshe Lemster, I became increasingly interested in precisely the free-speech segments. In addition to providing important dialectological data on the Yiddish language, these people were telling stories about Soviet Jewish life from a vantage point that I had never heard. The Jewish chess champions, scientists, writers, and dissidents that émigrés and urban intellectuals admired seemed to have little relevance here, where people tended to be most proud of how they persevered in their own homes and communities.

The communities this book studies are in dire straits. The younger folk have left or are in the process of leaving, either for Israel, America, Germany, or larger cities within the Former Soviet Union. As they depart, they usually leave behind the Yiddish language and the ways of their ancestors. Many will reject Judaism and Jewishness altogether in their new homes; others will come to appreciate their Jewish identity in new ways and take on leadership roles within world Jewry, a process already well underway. The focus of this book, though, is on the past rather than the future, and particularly on the ways the past is remembered.

This book strives to tell both the particular stories of a group of individuals and a collective history of their shtetl communities. In most sections I have sought points of commonality, drawing from our interviews to illustrate shared experiences and perceptions. At the same time, where differences occur either in opinion or experience, I have indicated those as well. As with all of us, the people in this book exist both as individuals and as members of a collective; I have sought to do justice to both sides of these identities. My lens, however, remains focused on the shtetls of Vinnytsya Province. Thus, when people leave the shtetl, as many more did than stayed, they exit the frame of my lens. Those who later return, reenter the picture, but I do not dwell on what happened when they were off camera, out of the shtetl.[18]

Part of this project, therefore, is concerned with the physical space of the shtetl in its Vinnytsya context. Other studies of individual provinces in the Russian Empire as a whole have helped us understand the provincial within a Russian imperial context, a context in which the provincial does not always orient itself toward the center but rather exists for its own sake. The best of these studies seek to do more than just add local color, but also force us to rethink fundamental assumptions about the operation of society. These microstudies have helped us move away from stereotypes and generalities in order to understand in greater detail the specifics of daily life and social interactions in specific locales.[19]

We conducted all the interviews "in situ," on location in our subjects' own homes, community centers, and neighborhoods. The shtetls in which our interviewees live are distinct realms of memory, in which the physical locale preserves what Pierre Nora calls a "residual sense of continuity."[20] This residual sense evokes specific memories, and shapes the ways in which the past is conceived. As we strolled by the sites of former synagogues, for instance, our conversations tended toward the religious life of the community. Even when our interview subjects were too frail to walk the streets, their familiarity with and continued proximity to these surroundings shaped their impressions of the past and guided the conversation. Familiar sites and objects helped evoke stories, memories, and the extraneous details of daily life that are not integral components of overall life narratives. Memory begins through association with one's physical surroundings. Memory cues, such as photographs, books, or buildings stimulate the mind and awaken the past. While these "testimonial objects" hint at a story, the narrative can only be fully articulated by a witness.[21] With a video camera capturing our every move, we toured towns with local residents, flipped through old sepia photographs, browsed through the ephemera overflowing from bookshelves and mantle pieces, and sampled family recipes, recording for posterity crucial memory prompts. Often—too often—these sites of memory included unmarked mass graves dating to the German occupation, the precise location of which is still largely unknown, or only vaguely understood as "in the forest" or "by the railway station." The video archive, which is available on the Web (www.aheym.org) and from which the material for this book was drawn, will therefore serve as an important supplement to the written word.

One other realm of memory that informs this book is the Yiddish language. In much of Eastern Europe, the Yiddish language itself has become the primary symbol by which the subculture of shtetl Jews differentiates itself from the larger community.[22] This has been particularly true since the decline of Jewish religious practice in postwar communist states. Although few Jews in the region—or indeed around the world—speak Yiddish today for everyday use, Yiddish often serves as a vital link for the elderly to the Jewish culture of their youth. By reminding them of their childhood through language, I believe we were able to help them retrieve memories that would otherwise have been inaccessible. Indeed, research on the saliency of the linguistic domain has demonstrated that certain memories can best be evoked in the language in which the experience transpired. By approaching our informants as a Yiddish-speaking group, we acted as a "saliency raising experience" and thereby called into consciousness memories that might be different from those they would recount in Russian.[23] At times, this difference is evident in comparisons between our Yiddish interviews and the Russian-language interviews that the USC Shoah Foundation Visual History Archive conducted with some of the same individuals. Language can also serve as an "activating event," allowing a core memory to resonate.[24] By speaking in Yiddish—the language of their childhood rather than their language of everyday use—our informants were also discouraged from retelling well-rehearsed life stories; their narratives were defamiliarized. Finally, Yiddish interviews capture the linguistic realm of memory and the past. There is no accurate way of recording prayers, songs, proverbs, folklore, and the "daily rounds of constant verbal interaction," to borrow socio-linguist Joshua Fishman's term, other than in their original language.[25]

Notably, our source base, restricted for the most part to Yiddish speakers, does not claim to speak for the entirety of the Jewish experience in the region. Those who grew up speaking Russian and have only a residual knowledge of Yiddish, or no Yiddish knowledge at all, were excluded from our pool of informants. We focused on Yiddish speakers because of the linguistic goal of the interviews, but there were also corollary effects of restricting our source base. For one, it provided us with a more manageable number of potential informants. We cannot claim to have interviewed every Yiddish speaker in the towns we visited, but I believe we did meet most of them. Second, those who spoke Yiddish fluently were also more likely to have been raised by parents who valued their Jewish identity and resisted assimilationist tendencies. The result is that this study likely emphasizes issues of Jewish identity more than would be the case than if we had interviewed a more representative sample of the Jewish population in the region, regardless of language preference. The smaller-sized and more cohesive population that we interviewed represents a subgroup of Jewish residents, who share some similar experiences and values, allowing for the construction of a collective life narrative.

ORAL HISTORY AND MEMORY

Extensive scholarly discussion has been dedicated to the vicissitudes of memory and the challenges of oral history. The study of oral history, which began largely as a democratic impulse to give voice to those overlooked in the written historical record, has expanded to include as well an emphasis on new modes of interpretation. Over time, scholars have come to understand oral history interviews as interpretative texts that demand narrative analysis. We now understand and appreciate the impact of social, political, cultural, and economic forces on the construction of life narratives, and the intervention of the interviewer on the conversation that constitutes an oral history interview.[26]

The social construction of memory has become a commonplace among historians and psychologists, most of whom have followed Maurice Halbwachs in recognizing that memory is a subjective experience constructed in collaboration with societal influences.[27] Decades of psychological research have shown that memory should not be imagined as a file cabinet in which raw facts can be retrieved at will in exactly the same form in which they were filed. Rather, memory is a process in which each articulation is created anew and reformulated for the purpose at hand. Psychological studies have shown that we have a great deal of difficulty with "source monitoring," that is correctly identifying the source of our memories; we are prone to confusing hearsay with our own eyewitness memories, and to filling in missing holes in our recollections with fabricated details. These lapses in our memory hold true for traumatic events as much as for the everyday.[28] Most of the studies that have been conducted on this topic, though, focus on traumatic events that have been highly publicized, showing how individuals confuse the public narrative with their own personal recollections. In cases where the events described have been less publicized—or even repressed—it is possible that personal visualizations may be more accurate. This holds true for oral history as much as it does for witness testimony. Elizabeth Tonkin coined the phrase "representations of pastness," an admittedly cumbersome phrase that alludes to the dialogic nature of the genre, which entails the conscious or subconscious representation of history by the teller, and the interpretation of that representation by the listener.[29]

Oral histories have proven to be particularly fruitful for understanding life in polities in which the public expression of personal opinion was suppressed.[30] Ideally, one can study "lived experiences" through diaries, letters, and newspapers, among other traditional tools of the historian. However, in a country such as the Soviet Union, in which many people were afraid to keep diaries and carefully censored their letters, and where newspapers routinely distorted their reports to tow the party line, the historian must look elsewhere for an account of lived experiences and daily life. Even archival reports are often unreliable, as government officials exaggerated figures and painted overly optimistic portraits for fear of reprisal if their quotas were not met, or for fear of accusations of sabotage. These official documents can reveal new information, but they can also conceal it.[31]

Since the collapse of the Soviet Union, an entire scholarship on "Soviet subjectivity" has emerged as historians have struggled with methods of obtaining access to the everyday lives of Soviet citizens.[32] One of the most productive avenues for accessing subjectivity has proven to be oral history. Oral historians have successfully mined life stories for insights into how individuals experienced Stalinism, the Second World War, and the Cold War, and how major historical events had an impact upon personal lives. These studies have provided us with rich descriptions of the daily lives of urban intellectuals and other privileged segments of society, those best placed to articulate and mold their experiences for public consumption, but have struggled to give voice to those located geographically and conceptually further from the centers of power.[33]

Oral history borrows from some of the theoretical tools developed by anthropologists in their field research. I have benefitted in particular from anthropologies of trauma and genocide, also conducted in places where memory was suppressed.[34] New scholarship on the Holocaust informed by anthropological and psychological studies of memory has promoted oral history as a means of getting beyond perpetrator histories, to study the events of the Holocaust from the perspectives of the survivors.[35] Scholars such as Jan Gross and Christopher Browning have utilized oral history to adopt microhistorical approaches to study the Holocaust "from below."[36] These scholars and others have considered oral history interviews, even those conducted many years after the events described, as a viable methodology that when approached critically provide much needed "thick descriptions" of events as they were experienced by survivors.

Indeed, psychological studies have shown that "flashbulb memories," particularly vivid recollections usually of traumatic or highly emotional events, remain detailed and specific many years after an event occurred.[37] Although it is difficult to determine how accurately flashbulb memories reproduce the events to which they refer, they have been shown to remain relatively stable across time.[38] In his study of oral testimonies recorded from Holocaust survivors, social psychologist Robert Kraft argued that "the most pervasive finding about memory for atrocity is its extraordinary persistence." Kraft differentiates between core memories, which are experienced vividly, phenomenally, and emotionally but also episodically and disjointedly, and narrative memories, which the individual constructs in order to string together a set of core memories into an intelligible narrative.[39] Christopher Browning similarly writes of finding a "core memory that has remained basically stable despite the passage of time and the geographic dispersion of the survival communities."[40] As Browning shows throughout his book, it is the small details that remain in the mind seventy years later, which most clearly define a life lived.

Oral history testimonies should be subjected to the same textual analysis as the written record. Like memoirs, inspector reports, and newspaper articles—all commonly mined by historians—each oral life story represents only the view of one individual at a particular point in time, and should therefore be triangulated with other sources. We were able to approach many of the people we interviewed in this book on multiple occasions, and in some cases could compare the testimony they gave us to that they gave to other organizations. This methodology helps mitigate the impact of a single interview. One of the benefits of oral history, as well, is that we can analyze the myriad of nonverbal signals that an interviewee provides. Careful scrutiny of facial expression, hand motions, velocity of speech, and other forms of body language and speech cues all provide important clues for interpreting the interview that no transcript can reliably reproduce.

As Paul Connerton has noted, few people bother to write down what they take for granted.[41] As a result, written contemporary documentary evidence tends to privilege the exceptional rather than the routine and the normal. It is only upon reflection long after events have passed that one notices in retrospect how norms have changed. In conducting our interviews, we did not ask for chronological descriptions of the interviewees' lives nor, with a few exceptions, did we ask about specific one-time events. Our interviews tended to ask more general questions, about the celebration of the weekly Sabbath, about schooling, about customs, and about relationships. We hoped, therefore, that the interviews would best utilize the natural contours of memory. They present not only a linear past, characterized by a succession of specific moments that build upon each other, but also a cyclical past, in which seasons and holidays recur year after year. Following Connerton, as well, our interviews sought to solicit not only personal memory—that is, the object of one's life history—but also cognitive and habit memory. The latter can be measured by the interviewee's Yiddish-language speech, as well as by their performance in prayer, song, and poetry recital, all of which provide clues to the daily life of the shtetl in the time of their childhood. To use some of the simplest examples, an interviewee who greeted us with the modern Israeli greeting of *Shalom* rather than the traditional Ashkenazic greeting of *Sholem aleykhem* or *a git elef* appeared as somebody who had little exposure to Jewish culture as a child, and had therefore adopted the modern Sephardic Hebrew pronunciation preferred in Israel rather than the customary Ukrainian Yiddish greeting. Most likely, the individual learned the greeting later in life, after the establishment of the State of Israel and after Sephardic Hebrew achieved its predominance among Judaic languages.

Many of the memories recounted in this book were told in the past habitual tense—"*me fleg . . .*" in Yiddish, approximately translated as "one used to." Although this grammatical formulation betrays vagueness to the memory, it is precisely this type of formulation that allows the historian to get a sense of the memory of everyday experiences. This is the grammatical tense used to describe unmarked routine. Those we interviewed were much more likely to recount individual extraordinary episodes in the simple past, but the quotidian details of daily life were less obvious to discern, hidden as they were in a flurry of habitual past formulations. I have sought to uncover the meaning behind these everyday occurrences.

I recognize that many of the stories we have recorded have probably been told and retold many times over the years, and were changed and reinvented with each telling. In interviewing the same person on different occasions, I have seen how certain phrases recur, while other details are added or omitted each time. Sometimes when we asked for clarification during a story, we found that when the same story was retold years later, the new details had been inserted. For instance, we once interrupted a story to ask, "Did he go to your school?" When the story was retold to us several years later in almost the same words, the story now began with the introduction, "I knew him because he went to my school." I imagine that at times our questions influenced the interviewee's storytelling in less benign ways as well, providing false suggestions, for instance, despite our best efforts to avoid these pitfalls. Sometimes uncomfortable details were often hidden from us, only to be revealed off-camera by the interviewee, or by a spouse or other relative who filled us in after the interview was over. The individual who actually experienced the episode left out a gruesome and traumatic detail when recounting the story to us, but the spouse who had heard the full story in all its details felt less emotional attachment to the episode and less shame in sharing it with outsiders.

On one occasion, when asked to describe her childhood, an elderly woman told us it had been a good childhood, full of family, friends, and civilized neighborly relations. Her middle-aged son, however, who was listening with us behind the camera, gruffly interrupted her to declare that her childhood had been miserable—she had been poor, hungry, and alone! The son was frustrated that his mother was whitewashing her childhood for outsiders. He had likely endured some forty years of listening to his mother complain about how difficult her childhood had been, and it seemed unjust to him that we were getting off easy. His mother, on the other hand, being confronted probably for the first time in her life with the invitation to succinctly summarize how she, in her twilight years, remembered her life experiences, chose to find joy in her youthful self.

I have also been able to compare some of our interviews with interviews conducted in Russian with some of the same people, usually a decade earlier, by the USC Shoah Foundation Visual History Archive. Comparisons between the two interviews demonstrate that on the whole, the core memory remains constant. Differences of emphasis, though, are apparent, reflecting both the timeframe in which the interview was conducted, the people conducting the interview, and the language of the discussion. When interviewed in Russian, for instance, people were more likely to talk about their youthful experiences in the Komsomol (the Young Communist League), whereas the Yiddish-language interviews brought out memories of Jewish holidays in greater detail. Part of this is a result simply of language—it is easier to detail the ritual of Jewish religious performance in Yiddish than in Russian, where one cannot easily distinguish between, say a *besmedresh* (house of study), a *shul* (synagogue), and a *kloyz* (house of prayer), all of which were different locales that served similar purposes. Our stated goals, to learn about Jewish life in the region before the war, also influenced how individuals told their stories.

When I began writing this book, I was intrigued by the small details of memory and forgetting, and planned to engage in deep analysis of my informants' constructed narratives. As I got deeper into the work, however, I became more empathetic to my informants' views. I began to accept and understand the trust that these individuals were placing in us by allowing us to record their narratives. I came to see my role as helping them channel their experiences into a coherent narrative, and I came to appreciate that they were telling us their stories so that their version of events would be known. Their experiences had been silenced for many years—marginalized in Holocaust historiography, which largely neglected the Soviet experience; marginalized in Jewish history, which saw the shtetl only as a product of a different era; and marginalized in Soviet history, which suppressed the unique experiences of Jews. I felt that to use their stories as raw data for a study of memory and forgetting would be to marginalize those stories once again.

I was inspired by Alessandro Portelli, who provides a model of how the historian can channel the voices of his or her subject as nonjudgmentally as possible. Portelli writes of the historian "constructing a coherent discourse" through the use of montage, sampling, and quilting in order to piece together fragments and bits and pieces of dialogue.[42] Most oral testimonies lack the coherence and sense of purpose that I was familiar with from written memoirs and autobiography. Written texts are usually the products of years of deliberate writing and rewriting in which the author ascribes meaning and relevance to a life narrative, whereas the oral testimonies we collected tended to be less coherent, less elaborated, and more open-ended than the written genres with which I was more familiar.[43] The fact that the primary purpose of the interviews was to acquire linguistic data also influenced the final result, both in the way those we interviewed framed their responses and in the questions we asked. As I wrote this book, I came to feel a responsibility for presenting, or channeling, the narratives of those we had interviewed, particularly as almost all those we had interviewed had died by the time I finished writing, in many cases leaving our recorded interviews as their only testimony. When asked at the end of their interviews if there was anything they would like to add, the most common answer was that they wanted their story to be told, as one individual put it: "Our children's children's children's children must know!"

It is for this reason that I have chosen to use real names in the testimonies rather than pseudonyms. After much reflection and discussion, I decided that the use of pseudonyms deprives individuals of their personal stories, of their lives.[44] The people in this book experienced their lives as individuals. It felt wrong to simply use them as data examples in some generalized and anonymous body of knowledge. These are their stories and should be told as theirs. In order to avoid the pitfalls of using real names, I have done my best to present their stories in an honest light as they themselves remember them. In order to ascertain the "core memory," I have chosen not to dwell on minor and insignificant variations in specific episodes or small anachronisms, except in a few cases where I could identify meaningful explanations for these discrepancies.

Recognizing the vicissitudes of memory, though, I have supplemented and corroborated our own oral histories with several major archival collections. I have used documents from the Soviet Extraordinary State

Commissions, which collected testimonies of war crimes in the immediate aftermath of the war, and from the archives of the Soviet Jewish
Anti-Fascist Committee, which include thousands of manuscripts sent
to the Committee during and immediately after the war about life under
Nazi rule in the occupied territories. The archival records of the Jewish
Sections of the Communist Party provided background to Sovietization
projects of the 1920s, and the archival records of the Council for Affairs
of Religious Cults provided information on the antireligious campaigns
of the postwar period. Local city archives, most of which I accessed
through copies at the Central Archives for the History of the Jewish
People in Jerusalem, also supplemented the historical record for the interwar period. Finally, newspapers, memorial books, written memoirs,
Soviet ethnographic reports, census records, and travel accounts provide
detail and corroboration throughout.

—⚹—

Following this introduction, the book is divided into nine chapters.
After considering the idea of the shtetl in myth and reality, chapter 1
focuses on the specific shtetls that this book discusses, introducing some
of the main characters and describing the differing traits of individual
towns. Chapter 2, "The Scars of Revolution," begins the chronological
narrative of the book in 1919 as pogroms terrorized the region and in-
augurated a decade of hunger and suffering. In chapter 3, we turn our
attention to the socioeconomic basis of the Jewish community, looking at the ways Jews in the Soviet shtetl sought to earn a living and the
impact that revolutionary change had on their occupational lifestyles.
This chapter deals mostly with the parents of our cohort. In chapter 4,
"Growing Up in Yiddish," our cohort begins their education; the chapter looks at the different school systems and modes of education of the
interwar years, and briefly addresses youth in the Soviet shtetl. Chapter
5 takes us into the synagogues to see the importance that religious life
continued to have despite the Soviet antireligious campaigns. In chapter
6 the impact of the anti-religious campaigns becomes clear, as Jewish
religious life is transplanted from the public to the private sphere, and
the home becomes a place of observance distinct from the synagogue.
Chapter 7 takes us into the Second World War. In Reichskommissariat Ukraine—the parts of Vinnytsya Province that fell under German

rule—Jewish communal life was destroyed and only isolated individuals were able to survive, each with his or her own harrowing story of escape and near-death. Only in Romanian-controlled Transnistria, the subject of chapter 8, was a semblance of Jewish communal life able to continue under occupation. This chapter looks at the fate of Jews in the ghettos of Transnistria with a focus on the Pechera concentration camp, on the banks of the Southern Bug River. The final chapter, chapter 9, looks at the postwar period, as soldiers returned victorious but weathered, to their hometowns, only to discover that they were no longer welcome.

NOTE ON TRANSLATION

I have tried to render the translations as accurately as possible, but recognize that much of the meaning may be lost in translation and that the process of translation and transcription is an interpretive act. Each translation was checked multiple times by multiple people. I apologize, nevertheless, if I have inadvertently misconstrued any interviewee's words. In choosing how to render an oral performance into a written transcription, I have made multiple choices. One of these choices was to omit needless repetitions and interjections. I recognize that this system implies a fluency in the conversation that was not always present, but I believe that this system more effectively renders the gist of the conversation to the reader and makes for an eminently more readable text.

In most cases, I have transliterated Yiddish and Hebrew words according to their pronunciation in Ukrainian Yiddish, with two exceptions: 1) I have transliterated Yiddish songs into standard Yiddish, maintaining dialect only if necessary to preserve a rhyme; and 2) I have used the *Oxford English Dictionary* spelling of Yiddish or Hebrew words that have made their way into English language usage (*Succoth* rather than *Sikes*; *heder* rather than *kheyder*; and *Sabbath* rather than *Shobes*). I have generally used the Library of Congress system for transliterating Hebrew and Russian and the YIVO system for Yiddish, but without diacritic marks. In order to preserve consistency in pronunciation, I have also generally rendered both *het* and *kaf* in Hebrew and Yiddish as "kh" when they are pronounced as "ch," as in the Scottish *loch*.

I have rendered most place names in Ukraine according to current Ukrainian usage, but without diacritic marks. I have made a few exceptions for place names commonly used in English: thus, I have rendered the Ukrainian capital as Kiev rather than Kyiv and have used Berdichev rather than Berdychiv. I recognize that the current Ukrainian usage may be unfamiliar to some readers steeped in Jewish or Russian history, but they reflect the reality of the geopolitical situation during the times I visited the region. I have given alternative names in parentheses at first mention. I have translated *oblast* as province and *raion* and *okrug* as district. I have generally rendered proper names of historical figures according to the *YIVO Encyclopedia of Jews in Eastern Europe.*

IN THE SHADOW OF THE SHTETL

1

The Shtetl

A HISTORICAL LANDSCAPE

Reading Yiddish literature as a child, I used to imagine the shtetl as a Smurf village, an oasis fantasyland populated with peaceful, joyous, and simple Jews, singing Yiddish songs and humming Hasidic tunes. This blissful flow of life would only be interrupted sporadically by the marauding Cossacks, who, I imagined, lived in the outskirts of the village, plotting like the Smurf's nemesis Gargamel against the Jews. My images were probably influenced by the likes of Maurice Samuel, who did much to bring the idea of the shtetl to American audiences in the 1960s, although I only encountered his writings much later. In 1963, he described the shtetl as an "impregnable citadel of Jewishness." "The Shtetlach!" he continued, "Those forlorn little settlements in a vast and hostile wilderness, isolated alike from Jewish and non-Jewish centers of civilization, their tenure precarious, their structure ramshackle, their spirit squalid."[1] In one of the first academic articles published on the shtetl as a sociological phenomenon, Natalie Joffe referred to the shtetl as "a culture island."[2] To Elie Wiesel, the Shtetl (spelled occasionally in his rendition with a capital S) is a "small colorful Jewish kingdom so rich in memories."[3] In Wiesel's imagination, "No matter where it is located on

the map, the shtetl has few geographical frontiers. . . . In its broad out-
lines, the shtetl is one and same everywhere."[4] It has become customary
to write about the shtetl as an ur-space located outside of any particular
time or place. Countless "composite-collective" portraits of "the Shtetl"
have emerged in the Jewish imagination, as though no further geographic distinction is necessary. Some refrain from naming individual
shtetls and instead write of an imagined "Shtetlland."[5] Wiesel's portrait
purposefully exemplifies the duality of this tragic and nostalgic image:

> Such was the fate of hundreds of communities. The enemy would sud-
> denly emerge with sword in hand, and in a frenzy of hatred, he would
> behead men, women, and children in the streets, in poorly barricaded
> homes, caves, and attics. The murderers would leave only when they
> thought the last Jew was dead. Then as if out of nowhere, a man, a woman,
> or adolescent would appear . . . life would once again begin flowing, bind-
> ing the abandoned survivors into a community. They would rebuild their
> homes, open schools, arrange weddings and circumcisions, celebrate
> holidays, fast on Tisha b'Av and Yom Kippur, dance on Simhat Torah,
> and make their children study Talmud: all that, while waiting for the next
> catastrophe. That was life in the shtetl.[6]

In Wiesel's colorful rendition, the shtetl lurches from tranquility to
catastrophe.

Today when most people think of a shtetl they think of Sholem
Aleichem's *Tevye the Dairyman,* or, more accurately, of Norman Jewison's adaptation of that story cycle as *Fiddler on the Roof.* Sholem
Aleichem's Tevye, though, lives not in a shtetl, but in a *dorf,* a village. It
was the non-Jewish Jewison who relocated him to a shtetl, as the small
town had become by the 1960s a synecdoche for Eastern European Jewish life. For American audiences in the 1960s, it was difficult to conceive
of Eastern European Jews living anywhere other than a shtetl.

The emotional impact that the Yiddish language and the shtetl continue to have on American Jewish culture is remarkable. Nowhere has
this impact been more evident than in the literary marketplace: modern novelists and nonfiction writers have continued to play with the
sentimentality of the shtetl, reworking these worn nostalgic themes toward new ends. They often portray the shtetl in epic terms as the focus
of a journey, a quest that will forever remain unfulfilled. In his debut
novel, *Everything Is Illuminated,* Jonathan Safran Foer imagines a fic-

tional character aptly named Jonathan Safran Foer, who travels through Ukraine in search of the elusive Trachimbrod, a shtetl that turns out to exist only in memory and ephemera. Similarly, Nicole Krauss—the spouse of the real Jonathan Safran Foer—writes, in her *History of Love*, of longing for an Eastern European past that can no longer be recovered. Daniel Mendelsohn's *The Lost: A Search for Six of Six Million* is, in many ways, a real-life version of Safran Foer's novel. Like Safran Foer's protagonist, the real Daniel Mendelsohn travels to Ukraine in search of his grandfather's world, to uncover the lost life of his great uncle known to the family only as "Shmiel. Killed by the Nazis." In the midst of all this searching for the lost, vanished, and erased, the real-life experiences of Jews who remained are often forgotten.

The Shtetl as an imagined space has trumped shtetls as real lived spaces.[7] Part of the blame can go to Mark Zborowski, a one-time Soviet spy and native of the city of Uman, who co-wrote the book *Life Is With People* in 1952, a pseudo-sociological study of "the Shtetl" that was produced in conjunction with a Columbia University Research in Contemporary Cultures project headed by Margaret Mead and Ruth Benedict. As Steven Zipperstein puts it, "*Life Is with People* examines shtetls not in their considerable variety but as instances of a single ideal type presented in the present tense, as if it still existed."[8] Zborowski and his co-author Elizabeth Herzog imagined a lost home in the midst of the Diaspora: "The small-town Jewish community of Eastern Europe—the *shtetl*—traces its line of march directly back to Creation," they wrote in the prologue, before speaking of "the road from Mount Sinai to the shtetl."[9] The shtetl for Zborowski and Herzog was one big happy family: "For the shtetl, the community is an extended family," they crooned.[10]

The shtetl also loomed large in the Soviet Jewish imagination, but with less bombast than in the West. For Soviet writers, the shtetl landscape was more than an imagined past; it was a sociological reality, rife with economic and political challenges. The Soviet passion for the industrial factory left the shtetl a spurned bride; small-town life was portrayed as exploitative, superstitious, and backwards. Although most Jews with roots in the shtetls of Ukraine had abandoned the region by the postwar period, and lived in the larger metropolitan cities—Kiev, Moscow, St. Petersburg—tens of thousands of others continued to reside in the shtetls of Ukraine. Soviet writers, as well, could still, on occasion, visit the shtetl and write about their travels through the region. Others used fictional and autobiographical genres to imagine their hometowns, sometimes doing so from abroad. Among them, Shire Gorshman, Fridrikh Gorenshtein, Shmuel Gordon, Itsik Kipnis, Hershl Polyanker and Elye Shekhtman all turned their gaze toward the shtetl, nostalgically lamenting the destruction of Jewish life.[11] Gordon, for instance, began publishing his story cycle *Shtetlekh: rayze bilder* (Shtetls: Travel Portraits) in 1966 in the Soviet Yiddish journal *Sovetish heymland* (Soviet Homeland). Like many American and Israeli writers, he grounded the shtetl in the literary imagination, associating the names of the Podolian towns with the writers who made them famous: Sholem Aleichem, Mendele Moykher Sforim, Dovid Hofshteyn, Avrom Goldfadn and Nahman of Bratslav. He wrote apologetically of traveling by bus instead of by horse-drawn carriage, as in the old days when travel was so slow that "you could count the branches on the trees."[12]

Most scholars now recognize that the shtetl has entered public consciousness not as a historical or sociological entity, but rather, in Arnold Band's terms, as "an imagined construct based on literary descriptions."[13] Historian Israel Bartal agrees, noting that "the literary image of the shtetl obliterated the historical facts and distorted the geographical maps."[14] Bartal notes the exclusion of non-Jews from the literary landscape of the shtetl, which, he argues, eviscerated the "complex ethnic mosaic" from the historical shtetl. Ben-Cion Pinchuk largely concurs, writing that the shtetl "became in the narrative of the Jewish people one of the more lasting symbols of life in the Diaspora,"[15] and that "the place of the *shtetl* in the dominant Jewish narrative was determined principally by those who left it, and frequently turned the small town into cliché stereotype, and symbol."[16] But Pinchuk is unwilling to see the shtetl solely as an invented landscape: "the shtetl was a real Jewish town, not a mythical Jewish world. There was nothing mythical about its portrayal as such in literature and in Jewish cultural and political discourse."[17]

In reality, a shtetl is simply the Yiddish word for *town*. It is a diminutive for *shtot*, or city. In other words, it is a little city. A town. A shtetl is sometimes defined as a market town, and indeed it was the presence of a market that most often distinguished a shtetl from its smaller cousin, a *dorf*, or a village. The definition of a shtetl, though, was always in the eyes of the beholder.[18] Historian Samuel D. Kassow defines it as a settlement "big enough to support the basic network of institutions that was essential to Jewish communal life" and yet small enough to be "a face-to-face community."[19] Historian Adam Teller, looking for a definition of the eighteenth-century shtetl, settled upon "a small settlement of less than 300 houses, which dealt mostly in agricultural produce, and at least 40 per cent of whose total urban population was Jewish."[20] Neither the tsarist government nor the Soviet government ever defined a shtetl, or a *mestechko*, to use the Russian-language equivalent. The 1926 Soviet census, for instance, distinguished between urban cities and rural villages, but invented no terminology to account for the difference between a major metropolis like Kiev and a small town like Teplyk, both of which were deemed to be urban. The shtetl did not exist as an administrative category in the Soviet Union, even though *mestechko* became a common Russian equivalent for the Eastern European shtetl. Nevertheless, official reports and publications discussed the shtetl extensively, even obsessively, and always recognized it as a distinct entity. They knew it when they saw it. The leading Party intellectual, Motl Kiper (1869–1938), for instance, after whom the Jewish colony Kiperovke was named before Kiper fell out of favor and was himself arrested, had estimated that in 1926 there were about 525,000 Ukrainian Jews living in shtetls, constituting about a third of the Jewish population of Ukraine.[21] The defining elements of a shtetl remained a small urban settlement with a large Jewish population, with both "large" and "small" to be determined by the expediency of the moment.

A shtetl is sometimes described as a Jewish town, and, in fact, many towns in Eastern Europe during the late nineteenth and early twentieth centuries were largely Jewish. Using data from the 1897 census of the Russian Empire, Ben-Cion Pinchuk identifies 462 shtetls with Jewish majorities, and 116 in which Jews constituted more than 80 percent of the total population.[22] "The single most important feature or characteristic of that settlement, the one that made it distinctive and unique," he argues, "was its being a Jewish town, a Jewish island and enclave, a world of its own. This basic fact, true for hundreds of towns, has to be emphasized, because while obvious to contemporaries who were familiar with life in the *shtetl,* it was treated as a literary concoction by later generations."[23] The fact of Jewish majorities in many shtetls was a significant attribute of the town. Gershon Hundert has even questioned whether Jews of eighteenth-century Poland should be considered a minority, since they tended to constitute a majority within their own communities and lived primarily among other Jews.[24] But despite the genuinely Jewish character of these towns, it would be an overstatement to insist that they constituted a world of their own. When he writes that the Jews were living in a "sheltered environment" or that they were "living in isolation from the surrounding societies,"[25] Pinchuk neglects the constant interaction with the outside Jewish and non-Jewish world that characterized most Jewish communities in small towns. In fact, there was constant interaction between the Jewish community of the shtetl and Christian peasants as well as Christian officials. The church that lurks in the background of most photographs and paintings of the shtetl has a purpose beyond providing linear perspective to frame the central scene. In recognition of the complex networks linking Jewish and non-Jewish communities around the shtetl, John Klier proposed that "the shtetl might better be envisioned as the centre of an economic-cultural zone, linking Jews to Christians and Jews to Jews."[26]

Shtetls, therefore, have too often been studied as abstract entities— either as historical places or literary myths—rather than as individual urban units. In the aftermath of the Second World War, survivors and émigrés published hundreds of memorial books, *yizker-bikher*, to memorialize their individual towns. These books, although containing valuable data and otherwise unobtainable reminisces of daily life in the shtetl, were often published haphazardly and usually lack a structured argument or scholarly direction. Because of the small number of émigrés from shtetls that fell within the prewar Soviet Union, there are also precious few memorial books for towns within Vinnytsya Province. Only a few studies have looked at individual towns or discrete regions during specific periods of time in order to help more clearly understand the nature of the shtetl.[27] While there are certainly commonalities within the shtetl experience across geographic borders, shtetl life also differed across regional expanses. Shtetls were profoundly impacted by their relationship to neighboring urban centers and rural settlements, their geographic setting, the political sovereignty under which they functioned, and a host of other factors. Sometimes, two shtetls across the river from each other would develop in radically different ways simply because political borders cut across the river. Never was this more true than during the Second World War, where one side of the Southern Bug River fell under Romanian control and the other under direct German control.

—∞—

The socialist writer Moyshe Olgin (Moyshe-Yoysef Novomiski), who left his native shtetl, near Sokolvika, just north of Uman, in the first decade of the twentieth century, described his hometown as follows:

> After a hill on the other side of the river you can see the shtetl in the valley. It seems as though someone playfully scattered around blue, red, green, white, and gray boxes. They are arranged in a beautiful pattern. They spread out from the river all the way to the edge of the hill. Perhaps they extend further still, but can't be seen because the sky begins. The boxes are the roofs of the houses. In my shtetl people cover their roofs with tin and they paint them, if they so desire. The shtetl shines with all types of colors.[28]

Olgin's description of the town's haphazard layout echoes the image of the shtetl portrayed by the Yiddish writer Mendele Moykher Sforim (Sholem Yankev Abramovitsh), who wrote, "The builders' art is despised there and its rules are never followed. Its houses do not stand upright, arrogantly challenging heaven, but are low. Some of them tilt precariously and their roofs are buried in the ground." Sholem Aleichem (Shalom Rabinovitz) described his fictional Kasrilevke similarly: "The houses themselves are small mud huts, low and rickety, and look like ancient gravestones in an ancient cemetery," and the streets, he continued, "are twisting and curving and wind about, running up hill and down dale, full of trenches and pits, cellars and caves, back lots and courtyards."[29] The Argentinean Yiddish writer Valentin (Velvl) Tshernovetski wrote of the houses in his native Teplyk: "There are three types of houses in Teplyk: the majority are orderly. That is, they are made of clay brick and are covered with a roof of tin or slate. Another group of houses, mostly in the backstreets, were built of earth and mud and the roof is covered with straw. A third group very few in number, are actually called palaces and are soundly built, have many rooms, several trees in front of the door, and are surrounded by a fence and a garden with flowers."[30] The same shtetl image persists across media: whenever the director of the

Moscow State Yiddish Theater, Aleskandr Granovsky, put the shtetl on stage it was always portrayed with a Constructivist set of ladders and platforms protruding at odd angles. In his 1925 film *Yidishe glikn* (Jewish Luck), the shtetl houses dissolved into cemeteries, with gravestones lackadaisically strewn about. Similarly, Marc Chagall's famous images of slanted houses in colorful panoramas provide pictorial reinforcements of Olgin's description.

The market, Olgin continued, consists of:

> two lines of stores that stand in the middle of the market. Opposite them are a few houses—Avrom Koretsky's inn, two other inns, and the big dry goods store. On the other side in a corner is the *besmedresh* [study house], surrounded by a picket fence. A little further is the church with its green spires. The non-Jews live on the mountain. There, past the pharmacy, one goes to the fields and vineyards. Along the way, on both sides, stand old high poplars.[31]

Shtetls of the Podolian region are typically nestled in valleys or alongside rivers. Established on the private lands of the Polish nobility, many also include a Polish noble palace and a Catholic church in the highlands on the outskirts of the town. Usually, the synagogue is on the opposite side of the town from the church, two bookends holding up the town. Sometimes, as in Sharhorod, a sixteenth-century synagogue was built as a fortress, outside the confines of the original town fortifications. These old stone "fortress synagogues" were built in part to protect the Jewish community from Tatar and Cossack invaders. The Sharhorod synagogue is located in the extreme southeast of the town—exactly opposite the church that dominates the upper northwest quadrant. Since Jews were usually forbidden from building their synagogues higher than the church spire, these original stone synagogues often had sunken sanctuaries beneath ground level, designed to allow for a spacious interior without violating restrictions on the height of the building.

The Jewish cemetery was usually separated from the town itself; the dead were put to rest on the other side of the river or in the hills above the town. In Bratslav, where the Jewish cemetery lies on a plateau overlooking a bend in the Southern Bug River, the dead have a stunning view of the meandering water as it flows past the mill. The Jewish cemetery was separated not only physically from its Christian counterpart,

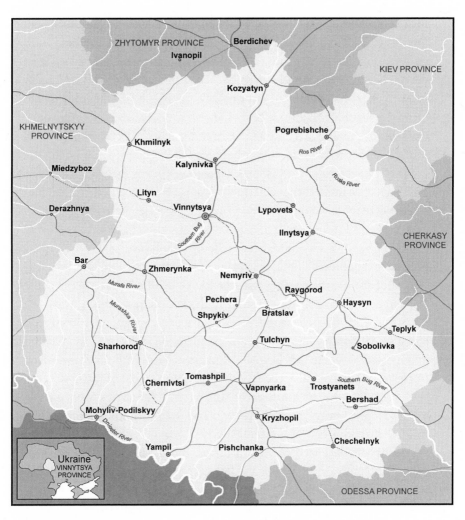

Vinnystsya Province

BRATSLAV

We first drove into Bratslav, a scenic town overlooking the Southern Bug River, on a scorching hot July afternoon in 2002. It was in Bratslav that Rebbe Nahman arrived in 1802 and "captured the city by clapping hands and dancing." Israel ben Eliezer, an itinerant faith healer and Nahman's great-grandfather, was known throughout the region as the Baal Shem Tov (Master of the Good Name), or the Besht, and was credited with establishing the pietist movement of Hasidism. As the Besht's direct descendant, Nahman had a credible claim to leadership of the rapidly growing Hasidic movement. To this day, the name Bratslav conjures to mind the Breslov Hasidim, a sect of Jewish mystics, who continue today to flock to Uman, where Rebbe Nahman, their *tsadik,* their righteous leader, was buried in 1810, to pay homage to his memory and spirit. The grave of Nahman's chief disciple, Nosn Sternhartz, ensures that Bratslav itself remains on the itinerary of many Hasidic pilgrims. We had already had a busy day, conducting interviews elsewhere in the region, and resisted the temptation to call it a day and head back to the regional capital of Vynnytsya, where we were looking forward to relaxing in the pub across the street from our hotel. As we approached the crystal-clear waters of the Southern Bug River, which meanders just north of the town in a southeasterly direction from the Podolian uplands toward the Black Sea, and watched a handful of children and Speedo-clad local men bathe in the cool waters next to the picturesque stone mill, we decided that we would search for Yiddish-speakers in Bratslav before rewarding ourselves with a swim in the river. We stopped an elderly passer-by on what seemed to be the main street, and asked if he knew of any Jews in town. "Not so many," he muttered, and pointed us in the direction of a small dirt road, where we found Moyshe Kupershmidt.

The first Jewish settlement in Bratslav dates back to the early years of the sixteenth century, when a Jew acquired a lease to collect taxes from the nobleman who owned the town, a common practice among Jews in early-modern Poland. Because of its strategic location on the river bend, Bratslav became a regional trading center that attracted Jewish merchants and artisans, who lived alongside the Polish nobility in the town. According to the 1765 census, there were thirty-five Jewish households in the town, comprising 101 individuals. The next decade saw a fire destroy forty houses in the town and a Haidamak pogrom that resulted in the deaths of several Jews. As a result, the Jewish population had declined modestly by 1776, the next year for which figures are available. By the early nineteenth century, the Jewish population had increased to 352 Jews, who now constituted more than 40 percent of the town's population. There were two synagogues in Bratslav by the early nineteenth century.[33] The town's fame today rests largely from the brief period between 1802 and 1811, when Nahman settled there. His arrival in Bratslav led one of his admirers, Natan Sternhartz, the son of a prosperous merchant from Nemyriv, to move to Bratslav in order to be near the great *tsadik*. Natan recorded Nahman's sayings and published them in his *Sefer hamidot,* and later edited Nahman's teachings, which he published as *Likutei Moharan. After his teacher's death in 1810, Natan published Nahman's fairytale-like stories in a bilingual Hebrew–Yiddish edition. These stories, with titles like, "The Lost Princess," "The Humble King," and "The Burgher and the Pauper" were not only instrumental to the spread of Nahman's teachings, but also to the development of Yiddish and Hebrew literature. They are even said to have influenced Franz Kafka.[34] By 1907, the Jewish population of Bratslav had reached 5,903, representing just over half of the total population. Jews continued to play integral roles in the economic life of the city, particularly in the mill and honey factory, which were owned by Jews.[35]

When we first met him outside his home on a small cobblestone road heading down toward the river in 2002, Moyshe Kupershmidt was in his eighties. His frame showed wear, but he had clearly been a muscular man in his youth. His intense eyes lit up at the sound of Yiddish as he greeted us wearing a tank top and beige ivy cap. Our driver, Petr, was waiting in his white Mercedes minivan on the cobblestone lane outside. The sounds of ABBA could be heard coming out of Petr's open window as we sat down with Moyshe: "You can dance, you can jive, having the time of your life / See that girl, watch that scene, diggin' the Dancing Queen." Moyshe inspected our van like a prospective buyer at a used-car depot before asking, "Did you bring the car with you from Israel?" assuming immediately that we were a group of Hasidic pilgrims from the Holy Land. We later learned that Moyshe was a professional driver and so his interest in our vehicle was more than just casual chit chat. When we told him it had been driven from Lithuania, he nodded and then, still assuming we were Israelis, asked if we knew of any news about Yasser Arafat.

He invited us in. We had to bend down to get into the front door, which led immediately into a tiny cramped kitchen. Glass jars of home-made compote sat on a rickety wooden table, next to a sink and tiny refrigerator. The living room, which doubled as a bedroom, was decorated with colorful rugs hanging on the wall. Souvenir American, Ukrainian, and Israeli flags were taped to the wall above his bed. Mezuzahs were clearly visible on every doorpost. The wide wooden floorboards looked about a century old, a reasonable estimate for the age of the house. The only running water in the house dripped through a spigot in the kitchen sink; an outhouse was accessible through the garden in the back. When we asked if he had been born in this house, he told us that he had actually been born two houses over, toward the river, but he had been living here for over half a century. When he returned to Bratslav after the war, he found that his house had been occupied by Christian residents who had assumed he was dead. The new occupants never imagined that the Jews who fled so suddenly in the summer of 1941 would find their way back. In the vast majority of cases, this assumption proved correct: the Yiddish speech that had echoed through market squares for generations was silenced overnight. When sound returned, it was overwhelmingly in Ukrainian, forever transforming the aural landscape. Rather than take his real estate claim to the courts, Kupershmidt had simply settled into a neighboring house whose owners really would never return.

As he led us into his living room, Kupershmidt inquired about our families and shared with us that his son and two grandchildren had left for Israel three years ago. His grandson, he proudly told us, was serving in the Israeli army. No sooner had we sat down in his living room than he boasted of his ability to write in Yiddish. Like a magician performing a card trick, he took out a pen and paper and began scribbling. A few seconds later he held up the paper: "This is Yiddish writing, not Hebrew," he asserted, as though he were showing us that our Six of Diamonds had turned into the Ace of Spades. As we set up our technical equipment, Kupershmidt continued his performance. He knows how to pray, he explained. His father had taught him when he was a child. And with that he launched into a list of the Judaic subjects he recalled from his childhood. "It's been seventy years since I learned to pray," he apologized. "I have forgotten so much."

BERSHAD

Bershad is situated on the bend of a small tributary to the Southern Bug River and is accessible only along a handful of winding roads that half-heartedly link it to neighboring regional centers. Even the roads to nearby Trostyanets and Chechelnyk are indirect, forcing drivers to go out of their way, past Olhopil, for instance, to reach Chechelnyk. Bershad has always been a bit out of the way. On our first visit there in 2002, Efim Vygodner, the head of the Jewish community, met us on the cobblestone street and took us on a tour of the Jewish quarter, Yerusalimka: "This was all Jewish," he boasted, "completely Jewish." "This was a Jewish house. This was a Jewish house," he pointed at each of the seemingly abandoned white brick houses, and assigned them an ethnic identification. In the geography of the shtetl, every street and every house has its own ethnic identity. This ethnic demarcation of public space was an important marker, serving as a reminder of the boundaries between communities, and was repeated wherever we went. Jews and non-Jews alike seemed acutely aware of the difference between a Jewish and a non-Jewish house. These differences were not just reflected in imagined ethnicities of past owners, but were also visible in architectural style.[36] Some of the Jews still living in these houses had inherited them from their parents or grandparents. They live there with a sense of permanence rare among contemporary Jews elsewhere around the world, who have made mobility one of the defining features of Jewish life in the twentieth century. But many of the Jewish houses in Bershad's Yerusalimka have not had Jewish owners for decades; entire Christian families have grown up in these houses, where mezuzahs mark the doorposts. There was no reason to believe that the erstwhile Jewish owners would ever return. There was a time before the Revolution, when the street itself had a Jewish name—the Jewish Street or the Synagogue Street—and the ethnic composition of the houses was explicit. But after the Revolution, the streets in the market were rebaptized as Proletarian Street and October Street, and the Jewish identity of the square was hidden beneath a veil of internationalism. Only the Jewish residents remember: they insist that even though the communists had confiscated the houses from the Jews, they remained indelibly Jewish houses. As one resident of a neighboring shtetl told us, as we strolled through her town, "This is a Jewish house, this is a Jewish house, this was a polyclinic of ours, this is a Jewish house. These were all Jewish houses. And behind that street are also Jewish houses. But now non-Jews live here." Much of the Jewish population had left the town since the collapse of the Soviet Union, leaving the architecture as the primary marker of the town's Jewish identity. Now even that was being lost. What had once been a Jewish shtetl was becoming a Ukrainian town.

In search of those Jewish houses in Bershad, we looked past the overgrown weeds that crawled along the collapsing fences. We slowly drove through the narrow cobblestone streets of Yerusalimka, bumping along what were supposed to be symbols of Soviet progress—Proletarian Street, People's Street, October Street—and made our way toward the center of the quarter, toward the synagogue of Bershad. "Look at the roof of our synagogue," mulled Efim as the peeling layers of roofing came into view. We would return to Bershad many times over the next decade and watch as the roof further deteriorated each year. In 2010, though, the sound of hammering echoed throughout Yerusalimka and a new roof was finally being installed with the help of money raised from abroad.

Even in its heyday, the synagogue was hardly spectacular: its white-washed pisé walls of earth, chalk, lime, and gravel blended into the surroundings: no steeple or turret alerted visitors from afar to the pride of the community. Like most synagogues of the region, the exterior architecture reflected the community's modesty. This was not the Main Synagogue, *Di hoykhe shil,* which was situated on the market square and had been turned into a communist club before the war. It was actually only a *shilekhl* (a little synagogue); it had once been the tailors' *shilekhl,* but since the war, it has been the only synagogue in town and one of the few in Vinnytsya Province. The plaster was peeling, the building's foundations were crumbling, the roof was leaking, and dampness pervaded every nook and cranny. The floor of weathered wooden planks felt spongy as our feet sank into the rot; in places, the earthen floor was visible beneath. Wooden benches faced the ark on the eastern side, where the Torah scrolls would be kept. Efim explained, however, that he keeps the scrolls in his home rather than the synagogue. There are a total of six Torah scrolls in Bershad, all of which are stored in private houses for safekeeping, he continued. The synagogue uses two scrolls: a small one that everybody agrees is kosher, and a larger one that a rabbi who once visited from Israel told them was not kosher. In the center of the synagogue is the *bime,* the elevated platform from which services are conducted. A string of small Israeli flags was suspended between two pillars in the back. Metal pails scattered across the benches collected water that was dripping from the roof. The walls were whitewashed with few decorations other than some posters of Hasidic rebbes taped to the plaster. Rabbinical objections to displaying human images in a place of prayer were apparently forgotten or ignored. A six-pointed star, a *mogen dovid,* with the inscription "How Goodly are Your Tents, O Jacob," the first line of the *Ma Tovu* prayer recited by Jews upon entering a synagogue and derived from Numbers 24:5, was painted on the ceiling.

Today the synagogue serves the tiny Jewish community of Bershad as a social hall, administrative center, and place of prayer. The Bershad *shilekhl* was one of only four synagogues in the entire province to remain open throughout the Soviet period; the others were in much larger cities, maintained in part as "showpieces," to counter accusations that the Soviet government discriminated against its Jews. The Bershad synagogue, though, was no showpiece. It is precisely its modesty in an out-of-the-way shtetl that allowed it to remain open, beyond the sight of Bolshevik bureaucrats in the capital.

Window slits were visible above the back wall where the women's section was located. Efim resisted our requests to go up to the women's section, warning us that it wasn't safe—the stairs were rotted and the floor above wasn't sound. He explained that there used to be a separate door and stairs to access the women's section from outside. After some persuasion, though, he ventured up with us. The attic room had become a storehouse of old sacred books, a *geniza:* boxes of frayed leather-bound books were piled atop each other, with holy texts overflowing from boxes and scattered around the floor—Talmud folios, Hebrew legal codes, prayer books. The storehouse in the women's section was an attempt to preserve this heritage and protect the folios. But time and neglect had foiled the plan. Torn pages were scattered across the floor, praising God's glory from beneath the dust. When we picked them up, the paper crumbled in our hands. Efim explained that books from all of the synagogues in Bershad had at some point been brought here for preservation. By now, though, there was little that could be preserved. In the corner, he pointed out a rusting *matsukah,* a machine for producing matzo.

The town of Bershad first appears in historical sources in the mid-fifteenth century as a fortress town. It subsequently came under noble ownership and by the seventeenth century had attracted a Jewish population. Like many other towns of the region, the Jewish community was devastated in the mid-seventeenth century. In 1648, a group of nomadic Cossack horsemen under the leadership of Bogdan Khmelnitsky rebelled against the Polish government ruling the region and attacked the Jewish communities, whom they viewed as agents of the hated Polish nobility. Ukrainians today credit Khmelnitsky with taking the first step in establishing Ukrainian political independence; his statue stands in Kiev's central square and his picture adorns the five-hryvna bank note. But in Jewish historical memory, the rebellion came to be known as *gzeyres takh vetat,* the evil decree of 1648–1649, and is remembered for the tens of thousands of Jews who were killed. The violence of the rebellion was followed quickly by war, which ultimately brought the town under the control of the Turkish Sultan Mehmet IV in 1676. It was returned to Polish sovereignty twenty-three years later. In 1776, a total of 267 Jews were counted within the city, and another 249 lived in the surrounding countryside.[37]

In the eighteenth century, Bershad emerged as a Hasidic center under the leadership of Rebbe Raphael, a student of Pinhas of Korets and one of the new charismatic leaders who were beginning to challenge the official rabbinical establishment of the region. Although Raphael did not leave any significant writings, his teachings circulated through stories told by his followers; several of his sayings were published posthumously. Raphael is best known for two things: honesty and smoking. Two stories, or perhaps two versions of the same story, relate how a police officer caught him smoking contraband tobacco. When he confessed that the tobacco had been smuggled, the officer commended him for his truthfulness and let him go without punishment. The freethinker, Abraham ber Gotlober, who spent time among the Hasidim of Bershad in the mid-nineteenth century and who personally claimed to have dined at Raphael's table and learned from his sermons, wrote of the Bershad rebbe: "'It is forbidden for a man to be proud' and 'woe to a man who speaks a lie,' etc. These were his teachings and these he brought in his words to all his relations all the days of his life."[38] Gotlober is also one of the sources of a story about Raphael's unusual death. According to Gotlober, the rebbe was called as a witness against a Jew he knew was guilty. Unable to present false testimony and unwilling to condemn a fellow man, Raphael is said to have died on the spot. While this story is likely apocryphal, it tells a truth about how the Jewish community of Bershad sought to present itself to the world and of the ideals that the followers of Raphael were exhorted to value.

The Bershad Hasidim, sometimes called the Breshter or Bershidir, prided themselves on their honesty and humility. Even the great Raphael himself is commonly commended for being a simple man of the people. He is said to have shopped in the marketplace and carried his own vegetables home, to have dressed in modest clothes, and to have sat in the back of the synagogue or stood behind the door during prayer. Raphael is said to have encouraged small-scale manufacturing and manual labor, which can be performed for the sake of God, and was likely instrumental in transforming Bershad into a local center for the manufacture of prayer shawls (talliths, or *taleysim* in Yiddish) and garment fringes (tsitsith). Because of their skills in tallith making, residents of Bershad were known as Bershad Taleysniks. Podolians from neighboring towns prided themselves on their Bershad-made prayer shawls.

When the freethinker Mikhah Yosef Berdyczewski, who was raised in Dubova, near Uman, visited Bershad in 1887, his impressions were dim: "A dark spirit hovers over the entire city and all the heads are bowed and bent." Berdyczewski looked back at the golden age of the city. "A long time ago the chief trade in our city was religious goods, they made talliths and tsitsiths and the majority traded in this plentifully," but now,

> in this entire large city, there are many poor folk and only a trifle few wealthy . . . even living conditions are very difficult because of the crowded conditions: twenty people live in a single house as a result of which no air gets into them . . . the majority of youth live in darkness because the Talmud Torah [Jewish public school] has deteriorated and Enlightenment has not made any inroads. In this entire city you won't find a single person with any concept of our books or our nation. In general, this city is isolated and has no connection to the rest of Israel.[39]

By the early twentieth century, the town was showing signs of growth, with the establishment of an independent bank, as well as a distillery, a brewery, a sugar refinery, a mill, an iron foundry, a printing house, a haberdashery, and timber and produce stores. A market and bazaar also fueled commerce in the town. During the violence and pogroms that accompanied the Civil War of 1918–1919, several Jews, inspired by Zionist self-defense ideology, organized a defense brigade, several members of which gave their lives defending the town during a pogrom on March

14, 1919. When the Bolsheviks moved into the city in April, the violence and rioting intensified, leaving thirty-one Jews dead. The city repeatedly switched hands during the spring and summer of 1919, and in August of that year, twenty-two Jews were killed in a pogrom as Soviet and Ukrainian forces clashed. Throughout the remainder of the year, Jews were forced to pay tribute to the Ukrainian conquerors until Bolshevik forces took the city in April 1920. During the two years of civil war, approximately 150 Jews were killed in pogroms and fighting. By comparison, the next few years brought peace, if not prosperity, to the small town.

The census of 1924 showed 9,371 residents in the city, of whom 6,979 were Jewish and 1,657 were Ukrainian, with most of the remainder identifying as Polish. The Jewish workers of Bershad seemed disinterested and distant from the revolutionary turmoil and excitement engulfing the region. Their hearts were more set on emigration, whether to Palestine for the many Zionists in the town, or to America. A correspondent who visited the town in 1925 was struck by the absence of Jews in the local revolutionary movement and commented that "all cultural and political work in the unions is done by Russians."[40] The Jewish Sections of the Communist Party tried to spread their message of communism, but Bershad proved to be infertile ground for revolutionary activism.

TEPLYK

In his book, *Teplyk, My Shtetl: Chapters from Fifty Years of Life,* published in Buenos Aires in 1946, Velvl Tshernovetski, who was born in Teplyk in 1898 and emigrated to Argentina in 1922 after a brief stint in Odessa, situates the geography of his hometown:

> If you look on a map of Europe or even just of Russia, you will not find Teplyk. You could take the biggest map just of Ukraine and prepare the biggest telescope and I'll be darned if you can find my shtetl, Teplyk. And you know why? Perhaps you think that Teplyk is not an important point in the world? Perhaps you believe that Teplyk has, God forbid, committed some type of sin before the geographic world so that it will be ignored and forgotten? God forbid! Teplyk is, on the contrary, a big shtetl with its own fair that takes place every second week (Mondays) . . . Why then doesn't Teplyk figure on the world map? Here is the explanation: Teplyk does not have its own train line! Teplyk is located seven versts from

a train station, and if this is still a small misfortune, then the second misfortune is even greater! The railway station carries the name of the shtetl "Kublitch." A shtetl that is as big as a yawn, and where there are more goats than houses![41]

Teplyk remains off the beaten track to this day; it is located 44 kilometers north of Bershad, and 63 kilometers from Uman by road. Highway M12, which connects Nemyriv to Uman, traverses about 20 kilometers north of Teplyk, leaving Teplyk accessible only by smaller roads. When we first entered the city in 2002, a horse and wagon with a family of five was trotting down the main thoroughfare, mingling with the faded green and brown Ladas spewing exhaust as they chugged around town. Our white Mercedes van with Lithuanian license plates was clearly out of place. We parked in the town square. As we opened the door of the van, we were greeted by Boris Chechelnitskii, who had noticed the strange car coming into town and, automatically assuming that we were Hasidic pilgrims—who else visits Teplyk from abroad?—wanted to introduce himself as the mayor of Teplyk. He told us there are only about forty Jews left in the town, and of those only about ten are "pure" Jews. The rest, he continued, are—like him—the offspring of intermarried families.

The Jewish community of Teplyk dates to the seventeenth century, when the town was incorporated into the vast holdings of the Polish noble Potocki family. The residents of Teplyk made a living mostly in trade and as artisans, working as cobblers, tailors, and smiths. The town is perhaps best recognized in Hasidic lore as the hometown of Rabbi Moshe Yehoshua Bezhilianski, better known by his pseudonym Alter of Teplyk. Bezhilianski, a follower of Breslov Hasidism, made his mark in neighboring Uman, where he was known for his writings on the importance of prayer and meditation. It is little wonder that Teplyk's most famous son achieved his reputation glorifying isolation and inwardness.

Another story tells of how the Breslov Hasidim, who formed the town majority in the early nineteenth century but were countered by a strong freethinking minority, invited a disciple of Natan Sternhartz, Yitzhak Ber Meir Trhovitse, to reside in the town. According to Breslov sources, Yitzhak arrived and convinced the freethinkers to abandon their heretical ways. The town also comes up in one of Sholem Aleichem's stories. In "The Convoy," the wealthy miser Sholem-Ber Tepliker of Teplyk is arrested for chucking his household slop onto the street, and is led to court with two other prisoners to nearby Haysyn. When their drunken guard takes a nap, Sholem-Ber Tepliker of Teplyk is forced to listen to the life stories of his two pitiable fellow prisoners, and comes to repent for his past sins, resolving to treat the poor with greater respect in the future.

By the turn of the century, Teplyk was still a small, largely Jewish town that figured in literature and memory mostly as one of several backwater towns deep in Podolia. Sholem Aleichem dubbed the railroad that ran by Teplyk "the Slowpoke Express." "What did Teplyk, Golta, or Haysyn need a railroad for?" he has the locals ask in a 1909 entry of his *Railroad Stories*.

According to Tshernovetski, the Jews of Teplyk were engaged predominantly in trade and handicrafts. Most Jews had no stable source of income, but earned what they could buying and selling in the Sunday afternoon market or at the small local fair that Teplyk hosted every second Monday. Those with anything left over to sell could travel to one of the other fairs hosted by neighboring towns on different days. Tshernovetski describes how "Sunday in the morning the gentiles would begin to gather in the shtetl and the Jews and Jewesses would already be in the street and the market prodding the gentile's wagon and asking 'what do you have there?' And the gentile who comes by foot on a market day carrying a chicken, has a hundred hands prodding and haggling."[42] He portrays the Jewish traders as swindlers, trying to outsmart the peasants who come to town on market day. Despite painting a generally idyllic portrait of Jewish life in the town, Tshernovetski does not shy away from praising Christians and chastising Jews. He describes, for instance, a gentile doctor who would visit Jewish homes and "sit by the bed of the patient, and with love begin to speak in such a way that the patient would start to feel better. For a visit he would take a half dollar. But if somebody put 20 kopeks in his hand, he would also say 'thanks' and if somebody had nothing to give he would also not be angry." The Jewish doctor, on the other hand, would quickly write a prescription and "stretch out his hand for money. And if someone gave him 20 kopeks, he would throw it in their face!"[43]

The 1897 census listed the town's Jewish population at 3,725. According to Tshernovetski, the town had seven prayer houses at the turn of the century, including a great synagogue where the wealthy prayed, a study hall, and several prayer houses (*kloyzn*), preferred by the Hasidim. The town remained predominantly Hasidic, but it had a noticeable Zionist inclination. Tshernovetski writes of one *melamed* (teacher), who taught his students to begin their prayers with "Barukh" rather than "Burikh," thereby utilizing the Sephardic pronunciation of Hebrew preferred by the Zionists rather than the Ashkenazic pronunciation that had been traditionally used in Eastern Europe and continued as the Orthodox mode of prayer. Another teacher kept a library with several dozen Hebrew books by proto-Zionist authors such as Abraham Mapu and Peretz Smolenskin, which he discreetly would lend out to intellectually adventurous students. The same teacher, though, delighted in telling the children stories of miracle workers.[44] In Teplyk, as elsewhere, mystical pietism coexisted with liberal nationalism. The town was one of many that suffered during the pogroms of 1919, with a reported 350 Jews killed in a single incident of violence.[45] In 1923, as Jews sought their fortunes elsewhere, the town's Jewish population was listed at 2,860, and had further shrunk to 1,233 in 1939, on the eve of the Second World War.[46]

TULCHYN

About 70 kilometers northwest of Bershad, past Trostyanets, is Tulchyn. The city itself is due west of Teplyk, but is accessible from Teplyk only by traveling north past Haysyn and Bratslav. In 1726, Tulchyn was purchased by the Polish nobleman Stanisław Potocki. When Potocki died six years later, he left the property in the hands of his heirs, who would come to amass enormous holdings in the region, and kept Tulchyn as a major trading center. Felix Potocki, who ruled the town in the late eighteenth century, oversaw its expansion and development as the largest Jewish center in the region. It was Felix, as well, who built the 1780 Palladian palace that still greets visitors to Tulchyn today. The building mimics the classical temple architecture of ancient Greece, with its symmetrical design and Ionic columns supporting a colonial balcony that stretches across the length of the immense palace. Behind the palace is a large park leading to the Selnets River, a tributary of the Southern Bug that flows along the northern edge of the town. The vast parks surrounding the palace—long held privately by the noble family who guarded their usage—became a symbol of progress during the Soviet era, when the government expropriated the palace and the park and opened them up for public access. Lacking the funds to build entertainment palaces and clubs, the best the local government could do to provide leisure facilities for its citizens was to tear down the park gates. Directly across from the palace to the south is the Cathedral of Christ's Nativity, constructed in the 1780s as a Catholic church on the spot of what was once a Dominican monastery. The Potockis would at one time have enjoyed the forests, land, and river surrounding their vast palace, and attended the church to the palace's south.

For most of the Jews in the town, though, the Potocki palace was of lesser interest than the court of Rebbe Borukh, the grandson of the Baal Shem Tov, who in 1781 moved from Miedzyboz to Tulchyn, where his father, the Baal Shem Tov's son-in-law, was born. Borukh followed the example of the Potockis and established an opulent court for himself in Tulchyn, earning the nickname the Prince of Tulchyn. His followers spoke his name with reverence, his critics with derision. Borukh hoped to establish himself as the heir to the Baal Shem Tov, but his quarrelsome nature and extravagant lifestyle failed to appeal to the broad public. Legends of Borukh of Tulchyn are rife with arguments and battles— between Borukh and his nephew, Nahman of Bratslav, and between Borukh and Shneur Zalman of Liady. Nahman would become a leader of Breslov Hasidism and Shneur Zalman of Habad Lubavitch Hasidism, both vast movements still highly influential today. Borukh, though, is largely forgotten, not even famous in Tulchyn. According to Hasidic legend, the Baal Shem Tov stopped appearing to Borukh in his dreams and instead interrupted the sleep of Nahman of Bratslav, thereby anointing the younger *tsadik* as his heir and bypassing the arrogant grandson.

By the early nineteenth century, the leadership of the Tulchyn Hasidim had passed to the students of the Seer of Lublin, who trumpeted the mystical and supernatural abilities of the *tsadik* to intervene with the Divine and annul Divine decrees. But with the growing popularity of the Breslov school of Hasidism in the region, followers of Natan Sternhartz soon set up camp in Tulchyn, becoming the dominant Hasidic court in the town by the middle of the century, only to be surpassed by the Talne Hasidim toward the end of the century. There was also a small group of Hasidic opponents, led by Akiva Sholem Chajes, at least until

Chajes himself renounced his opposition and joined the followers of the redoubtable David of Talne.

The 1,300 Jews who resided in Tulchyn in the early nineteenth century failed to make a positive impression on Tulchyn's most famous son, Colonel Pavel Pestel. After taking part in the Napoleonic wars of 1812, Pestel became commander of the Vyatka Infantry Regiment, quartered in Tulchyn. While abroad, he imbibed Republican ideas and, when he returned intoxicated with Revolution, wrote a proposal for the establishment of a liberal constitutional government in Russia. The "Southern Society" he established advocated the overthrow of the monarchy and the installation of a new government modeled on Pestel's constitutional proposal. He had no place for the Jews in the liberal utopia he hoped to establish, though. He recommended the Jews be expelled to Central Asia. After the failed December 1825 rebellion, Pestel was arrested in Tulchyn and later hanged in St. Petersburg's Peter and Paul Fortress. The fact that the most radical ideas of the French Revolution could be heard even in "faraway" Tulchyn provides clear evidence that the shtetl was never an isolated island of tradition.

Tulchyn continued to expand throughout the nineteenth century as a trade and manufacturing center, particularly of sugar, beer, soap, and leather. Its status as a leading trading post, however, was threatened when the new railroad passing through southwestern Russia bypassed Tulchyn. The anti-Jewish vandalism that took place in the city in late May 1882 further led to the town's decline, damaging the market where the Jewish stores and houses were concentrated. In 1896, the city had about 22,000 residents, 18,000 of whom were Jews. A report from the time noted that the "economic condition of the shtetl is not bad" and "on a par with, even better, than many other shtetls of Podolia."[47] The town's economy was buoyed by the tobacco factory, brewery, soap factory, and leather factory. By the early twentieth century, the Jewish community was supporting a synagogue as well as eighteen prayer houses and a hospital. Boys received traditional educations in one of the city's seventy heders, and girls had since 1867 benefited from the opportunity to study in a modern private school. Tulchyn was not bypassed by the flowering of cultural activity that followed the 1905 Russian Revolution: a library was established in the town, as well as a private Jewish boys' school, another Talmud Torah, and rival Zionist and Bundist youth movements. Before the First World War, there were some two hundred stores in Tulchyn, almost all owned by Jews. Jews also worked in town as professionals: doctors, dentists, midwives, apothecaries, teachers, and insurance salesmen. There were 262 Jews left in Tulchyn when we first visited in 2002, only a handful of whom spoke Yiddish.[48]

SHARHOROD

Sharhorod is located 70 kilometers west of Tulchyn, past Shpykiv, at the confluence of the Murashka and Kolbasna rivers. When we visited in 2002, we strolled up and down Lenin Street and Karl Marx Street, the former Yidishe Gas (Jewish Street), which brackets the main market square. Although the communist duo had been out of favor for more than a decade, nobody had yet bothered to rename the streets in this out-of-the-way hamlet. Abandoned houses still bore the marks of mezuzahs on their doorposts, but inside only chickens made their homes. In one house, feathers gently floated around the empty room, circling with the wind that blew through the broken windows. Outside, a goat bleated, tied to a tree with rope. A lone chicken roamed through the empty square. In the early twenty-first century, the town still retained its nineteenth-century layout and residential area. The historic preservation of the town center has come at the price of modernization—many houses still have outhouses, and urban amenities are hard to come by, but it has made for a very scenic background, earning it a place in numerous recent films about the shtetl. Among the city's most noticeable highlights are the Orthodox monastery, the Catholic church, and the sixteenth-century fortress-style synagogue. The synagogue still stands in the southern portion of the town, even though it was converted into a juice factory after the war. The synagogue had undergone several renovations over the centuries, leading to numerous legends about its longevity. Many of these legends tell versions of how the synagogue was "discovered" rather than built. In one variant recounted by Mordechai Cooper in his book about Sharhorod, some children were playing on a hill, digging into the ground when they hit upon the tip of a cornice, and "when they started to dig further, they found the synagogue just as it stands today, in every detail."[49] Asya Barshteyn, an energetic woman who was born in the town in 1928, traveled with our team from her home in Vinnytsya back to Sharhorod in 2005 to show off the sites. She told us a similar story she heard from her mother, about how the synagogue survived calamity because it was buried underground. Cooper insists that its Torah scrolls were five or even six hundred years old. The souls of the dead were said to come to the synagogue from the cemetery at night—it was therefore always advisable to knock before entering in order to allow them to disperse. In its day, the synagogue was but one site of prayer, surrounded by several prayer houses used by the various Hasidic groups that vied for supremacy in the town.

The town was established in the sixteenth century by the Polish crown as a bulwark against Turkish invaders and as a trading center on the crossroads of several trade routes through the region. The territory was granted to Jan Zamoyski in 1579 and given the rights of Magdeburg Law in 1588. The fortress-style synagogue was built the following year, and the Jews coexisted with Catholic and Orthodox Christians in the town. In the seventeenth century, the town emerged as one of the largest in Podolia, largely due to its location along the wine- and cattle-trading routes between Wallachia and Piast Poland. When the town was occupied by the Turks between 1672 and 1699, it was dubbed "Little Istanbul," a name that allowed for an opportune pun on the names of Sharhorod and Tsargrad (a Russian name for Istanbul). By the time of its return to Polish hands, the town had developed a reputation as a center of mysticism, owing in part to the local influence of Sabbatianists, followers of the seventeenth-century false Messiah Shabetai Tsevi. The famous German rabbi Jacob Emden spread reports of orgies, wife-swapping, and black magic taking place in Sharhorod under Sabbatian influence. Among the miracle-working rabbis who resided there during this period were Naftole Herts son of Aaron Kohen, and Avrom son of Meir, both of whom are buried in the old Jewish cemetery. Dovid Tzevi, the father-in-law of Natan Sternhartz, served as rabbi and head of the yeshiva in Sharhorod, thereby tying Sharhorod to the Breslov Hasidim. Sternhartz himself got married in Sharhorod in 1793 and lived in his father-in-law's home there for two years. Ya'akov Yosef of Polonne, the author of the seminal Hasidic text *Toldot Ya'akov Yosef,* served as Sharhorod's rabbi for four years before being driven out by the community. Legend has it that upon his exit from the town, under police escort, he turned back and cursed the residents who had expelled him. Later in the nineteenth century, the town became a center of Sadagora Hasidism—the opulent and ostentatious leader of the Ruzhin dynasty, Israel Friedman, even visited the city himself in 1825, thirteen years before his arrest for the murder of two Jewish informants, a charge that was never substantiated. The Jewish community, as well as the Christian community, continued to grow throughout the eighteenth century; there were 283 Jewish houses there in 1799. A survey of that year noted that "Jews carry out trade in goods brought from Berdichev and other locations" and counted among Jewish artisans fifteen tailors, eight cobblers, and ten bakers, as well as furriers, glaziers, silversmiths, a coppersmith, and a watchmaker. A salt storehouse, three distilleries, a copper smelting works, and a tannery were also run by Jews.[50]

Relations between Jews and Christians in the town remained generally cordial throughout the nineteenth century. Sharhorod was spared violence during the wave of pogroms that swept the region in 1881–1882. The closest the town seems to have come to experiencing a pogrom was in April 1885, when a group of drunken peasant military recruits began harassing Jews on the street. According to one newspaper report,

> A crowd of Jews gathered to defend themselves and then a genuine fight broke out. All the stalls and stores were closed in an instant, and the women took cover in cellars. A rumor that they are beating the kikes quickly spread through the entire city. The local peasants instantaneously ran into the bazaar, and were already prepared to make a run for the stalls, but word that a boy had been killed quickly cooled the crowd of burghers and peasants, who feared responsibility for the murder, and quickly dispersed to their homes.[51]

After the May Laws forbade Jews from residing in villages, Jewish refugees from surrounding villages began to settle in Sharhorod. Many who came to reside there temporarily during the High Holidays were not permitted to return to their village homes. The town was then engulfed with endemic poverty and homelessness as the new refugees sought work and shelter. In response, in the 1890s, the Jewish community engaged in several communal building projects, including a renovation of the synagogue, the construction of a new bath, the establishment of a private school, and the building of other facilities. Many Sharhorod Jews, however, believed their only future lay in America and sought to emigrate. By the turn of the century, the Jewish community numbered five thousand people. The marketplace was full of Jewish stalls, including twenty-seven grocers, eight flour merchants, three butchers, and two fishmongers. There were also eleven Jewish haberdasheries, eight tanners, seven smiths, a watchmaker, a book and paper store, and several other stores, including one that manufactured goods from hemp.[52] The generally peaceful relations that had reigned in the town between Christians and Jews were briefly broken when Ukrainian soldiers carried out a pogrom in the town on September 3, 1919. The number of dead was estimated at about one hundred. The Soviet government took control of the town in spring 1920.[53]

At the end of our visit in 2002, we went to the old Jewish cemetery. It was overgrown with weeds; even fully mature trees had grown over time amidst the underbrush. Only a handful of gravestones remained, jutting out of the earth at slanted angles sporadically throughout the field. Most of the stones had been carried off long ago to pave streets or repair broken walls. I decided to wander off on my own to see if any old stones could still be found protruding from the ground. In an isolated corner of the graveyard, I found a few inches of stone, surrounded by earth and foliage. I squatted down to see if I could make out any of the epitaph, but the inscription was concealed behind layers of thorny weeds. Lost in my thoughts, I felt a shadow creep over the tomb and heard heavy breathing behind me. I glanced up and saw, standing over me, a somber-looking man in black, brandishing an enormous scythe—the image of Death Himself. In a moment of terror, I saw in the rusting blade the blood of all those Jewish martyrs who had been murdered by Cossacks, Haidamaks, pogromists, Stalin's agents, and Hitler's henchmen, on the outskirts of Ukrainian villages just like this one. The peasant from the neighboring field, aware only that he had inadvertently startled me, smiled, revealing a mouthful of gold and silver teeth, and gently lowered the tarnished blade to help clear the brush away from the stone. I thanked him with a dollar bill as the name of the deceased came into view.

2

—⨏—

The Scars of Revolution

"YOU CAN SEE A SCAR"

When we met Nisen Yurkovetsky in 2009, he was ninety-one years old—
still too young to remember the violence of the revolutionary years.
But the physical and metaphorical scars of that violence were still very
much with him when we sat down with him in his home in Tulchyn,
ninety years after his parents, aunt, and grandfather were murdered by
a crowd of Ukrainian nationalist fighters—the Lyakhovich gang—in
his town. He broke down in tears as he rolled up the sleeve of his navy
plaid lumberjack shirt to show us the long scar across his forearm that
marks the path of the bullet that killed his mother, as it ricocheted off
her and grazed his arm. Only a baby at the time, he was being carried in
his mother's embrace as the bullet felled her. "They killed my mother and
father. The bandit shot and the bullet went up my arm—you can see the
scar [*simen*]—a Pole, a priest took me in and saved me. . . . They killed my
father—he was a barber—and my mother, and my grandfather—a tailor.
. . . I didn't know my mother. I didn't know my father." Later he added,
"I was only one year and three months old. . . . When they shot them

30

the bullet went off me and I fell into the grave. My mother was holding me." Nisen was left an orphan with his two older brothers, Shumi and Zoye. The Polish priest who found him lying among the corpses brought him to an orphanage in neighboring Nestervarka. Nisen's grandmother eventually took him in, and raised him, back in Tulchyn.

Yurkovetsky, like many Jews born during the agonizing birth pangs of the Revolution, was weaned in violence and destruction. His story is, in many ways, the story of the revolutionary generation. As the Bolsheviks declared victory in faraway Petrograd, the fighting was only beginning in Right Bank Ukraine. Podolia was in particular turmoil, with a bulk of the violence and disorder falling along the path of the Dnieper. Most of this territory came under the control of the Central Rada, a Ukrainian parliament that established itself as the preeminent authority in Right Bank Ukraine after the abdication of Tsar Nicholas II during the February Revolution of 1917. Over the course of that spring, the Rada became increasingly adamant in its demands for Ukrainian autonomy within the new Russian state. The Provisional Government that ruled in Petrograd after the tsar's abdication reluctantly negotiated with the Rada, but was unable to come to a definitive agreement on Ukrainian autonomy before the Provisional Government itself was overthrown by the Bolsheviks in the October Revolution. The Central Rada responded to the Bolshevik takeover in Russia by declaring itself the supreme political authority in Ukraine and establishing the Ukrainian National Republic (UNR) as an autonomous entity within Russia, consisting of the provinces of Kiev, Podolia, Volhynia, and six other provinces within what had been the Western Provinces of the Russian Empire. A few months later, in January 1918, the UNR declared independence and requested German assistance in staving off Russian forces. But a group of communists in Ukraine who sympathized with the Bolsheviks formed the All-Ukrainian Congress of Soviets of Workers', Soldiers' and Peasants' Deputies, which met in Kiev as an alternative power to the Central Rada. Tensions between the Central Rada in Kiev and the Bolshevik authorities in Petrograd were exacerbated by the Bolsheviks' vocal support for the rival Congress of Soviets. In December 1917, the Congress of Soviets established its own separate government in the city of Kharkiv, subordinate to the Petrograd Soviet. Ukraine was thus divided between two political entities: a Ukrainian National Republic, ruled by the Central Rada in Kiev in Right Bank Ukraine, and a Ukrainian Soviet government based in Kharkiv in Left Bank Ukraine. The clashes between the dual powers quickly led to civil war, first between the Bolshevik Red Army fighting for the Soviet state and the irregular forces that constituted the Ukrainian standing army under Semyon Petliura, and later between numerous other forces that joined in the fighting, including conservative monarchists (the White Guard) and anarchists (the Greens). Real power in the region—if there was such a thing during this turbulent time—resided primarily with the German military occupation that continued as a holdover from the Great War still being waged to the west. In December 1918, Petliura managed to establish a new Ukrainian national government, the Ukrainian Directorate. Like the parade of governments that preceded it, the Directorate was unable to seize lasting control of Kiev, let alone all of Ukraine. The Civil War intensified.[1]

Jews, who tended to reside in the borderlands most devastated by the fighting, were disproportionately affected by the war. During the Great War of 1914–1918, they had been distrusted by the German and Russian military alike, both of whom imposed debilitating discriminations upon Jewish residents of the borderlands and sometimes even deported entire communities.[2] As the Great War gave way to the Civil War, the sufferings of the Jews continued. Although the Provisional Government that had been established in February 1917 removed all legal restrictions on the Jewish population from the tsarist era—a policy that was maintained by both the Ukrainian Directorate and the Soviet government—Jews continued to bear the brunt of governmental economic policy by dint of their sociological standing and the particular niche they played in the market as merchants and sole-proprietor artisans.[3]

Each time authority broke down in the urban centers, nationalist fighters, criminal brigands, and disgruntled mobs took advantage of the power vacuum to loot Jewish property and vent their frustrations on Jewish civilians. They garnered support for their violence in large measure by linking popular distrust of the Soviets with latent Judeophobia, claiming that the Jews were ushering in the communists. The pogrom perpetrators saw the Jews as the source of much of their misfortune: some blamed the Jews for the communist onslaught, some blamed the Jews for the war, some blamed the Jews for the economic collapse, and others blamed the Jews simply for being Jews. Still other bandits felt no particular compulsion to blame the Jews for anything, but saw potential loot in Jewish-owned holdings. These perpetrators repeatedly plundered and destroyed Jewish property, and killed and maimed with impunity in outbursts of violence. This wave of anti-Jewish violence came to be known in Yiddish as the *khurbn,* or destruction, a term that evoked the destruction of the Jewish Temple in Antiquity, and that would later come to be associated most saliently with the Holocaust.[4]

The first pogrom in Tulchyn took place in February 1918, when the city government, which had been loyal to the Central Rada, fell to the Soviets. In the ensuing chaos, disbanded soldiers attached to the 132nd Benderskii infantry regiment attacked the Jewish quarter of the city, destroying and burning Jewish homes and killing two people (a third person died in the fires). But this was only the beginning of the violence. Eighteen months later, in May 1919, a group of peasants and bandits attacked the city, killing fourteen Jews and looting Jewish homes. As the weather warmed, the violence heated up. In June, as all authority broke down, the Christian Orthodox population of Tulchyn, with the local priest Nestervarka Afanasii Braduchan at its helm, took action to curb the violence and expel the bandits who had shattered the town's peace. According to one report, Braduchan spread false rumors that the Red Army was approaching the city, forcing the violent brigands to flee. But the local Christians were only able to keep the bandits at bay for so long. On the night of June 14, 1919, another gang of Ukrainian nationalists, this time under the command of a Cossack ataman by the name of Lyakhovich, moved into the city, chanting, "Long Live Independent Ukraine!" and attacking the Jewish quarter of the town. When the night was over, Lyakhovich and his gang had murdered 260 Jews, and left the baby Yurkovetsky an orphan, bleeding in a mass grave in his dead mother's arms.[5]

Yurkovetsky's account, like many other pogrom narratives, even those dating back to Nathan Hanover's famous account of the 1648 Khmelnitsky pogrom in Tulchyn, demonstrated the complexities and ambiguities of Jewish–Christian relations in the region. In both the early modern prototype and the modern manifestation, the local Christian population sought to defend the Jews against invading bandits. In Hanover's telling of the seventeenth-century pogrom, however, the Christian nobility succumbed to the invaders and betrayed the Jews, only to be betrayed themselves by the Cossacks. The Christian clergy of 1919 were more stalwart in their defense of the Jewish victims, even though the majority of the population chose not to intervene.

Yurkovetsky's account, told to him by other survivors and authenticated by the physical evidence that scars his arm, is further corroborated by contemporary reports. A 1921 investigation into the Tulchyn pogrom found that there were instances of Jews being concealed, "primarily on the part of the intelligentsia class," and that there were some Christian efforts to avert the pogrom. But despite these exceptional cases, the report concluded, the general attitude of the surrounding peasants was indifference. The report notes that the pogrom led to a deterioration of relations between Jews and Christians in the city, as well as a wave of Jewish emigration, primarily to America, and a worsening of the local economic situation.

It is difficult to determine the precise number of victims of the 1,200 pogroms perpetrated during this era, but the estimate of 100,194 deaths reached by the Commissariat of Nationality Affairs in its 1922 investigation into the violence is likely within range. An estimated 76 percent of the victims were male, meaning that the pogroms continued to have a measurable demographic impact for a generation, resulting in countless children who grew up without a father, and a surfeit of marriageable women.[6] The pogroms were not only more lethal than the previous outbreaks of anti-Jewish violence that had sporadically punctuated Jewish life in the region for hundreds of years, but they were also much more widespread, affecting almost every town that had a Jewish community.[7]

One of the worst pogroms occurred in Proskurov (now Khmelnytskyy), where rumors were spreading that the Bolsheviks were about to launch an uprising in the city and appoint a Jewish socialist as its leader.[8] Christian residents responded by attacking the city's Jewish population. The pogrom began on February 15, 1919, and lasted three days. Naum Gaiviker, who was six years old at the time, remembered the events of that terrible day when we spoke with him in 2007. At the age of ninety-five, he retained his boyish rebelliousness and good humor, even while sharing with us some harrowing stories from his past. But this one he found too upsetting to talk about, so his wife, Sonia, told us what had happened to him as Naum sat next to her, leaning against his cane, nodding and wincing. According to Sonia:

> They came into their house:
> "Give gold or diamonds!!"
> They were very poor. They didn't have anything. So they said: "We don't have anything."
> "If you don't give us anything, we'll chop off your head."
> They had no idea what was going on outside. They only heard how people screamed "gevalt." At that point, whistling began outside, [signaling] the leaders to convene, to gather together. The bandit, who wanted to kill them, took his saber and put it inside his sheath, and left. This time they survived. But when they went outside, they saw that over there were heads, over there were hands, over there were feet. And all of his friends were killed off. And he, just a boy, stayed alive. It tormented him his entire life.

Gaiviker finished the story, adding, "Afterwards the Poles came in and took away my father for one-and-a-half months. When he wasn't there anymore, we thought he was murdered." But Gaiviker didn't want to end the story here; instead he concluded with the comment, "In general, things were joyous here." Sonia Yarmulnik, who was born in Khmelnytskyy in 1929, shared some stories about the pogrom that she had heard from her mother. One story tells of a priest who sheltered a group of Jews in his chapel. When he was discovered, though, she told us, he was killed together with the Jews he had tried to save.

Khayke Gvinter, a nurturing and spirited woman we interviewed in her hometown of Bershad, endured enormous sufferings in her life. She was spared the pogroms of the Civil War, though, by virtue of being born too late, in 1930. But she told us a story she had heard about her grandfather, who she claimed was murdered in a pogrom at the age of 115: "My grandfather lived a long time. The Petliurists killed him. 115 years old. He hid 200 people in a storage room. . . . Since he was already a very old man, he figured, 'It makes no difference. I might as well die here.'.. Then the Petliurists killed him, they cut him to pieces and they threw him out. They were looking for the secret room." Gvinter's secondhand account includes numerous common features of pogrom violence. The old man who sacrifices himself to save his community or his family is a stock character of pogrom narratives. In this case, the old man is presented as having reached the biblical age of 115, just five years short of the 120-year lifespan the Bible accords Moses. "May you live to be 120" is a common Yiddish blessing. The tragedy of Gvinter's portrayal of her grandfather's self-sacrifice is thereby mitigated by his old age. His venerability also bestows added communal status upon him and attests to his standing in a culture that still reveres the elderly. Gvinter's second-generation link to the narrative and the pogrom provides her with a genealogical connection to this formative moment in the community.

The "secret room" is another common motif of pogrom narratives: bandits searching for loot commonly believed that Jews had hidden rooms inside their homes where they kept their treasures. In fact, many houses in the densely populated central urban streets did have hidden passageways beneath the ground; these were used for storing foodstuffs, such as mushrooms, root vegetables, preserves, compote, moonshine, and occasionally valuables as well.[9] In Gvinter's narrative, the cellar, hidden underneath the floorboards, protects the family and their valuables.

In another pogrom narrative we recorded, Sonia Litvak, who was born in Volhynian Novohrad-Volynskyy (Zvhil), told us that during a pogrom her grandmother was fatally beaten for refusing to give up a fur coat into which she had sewn money. She told us her grandmother first tried to trick the bandit, but when that failed, she managed to hold on to the coat and withstand the beating, only to die of her wounds a few days later. The money inside the coat, Litvak continued, is what saved her family during the famine that scourged the region over a decade later. Like Gvinter, she presented the death of her elderly grandparent as a sacrifice intended to protect the family valuables, which in this case ultimately saved the family years later.

The pogroms that accompanied the Civil War far surpassed earlier bouts of violence in Ukraine. In addition to the psychological impact on the survivors, the devastation set back the economy of the shtetl and made recovery from the cataclysm of the Great War and the Revolution even more difficult than it would otherwise have been. The pogroms also provided a convenient excuse for Soviet officials to explain away the devastation wrought by the first decade of communist power. Blaming the slow pace of development in Ukraine on the pogroms, official histories thereby distracted attention away from the failure of Soviet economic policy. Typical of this type of explanation was that of V. G. Bogoraz, who wrote in 1926: "Soviet authority in the shtetl, thanks to strong brigandism, was weak and feeble."[10] Regardless of the effects of the pogroms on the economic devastation of the region, they played an important symbolic role in the twentieth-century development of the Ukrainian shtetl. The pogroms were the metaphorical birth pangs of the revolution in Ukraine and the very real beginning of life for the cohort of Ukrainian Jews born in the shadow of the revolution.

The violence and economic devastation wrought by the pogroms fueled rampant emigration from the region. In Podolia, Jews in search of better lands took flight across whatever border seemed most porous. Most refugees fled south, across the Dniester into Romania, where 73,000 Ukrainian Jews assembled in Bessarabian towns. Some Podolian Jews may also have been among the 200,000 Jews who fled westward to Poland between 1918 and 1921.[11] Many of those who escaped into neighboring countries eventually migrated to the United States, Canada, Argentina, or Palestine. As a result, by the early 1920s, many Jews living in small towns and villages throughout Ukraine had family networks scattered around the globe. These transnational connections were vital links that would provide crucial and sometimes lifesaving information from abroad, as well as vital hard currency that could be used to purchase survival rations during times of famine. The government initially welcomed the flow of hard currency, which it recognized would eventually end up in the state coffers. Relatives could even send foreign currency directly to the special hard-currency stores, called Torgsin, where the best-quality produce and goods were available at grossly inflated prices.

For many people, the few dollars received from American relatives were enough to help them through the winter and stave off hunger during difficult times. Despite the lifesaving advantage of receiving funds from abroad, though, the recipients had to face the fact that the Provincial Central Committee feared that this type of dependence on foreign aid would lead to anti-Soviet sentiment among the recipients. The government began to view those with foreign connections as potential "enemies of the people" and began discriminating against them. As one report put it, "It is important to note that the poorest segment of the shtetl population is connected by family and friendship ties to their foreign relatives and the transmission of these conditions abroad promotes the spread of undesirable and damaging information about the situation of Jews in the Soviet Union."[12] The government therefore started to cut back on opportunities for engagement with the world at large, thereby furthering the dire economic devastation of those who were often the poorest segments of the shtetl population. What had once been vital survival lines instead became paths to persecution, imprisonment, and exile, fueled by the paranoid rumors and accusations of spy networks that perverted public discourse. By the time of the German invasion in 1941, few Soviet Jews had regular contact with their families outside of the Soviet Union.

But most Jews fled internally, migrating from one town to another, hoping to find solace and opportunity without abandoning the land that was all they had ever known. The first Soviet census of 1926 provides us with an idea of the extent of internal migration among Jews in the region. Compared to the general population, Jews in Right Bank Ukraine—the geographic division employed by the census—were almost twice as likely to be living in a locale other than their birthplace: 36 percent of Jews compared to 14 percent of non-Jews reported that they had been born elsewhere. In urban centers, these figures were even more dramatic: 60 percent of Jews were not local, compared to 23 percent of non-Jews. The 1926 census also confirms that most Jewish migrations took place during the period of the pogroms, and that Jewish migration slowly declined after the formal consolidation of Soviet power in the region: 26 percent of the nonlocal Jews had arrived between the years 1917 and 1920; 17 percent between 1920 and 1923; and 16 percent between 1924 and 1926. Jewish migration was dwindling. By contrast, non-Jewish migration continued to increase: 10 percent of migrant non-Jews had arrived between 1917 and 1920; 14 percent between 1920 and 1923; and 20 percent between 1924 and 1926. Whereas the largest waves of Jewish migration took place during the revolutionary years as a result of the pogroms and accompanying discord, non-Jewish migration was more recent, as peasants from the countryside moved into the cities to take advantage of economic opportunities and to work in the new factories. By and large, Jews moved to flee persecution and violence; non-Jews moved for economic advancement.[13]

"WHAT CAN YOU EAT WITH THIRTY-SIX RUBLES?"

Despite having served during the Second World War in an elite unit, Isaak Vaisman, who was born in Berdichev in 1925, was never able to escape the poverty of his childhood. When we first met him in 2002,

Vaisman was seventy-seven years old and still doing backbreaking work selling seltzer water in the Berdichev marketplace. On a sweltering summer day, in the company of the city's Hasidic rebbe, whose long black cassock and skullcap seemed out of place in the bustling marketplace, we sauntered through the market, past stalls hawking fabrics, wallpaper, cheap toys, metal pipes, and clothing, to Vaisman's soda stand. Wearing a white short butcher's coat and cap, Vaisman was hunched over his gas canister: "Sholem aleykhem," he grinned as we approached the stall from the back service entrance. We watched him pry open the heavy rusting canister with a wrench and pour seltzer into glasses for the waiting customers who tossed him a couple of kopecks for a swig. He worked silently, rarely exchanging pleasantries with his thirsty customers, and only turning his attention from the queue to glance at the canister's gauge and adjust the pressure of the gas. Vaisman's pride in serving his country during the war was evident, but when asked when he had experienced the best times of his life, he answered without hesitation, "My youth." After hearing him describe his childhood, I could only imagine how much worse things must have become for these to have been his best years:

> We couldn't even get a piece of bread. We were so poor. My mother worked and earned only thirty-six rubles. From one paycheck to the next she had to borrow money. She worked at a leather factory. . . . It was very difficult. She couldn't get married because she had to bring us up. . . . I lost my father in '28. I was only three years old, and my mother was left with two of us, me and my disabled sister. And [my mother] worked at the Schlanger factory. Thirty-six rubles she earned. And what can you eat with thirty-six rubles?

When Vaisman was a child he lived in the same building block as Beyle Rainsdorf, who would become his wife after the war. Beyle came from a wealthier family; her father, born in Warsaw, had come to Berdichev as a refugee during the First World War, but was able to make a living for himself in the Soviet Union as a bookkeeper. "We lived well in the courtyard," she told us. "My father graduated from two institutes before the war, and he knew a lot of languages. He had degrees in economics and finance. In Warsaw, he studied at a yeshiva and studied music. And then, here, he studied accounting. Our whole family was very educated, the aunts and uncles. And we didn't live too badly." When we interviewed Beyle, she was sitting next to her husband on the couple's divan. Beyle teased her husband about those days, about how her family could have helped his out: "We lived in the same courtyard. Now he complains to me. Why? Because before the war, I didn't support him: 'You lived well, so why didn't you [help me out]?'" In fact, they both tell us, her family did provide some charity for the poorer families, like the Vaismans, who lived in the same building bloc. Those who grew up poor often relied upon the beneficence of those who were a little more fortunate. At least until the government began arresting the wealthier members of the community, there was often a philanthropist in town who helped alleviate the struggles of the destitute.

Although it was by no means the poorest locale in the region, the city of Berdichev became synonymous with poverty in the 1920s. Chaim Skoblitsky, another war veteran we interviewed in Berdichev who in his retirement helped out leading services at the synagogue, was born in the city in 1919 and was raised in destitution. He spoke to us in an authoritative voice that hinted at the powerful role he once played in the military, and the influential position he continued to hold in the Jewish community. Wearing a pale pink shirt and a straw hat, he reminisced about Berdichev of old. His memories of youthful poverty, though, were tempered with nostalgia. He began his lament to us with the phrase "We didn't live badly [mir hobn nit shlekht gelebt]" before continuing:

> There were such poor people. Oy! . . . There were plenty of poor people. And in our kitchen we had a cupboard. On top of it, there would be pieces of bread smeared with butter. There were four of us, four boys at home. So, we were hungry all the time. When we came into the kitchen, we would pour a glass of milk and take a piece of bread with butter. And we considered that to be stuffing ourselves.

In Berdichev, Skoblitsky told us, there was a philanthropist named Magazanik, who exported leather from the leather factory, where Vaisman's mother worked, to Czechoslovakia. Magazanik, he told us, "was a great landowner. He would lead his cattle along the entire street and would carry dairy products, like butter and sour cream, to sell in Zhytomyr and Kiev. And over there, he planted an orchard with all kinds of trees. Now it's a street where they have added new buildings. It used to be a long orchard along the street." Magazanik, Skoblitsky went on, lost most of his wealth when it was expropriated by the Soviet state and his property was seized for communal use. It is perhaps in tribute to Magazanik that the Berdichev-born writer Vassili Grossman gave the name of Efim Magazanik to the poor Jewish blacksmith who is forced to host a pregnant Red Army soldier during the Civil War in his 1934 short story, "In the City of Berdichev," a story later made famous by Aleksandr Askoldov's 1967 film *Commissar*. Grossman was, perhaps, making an ironic comment on the fate of the wealthy under Bolshevism, by taking the name of this locally famous aristocrat and philanthropist for his poor blacksmith.

Poverty was even more endemic in smaller towns, where many residents lived in overcrowded houses on mud streets. Donia Presler, who grew up in Tulchyn in the 1930s, boasted of how her family lived in a house with a dirt floor and sparse furniture:

> Back then, before the war, I remember we were really paupers. They called the street we lived on the "Paupers' Street." . . . There was one house on top of another . . . we didn't even know what a bathroom was, there were so few. On our little plot of land there were eight families. Eight! One house on top of another. . . . The house was small. We had just a dirt floor. Before the war, we didn't know what a floor was. We would smear clay on the dirt. I did it myself. We bought a kind of lime clay. We would spread it with a cloth. I did it myself as a child. I would spread it around and around the dirt floor, and it would turn yellow. It was a little house, but we had a big table. We would gather together, all the brothers and siblings. Someone would cook and bring it over and we would sit. There were a lot of children at the table, so the kids sat and the grown-ups stood around. We didn't know what a plate was. We didn't know what a spoon was. We didn't know of these things. [We ate] from a wooden ladle and a big round bowl. People prepared dumplings [varenikes] with their fingers and the kids and the adults ate with their hands. And a samovar would be there with tea and we would drink. . . . In the summertime, one person would take a cover and sleep outside; someone else would sleep on the floor, and another person would sleep on the bed.

During the Civil War, the fledgling Soviet State sought to orient all its resources toward fueling the Red Army's efforts by instituting an economic policy known as "War Communism." In the infancy of the Revolution, the engineers of Soviet ideological and economic policy believed they were implementing pure communism and foresaw world revolution close behind. The state nationalized the banks and large industry, centralized industrial management, introduced a state monopoly on trade, and criminalized private enterprise and exchange. These policies disenfranchised anybody who employed hired labor, received income from sources other than employment, or worked as private merchants, brokers, or religious functionaries. Jews predominated in each of these categories. Living mainly in the urban centers, where commerce and industry were most concentrated, Jews were subject to the worst of the military requisitions and property seizures. Relying overwhelmingly on private enterprise and trade for their livelihood—the two occupations most targeted for elimination by the new government—the Jewish middling class was one of the major victims of the Revolution. Jews, who accounted for just 5.4 percent of the total population of Ukraine, constituted 45 percent of disenfranchised people, based on figures from 1925–1926.[14] Many Jews thereby lost the emancipation rights that the Provisional Government had only just recently awarded them. Previously persecuted for their religious beliefs, they now faced persecution instead for their sociological and economic status.

The suffering of the largest segment of the Jewish population could be contrasted with the benefits that the Revolution brought to the select few who attained leadership positions within the new government. The most visible of these was Leon Trotsky, who headed the Red Army. But on a smaller scale, local Jewish intellectuals often took on leadership positions within the city councils (soviets) and party cells emerging throughout Ukraine. Long denied upward professional mobility and civic leadership roles, many educated Jews embraced the promise of equality the new regime offered. The sudden presence of Jews in the local governments of small towns had a palpable effect on the peasant population, which came to associate the Revolution with the Jews. As Yurkovetsky told us of 1920s Tulchyn: "The president of the regional executive committee was a Jew, the president of the city council was a Jew, the director of the regional cooperative was a Jew, the director of the city cooperative was a Jew, there was a Jewish editor." Jews were overrepresented both among the biggest losers of the Revolution and its biggest winners.

By the time the Red Army's victory in eastern Ukraine was ensured in 1921, the economic devastation caused by the nationalization of finance, industry, and trade was too obvious to ignore. The state, which had only just come into being, still lacked the resources and experience to control the economy it claimed: black market, barter, and subsistence farming had come to replace a functioning modern economy. In 1921, Lenin instituted a strategic retreat designed to allow the economy to recover; he retained state ownership of large industry and banking, but allowed for limited privatization, particularly in petty trade. The New Economic Policy (NEP) brought the marketplace to life again and allowed artisans to resume their handicrafts: tailors could purchase the wool they needed, cobblers could once again acquire leather, and bakers could buy wheat from the peasants in the countryside. Although the vast majority of the Jewish population in Ukraine continued to languish in poverty, popular images of the Jew as the prototypical NEP-man, who benefited from and manipulated the new economic leniency for his own benefit, proliferated in popular culture.[15]

The difficult economic situation in the shtetls of Ukraine, and particularly the Podolian region, was evident throughout the early 1920s. In 1924, the leading Yiddish Moscow paper, *Der emes,* reported: "The situation of Jews, particularly in the shtetls of Right Bank Ukraine, is terrible. In connection with the development of cooperatives and state trade, the shtetl population was crushed out of its former economic position. The poverty of the shtetl has reached colossal proportions."[16] A year later, a secret report to all regional executive committees and to the Jewish Section of Vinnytsya noted that "the economic situation of several significant segments of the Jewish population is very severe."[17]

The poverty of the shtetl was exacerbated by excessive taxation. Because taxes were assessed at a higher rate in towns than in villages, the brunt of Soviet taxation policy fell upon urban residents, among whom the Jewish population was concentrated. The Provincial Central Committee noted that local organs were overtaxing shtetl craftsmen, and recommended that taxes on all artisans be set at the same level, regardless of whether they lived in villages or towns. The report indicated that the disparity between taxes on town craftsmen and village craftsmen amounted to an effective discrimination against the Jewish population.[18] At a meeting on April 8, 1925, the main office of the Ukrainian Jewish Section reaffirmed this recommendation and argued for leveling taxation for artisans and craftsmen in villages and small towns.[19] These reforms notwithstanding, the failure of the 1925 harvest led to what one report called an "exceptionally difficult situation" in certain districts of Podolia.

The endemic poverty was most visible in the housing sector. A 1927 survey of houses in two shtetls in Vinnytsya province, Lypovets and Ilnytsya, found that only 9 of the 193 houses in the two towns were built on stone foundations. In larger towns, such as Sharhorod and Tulchyn, it was more common to find houses on limestone foundations. Most Jewish houses, whether built on a foundation or not, had timber frame walls stuffed with mud, lime, and thatch, covered with clay and whitewash. Only eight houses in the two shtetls surveyed had walls made entirely of timber. Roofs were thatched or tiled, and were in need of constant repair to protect against leaks. Most houses also had walls plastered from the inside that required regular whitewashing. Earthen floors were common; they were usually covered with clay and lime that needed to be cleaned and smeared with new clay on a regular basis. The inspector who compiled the 1927 report noted that well over half the houses surveyed were damp inside.[20] The 1926 census revealed similar living conditions. In Tulchyn, for instance, the census counted 2,242 houses, 89 percent of which were made of wood. Only 79 houses were made of brick, and 158 were composed of mixed materials (usually lime, clay, and thatch). In Bershad, 58 percent of the 1,569 houses in the city were made of wood and 38 percent out of mixed materials.

Electricity was still rare in Ukraine in 1926. In Tulchyn, only about 15 percent of the population lived in one of the 251 dwellings in the city that had electricity. In Sharhorod, 21 percent of the population had electricity, in Kryzhopil the total was 16 percent, in Tomashpil 23 percent, and in Bershad 37 percent. Even in a large city like Uman, close to the Gnilii Tikich hydroelectric plant, which was one of the first in Ukraine, only 45 percent of the population lived in dwellings with electricity.[21] Many of those whom we interviewed remember when electricity was first brought to the shtetl in the late 1920s or 1930s. Some recall how tractor headlights illuminated the town square for evening events prior to urban electrification. Indoor plumbing was a real luxury; to this day, many of the houses in which we conducted our interviews were served only with outhouses across the yard.

In addition to the poor sanitary and physical condition of the shtetls, many towns were overcrowded. The 1927 inventory of houses in Ilnytsya counted 407 houses and estimated that 10.7 people resided in each house, or 4.8 people per room. The situation was similar in Lypovets, where 4.6 people on average resided in each room. In both towns, the majority of the houses inventoried had been built before 1900. The same inventory looked at the caloric intake of the population and estimated that 74 percent of all families were consuming less than two thousand calories per day, with about half of those calories derived from bread products.[22]

The stark poverty led to malnutrition. Maria Yakuta laughs at how accustomed her great grandchildren are to eating bananas today when she recalls the types of fruits that had been available to her as a child: "I lived my whole life without knowing what a banana is, and I didn't known about oranges. How a Jewish child should eat an orange! Lemons, I knew. . . . We used to each get half an apple. There were six children. Where was there to even buy an apple? And our mother would buy one and she would peel it and divide it up for us. It was such a great joy! We didn't have any pastries or oranges."

Malnutrition contributed to rampant disease, high rates of infant mortality, and childhood death. When we asked about familial background during our interviews, parents wept over the children they lost in infancy seventy years ago, siblings trembled when talking about their brothers and sisters who didn't make it, and children routinely lamented the sorrows of orphanhood. Many children were born after older siblings had already died in infancy, and recall being brought up in houses full of melancholy and a sense of loss that would never be overcome. In the expectation of losing at least some of their children, parents planned for large families. Those whose households were blessed with a respite from disease were left with more children to care for than their meager economic situation could reasonably accommodate. Those who were orphaned as children remember not only the pain of losing a loved one at such a young age, but also the economic cost that the loss had on their household. Widows and widowers had a difficult time managing with half the earning potential of a two-parent household.

As a result of the tragic losses that most Ukrainian Jews suffered in their lives, even the most nonchalant of questions we posed could elicit heartbreaking stories of tragedy. When we began our interviews with preliminary questions about family backgrounds, the simple task of listing one's family members inevitably resulted in tears of sorrow and tales of lives lost. When we met Khayke Gvinter on the streets of Bershad outside her home, she launched into an emotionally wrenching story about how she climbed out of a mass grave during the Second World War. She was becoming visibly upset and agitated, so we tried to turn the conversation to happier times. We asked Gvinter about her childhood and about her mother: "[She was] so young and she had three children. There was another one before me, and my sister. One from '28. Her name was Malka. She died." Gvinter continued: "My mother was a simple woman. And she was a real *baleboste*. Oh! But not for long, not for long. I don't even remember my father. Just a bit. My father had already buried the child that had died from smallpox. [She was] older than me, born in '28. And afterwards my mother also had me." Her father died soon after Khayke was born: "I used to ask my mother, 'Where is my father? Where is my father? Everybody has fathers, but woe is me.'" She tempered the memories of the sufferings she endured as a child with the phrase "We did have some good years," with which she ended her story. In comparison to what came later, her childhood was not altogether bad.

Tseytl Kislinskaia's father also died when she was young. When she was nine years old in Korsun-Shevchenkivskyy, in Cherkasy Province, her mother was left alone with two children: "Our life was very difficult. Very difficult. My mother . . . would earn thirty rubles a month and we were two children." In the absence of any social safety net, the ability to survive was so closely tied to one's paycheck, that eighty years later, children still remember their parents' precise monthly salary to the ruble—an ironic detail for what was supposed to have been a socialist and egalitarian society.

Many Yiddish songs that shtetl Jews sang in this period bemoaned the poverty of the shtetl. The same melancholy phrases and idioms of poverty recur in numerous songs. Young orphan children are always wandering through the dark and cold streets of the shtetl barefoot, dreaming only of a pair of shoes, for which they would pawn their last shirt. Evgeniia Kozak, who grew up in Bershad in the 1920s, sung several songs for us incorporating these themes. One, in particular, weaved them all together in a lament of poverty, want, and destitution:

In droysn iz finster un nas un kalt
Ikh hob shoyn nit keyn shikhelekh.
Aroystsugeyn in gas.
Ven mayn oreme muter volt atsind gelebt
Zi volt farzetst dos letste hemd,

Arayn in tifn noyt,
Un volt far ir yoseml a por shikhelekh gekoyft.
Der lerer fun der shul zogt ikh bin a kind, a brilyant
Un ale raykhe yingelekh lakhn fun mayn shand.
Azoy iz avekgon tsvelef yor derkhanand
Un fun dem oremen yosem iz gevorn . . .

. . .

Di oreme muter hot farzetst dos letste hemd
Un hot far dem yoseml a por shikhelekh gekoyft.
Azoy iz avekgon tsvelef yor derkhanand
Er zitst in tsimer un drikt im di hant.
Tsi gedenkstu shoyn tatenyu tsurik mit tsvelef yor
Ven du host mir gekoyft shikhelekh a por?
Un derfar vos du host mir gekoyft shikhelekh a por
Vel ikh dikh gliklekh makhn ale dayne yor.

Outside it's dark, and wet, and cold.
And I have no shoes,
To go out on the street.
If my poor mother were still alive,
She would pawn her last shirt.
Never mind her extreme need,
And would buy a pair of shoes for her little orphan.
My school teacher says I am a precious child,
And all the rich children laugh at my shame.
So twelve years passed,
And since then this poor orphan has become . . .

. . .

My poor mother has pawned her last shirt,
And bought her orphan a pair of shoes.
So, twelve years have passed,
He sits in his room and wrings his hands,
Do you still remember your son after twelve years?
When you bought me a pair of shoes?
And because you bought me that pair of shoes,
I will make you happy for all your years.

The Jews of the Podolian shtetls remember the 1920s and 1930s as a time of great need and want, but they also recognize that within this period there was a sense of community and mutual aid. Many recall their fellow Jews sharing food and helping out. At least in the early 1920s, they claim, the community was close-knit and neighbors helped one another.

Kislinskaia told us, "There was this Jew who would cook us soup every Friday. What was in the soup? The feet of the chicken, the head of the chicken, I don't remember what else. Every Friday my mother would go there and every Friday he would give it to us because we were so poor. We had nothing." Others told stories of their Christian neighbors helping them in their time of need, whether it involved rescuing them from the mass graves during the pogroms or simply bringing them hot tea on the Sabbath. Jewish–Christian relations before the war, we are often told, were friendly. "We were too poor for antisemitism," recalled one interviewee. Many of those who recall times of intense poverty portray life as having been somehow more "pure" in those days. These sentiments can be found in the written accounts left by emigrants as well. Many emigrants remember the poverty of the shtetl, but associate that poverty with idealized notions of lost values. In his written memoirs, Moyshe Olgin, for instance, remembers:

> My shtetl longed only for beauty. It was a gloomy life with muddy streets, damp houses, earthen floors, smoky ovens, shoes without rubber, pillows without pillowcases, and evening meals of bread with a bit of herring. Poverty abounded. One was never sure about the next day. And amid this desolate life, people carried a thirst for beauty, for refinement. People envied the wealthy not for their mansions, but for their education, for their life of beauty.[23]

For many residents of Podolia during the early revolutionary years, the 1920s were a time of lawlessness and anarchy, during which the community had to come together to help each other out. It was only during the 1930s, as the Party began to assert its authority in the region, that conditions worsened. Residents of the shtetls commonly refer to the 1930s as the beginning of Soviet times, despite the reality that the Revolution was already more than a decade old. As Kislinskaia put it, "and then during Soviet times, everybody was just for themselves."

"IF YOU WANT TO EAT, GO AND DANCE!"

Conditions continued to worsen throughout the decade as the Soviet government embarked upon its collectivization drive in 1929–1930 in order to force all peasants into collective farms. The immediate impetus for a change in course was the grain procurement crisis of 1927–1928. Unwilling to admit the failures of its economic policies, the state laid the blame for its inefficiencies on private traders in urban centers and "kulaks," a term connoting the wealthier strata of the peasantry, in rural regions. Despite the rhetoric coming out of Moscow, however, most merchants and kulaks along with most petty bourgeoisie were only marginally better off, and sometimes even worse off, than their neighbors. But both were a convenient scapegoat to explain the state's poor economic performance over the last decade. Over the summer and fall of 1927, the state began arresting "anti-Soviet elements" in the countryside and towns, effectively ending the New Economic Policy that had allowed for private trade to continue. In a series of decrees issued in January 1928, Stalin called upon local officials to take repressive measures to combat private trade, speculation, and grain hoarding. Private trade, the state argued, was interfering with the central procurement efforts of the government by inflating prices through speculation. The state responded by instructing the secret police to embark upon "extraordinary measures" to rout out the last vestiges of private trade: some 16,000 individuals were arrested by April 1928. The grain shortage, however, only worsened as peasants resisted the forcible seizure of their harvests by hiding their grain.

In an effort to carry out the First Five-Year Plan initiated in 1928, the Soviet government sought a radical reorientation of the economic basis of the country. Private landholdings were to be seized by the government, acting in the name of the people, and all land was to be transferred to public ownership. In December 1929, Stalin called for the "liquidation of the kulak as a class," initiating a campaign of "dekulakization" that would leave tens of thousands dead, and hundreds of thousands relocated or "administratively dekulakized" through property expropriation. In order to carry out these draconian measures, the state sent some 25,000 factory workers and Red Army soldiers into the countryside to organize the peasantry into collective farms. As suspected kulaks and speculators were arrested in 1929–1930 and exiled to "special settlements" in Siberia, a new decree subjected the families of those arrested in Right Bank Ukraine to exile. A total of 10,000–15,000 families were exiled from the region.[24] By March 1930, 60 percent of peasant households in Ukraine had been collectivized.[25] Throughout the Soviet Union, peasants responded to the seizure of their property with mass resistance, compelling the state to increase its use of force. Resistance was most severe in Ukraine, where more than four thousand disturbances were recorded in the spring of 1930.[26] In 1931, the state introduced a hierarchical rationing system that privileged the party elite, urban workers, military personnel, and state farmers. Peasants and the disenfranchised did not receive ration cards. Instead, they were forced to rely upon the market, which was severely depleted by state procurements. Only goods and produce left over from procurements made it to the market, where prices were grossly inflated. Connections, theft, freeloading, and illegal private plots of land helped supplement the market, both for those with ration cards and for those without.[27] The central government's insistence on meeting outrageous procurement quotas and their obstinate refusal to yield to local needs, combined with climactic conditions, created a massive famine in 1932–1933.

Donia Presler, who was born into a family of musicians in Tulchyn in 1929, was still a spirited woman with a vivid memory of her childhood hardships when we spoke with her in 2003. She told us: "In '33 during the famine, my father's brother, Utler, died. Khane died. And also their son died from hunger. Our salvation from '33 was the dry weather. The soil was dry and you could work on the fields. They would give us a bit of soybean soup. You could take a little jar with you and for a day['s work] they would give you a bit of soup." Binyomin Geller, who was born in Pyatka in 1923, began his interview with us in a lively mode, smiling, winking at the camera, putting on a show. But the twinkle in his eyes diminished quickly when talking about his two-year old brother, who succumbed to the famine in 1932. Now squinting, gazing at the ground, and fiddling with his glasses on the table, he explained that his father, who had worked in the local sugar factory, lost his job when the factory was closed during the famine. He traveled to Dnepropetrovsk in search of work, but became ill and passed away within the year. When we interviewed Chaim Rubin in the antechamber of the Breslov chapel in Uman, where the grave of Rebbe Nahman of Bratslav resides, he recalled the famine in Buki, a shtetl about 50 kilometers from Uman. Rubin remembered how his uncle, Hershl Bondar, who played the tin flute, would try to calm the hungry children with distracting entertainments and music during the worst years of the famine: "There were years, in 1933, when there was a famine. There was no food. People dropped like flies. The children would beg: 'We want to eat.' 'If you want to eat, go and dance.' He would start playing and they would dance, the hungry ones. They should be merry. . . . People were falling. They were eating frogs from the river. They ate whatever they could get." Yosl Kogan's father, Avrom, who had been a soap-maker, died in 1933 in Bershad, when Yosl was six years old: "He died in '33, during the time of the famine. He went to these peasants. They treated him to vodka and whatever else. He got dysentery and he died." His mother, who made a living making and selling almond candies, brought up Yosl and his two siblings on her own. In the collective farm, Gigant, near Tomashpil, Nisen Kiselman's father died of hunger in 1933, leaving his wife with six children to care for. "The Jews compelled him to go to synagogue to pray, to say kaddish after his father. He was a little child, so he just said whatever they said," explained his wife.

Raisa Chuk, an elegant and businesslike woman who was born in Berdichev in 1919, remembered the famine in her hometown:

> It was such an enormous disaster. I remember well how we children were so hungry. Back then, I was twelve years old and my brothers were nine and seven years old. My brothers were always lying down and sleeping because they were starving. I was still studying at school, so I had to keep going. . . . My mother saved us from starvation. How? She took out the linens from a featherbed, and she took the thread from an old blanket. She sewed a blanket. At night, she would sit and sew the blanket and carry it to the market. She sold the blanket and bought material for another blanket and bought us a loaf of bread. Our mother saved us from hunger. I remember it very well. She would buy a glass of millet and cook a soup and [give] us a piece of bread. This was our meal.

Frida Pecherskaia was born in Bratslav in 1927. Her father was a coach-man. When we interviewed her in 2009, she reminded me of Whistler's Mother—she had the same noble poise and lanky figure, and she sat with her scarf flowing over her shoulder and her hands folded across her lap just like the iconic figure in the painting that hangs in Paris's Museé d'Orsay. She scolded me for not eating enough, and told us that during the famine, her parents sent her over to an orphanage because they couldn't feed her: "My mother was swollen. She would throw herself down on the grass and eat the grass, and she turned me over to an orphanage. I was about two years old. I was in the orphanage until it ended, and my mother and my father came to pick me up."

Some of the most detailed descriptions of Jewish life during the famine, though, come from the writings of American Jews who visited during that time. Nahman Huberman describes the situation in Bershad: "For heating material people used paper, newspapers and old books . . . those who were wealthy enough to still have some furniture or household goods that had not been confiscated, delivered them to the villages in exchange for a bit of flour or potatoes."[28] Mendl Osherowitch, who visited Tulchyn in 1932, recalls,

> I spent a night in a worker's dwelling in Tulchyn. The dwelling was so terrible that I cannot imagine how somebody could live there. It had the absolute worst sanitary conditions a person can come out of. The house was narrow, dirty, and suffocating, and the poverty was so great that it seemed to leap out of all corners. There was not a single piece of bread with which to calm the hunger. And everybody—the father, the mother, the children—were dressed in such torn, old, and dirty clothing that it was a fright to look at them.[29]

"Wherever I went and wherever I stood," he continues, "people were talking about hunger and poverty, about sickness and death. Everywhere people told terrible things about a life that one can no longer bear, about suffering that is worse than hell."[30]

While those shtetl Jews who lived through the famine all recall the sufferings that the Jewish community endured, many admit that conditions were worse in the villages. Raisa Chuk told us, "Especially the Russians in the villages would die. Over there they were in a terrible [condition]. And in the town, we tried to do something about it. . . . Afterward they provided breakfasts at school, so we wouldn't die of hunger." Maria Yakuta recognized that the Jews were tormented with hunger, but her most vivid memory is of the Christians who died near the distillery:

> There was a distillery near us, where they would make spirits from wheat, oats, and corn. There was [spent] sour mash there, from the wheat. And they would throw the sour mash in a ditch. The hungry people would go to eat the sour mash in the ditch, they would eat it up and die. And the

road between the distillery and Teplyk was covered with corpses, with dead people. I used to take a wagon with those who could still make it. And they used to gather at the cemetery, at the Christian cemetery, and there was a ditch there and they would throw them into it.

Klara Sapozhnik knew of those in Tomashpil who resorted to cannibalism during the famine, but she quickly clarified that she was referring to "Russians," not Jews. Fania Braverman, who grew up in the town of Salnitsa, also identified the main victims of the hunger as non-Jews. Her own father worked as an inspector at a metal factory in Vinnytsya, from where he was able to bring some flour and barley to the village where his family lived: "I remember how the swollen gentiles from the village would pass by our house, so swollen," she told us. She remembered one non-Jewish woman her mother fed: "She didn't know how to thank my mother. We were a little better off." Chaim Rubin, who recounted the terrible suffering in his native Buki, could not recall any Jews who actually died of hunger. Motl Derbaremdiker of Berdichev, though, insisted that "it is a lie that only Ukrainians died in the hunger." When asked if he could recall any particular Jews who died, he answered affirmatively, but then went on to tell of several Jews who suffered during the hunger but ultimately survived.

Some Jews managed to survive because they still had relatives in America who could help provide for them. Tsilia Khaiut, who was born in Mohyliv-Podilskyy in 1917, explained that her maternal grandparents would send money from America, which her parents would keep in U.S. funds, recognizing that the exchange rates rendered their remittances worthless:

> When the Soviet government came in, they were exchanging dollars for sixty-six kopeks to the dollar. And they were afraid. I remember the last time very well: we received several dollars and my mother paid rent with it; we rented a house. Everybody started with: "What do you need it for?" "What would you gain from it?" They sent two hundred dollars and it would be worth nothing when you put it into kopeks.

Yurkovetsky also shared that he survived the famine because his family received money from America. He told us that his mother had a brother in Chisinau, but since there were no relations between the Soviet Union and Romania, his uncle would send dollars to America, and they would be forwarded to him. Those who had gold, platinum, or diamonds, he continued, could survive. Donia Presler also survived with the help of relatives abroad, who sent the funds that were needed to make purchases at the special Torgsin stores, which sold goods for hard currency:

> We wouldn't have survived except for two sisters, Zisl and Gitl, who left for America just before the [First World] War. They left for America and from America they learned that there was a famine here. During the Soviet regime, there was a store, a canteen, where they had food—flour and corn—and if you had a dollar you could go and exchange it for food. So they sent us—there were four sisters and two brothers—and they would send us twenty-five or twenty dollars or so, and we would go and buy the food. We would mix the cornmeal with some water and a little salt. We would make a punch of water, cornmeal, and salt, and slowly, slowly we would drink it. . . . And this is what saved us. Without it we would not have survived. They were falling like straw in '33.

The Torgsin stores remained stacked even during the worst times of the famine, a scene that taunted the starving masses. In fact, the Torgsin stores were available to the political elite and those with connections as well as to those with access to hard currency or valuables. Money sent by relatives abroad saved many Jews who would otherwise have surely starved to death.[31] Many believed that these storehouses were the secret reserves of the "bourgeoisie." Pesia Kolodenker recalled that her mother insisted there were secret storehouses of food that the "bourgeoisie" held onto.

Motl Derbaremdiker, though, insisted that Jews had not benefited from foreign assistance: "The Jews in the small towns starved like every-one else," he told us. "The only support they got was when people went to the big cities, to Moscow and Leningrad, and sent packages from there with sugar and bread, and it was already moldy." Although an untold number of Jews died of starvation during the Great Famine, the ability of some to survive on the basis of foreign currency and political clout has contributed to the false perception, often manipulated for political reasons today, that Jews were the instigators rather than among the victims of the Great Famine.

—⁂—

The famine of these years has become a hotly contested historiographical issue: today, many historians believe the famine was manufactured as a deliberate policy to punish the people of Ukraine for their resistance to collectivization. Some view it as a counterpart to the Holocaust and have come to understand it as "the Hidden Holocaust" or the "Unknown Holocaust."[32] Even the neologism commonly used to describe the 1932–1933 famine, Holodomor—literally, murder by famine—is a semantic counterpart to Holocaust, complete with the same first four letters of the word. Although the most comprehensive research on the number of fatalities during the Holodomor have put death rates at between 2.5 and 3.5 million, many Ukrainian nationalists have taken to utilizing the figure of seven million—tallied as one million more than the number of Jews killed in the Holocaust—as the definitive victim count.[33] However, it is not just a case of victimhood one-upmanship that shapes the debate over these figures. Rather, there is a deliberate link between this Holocaust equivalency or "double genocide" and the common assumption that "the Jews" were to blame for the Holodomor, or this claim's corollary that Jews did not suffer during the Holodomor. In his memoirs, Miron Dolot describes how the Party blamed the Jews for the hunger at the time, recalling how a local Party chief explained to an assembly that "the real culprits who distorted the Party line and brought so much suffering to your village were the Jews. Yes, it was the Jews who did it; not our dear Communist Party."[34] As historian John Paul Himka has shown, this myth remains a common misconception, fueled by the writings of Ukrainian nationalists, and, at times, maintained by the Ukrainian government itself.[35] The battle between the Holodomor and the Holocaust all too often takes the form of "victim competition." In reality, both atrocities were perpetrated predominantly by outsiders. While there certainly were individual Jews acting on behalf of Moscow who prevented grain from reaching the neediest segments of the population, the Jews as a group bear no blame for the Holodomor. Similarly, we need to balance the atrocities committed by many Ukrainians during the Holocaust, often acting in the name of Ukraine, with the stories of Ukrainian heroism that saved many of the Jews we have been able to interview. While academics and journalists from the Ukrainian diaspora as well as nationalists within Ukraine launch diatribes, the Jews who live in the small towns that suffered during the famine, recall the misery and despair they shared with their Christian neighbors.

Despite the much-vaunted building of new power plants and industrial factories, the first decade of Soviet power in Ukraine did little to alleviate the day-to-day sufferings of the shtetl Jews. To the contrary, state policies deprived them of the little livelihood they had, and led to a generation reared in poverty and want.

3

—ꟷ—

Social Structure of the Soviet Shtetl

In 1924, the Soviet ethnographer Vladimir Bogoraz, better known by his pseudonym V. G. Tan, led an ethnographic expedition to some of the shtetls of Ukraine. Bogoraz's report on the expedition, published in 1926 as *The Jewish Shtetl in Revolution*, jubilantly celebrated the victory of socialism during the first decade of the Revolution: "Socialist construction has taken off completely among the Jews," who, he continued, were working as "stonemasons, coachmen, carpenters, bathhouse attendants, street beggars, ex-convicts, prostitutes, pimps, an entire mass of petty and even pettier traders and, as if to make up for it, two or three wealthy people." Bogoraz contrasted this situation with the prerevolutionary shtetl, where there lived "Jewish holy people, prophets, and soothsayers; women walked around in wigs; men in long caftans. Elderly people spent the last years of their lives in synagogues in prayer and Bible reading."[1] Bogoraz was, in many ways, returning home—he had left his hometown of Ovruch, where he was born the son of a Jewish schoolteacher in 1865, in order to attend a gymnasium in Taganrog. There, he had become a revolutionary activist in the People's Will Party, a crime for which he was imprisoned and exiled to Siberia. In Siberia, he became interested in the Chukchi peoples, studying their folklore and anthropology, and eventually emerging as one of the most prominent ethnographers of his era—beginning in 1897 he collaborated with Franz Boas on the Jesup North Pacific Expedition across the Bering Strait, for five years. After the Revolution, Bogoraz returned to St. Petersburg, where he became a professor of ethnology at the Leningrad Geographical Institute. It was in this capacity that he led his 1924 expedition to the region in which he was born. His optimistic impressions of the pace of revolutionary change, though, were tempered by ambivalence about the social costs of change, as he observed stonemasons and carpenters coexisting with pimps and beggars. Indeed, despite the impetus to celebrate the achievements wrought by a decade of communist rule, Bogoraz and his team could not but note the sorry economic state of the contemporary Soviet shtetl.

Few of the people we interviewed were old enough to have been working before the war—most had just finished their schooling when the Germans invaded—but the picture they paint of their parents' livelihoods demonstrates that the factory jobs the Revolution had promised had yet to materialize. Traditional Jewish occupations continued to dominate the Podolian shtetls and surrounding cities. The evidence suggests that at least in the small towns, few adults had managed to fulfill the educational dreams of their youth. Whereas prior to the Revolution and Civil War the shtetls had been full of young people eager to engage with the world, become educated and cultured, and live better lives as members of the "free professions"—doctors, lawyers, dentists, or even writers or actors—by the first decade of Soviet rule, many of those with ambitious dreams had either left the shtetl or abandoned those dreams in the face of a stark reality.[2] Although education and the pursuit of a professional life remained an ideal in the Soviet shtetl, the vast majority continued to work in traditional handicrafts and trade.[3]

According to the 1926 census, Jews constituted 74 percent of all artisans in Tulchyn and 69 percent of all artisans in Vinnytsya district.[4] Put differently, 29 percent of all Jews in Tulchyn and 34 percent in Vinnytsya were artisans.[5] Jews also dominated the trade and credit industries—ac-

1926–1932 District borders

cording to census figures, Jews constituted 64 percent of the trade and credit industry in Tulchyn and 60 percent in Vinnytsya. In Tulchyn as well, 59 percent of coachmen and porters were Jewish, and 37 percent of those in the free professions were Jewish. On the other hand, only 5 percent of Jewish workers were engaged in agriculture, and only 3 percent of railroad workers were Jewish. Jews also comprised only 20 percent of all industrial workers in Tulchyn, the most favored profession in the hierarchy of the proletarian state. Notably, Jews also comprised about half of those who were classified as "unemployed," a category that likely included many engaged in trade and credit on the black market.[6]

Within the general category of artisans, certain handicraft fields in Tulchyn district were overwhelmingly dominated by Jews: 132 of 144 barbers were Jewish (92 percent); 108 of 140 coopers (75 percent); 80 of 82 glaziers (98 percent); 102 out of 141 coachmen (72 percent); and 1,372 of 1,639 tailors (84 percent). White-collar occupations were less common in Tulchyn than in Ukraine as a whole, but even in those fields Jews were disproportionately represented. Half of the prosecutors, almost half of the defense lawyers, and one-quarter of the judges in the district were Jewish; 10 of the 12 dentists, 5 of the 7 doctors, and 37 of the 73 musician-swere also Jewish.[7] In other words, Jews were differentiated not only by religion and language, but also by the trades in which they worked.[8] The Jews were almost as much a socioeconomic class as they were followers of a religious faith.

Indeed, almost all the people we interviewed came from artisanal backgrounds and equated the essence of Jewishness with such occupational skills. Maria Yakuta told us that most of the Jews in her native Teplyk were artisans: cobblers, tailors—"there were such great tailors"—"tinsmiths, there were many of them. They used to make tins for baking bread and pails for carrying water and tin for fixing the roof." Her own father was a hat maker, who specialized in caps and fur hats for winter. He would also make linings and cuffs for winter coats and muffs. Evgeniia Kozak's father, Avrum Gershkovitch, was a furrier: "He would go out to the villages, take an automobile, and make pelts. By hand, not with a machine—he would sew them by hand." Chaim Skoblitsky's father "was a locksmith. He knew how to make machines and all types of things." Moyshe Kupershmidt's grandfather was a mason in a mill: "He hewed the rocks there. . . . And later my mother became a little wealthier. They bought a cow and my mother used to milk it. And they would bring it to the market." Raisa Chuk's father worked out of the home, making and selling colanders for flour. Her mother was the manager of an artel, a workers' cooperative, that knitted blankets: "All the blankets in the city were hers." Moyshe Vanshelboim remembered, "Life was quiet in Berdichev. There were butchers, cobblers, tailors, watchmakers. There were jewelers, leather workers. There were a lot. There were carpenters." Chaim Rubin listed the occupations he recalled from Buki: "There were a lot of artisans: there were many tailors; there were leather workers; there were cobblers. People worked." His cousin Motl, who was sitting next to him, added to this list, "coopers [*bonders*], wagon-wheel makers [*shtelners*]," at which point Chaim clarified, "Coopers are the ones who make barrels, in which you put apples and all types of stuff to ferment."

The occupational distribution that current residents remember from their childhoods mimics the prerevolutionary structure of the town, in which Jews had been engaged in the same handicrafts for generations. Whereas these occupations were once regarded with low esteem, residents today recall them fondly. Some do so as part of a general nostalgia for a world that is disappearing, some do so out of respect for their parents who earned their livings in this way, and others do so because they remember that it was these "specialists" who were permitted to remain in the ghetto during the war, whereas the intellectuals and Party leadership were sent to camps.[9]

In addition to labor-intensive handicrafts, such as those associated with cobblers and tailors, Jews were also among the first to embrace newer technologies that did not impose upon them the restrictions built into some of the more established professions. With less to lose, Jewish artisans tended to be more willing than their neighbors to take on risk and to jump into newer labor markets. One such area was photography, and studios attracted those with artistic bents, like the artists Marc Chagall and Solomon Yudovin, both of whom began their careers by retouching photographs, as well as other laborers who had sufficient education to navigate the new technology. Skoblitsky recalled working in a photography studio as one of his first jobs. He would prepare negatives on glass plates: "In those days they would photograph on glass, it was called 'making it positive.' I used to retouch them. There was a white print, and it had to be made black."[10] In Sharhorod, one of the last remaining home-workshops in the old town square when we visited in 2002 was Abram Vaisman's photography store, from which a sign hung that was visible from the street. Vaisman had worked as a photojournalist for the local newspaper, having learned the occupation from his brother: "I used to travel around the villages. Their bosses would honor the people who were working better than others; those who received the

Order of Lenin or other orders or medals. . . . Heroes of work, heroes of the war. I would photograph them."

In practical terms, this occupational distribution fared poorly for the Jewish population. It was to the detriment of the Jews that handicrafts and trade were precisely the occupations accorded the least value and prestige in the Soviet hierarchy of professional life. About one-third of all Jews worked in the occupations that the Soviet government targeted for elimination—trade and traditional handicrafts. These occupations were already facing challenges from the late nineteenth century onset of industrialization. The nationalization of private enterprise and the criminalization of private trade during the period of War Communism had severely disrupted Jewish occupational life in the shtetl, forcing hundreds of thousands of Jews to flee across the borders or to seek a better fortune in the big city. Those who remained had to eke out a living amid rampant unemployment and severe shortages. Tailors needed material to stitch, bakers needed wheat to bake, and smiths needed metal to forge. The few wholesale goods that made their way into the shtetl from nearby villages were quickly snatched up by the state factories, leaving those engaged in private artisanal work in desperate need of raw materials. The life of Soviet artisans was not easy.

When the state began its campaign against individual artisans, the Jews who made their living in handicrafts and whose very identity was intimately tied to their artisanal skills suffered heavily. The Jewish Sections of the Communist Party and Party cells encouraged the formation of collective labor brigades, or artels, forcing individual artisans to give up their private businesses and throw in their lot with a collective. In practice, many artels provided little more freedom than the worst sweatshops. The journalist and son-in-law of Sholem Aleichem, B. Z. Goldberg, who visited the Soviet Union in 1934, wrote:

> Where there had been a score of small Jewish shops there was now one large state store, and the Jewish shopkeepers had become superfluous. State agents picked up all the surplus the peasants could spare, or be compelled to give up, and the Jewish trader in agricultural produce was now unnecessary. Transport had been taken over by the state; besides, nobody went anywhere unless sent on a mission—and so the Jewish coachman had nothing to do. Even the artisan had a desperate struggle, with competition from the new factories, scarcity of raw materials, and the tax on 'private enterprise' eating up whatever he earned.

There were only two alternatives, Goldberg continued: to join a Jewish collective farm or to join an artel, where "a man worked harder than before, and earned less."[11]

Although some Jewish artisans joined artels that were encouraged by the government, the majority continued—at least initially—to work in isolation out of their homes as their parents and grandparents had done. Only 176 of 1,581 Jewish tailors and 38 of 394 Jewish cobblers in Tulchyn district were members of artels in 1926. By contrast, 913 Jewish tailors and 224 Jewish cobblers were sole proprietors.[12] Most of the individuals we interviewed recalled their parents and others within the community working out of home workshops rather than communal artels. Some, like Donia Presler's mother, began working as a glazier in the family shop, but then moved into an artel. Tseytl Kislinskaia talked about the industrialization of the shtetl in the mid-1930s, after her father had died in 1933: "Afterward there was progress and people would go there to work. But he didn't go anywhere. In those days, in general, immediately after the Soviet government came in, people worked in their homes. Tailors worked in the home, cobblers worked in the home, and then later factories started appearing and plants started appearing. Even then my father worked out of his home." In the prewar shtetl, most Jews continued to work out of the family home and in the family business. Even in Kiev only 300 of the 1,500 Jewish cobblers in the city had joined workshops—the remainder worked out of their residences.[13] Ultimately the advantages of remaining independent outweighed the benefits of joining a collective. Even those who joined the collectives during the 1928–1932 campaigns often left a few years later, either for a factory job or to migrate to the city. Those who remained in the collectives often supplemented their incomes with independent work on the side.[14]

Occupations were an important identity marker and continued to have caste overtones—there was little separation between work and home, and communal status was heavily dependent upon one's occupation. The divisions between occupations were further enhanced by the structure of communal life that segregated people based on their trades. Tailors went to the Tailors' Synagogue; cobblers to the Cobblers' Synagogue, and coopers to the Coopers' Synagogue. As ethnographer Marina Khakkarainen reminds us, every occupation had its own reputation, its own indelible traits that were imagined to be ingrained in the blood of its practitioners. Coachmen were said to be melancholy, and because they traveled at night through the forests in peripheral, borderline spaces, were sometimes believed to possess magical abilities and to practice dark arts; smiths were strong and were sometimes credited with defending the city from pogroms and bandits; tailors were lucky; and barbers were independent.[15] The caste nature of occupational distribution was reinforced by marriage customs, which encouraged young people to marry within their family's profession. As Tsolik Groysman put it, "We were four brothers and a sister. My father was a watchmaker, and all the brothers were watchmakers, and my sister married a watchmaker."

Even when pioneering young folk sought out new occupations, they tended not to stray far from those of their parents. Moyshe Kupershmidt's father was a coachman: "My father had a horse and wagon. When people had to travel to the mill, for grinding, he took them." Coachmen were often regarded as the lowest rung on the social ladder, but they were also believed to have influence beyond their evident means: it was widely believed, for instance, that the reason the railroads had bypassed Tulchyn in the nineteenth century was because of the influence of the coachmen who protested.[16] Bratslav, where Kupershmidt was born, had also been bypassed by the major railroad built through the region. Like Tulchyn, it was a town best reached by road rather than rail. As a result, coachmen like Kupershmidt's father were much in need in the early twentieth century. It was common for children to follow in the footsteps of their parents, but to be a coachman would have been to look backwards, and the Soviet Union was all about looking forward. So Kupershmidt learned to drive a truck instead of a horse, and became a chauffeur—a "new coachman"—an occupation so romantic that its French name transcended linguistic boundaries. Because of the rarity of highways (the USSR had ten times less highway mileage than Britain), the poor condition of existing roads, the scarcity of automobiles, and the unreliability of Soviet models, most of those traveling by car or truck during the prewar period were professional drivers. In regions poorly served by the railway network, the need for a chauffeur was even more urgent. These chauffeurs commonly doubled as mechanics, able to repair the prewar Soviet trucks that tended to break down on too regular a basis to make them practical for the casual driver. The occupation of chauffeur attracted young men who were in search of adventure, those with a love for the open road, and those with a rugged sense of individuality. A chauffeur also needed to be industrious, mechanically minded, and not mind the smell of benzene in their hair and grease in their fingernails. Alexei Futiran of Tomashpil, whose father was a coachman, told us that coachmen even had to work on the Sabbath to earn money. He remembered several songs about the difficult life of the coachman. Kupershmidt followed his father's line of work, but he adapted to the new world and embraced new technologies.[17]

Nisen Yurkovetsky, on the other hand, did not go into his family's barber business, probably in part because he had been orphaned during the 1919 pogrom and had been brought up partially in the Nestervarka orphanage. Instead, he attended the same driving school as Kupershmidt in Bratslav, and became a professional chauffeur as well. "In '36 they sent me to a Machine Tractor Station and from there to Bratslav to attend a school for chauffeurs, and there I learned to be a chauffeur." But his two brothers did follow in his father's footsteps and became barbers: "We were left with a barbershop. My father was a barber. We were left with the salon, the premises, the mirrors. There was a worker with us, Isaac. He has since passed away. And when my elder brother was fifteen or twelve years old, he started to work step by step as a barber. That's how we made it through the Soviet period." The family kept a barbershop in their home on Lenin Street, opposite the market. The children took on this profession simply because they inherited the salon, and so many of the start-up costs had already been paid. Naum Gaiviker of Proskurov (Khmelnytskyy) also became a barber just like his father: "My father opened a barbershop and I learned with him." He worked as a barber for seventy years.

Practicing traditional crafts, however, was not a generally efficient way to earn a living; a craftsman had to be able to sell his or her wares as well. Arkadii Gelman, who made his living as a cattle dealer in Kamyanets-Podilskyy, explained: "That's how it was with money. A craftsman was always poor. A rich craftsman had to be both a craftsman and a merchant. You see, the cobbler who could make a pair of boots and sell them was both a cobbler and a merchant. But the cobbler who just stood and worked in his stand was a pauper. The locksmith, to whom you would come and bring a key to fix, or a frying pan, or a samovar, was a real pauper if he was only a craftsman." Many Jews dabbled in multiple jobs, buying, selling, and making whatever they could manage. As a result, the social status of Jewish artisans was ambiguous: on the one hand they could be considered productive, albeit at the low end of prestige as artisans, but on the other hand, their involvement in petty trade subjected them to scorn from a society that aspired to eliminate the free market.[18]

Only a small percentage of Jews were engaged in agriculture, the archetypical Ukrainian occupation, where the peasants' ties to the land helped define what it meant to be Ukrainian. In Ukraine as a whole, just 9 percent of all Jews farmed the land compared with 85 percent of all non-Jews.[19] The Revolution and the alleged alliance it forged between workers and peasants enhanced the peasants' standing in the strict hierarchy enforced by the communist state. On a more practical level, Jews who lacked access to the countryside usually had fewer opportunities to acquire basic foodstuffs during difficult economic times, as proximity to the fields and orchards often provided farmers with a built-in advantage. Only during the Great Famine of 1932–1933, during which forced requisitions starved the countryside, did the cities fare marginally better.[20]

Despite their artisanal skills, Jews were poorly represented among factory workers, and remained so through the 1930s. Rather than recruit from among the artisanal class to staff the growing factories, the major plants sought workers from among the peasantry. A skilled tailor had less of a chance of getting a job in a textile factory than a farmer from the village. Jews comprised less than 10 percent of the workers on the floors of the large industrial factories that were established in cities throughout Ukraine. In poorer regions, Jews were even less likely to work in factories: in Podolia as a whole, only 12 percent of Jews worked in factories compared with over 16.5 percent in Kiev.[21] By 1935, Jews were still less represented among workers than non-Jews, with only 17 percent of Jews working as blue-collar workers in Vinnytsya Province.[22] Most of those who benefited from the jobs created by urban manufacturing plants were peasant migrants to the city rather than urban Jewish artisans. In short, Jews were less likely than Christians to be getting jobs in the most dynamic sectors of the economy, and were more likely to be working in traditional handicrafts.

"ONLY JEWS LIVED HERE"

The Jewish Sections of the Communist Party embarked upon a massive campaign in the mid-1920s in order to restructure Jewish life, turning Jewish petty traders into factory workers and farmers.[23] Tulchyn, as a district capital, was one of the towns most heavily targeted by the Jewish Section and its "face to the shtetl" movement.[24] In 1925, Tulchyn was chosen as one of two sites—the other was Mohyliv-Podilskyy—for the establishment of Yiddish-language judicial courts in the region.[25] Mendl Osherowitch wrote of Tulchyn during his visit:

> Tulchyn is one of the shtetls where one sees signs not only of destruction but also of new construction. On the broad "Lenin Street," where there are still today two "stoops," the large stoop and the small stoop, a beautiful "Soviet House" has been built, where the activities of the various governmental institutions are concentrated. There is also a bank in Tulchyn, a "Museum of the Revolution," Jewish and non-Jewish schools, where all the children learn for free, and there are also factories and worker cooperatives from various occupations in Tulchyn that fall under the category of Soviet light industry.

But, he noted, most factory workers weren't actually working. The factories he visited lay half empty, lacking supplies of raw materials with which to produce. He was appalled at how much time workers wasted waiting in line for basic necessities like bread and eggs.[26]

Many of those we interviewed identify handicrafts with the very essence of the shtetl itself, drawing a sharp distinction between the Christian peasants who lived in the countryside and the Jews who lived in the urban centers. In this sense, the shtetl is defined as the place where Jews lived; and Jewish men, in turn, are equated with artisans. Arkadii Burshtein, a matter-of-fact fellow with a pleasant smile, spoke of Sobolivka, where he was born in 1928, in these terms: "Sobolivka was a beautiful shtetl. All the Christians lived surrounding the shtetl and in the middle was the shtetl. About one thousand people lived there. There were one thousand Jews there. There were Jews who worked in the sugar factory. There were tailors, cobblers, carpenters, glaziers, barbers, and shopowners. And the women were homemakers. They cooked dumplings (*varenikes*) and baked *pirogis* with cherries." Brukhe Gammer told us that her father was a "*goyishe* tailor," by which she meant that he was a tailor who worked in the village rather than in Khmilnyk, the town in which she was born in 1924. In her terminology, the village was again equated with non-Jews, even though it was also the workplace of her own father. The rich tailors, she went on, worked in town and the poor tailors in the village. Khone Poberevskaia, a soft-spoken and elegant women we interviewed in 2002, remembered Stanislavchyk, a shtetl near Zhmerynka where she was born in 1914: "The non-Jews lived separately in the villages. Only Jews lived here [in the town]. There was a tailor, a cobbler . . . everybody had their own way of making money. But the Christians—they worked in the fields. In the shtetl there was a market where people would buy and sell." Her mother, she explained, learned how to make yeast, which she would sell in the market to help make ends meet and provide for her eleven children. Shloyme Skliarskii also sharply differentiated the village of Ivanka from the shtetl of Zhorn-ishche. Zhornishche, he explained, was a Jewish town (*shtetl mit yidn*) with some two thousand Jews. There was a synagogue and "we used to go dancing and all that—*davening* [praying]." But the Jews, he says were not a majority: "There were goyim all around—there were no Jews there, surrounding it. Maybe there was a blacksmith there. . . . All around were goyim. In the shtetl, it was only [Jews.]" In other words, the town itself was completely Jewish, but it was surrounded by rural areas of Ukrainians. The only Jew in the rural regions was the blacksmith, who, because he was an artisan, Skliarskii took for granted was a Jew.

This impression of two starkly demographically distinct regions is supported by census data. According to the 1926 census, only 11 percent of all Ukrainians—Jews and non-Jews—lived in urban centers. However, 91.4 percent of Ukrainian Jews were urban.[27] Thanks to a series of campaigns that settled urban Jews in rural farmland, by 1939 the number of urban Jews in Ukraine had decreased a little; but still 85.5 percent of Jews lived in urban centers on the eve of the Second World War.[28] These figures were replicated in Vinnytsya Province, where the shtetl remained the central locale of Jewish life until the war.

The census data lend credence to the common perception of the shtetl as a largely Jewish town. The Jewish population of several towns, including Khmilnyk, Nemyriv, Sharhorod, Bershad, Kryzhopil, and To-mashpil, totaled more than 50 percent of the residents. By contrast, the countryside surrounding these urban centers was largely absent

Table 1. Jewish Populations of Select Shtetls in 1926

	Total Population	Jewish population	% Jewish
Bershad	11,757	7,016	60%
Bratslav	7,842	1,840	23%
Chechelnyk	6,463	2,301	36%
Haysyn	15,330	5,190	34%
Ilnytsya	11,552	5,407	47%
Khmilnyk	10,792	6,011	56%
Kryzhopil	2,986	1,538	52%
Lypovets	8,638	3,611	42%
Nemyriv	7,300	4,176	57%
Sharhorod	4,416	2,697	61%
Tomashpil	5,985	3,252	54%
Tulchyn	17,391	7,708	44%
Vapnyarka	1,433	667	47%
Yampil	6,289	1,823	29%
Zhmerynka	22,241	4,380	20%
Zhvanets	3,445	1,383	40%

Source: *Vsesoiuznaia perepis naseleniia 1926 goda,* Vol. 12, 202–213.

of Jews. Even the rural villages in the immediate vicinity of the most heavily concentrated Jewish towns, among them Sharhorod, Bershad, Vapnyarka and Lypovets, had only a handful of Jewish residents. Thus, for instance, in Sharhorod, where the urban population was 61 percent Jewish, the surrounding rural population was only 1 percent Jewish. Similarly, 7,016 Jews were living in the city of Bershad, according to the 1926 census, constituting 60 percent of the urban population, whereas only 190 Jews lived in the surrounding countryside, where they made up less than half a percent of the population.[29] The common picture of Jews living in the urban center and peasants living on the periphery is therefore verifiable through the census data.

Table 2. Rural Areas of Town Districts

	Total Population	Jewish Population	Percentage
Sharhorod	27,166	158	1%
Bershad	39,945	190	0%
Vapnyarka	39,525	816	2%
Lypovets	30,477	576	2%

Even though we lack census data about precisely where Jews lived within the city, oral histories and architecture indicate that Jews were overwhelmingly concentrated in the center around the market square, where the population around the main streets was nearly 100 percent Jewish.

The major cities within Vinnytsya Province and its immediate environs also had significant Jewish populations, informing the identity of the cities and their relationships with surrounding satellite shtetls. Uman was 49 percent Jewish, Berdichev was 56 percent Jewish, and Vinnytsya was 41 percent Jewish. Each of the cities became a focus of attention for the Jews in the shtetl, and often was a target of migration. Throughout the twentieth century, the general demographic trend was to migrate to larger locales: Jews from Bershad migrated to Vinnytsya; Jews from Vinnytsya to Kiev; and Jews from Kiev to Moscow.

Elizaveta Bershadskaia was among the few Jews born in the rural villages around Bershad. She was born in the village of Chernyatka, 30 kilometers across the Southern Bug River, in 1927. Her father, Kalmen, was a barber, and her mother, Khave, a seamstress. Elizaveta, too, recalled how few Jews lived outside the town. She explained that her father's clients were predominantly non-Jews: "The goyim would go to him. . . . He had a store there in the village." But even in the village, Jews, she told us, tended not to engage in agrarian work, but rather worked as artisans: "There were very few Jews there [in Chernyatka]. One was a tinsmith, one was a barber, one did something else—sewed, and a cobbler. Those types of occupations." Bershadskaia believed that the Jews of the village were valued for their skills: "They [the Christians] liked having Jews there. They liked having the Jews there because they did—they worked the types of jobs that a non-Jew can't do—work that only a Jew can do." For Bershadskaia, artisanal work was the very essence of Jewishness, indivisible from Jewish ethnic identity; it was a skill set inaccessible to her gentile counterparts.

Occupational prestige was part of a complex and ambiguous social hierarchy in the Soviet shtetl. Whereas many aspired toward higher education and professional lives, the practical value of possessing a set of artisanal skills was obvious. This occupational opacity was most evident in occupations that possessed both professional and trade characteristics. Donia Presler's father was a professional musician. Like many other trades, musicians learned their skills in the family: "They would go out and sing and play in the theater and that's how they made a living. It's not a profession; it's a trade. One doesn't learn in institutions. It's self-taught. His father could play the fiddle and taught the children music. They were musical; the daughter could sing well. It's not the type of thing you can learn in institutes," she mused. "My father came from a family of musicians," she continued:

> My father's father's name was Itzik . . . and his mother's name was Esther. They were descended from musicians. His father played the fiddle, he did. Itzik played the fiddle, and so did their older son; he also played the fiddle. And my father also knew how to play the fiddle, but he learned to play the flute. They said it was a more difficult instrument to play. They also had a daughter named Khone. They would drive around. They had their own production. They would drive out to the shtetls and put on shows. My father would play the flute, and his brother Utler—that was his name—played the fiddle. My grandfather also played the fiddle, and Khone, the daughter, would sing. So many Jews came out to see them.

She explained that her father was living in Odessa at the time, about 1920. He even played with famed Jewish Jazz musician Leonid Utesov, she boasted, a fact confirmed in Utesov's own memoirs. When her father moved to Tulchyn, he also played in a band:

> There was Simcha, the clarinetist. There was Shmuel-Chaim—he played the fiddle. And my father played the flute. There was Pinia, a drummer. On Purim they would go to the wealthy people, stand outside, and play. They were doing it up until the war. They would go around and, in Tulchyn, there were such wealthy people, too. And they would go from house to house and put on a Purim play for each one: one person would give them a couple of bucks, another would give them some cake. They would give to the paupers, to the klezmers. They were paupers. They would go around to the houses on holidays, they would take the two or three children who could play music, and people would throw something into the basket. Some would throw in baked goods and others would give money. That was their livelihood.

Since gigs were hard to come by, Presler's father had to supplement his income with artisanal work: "Once every three months there would be a wedding, or once every half-year. It was a small city," explained Presler. Presler's maternal grandfather had been a glazier and taught her mother the skills of the trade. As Presler went on:

> My mother's father, Avrum-Yosl, was a glazier. He had six girls and two boys. And he just made windows. . . . Their mother died and left behind eight children, some of them were small. My mother learned how to [do

the work] and she would work right beside him cutting panels. He would cut them. They would bring the windows and put the glass in, and my mother worked with him. . . . My mother taught my father how to be a glazier. They would take these cartons and put pieces of glass in them. At night they would go to the villages in order to meet the non-Jews very early because they went into the fields. This one needs a panel and that one needs a panel. They would leave at night and very early they would be in the village. They would start up with: "Windowpanes, windowpanes. Who needs windowpanes?" This one would need. That one would need them to do their glasswork. And afterwards they would return by foot.

Jewish traders and artisans wandered through the dark fields of Ukraine and along the village roads in search of customers. The situation in Ukraine was undoubtedly similar to that described by Bogoraz from his 1924 expedition to Sirotina, a village near Vitebsk in Belarus: "During the day everybody sleeps. At night, in the darkness, everybody wakes up. People get bread from the village. At night, they grind in the mill. At night, the coachmen go to Vitebsk with their goods, and the next night return. At night, they slaughter the animals. At night, they make deals with the poor peasants. They won't admit that vodka production takes place in the darkness of night. Even the artisans go about work at night, in order to avoid registration and requisitions."[30]

Women were kept busy at home caring for the children and keeping the house, but many women also had responsibilities for earning income, particularly through helping out or managing the family store or market stall. Skoblitsky described his mother's world:

The women in those days didn't study. It was a village, a little town, Chernove, where my grandfather lived. And so they learned to become merchants. They had stores. They would sell various things. . . . They used to come to Berdichev to purchase herring, fish, various materials, pelts, various types of clothing. They would sell it here and there and that's how they made a living.

In Tulchyn district, most working women helped out in the family business, with the largest group (505 women) identifying themselves as traders. Another 146 Jewish women helped out with the family hat-making business and 119 with the family tailor business. Many women also managed their own businesses: 498 Jewish women identified themselves as sole-proprietor traders, 32 were sole-proprietor bakers, and 323 were sole-proprietor tailors. There were also 72 Jewish women working as maids or household servants, 80 as teachers or teacher assistants, and 54 as office workers in doctors', dentists' and surgical clinics. Many Jewish women also worked in the region's textile factories: 828 classified themselves as textile workers and artisans.[31]

In part because of their work duties, Jewish women tended to marry later than their non-Jewish neighbors. According to the 1926 census, Jewish men were getting married in their mid-twenties and Jewish women in their early twenties. In Right Bank Ukraine, most Jewish men were married by the age of twenty-five and women by age twenty-two. Non-Jewish women, by contrast, were marrying at an even younger age; they were four times more likely to be married at the age of nineteen, and more than twice as likely to be married by age twenty.[32] Often the only respite from one's family was marriage. Asya Barshteyn of Sharhorod told us:

> Our house was very small. It was one room. There were three children, all girls, me—Asya—Fanya, and Sore. And all the girls had to be brought up and we had to be married. My father worked as a turner. We had a small room. We didn't live richly, just comfortably. My father was handy. He would prepare everything for winter. He would buy a little sugar. We didn't, thank God, experience hunger. . . . But we had such a small room. There were two beds. But we lived, and made it through, and got married.

Yet, for many women, marriage was not so easy. As a result of the violence that plagued the region—76 percent of the victims of the pogroms were men—there were 1,140 Jewish women for every 1,000 Jewish men in 1926, and 1,160 Jewish women for every 1,000 Jewish men in 1939.[33] Although women outnumbered men in the general population as well, the figures were starker for the Jewish population. The marriage market was a competitive one, and many women never married.

"AND A GOAT ON A CHAIN"

Between 1928 and 1933, the period of the First Five-Year Plan, the Soviet Union underwent a radical transformation from a mixed economy to a planned one: the state outlawed all private capital and launched a massive campaign to promote heavy industry and collectivized farming. The increased intrusion of the Soviet state into the Podolian shtetl was so transformative that people often indicate this break by referring to the post-1933 era as "the Soviet regime" in contrast to the earlier decade, during which the Soviet government had not yet fully infiltrated the shtetl. This popular periodization reflects the real difficulties the Soviet central government had in establishing full control over the small towns in Ukraine. Prior to what many people refer to as "the Soviet regime" the impact of Soviet institutions and policies was limited. Certainly for those who paid attention to politics, the communist government was instituting numerous changes, but for ordinary folk who struggled on a day-to-day basis to make ends meet, the period before the early 1930s was characterized only by economic insecurity, and at least in the initial revolutionary years, a dizzying array of governments that came and left. For about fifteen years following the Bolshevik Revolution in faraway Petrograd, the struggle for food security, shelter, and survival continued unabated in small-town Ukraine.

It was only during the 1930s that the region began to pull its way out of poverty and slowly transform itself into a modern industrialized region, just in time for a new devastation, whose terrors would completely surpass the Civil War and pogroms of that earlier era. In Ukraine, collectivization and dekulakization were the most invasive effects of the First Five-Year Plan, radically transforming the Ukrainian countryside. In addition to the subjugation of the peasantry, though, collectivization unleashed a wave of repression against individuals the state believed facilitated the peasant economy: priests, village elites, private traders, and the petty intelligentsia.[34] Repressive policies were replicated in urban centers, where religious functionaries, including rabbis and Jewish elites, were persecuted together with merchants and small shop-owners, who were accused of aiding the kulaks and preventing grain distribution. In short, those who had managed to sustain the economy during the first decade of the Revolution were rewarded for their efforts with arrests and expulsion.

The First Five-Year Plan was also finally able to disrupt traditional Jewish artisanal life. By 1929, a survey of occupational distribution in select cities demonstrated that Jewish involvement in trade and handicrafts was declining. Jewish workers started to join the industrial working-class, but still at a lower rate than their non-Jewish counterparts.[35] Binyomin Geller told us about how in 1930 the artisans in Pyatka were

forced into collectives: "In 1930 they gathered all the artisans into collectives: the carpenters had a collective, the cobblers together, the tailors
together. It was really bad. People began to flee to Kiev, to Zhytomyr,
to Odessa."

One target of the Teplyk collectivization drive was Maria Yakuta's
uncle, Khotskl. She remembered that Khotskl had a goat, and thus was
able to get milk whenever he wanted. This was a luxury in Teplyk during
the 1920s, and reason enough for the children to visit Khotskl as often
as possible: "He would welcome us with dumplings and milk. It was so
delicious." Khotskl's goat and the "luxurious" lifestyle he enjoyed with
his dumplings and milk attracted the attention of the authorities, who
were hunting "kulaks." Most of Khotskl's meager wealth came from his
small shop: "My mother's brother had a small shop. There were pencils
there and notebooks and herring, kerosene, candles. It was a poor little
shop, a little canteen. And he was a pauper with a big family." But since
he personally owned his shop, he was regarded as a speculator, an enemy
of the people. As Yakuta explained, "The president of the Jewish government, Stratievski, was given the task of collecting gold from the Jews. He
searched my uncle, Khotskl—his name was Khotskl Vitniatski. And he
was arrested. He didn't have any money. He was thrown in prison. He
was left there for an entire winter; his beard was overtaken by lice. He
barely made it out of there alive. It wasn't just his money they were after
but also that of his brothers. They wanted him to sell out his family."
Yakuta was indignant that Khotskl was targeted as one of the moneyed
elite, when he had so little with which to feed his family: "They were all
very poor people. Who were the Jews with money?! Those who had a
business with large stores, or large businesses of course. But he just had
buckwheat dumplings boiled in milk. And a goat on a chain."

The Palatnikov family of Teplyk was also targeted for expulsion.
Tatiana Marinina (née Palatnikova) was born in 1921. She completed
three grades in the Yiddish school and was doing well in her studies
when suddenly, in 1930, her family was forcibly uprooted and sent to the
Lunacharskii collective farm in Crimea, named after Anatolii Lunacharskii, the first Soviet People's Commissar of Enlightenment. Tatiana's
sister, Sofia, told us that in his youth her father was so poor that all the
children in his family shared two pairs of shoes between them; in the
winter, only two children could leave the house at a time, while the rest

remained at home barefoot. When she was thirteen, her father was apprenticed to a butcher; he eventually managed to open his own butcher shop and earn a good living. He bought a large house in Teplyk and a Primus stove, one of the first in the town. He "had a butcher shop. He had a permit for the butcher shop. But he was already considered to be part of the unreliable element. So they sent us to Crimea. At that time I was nine years old. My sister was two years old. There was nowhere to live there. They led us in to a barn."

In Crimea, the Palatnikov family had access to an orchard with apples, pears, peaches, and apricots; fields of cantaloupes and watermelons; and thousands of sheep. Both sisters attended a Russian-language school in a Tatar village about 1.5 kilometers away from the collective farm. They remembered that the school had Jewish, Tatar, and German students, as well as a group of converts to Judaism, and they recalled relations as being friendly: "We all played together. Nobody knew who was a Jew or Tatar or German there. We were all just children . . . we were happy," she told the Shoah Foundation during her 1997 interview. In the late 1930s, the Palatnikovs returned to Teplyk, now poor and "rehabilitated" as agrarian workers. Her father, though, returned to his previous line of work, selling meat and produce. The Palatnikovs' brief venture from shop-owners to collective farmers and back is a typical mark of the vicissitudes of the era and of the ineffectiveness of Soviet power in the shtetl. Many disenfranchised Jews in the shtetls migrated to collective farms in the late 1920s and early 1930s only to return to the shtetl when it became possible to do so.[36]

The roundups of the late 1920s severely disrupted shtetl life, but when the dust settled a decade later, many of those who had been forced to flee to the collective farms and the big cities found themselves returning to their hometowns. When we interviewed ninety-five-year-old Naum Gaiviker, he recalled: "In '30, when I finished my apprenticeship, I wanted to live in a big city. Only in a big city. And my father had a license, and they gathered up all the barbers together with the tailors, the cobblers, and the tinsmiths. I didn't go. I was a courageous lad. I went to the station and got a ticket to Moscow." Yet, ultimately, three-quarters of a century later, he was still in Khmelnytskyy, the city in which he had been born.

—⚊—

The "Great Terror" that Stalin unleashed in 1937 had less of an impact in the out-of-the-way shtetls of Podolia than in major urban centers. The relative paucity of Party members and intellectuals, the primary targets of the violence of 1937–1938, shielded the craftsmen and workers of the region from the worst excesses of the violence. In Ukraine, the primary ethnic targets of the terror were Poles. Those Jews who were targeted left no heirs in the shtetl. As a result, those with whom we spoke rarely had much to say about this tragic episode.[37] Those who were affected by the Terror tended to come from more intellectual backgrounds. Fania Braverman, for instance, revealed that when she joined the Komsomol in 1937, the local newspaper exposed her grandfather as a shop-owner and publicly chastised her for concealing this inconvenient fact.

Still, on the eve of the Second World War, the Jewish character of the shtetls of Vinnytsya Province remained largely intact. Some towns saw slight declines in the Jewish proportion of residents: Jews constituted 44 percent of the population of Tulchyn in 1926 and 42 percent in 1939, for instance, and 34 percent of the population of Haysyn in 1926 and 28 percent in 1939. And in several other towns of the province, the Jewish proportion of the population actually increased, from 61 percent to 74 percent in Sharhorod, and from 54 percent to 62 percent in Tomashpil. Most towns retained their Jewish character, but in almost all cases, there were fewer Jews in town on the eve of the Second World War than had been there a decade before.[38]

In contrast to the situation in Vinnytsya Province, in Ukraine as a whole rapid industrialization was well underway and the Jewish population was being transformed. By 1939, about six million ethnic Ukrainians had moved from the countryside to the city, so that on the eve of the war, many cities and towns throughout Ukraine that had been largely Jewish were becoming Ukrainian.[39] Whereas Jews constituted 23 percent of the urban population of Ukraine in 1926, the influx of Ukrainians into the cities and shtetls had dropped that percentage to 12 percent by 1939.[40] Jews were on the move as well, with many leaving the shtetl for Moscow and Leningrad. Although we do not have figures on Jewish departures from the towns of Ukraine, the growth of the Jewish population of Moscow from about 131,000 in 1926 to 400,000 in 1940 is indicative that Jews were coming from elsewhere, mostly from Ukraine and Belarus.[41]

While the Soviet state was making some progress in turning Jews into factory workers and farmers, the process was slow. In a survey of twelve Ukrainian shtetls conducted in 1935, only 26 percent of the Jewish inhabitants were identified as workers, 33 percent as white-collar workers, 30 percent as artisans, and a mere 3 percent as collective farmers.[42] The results of this survey were analyzed by Soviet historian Lev Zinger in his work, *The Renewed People,* published on the eve of the Second World War. Zinger, writing during the height of Stalinist euphoria following the completion of the Second Five-Year Plan, expressed great enthusiasm for Soviet progress in the shtetl: "The great socialist October Revolution that freed the downtrodden people and nations and radically solved the national question in the spirit of Leninism-Stalinism, also created the broadest possibilities for Jewish workers to join socialist construction," he wrote.[43] He also noted the following:

> Jewish shtetl workers are occupied in various undertakings like the lumber factory in Letichev, the sugar factory in Tomashpil, the cloth factory and the state mechanical factory in Dunaevets, the porcelain factory in Slavuta, the furniture factory in Ovruch, the flax factory in Drise, the paper factory in Tshashnik, etc. Jewish shtetl workers are employed in the local electric stations, the distilleries, the mills and the printing presses, in the nearby state farms and Machine Tractor Stations. . . . The old shtetl with its heder, with the *besmedresh* as the 'communal center' of the Jewish population has been left in the past. Today's shtetl is truly an advanced cultural-economic settlement.[44]

This euphoric portrait of socialist construction in the shtetls was part of the vast Soviet propaganda campaign to discredit the old way of life and celebrate the new. However, despite the radical process of industrialization and collectivization that had taken place in the decade preceding the war, the oral histories we have collected suggest that Jews in the Podolian shtetls continued to lag behind the general population in joining the urban factory working class, and agricultural sector.[45] Jewish occupational patterns as a whole remained remarkably stable despite the radical transformations taking place around them.[46]

4

—ɯ—

Growing Up in Yiddish

Naftoli Shor was born in Bershad in 1922. His father, Pinhas, was a leather worker—"he sewed pelts," Shor told us. Pinhas was also one of the core members of a Hasidic group of pietists in town that met secretly in the 1920s and 1930s in a private house near the synagogue. We interviewed Naftoli on Tishah b'Av, the Jewish holy day that commemorates the destruction of the ancient Temple, in 2002 in his living room in a Soviet apartment complex on Lenin Street in Bershad. He had an endearing toothless smile and a face full of expression. Newspapers, books, photographs and other ephemera cluttered the apartment, pouring out of bookcases and cabinets. Naftoli would pace around as we spoke with him, picking up books or photos and idly examining them. We occasionally had to ask him to return to the interview chair. His mind was sharp and his demeanor welcoming; his patience, though, was short. We began the interview by asking Naftoli about his education. He told us he had attended the local state Yiddish-language school for four years, and then finished his education in a Ukrainian-language school. "But I can read and write in Yiddish well," he insisted. The Yiddish school, he boasted, was located in the central square, right next to the Regional

Naftoli Shor reciting from his prayer book
in his Bershad apartment, 2002.

Executive Committee's building. Its placement in the center of town was
a visible manifestation of the Jewish presence in Bershad and a proud
public statement of the importance the Communist Party initially ascribed to Yiddish-language schooling.

Yiddish-language education was an integral component of the Soviet
shtetl in the 1920s and 1930s, and remains today a source of pride to
those who benefited from it.[1] The Soviet Union was the only country in
the world with a state-sponsored system of Yiddish-language schools.
In 1930, almost 95,000 children were studying in more than eight hundred Yiddish-language schools in Ukraine alone.[2] Many of these were
concentrated in the districts of Vinnytsya Province. In the twenty-one
shtetls that comprised Tulchyn district, for instance, there were fourteen
four-year Yiddish schools and eight seven-year schools in 1926.[3] One of
these was the seven-year Yiddish-language school that Shor attended,
which had been established in 1923 and counted an enrollment of 386
children in the 1925–1926 school year.[4]

Jewish Section archival documents give us some insights about the growth of the Yiddish school movement in select districts. In Berdichev, for instance, the Jewish Sections counted 1,621 students studying in ten Yiddish schools during the 1923–1924 academic year. That figure had more than doubled five years later, when, in 1927, there were 5,126 students studying in twenty-five Yiddish schools. According to the Jewish Section figures, in 1927, a total of 65 percent of Jewish children in Berdichev district were attending Yiddish-language schools, 17 percent were attending Russian or Ukrainian schools, and an estimated 5 percent were attending heders (Jewish religious schools); the rest were not being schooled at all.[5] Since heders had been outlawed, though, the true figure for heder attendance was probably much higher as it was difficult to track the number of students who attended them clandestinely. Although the percentage of Jews attending Yiddish-language schools was relatively high in Berdichev—well above the norm for Ukraine—the schools were attracting mostly the children of workers, artisans, and paupers; the reports state that parents with means preferred to educate their children in Russian.

The movement to school Soviet citizens in their mother tongues was part of the policy of *korenizatsiia,* or nativization, which encouraged national minorities to use their own languages for local governance, cultural development, and education.[6] Soviet ideologues rejected the Herderian notion that language is the primary receptacle of a nation's cultural heritage, and instead believed that language was simply an empty vessel into which any ideology could be inserted. The Commissariat of Enlightenment had decreed that schools for national minorities be opened wherever there were a sufficient number of pupils to warrant the organization of such a school, and that these schools be afforded the same rights as schools of the majority language. The Commissariat of Nationality Affairs and the Commissariat of Enlightenment called for the formation of educational institutions in the languages of the national minorities as the most effective means of reaching these students. In addition to schools, the policy encouraged the formation of theaters, party cells, films, cultural clubs, and courts, all of which functioned in minority languages. Ukrainians were encouraged to attend Ukrainian-language schools; Germans were encouraged to attend German-language schools; and Jews were encouraged to attend Yiddish-language schools. The latter, though, were not to be confused with Jewish schools, as they deliberately avoided teaching children anything about the Jewish religion, preferring instead to promote a completely secular de-Judaicized vision of Jewish life. The Hebrew language, which had for centuries served as the predominant written language of Jewish erudition, was rejected as the language of the hated bourgeoisie and Zionist agitators. The bedrock of a traditional Jewish education—Bible, Talmud, and rabbinical knowledge—was excised from the school curriculum and instead a new secular curriculum was constructed ex nihilo. Many Jewish cultural traditions were thereby made inaccessible to graduates of Yiddish-language schools.

When we asked Naftoli Shor what he had learned in Yiddish school, he summarized four years of education: "I would write slogans there. And placards in Yiddish." While the language of instruction varied across different Soviet schools, the curriculum and ideological orientation of all schools was in complete accordance with Soviet ideals.[7] Soviet schools were designed to mold individuals into useful citizens. Maria Yakuta highlighted the Soviet citizenship skills she had learned: "Comrade Motl was our teacher. . . . We used to call everyone 'Khaver' [Comrade]. Khaver Motl. . . . At the age of nine I was taken into first grade and I finished seven grades. When I graduated I was already a healthy young woman." She remembered very little, though, of anything else she had learned in the school: "I don't remember back to those years," she told us. Later she added, "We learned how to write an official letter and document [in Yiddish]." Students learned to mimic the slogans of the times, but many failed to fully assimilate the ideological content. The curricula of Yiddish-language Soviet schools prioritized citizenship skills and practical agricultural and industrial work. As one set of instructions put it: "It is the duty of the school to acquaint the child with all that is necessary for existence, and with those things that play the major part in life—with agriculture and industrial work—in all its phases and forms."[8] Teachers became agents of revolutionary change and the classroom was one of the revolution's most important battlefields.

Party ideologues cherry-picked literature from prerevolutionary Jewish culture on the basis of its utility and ideological consistency with the communist message. The curriculum was filled with works of contemporary Soviet Yiddish writers, whose ideological commitment to the communist cause was reflected in their writings. Jewish history was systematically purged of its nationalist and religious connotations and reoriented toward the needs of the Party.[9] Even Yiddish orthography was reformed with political motivations. The Jewish Sections and Yiddish schools helped promote a vast Yiddish orthographic reform designed to transform Yiddish spelling, removing any components that would remind readers of the Hebraic roots of many Yiddish words and expressions. Students were taught to spell even obviously Hebrew stock words like *shobes* and *sholem* in a purely phonetic orthography, thereby hiding their Hebraic roots. The educational system presented the shtetl and its milieu as the archaic remnant of a bygone world, destined for complete extinction. The schools shunned any religious expression of Jewish identity. Etia Shvartzbroit, who was born in 1928 in Mohyliv-Podilskyy, explained that "there was no religion. It was a Yiddish school." Tseytl Kislinskaia added, "In the school we learned everything Soviet.... There were Jewish teachers ... they taught us to read and write, arithmetic, all of that—but they didn't teach us Hebrew like they do now.... We learned history, mathematics, physics ... nothing Jewish only Soviet." Émigrés, who have become more accustomed to religious education, are more likely to view the Soviet system as anomalous. In her 1997 interview with the USC Shoah Foundation, for instance, Minna Varshavskay, who was born in 1925 in Mohyliv-Podilskyy, said in broken English:

> In the Soviet Union was a rule there is no God, no religious, and in school they didn't have any lessons about religious nothing. Only just atheist.... Not believing in God. But my father was an Orthodox. Real Orthodox. He prayed every day at home before going to his job and every Saturday he went to synagogue. He was even a cantor in synagogue.... Not his job, but he sang in synagogue. He had a good voice. It was a Jewish house and we before the war celebrated Passover and Purim and Hanukkah and our father told us the story about Jewish folk and we knew a little bit about it.[10]

Indeed, the record of Soviet schools in eradicating religious faith among the youth is mixed: whereas most school children learned to deny the existence of God when asked, and to classify themselves as nonbelievers in surveys, they retained deeper religious beliefs, and often continued performing traditional religious rituals in the home.[11] They lost knowledge of Jewish religious practices, but many held onto their faith. Few of those who remain in the region today recall the details of the antire-ligious curricula, or else they preferred not to share them with us. Those who did, recall it with a chuckle, but dismissed these lessons as having had no value. The Yiddish-language schools' success in instilling Soviet ideology into the hearts and minds of the youth is questionable.

Despite the assimilating drive of these schools, their students emerged highly conscious of themselves as Jews. Shor was gratified that he had learned to read and write in Yiddish. He knew how to type in Yiddish, he told us, tapping his fingers on a table as though it were a Remington typewriter. When we asked him to show us how to write in Yiddish, he took pen and paper and very deliberately wrote the words *shobes* (Sab-bath) and *khaver* (friend), in both cases using the Soviet orthography. We started asking Naftoli more about his education, about what poets he remembered reading as a child. He became frustrated, shooing the names aside, indicating that we were asking irrelevant questions. "Do you have your old workbooks from school?" "Neh! Why would I have such things!" he stammered.

Among those we interviewed, memories of state Yiddish schooling were vague. Most were just pleased to have been schooled in their mother tongues, and recognized how rare Yiddish language schooling was at the time. Chaim Skoblitsky was proud that he had learned to read and write in the Berdichev Yiddish school he attended. He even took us on a tour of the crumbling baroque building that had once housed his Yiddish-language school. It was near the church where he excitedly informed us Balzac got married. The building, built in 1891, had formerly belonged to the wealthy Jewish Magazanik family, but had been expropriated by the Soviet government and converted into a school. When we visited, the building was mostly abandoned save for a small store—the Victoria—in one corner of the building. "There was a Jew who taught us physics, in Yiddish. Everything was in Yiddish. There was a woman who taught mathematics. Also in Yiddish. Everything was in Yiddish. Botany. There were books in Yiddish. Yiddish books." In Bershad, Khayke Gvinter brightened up during our interview when she reminisced about the two-story Yiddish school she attended as a child. She was emphatic that she had learned to read and write in "Yiddish—not the Holy Tongue!" Chaim Rubin had gone to a Yiddish school in his native Buki: "I was a young boy in Buki. I studied for four years in a Yiddish school. A Yiddish school! Four years! And then the communists closed it. . . . Now even though some eighty-one years have passed, I still remember how to read and write in Yiddish. . . . Everything I learned is now recorded in my head like in a tape recorder. I remember from when I was eight until now. It's been some seventy-something years. I remember what I learned as a child."

Yosl Kogan, who also went to a Yiddish school in Bershad, remained a Yiddish enthusiast his whole life: "I love Yiddish," he told us with a broad grin. His love of the language encouraged him to dabble in Yiddish poetry throughout his life. He told us that he had filled up notebooks and scraps of paper with Yiddish poetry and musings, all of which he cherished and stored at his mother's house. When her house tragically burned down after the war, all he was left with was a single notepad he kept by his bed. He had learned to read and write in a Yiddish-language school in Bershad: "It was Yiddish School Number 3. There were three floors. They taught a little German. They thought that German was Yiddish; but [Yiddish] is Yiddish. Yiddish is simpler than that. The language is a Jewish one. But I learned German myself. I don't know any English. I only know Yiddish. I know Ukrainian. I know Russian, grammar. They taught all kinds of things: physics, algebra, geometry, trigonometry, chemistry, and other such subjects." Moyshe Vanshelboim remembered the Yiddish school he attended in Berdichev: "In the Yiddish school we had a big hall, and we would sing Yiddish songs and tell stories, Yiddish stories. We used to put on plays . . . one play was *The Golddiggers* and later there was *Two Hundred Thousand* by Sholem Aleichem." The Yiddish schools adapted the writings of Sholem Aleichem and a few other prerevolutionary Yiddish writers, selecting only stories that could be tweaked to serve Soviet propagandist purposes.

Aba Kaviner was and remains an avid reader and Yiddish enthusiast. Among his favorite writers from his schooling in 1920s Derazhnya are the "classical" Yiddish writers: Mendele Moykher Sforim, Sholem Aleichem, and Yitskhok Leybush Peretz, as well as more contemporary Soviet Yiddish writers such as Peretz Markish, Hershl Orland, Dovid Bergelson, and Leyb Kvitko. His love of Yiddish is accompanied by a skepticism about Hebrew. He shuns the Sephardic pronunciation of Hebrew adapted by the Zionist movement as false, and adores what he regards as the purity of the Ashkenazic pronunciation of the language that was common in his childhood shtetl. He remembers the Yiddish library in the city, as well as the larger library collection in the synagogue, all of which were burned during the war. He himself used to enjoy writing prose and poetry in Yiddish, but "after the war I stopped writing and before the war I burned everything because you never know what you're going to be thrown into prison for."

Some noted that Yiddish-language schools gave them the tools to connect with relatives abroad when it was still possible to do so. Yiddish is an international language, knowledge of which provided many with access to a world largely inaccessible to their Ukrainian neighbors. Kislinskaia told us about how she corresponded with her uncles in America in the early 1930s: "When I was a child, in third grade, I would write letters to America in Yiddish and they would understand me. [My mother's] brothers would write that they were very pleased that I could write Yiddish. But my mother couldn't write. She was barely literate. She was only able to sign. But I was able to write them letters in Yiddish and they could understand me, and I would read the letters from them and I could understand them." This attachment to America—accessible thanks to a Yiddish-language education—was a critical link that many had with the world beyond the shtetl. Indeed, many of those who attended these schools were the first in their families to acquire literacy in the Yiddish language, and they appreciated this as a positive step forward toward a cultured life.

Schools made up for their academic shortcomings with material rewards. Students who showed up for classes were provided with food and hot soup. As Kislinskaia told us: "We used to go in the morning at around 8:00 or 8:30 to school. What was the school like and why did I actually go to school? They would give warm soup to the kids who didn't have a father. Only to the little ones, up until the fourth grade. After the fourth grade, they wouldn't give any more." Pesia Kolodenker of Tulchyn also remembered how the school provided basic necessities for the poverty-stricken children: "All Jews attended the Yiddish school. There should be a school for Jewish children. So, I attended the Yiddish school. We were common folk. We were four children. The principal of the school approached us when we came into school and gave us a coat to put on, sheets of paper, books, and a bag. He dressed us from top to bottom for as long as we attended school." "The Yiddish school did a mitzvah. They clothed those who went to the Yiddish school," she clarified on another occasion.

"WE CAN ANSWER THE QUESTION, BUT ONLY IN YIDDISH"

Despite some initial successes, the state Yiddish school experiment was short lived, and Yiddish schools never managed to attract a majority of Jewish children. At their peak, in 1931–1932, only 49.6 percent of Jewish school children in Ukraine were attending Yiddish schools. By contrast, 84.6 percent of ethnic German school children were attending German language schools, and 93.9 percent of Ukrainians were attending Ukrainian-language schools.[12] According to 1927 figures, in the city of Vinnytsya, 95 percent of Ukrainian children attended Ukrainian-language schools, 89 percent of Russian children attended Russian schools, 66 percent of Polish children attended Polish schools, and only 44 percent of Jewish children attended Yiddish-language schools. Yet 45 percent of all students in the city were native Yiddish-speakers. The problem is even more apparent when the concentration of the Jewish population is taken into consideration: in the Vinnytsya district of Yerusalimka, Jews constituted more than 87 percent of the population, and in the city center, they accounted for more than 60 percent of the population. No other minority so clearly dominated particular districts within the city. The concentration of the Jewish population in two districts should have made it even easier for Jewish children to receive education in Yiddish in their neighborhood schools.[13] Further, although in Ukraine as a whole Yiddish-language usage was already on the decline by 1926, it remained the language of the vast majority of Jews in the Podolian region. Whereas 76 percent of Jews throughout Ukraine listed Yiddish as their mother tongue in the census of that year, 97 percent of those in the Tulchyn district and 94 percent of those in the Vinnytsya district did so.[14] Many Jewish children spoke Yiddish, lived in very Jewish neighborhoods, and had access to Yiddish-language schools, but chose to attend Russian ones instead.

Parents realized that the Yiddish schools were underfunded and starved for resources. In 1923, the entire Berdichev Yiddish school system had only thirty-two teachers, leading to a student–teacher ratio of one teacher for every fifty-one students. By 1927, the student–teacher ratio had improved significantly, but was still relatively high: there were 151 teachers in the system, amounting to a ratio of one teacher for every thirty-four students.[15] However, the rapid hiring of new teachers meant that few had significant experience or credentials: only 29 of the 151 teachers active in 1927 had received any type of higher education, and 71 had been teaching for five years or less.[16] Material resources were also in short supply: only 16 of the 25 schools functioning in 1927 had their own building, and the entire district had only 868 student desks to share among 5,126 students.[17]

Parents filed numerous contemporary complaints about the poor quality of Yiddish schools and about the low priority they were given in state allocation of resources. The government seemed to have essentially given up on Yiddish schools in the early 1930s, leading to the steep decline in enrollment noticeable after the peak of 1931. One letter in *Der emes* complained that even the director of the Yiddish school in one town sent his own children to the Ukrainian-language school. He had seen too many of his best teachers transferred from the Yiddish school to the Ukrainian one. This practice, complained the letter-writer, was rampant throughout the Kiev and Vinnytsya regions.[18]

Dora Yatskova of Kopayhorod (Kopaygorod, Keparet) told us that she attended a Ukrainian-language school even though her father was the director of the Yiddish school in town; he had received the post after studying in a yeshiva in Chişinău and a Russian-language gymnasium in Zhmerynka. She told us that when she was young everybody spoke Yiddish in Kopayhorod, but even many of those who spoke Yiddish went to the Ukrainian school. Binyomin Geller also attended a Ukrainian-language school in Pyatka even though there was a Yiddish school in the shtetl. He explained that the Yiddish school "was closed because there were no children. Some left [the shtetl] and the others wanted to go to the Ukrainian school." His older brother, however, had attended the Yiddish school. Pinia Golfeld also attended a Russian-language school in Tulchyn in the late 1930s because "it was fashionable to go the Russian school. Nobody wanted to go the Yiddish school. That's the kind of time it was; everybody only wanted Russian." Golfeld did receive some Yiddish education from an elderly townsman—Leybish Kishke [Leybish the Guts] they called him—and reported that "he said to me, 'Pinia, I have to teach you how to write, how to read. In short, he taught me the ABCs (*aleph, beys, giml, doled*)." When he told his Russian teacher that he was learning Yiddish, though, the teacher called his mother and chastised her: "You either learn Yiddish or you learn Russian. There is no such thing as two languages!"

Instead of bolstering Yiddish-language education, the state undermined it. In 1935, the government began closing the Yiddish schools it had opened only a decade before, a process that was accelerated in 1937.[19] "In early 1935 they started taking away one teacher after another," explained Fania Braverman: "I finished the fourth grade. There were only four grades and then they would transfer you into the Ukrainian school." Kislinskaia told us she went to a Yiddish school for seven years, but her younger brother only went for five years because "at that point there were no longer any children there, since they put them all into the Russian [school]." She explained that the Yiddish school was closed "because there were no longer any children who would go to the Yiddish school. . . . It was closed and then they sent them to study at the other school, the Russian school." Avrom Furer, a shop manager and veteran of the Second World War, attributed the interruption of his own education, when he was transferred from a Yiddish to a Ukrainian school in Kryzhopil, to the authorities: "I learned in a Yiddish school for four years and then they took all the Jewish children and put them in a Russian school. They didn't let the Jews live their lives," he lamented. Chaim Rubin, who had assured us he remembered everything he ever learned in Yiddish school, switched over to a Ukrainian school after fourth grade, and continued there until he was drafted into the army. By 1940, there were only about twenty Yiddish schools left in all Ukraine.[20] Most students who had begun their education in Yiddish were forced instead into Ukrainian- or Russian-language schools to complete their studies.

Parents had numerous reasons for wanting to avoid sending their children to a Yiddish school. Those parents with lofty career goals for their children recognized that fluency in Russian would be an important skill for occupational advancement. These parents, many of whom were themselves urban and educated and who aspired towards acculturation, likely worked hard to help their children overcome their Yiddish accents—to roll their "r"s like a Russian—and viewed Yiddish-language schools as a barrier to advancement rather than as a ladder to success. A lack of higher educational institutions in Yiddish also meant that graduates of the primary schools were at a disadvantage when they tried to continue their educations in Russian or Ukrainian. Raisa Chuk explained to us how difficult it was for graduates of the state Yiddish schools to continue their education: "In the technicum at which I studied there were young Jews who were very learned—they knew mathematics and physics very well—but they didn't know any Russian. The teacher would ask them a question and they would say, 'We can answer the question, but only in Yiddish.' So the teacher would say: 'Speak in Yiddish and someone else will translate it.' Those schooled in Yiddish were at a distinct disadvantage when they sought higher education in Russian. Chuk continued to explain how students embraced the switch to Russian: "we spoke in Yiddish and then when the schools stopped being Yiddish and they all became Russian, we started speaking Russian. I had already finished the technicum in Russian." As she uttered this sentence, she switched from Yiddish to Russian herself. "I used to say to my mother," she told us, "Mother, speak with me in Russian. I am already going to a Russian technicum, but I still speak in Yiddish. There [in the technicum] I had to speak Russian. So, I told my mother to speak Russian to me. But she herself couldn't speak any Russian. This is how we communicated."

Many Jewish children in Ukraine viewed the opportunity to enroll in an institution of higher education as one of the benefits of the Revolution. On average, Jews were better equipped than their neighbors for admission into coveted institutes and universities: 70 percent of Jews in Ukraine were literate, compared with 56 percent of Russians, 48 percent of Poles, and 42 percent of Ukrainians. The educational advantages of Jewish women were even greater: 67 percent of Jewish women were literate, compared with just 45 percent of Russian women and 28 percent of Ukrainian women.[21] Jewish parents likely expected that both their sons and their daughters would pursue some type of higher education. They also knew that any such higher education was likely to be in Russian or Ukrainian.

When Maria Yakuta's Yiddish school was converted into a Ukrainian school, the Jewish community was supportive: "They wanted to go to the Ukrainian school, because the Yiddish language was not used anywhere. So, why should children struggle to learn Yiddish when there is nothing they can do with it? There were no jobs or [higher education] schools anywhere [for Yiddish-speakers]." Before the Ukrainian school was opened in the shtetl, some Jewish children from Teplyk—she remembered Manye, Klave, and Dania—were even sent to the Christian school in the neighboring village to receive a Ukrainian education. But why, we asked, did they prefer a Ukrainian school over a Russian school? "Because we are Ukrainians!" she answered. Yakuta, who was one of the few people we interviewed whose speech tended to drift into Ukrainian rather than Russian, was also one of the few to express a national identification with the Ukrainian state she called home.

The more traditional and religious Jews, on the other hand, saw the Yiddish-language schools as an antireligious propaganda ploy. These parents likely feared the ideological pressure that was placed on students in schools run by the Bolshevik Party, and so preferred to keep their children away. Parents likely preferred that, if their children were going to be indoctrinated in a Soviet school, they did so in a Russian- or Ukrainian-language school, where the antireligious propaganda would at least not be geared specifically toward the Jewish population.[22] Aba Kaviner remembered that the rabbi in Derazhnya refused to send his children to the Yiddish school, despite the Yiddish school director's constant pestering. Instead, the rabbi sent his children to the Ukrainian-language school, where they would be spared anti-Jewish propaganda, and instead imbibe the anti-Christian polemics of the atheist state. Consequently, the Yiddish-language schools were populated predominantly by poor children who had few other options, or whose parents lacked the social capital to consider other avenues for education.

About 40 percent of all school-aged children were not registered at any school at all.[23] Some of these children likely attended clandestine heders, but others—more commonly young girls than boys, and usually in smaller towns—attended no school because they were too poor, lived too far from a school, or were needed at home to help work. One of the few people we interviewed who had not received any formal education was Klara Sapozhnik. She was born in Tomashpil in 1924 but grew up on the nearby Gigant collective farm, and told us she never had gone to school nor learned to read. The majority of those who grew up in the types of shtetls in which we conducted our research, though, did go to school.

"IN HEDER WE LEARNED TO PRAY"

When we were interviewing Naftoli Shor about his Yiddish-language schooling on Tishah b'Av 2002, he had seemed disengaged and frustrated with the interview. Looking around his cluttered apartment for any items that could stimulate further conversation, we found an old prayer book, a *siddur*. We passed it over the table to him and his agitation instantly turned into exhilaration. This is what he wanted to discuss! He put on a hat to cover his head and began to recite the *Shema*, the centerpiece of the Jewish liturgy. He continued to absentmindedly flip through the prayer book, paying little attention to the questions we continued to toss his way. When asked how he celebrated the Sabbath as a child, though, he perked up to describe to us the tastes of the holiday: "Sabbath: we celebrated in the old days. One would cook fish, soup, meat, a soup, a *tsimes*. . . ." He went into the kitchen to grab a wood chopping block and a wooden mallet to show us how he would chop fish to make *gehakte* (chopped) fish. On the way back into the room, he explained, "And when you wake up, you say *moyde ani* (I give thanks)," at which point he launched into the *moyde ani* prayer customarily recited upon waking. "Who taught you to say that?" we asked. "In heder," he answered, as though it were the most obvious of things.

Heders, the traditional system of Jewish education in which sacred texts were given exclusive attention in the curriculum, had long been the bedrock of Jewish education in Eastern Europe. At the turn of the century, the St. Petersburg Free Economic Society together with the Society for the Promotion of Enlightenment Among the Jews of Russia counted 9,788 heders in the Pale of Jewish Settlement (not including Poland), which were attended by 135,134 students.[24] Many proponents of Enlightenment, however, had derided the heders for retarding the growth of Jewish secular education—for failing to supplement Talmudic erudition with the natural sciences, mathematics, geography, and other tools deemed essential to function in the modern world. The heders, the critics contended, fostered Jewish segregation.[25] In the mid- to late nineteenth century, Jewish freethinkers, often with the support of the tsarist government, offered several major reforms of Jewish schooling, all intended to introduce secular subjects into the curriculum. At the higher educational level, colleges like the Zhytomyr and Vilna rabbinical schools succeeded in training a cadre of reform-minded elites, like the playwright Avrom Goldfadn. At the elementary education level, reformers often had more success introducing secular subjects into girls' schools, where rabbinical elites had less interest.[26] Zionist efforts to modernize the heder, to establish a *heder metukan* (reformed heder), started to spread in the early twentieth-century. These schools, which were particularly prevalent in southern Ukraine, where the Zionist movement was strongest, emphasized the study of the Hebrew language for its own sake, and were geared toward cultivating a sense of Jewish national awareness and identity among the students rather than strict religious adherence. Because of their nationalist orientation and emphasis on the revival of the Hebrew language, however, these schools were inappropriate models for Soviet educational efforts. Hebrew, communist reformers insisted, was the obsolete tongue of the rabbinical elite and bourgeois Zionists. The Soviet government, acting at the behest of the Jewish Sections of the Communist Party, accelerated the liberal critique of the heder, and turned the liquidation of this religious educational institution into a hallmark of its education policy. The government outlawed heders in 1918, and began an intensive campaign to close them in 1920, when the Central Jewish Bureau of the Commissariat of Enlightenment urged that Jewish children "be liberated from the terrible prison, from the full spiritual demoralization and from physical deterioration."[27] But the heder remained a common source of underground education through the 1930s. One report that appeared in the Yiddish newspaper *Der emes* commented on the continued influence of Jewish religious education in Vinnytsya Province. After remarking upon the success of the Yiddish-language schools in places like Bershad and Tulchyn, the report also noted that there are "heders with teachers and rabbis, who organize their own 'children's brigades' and take them twice a day to the synagogue to pray."[28]

Still flipping through the prayer book, Shor explained that he had started heder at age six and attended for three to four years. There he had studied the Pentateuch and the classic rabbinical commentaries. With us, he stumbled upon the *Shminesre* (Eighteen Benedictions, or Amidah, one of the central prayers of the Jewish liturgy) in the *siddur* and again launched into prayer. Shor came alive again reciting little ditties he remembered from heder. One well-known rhyme playfully provided Yiddish translations for Hebrew words interspersed with religious obligations:

Buser iz fleysh
Fleysh iz buser
Khozer iz user
User iz khozer
Mayim iz voser
Voser iz mayim
Lomir trinkn a lekhayim!

Buser means meat
Meat means *buser*
Pork is forbidden
Forbidden is pork
Mayim means water
Water means *mayim*
Let's drink and say l'chaim![29]

He laughed as he recited some of the more raunchy rhymes that the boys in his heder had enjoyed, several of which hint at the well-developed sexual knowledge that little boys in the shtetl obtained in this community with little familial privacy. Shor, though, was more interested in showing us how he was able to pray: he put away the *siddur* we had handed him and brought out his father's *Mahzor,* his High Holiday prayer book, to show us. He stood in prayer and recited the *El Malei Rakhamim* (God full of mercy) with the fluency of a yeshiva student:

O, God full of mercy, Who dwells on high,
Grant proper rest on the wings of the Divine Presence
In the lofty levels of the holy and pure ones
Who shine like the glow of the firmament . . . [30]

We handed him a Yiddish book and asked if he could read it. Hesitantly and now with the fluency of a first-grader, he sounded out the syllables of the Yiddish text, demonstrating comfort only when he came upon a Hebrew root word: "It is cus-to-mar-y to vis-it the graves of tsa-diks on the eve of Rosheshone and the eve of Yonkipper. . . ." A few minutes later, with a Passover Haggadah in hand, he again erupted into song, singing the series of songs that traditionally concludes the Passover seder:

Ki lo nohey, ki lo yohey [To Him it is fitting; to Him it is due]
—do you know this one?—
Mighty in majesty, supreme indeed!
His legions sing to him:
Yours alone, O God, is the world's sovereignty.
Ki lo nohey, ki lo yohey [To him it is fitting; to Him it is due].

After another verse, he skipped ahead to the "Adir hu" (God is Mighty), singing:

God is Mighty!
May he soon rebuild His Temple.
Speedily, speedily.
In our days soon.
O God, rebuild, O God, rebuild,
Rebuild Your Temple soon.

And then skipping again, he sang the opening words of the well-known call-and-response song "Ekhod mi yodeyo?" (Who Knows One?) before interrupting himself, looking at us, and explaining "*Ekhod* means one." He continued the song through all thirteen verses, stopping occasionally at the beginning of a verse to explain to us again: "*Shnayim* means two." When he came to the segment of the song that lists "eight" as the number of days until a baby boy is circumcised, he explained: "*Shmoyne* means eight," and then made a snipping motion with his hands to explain the relevant phrase. Following the custom of the recitation of the Haggadah, he hadn't so much as ended the "Who knows one?" before he began singing the Aramaic song "Khad Gadya" that concludes the seder.

Naftoli Shor spent his formative years studying in a state Yiddish school where he learned to write slogans and placards. When he was not at school, though, he attended an underground heder, where he was immersed in the Jewish tradition. At home, prayer was reinforced by his Hasidic father Pinhas, who ensured that his son recited the *moyde ani* before getting out of bed each day, and by his mother who cooked a special meal for the Sabbath. He remembered virtually nothing of his education in the official Soviet Yiddish school, but his heder education, which he didn't even think to mention to us when we had first asked about his educational background, was second nature to him. To the end of his days, Shor cherished his Jewish identity and retained his faith and enthusiasm for its ritual and prayer. Like so many of the people we spoke to, a profound and deeply embedded sense of Jewish identity persevered in his psyche throughout his life, reemerging in full as he aged. Naftoli Shor passed away soon after we visited with him in 2002.

Shor was not alone among his generation. There were others, born in the late 1910s and early 1920s, who also received religious instruction that counteracted their state education. Aba Kaviner, who was born in Derazhnya in 1921, attended a Yiddish school for ten years between 1929 and 1939 while simultaneously studying in what he called an underground yeshiva. He told us that he had first studied Hebrew and religious subjects with private tutors and was then sent to a Talmud Torah (public religious school) before moving on to the higher-level yeshiva. "I had no childhood. I studied day and night. The more I studied the more I learned. And the deeper I studied, the more I was drawn into it." In the yeshiva, he studied "Rashi, gemore, tanakh, mishnayes, medresh," he told us, using familiar terms for the commentary of the eleventh-century rabbi Shlomo Yitzhaki (Rashi), the Talmud, the Hebrew Bible, the Mishnah, and homiletic teachings. He explained that the yeshiva had originally functioned openly, but later went underground: "The government knew that it existed underground, but pretended that they didn't know about it. And then later when times worsened, they ordered it closed." Even after the yeshiva was officially closed in the mid-1930s, Kaviner insisted that it continued to function underground for several years. In the Derazhnya yeshiva, Kaviner explained, the teachers were knowledgeable about secular matters as well: "In the yeshiva, the teachers can't be ignorant. A teacher in a yeshiva must know mathematics, physics, chemistry, history . . . in prayer, in the Torah, in the Mishnah, in midrash there is physics, mathematics . . . medicine." When the yeshiva was finally closed, Kaviner continued, the teachers were not punished; rather, they received esteemed positions: the head of the yeshiva, Dovid Nisenboym, became the chief bookkeeper of a bank, and another was able to continue his career as a teacher. The authorities in Derazhnya, it seems, were protecting the religious educators from the fates that befell most of their peers. Until the arrival of the Germans in 1941, Kaviner insisted, there were also underground heders functioning in Derazhnya out of private homes.

Chaim Skoblitsky, born in 1919 in Berdichev, also told us that until second grade, he attended both a Yiddish school and a heder. "First I would go to heder and then at noon I would go to school . . . to a Yiddish school. . . . We learned the two Pentateuchs (*di tsvey khimushim*). In heder we learned to pray." The two Pentateuchs, he explained, are the first two of the Five Books of Moses: Genesis and Exodus. The heder Skoblitsky attended was led by a *melamed*, a teacher, named Leybl: "I have forgotten his family name, but there were about twenty children in the heder. . . . There were a lot of heders. In every synagogue there was a heder. . . . What do children learn in heder? We learned to pray. . . . I can pray with the text of almost anything. Nowadays, when the rabbi is away, I pray at the podium [lead the services] and when they need someone for the podium, they call me," Skoblitsky proudly told us, a fact confirmed to us by the Berdichev rabbi. "When my father used to take me to synagogue," he continued, "we would wash hands and we would say the *moyde ani*. And that's that."

Skoblitsky's heder was closed in 1928, when he was nine years old. For three and a half years, though, between 1924 and 1928, he would spend his mornings immersed in the Jewish religious tradition, studying the Pentateuch, the rabbinical commentaries, and Jewish prayer. Then in the afternoon, he would go to the Soviet Yiddish school where he was taught that everything he had learned in the morning was false.[31]

This dual educational system recalls how Jews had lived in numerous other situations throughout their history, developing strategies of existing simultaneously within two seemingly incompatible worlds. Whether it was the Jews of Sasanian Persia, who wrote the text of the Babylonian Talmud while living in fear of the demons and spirits that populated the trees, roofs, air, and water that surrounded their rabbinical academies, or the nineteenth-century freethinkers who brought kosher meals with them to study in Protestant seminaries, Jews have often carved a separate space for their religion and tradition within a broader non-Jewish world.

Skoblitsky, Kaviner, and Shor, though, were probably not typical of their generation. All had the religious traditions of the heder deeply enforced in their respective homes: Shor's father was one of the leaders of the clandestine Hasidic circles of Bershad; Skoblitsky's maternal grandfather was a rabbi, and his uncle a cantor. But they saw their heder education in the early 1920s as completely ordinary and unremarkable, and presented it as part of a normal process of growing up Jewish in the early years of the Soviet Union. They regarded their ability to pray and read in Hebrew as too prosaic to bother mentioning unless they were asked specifically about it. The fluency with which the words and tunes came to them today, albeit with the assistance of a written text, indicates that their religious upbringing played a prominent role in their lives. The local inflections that accompany their mode of recitation—subtly different from the way the tunes are commonly taught today—provide evidence that the melodies of childhood stayed with them until the final years of their lives. Afternoon attendance at the Soviet Yiddish schools did little to erase habits and values formed in deeply pious homes.

Others who received a heder education, however, did view it as anomalous, and were affected by the antireligious morals and values the society enforced. Avrom Furer bitterly remembered how the children at the state Yiddish school he attended would mock him mercilessly for receiving private religious instruction from a *melamed*:

> At age six or seven I was sent to a heder. There was a *melamed*. Do you know what a *melamed* is? So, I went to heder, and then they began with the laughter and the stories. I also went to school. . . . My grandfather said that the *melamed* should come to us at home, to teach me the ABCs. So we started to learn at home. And I went to a Yiddish school. . . . There were Jewish teachers, and all. And when the children found out that a *melamed* was coming to me, they started to laugh at me. I ran away from the *melamed* and my father beat me, my grandfather yelled at me, and my mother—they laughed at me. And we sent away the *melamed*.

It was not just boys who were receiving religious educations. Rakhil Shames, who was born in Ivanopil (Yanushpol) in 1915, told us that a private tutor would come to her house and teach her a bit: "When I was eight, nine, or ten, a man would come to me and teach me Hebrew [Ivrit]. I knew it very well, but now I don't remember a word." Tsilia Khaiut in Mohyliv-Podilskyy also remembered how her parents supplemented her education in the Soviet Yiddish school with private instruction in her home.

—◊◊◊—

When he returned from his 1924 ethnographic expedition to the shtetls of Ukraine, Vladimir Bogoraz wrote of what he saw as the futility of individual efforts to keep religious education alive in the absence of a sizable religious community to support those traditions: "Currently there is no rabbi in the shtetl Sirotino," he wrote. "Apparently, they have no sense of a particular need for one. The two last religious teachers— one a former shopkeeper, the other a butcher—go from home to home and secretly teach children Jewish literacy. The teacher arrives with the wife. The wife stands on the street, keeping watch for the police." But ultimately, Bogoraz was confident that "the young boy strives to become a Pioneer and doesn't accept what he is learning from religion."[32] Bogoraz was probably right. There is no reason to doubt that most young boys preferred the red tie and badge of the Young Pioneers to the side curls and skullcaps of the heder. People we interviewed recalled with fondness the outdoor marches, the bugles and the drums, and the dancing of the Pioneers and Communist Youth. But for many of those who were forced by their parents—while their mother stood watch for the police—to attend clandestine heders, it is the heder experience that remained with them longest and that evoked the deepest devotion. Ultimately, the educational offerings of the Soviet state often amounted to little more than the placards and slogans that Shor learned in his Yiddish school. For them, the new "red rituals" offered by the Soviet state were never fully embedded within their daily routines and seasonal cycles, nor were they venerated with the force of tradition. In their final years, men like Naftoli Shor, Chaim Skoblitsky, and Aba Kaviner presented themselves as pious Jews and relished the traditions they had learned in the heder as well as the Yiddish language literacy that they acquired in the state school.

"WE ALL LIVED TOGETHER IN FRIENDSHIP"

Although they were designed with the goal of better integrating Jews into the Soviet system, Yiddish-language schools often had the opposite effect. As Avrom Furer remarked, "All my friends were Jewish." By removing one of the most important venues of interethnic and intercultural exchange the modern state offered—integrated public schools—Yiddish-language schooling heightened the ethnic divisions between Jews and Ukrainians. Those who attended Yiddish schools were surrounded almost exclusively by other Jews and had their Jewish identity reinforced despite the curricular efforts to erase parochial ethnic identities. Many Jewish children socialized only with other Jews.

But there were many who managed to traverse these ethnic boundaries. Sometimes, if they happened to live in Yiddish-speaking neighborhoods, non-Jews also enrolled in Yiddish-language schools. Yosl Kogan told us there were several non-Jewish children who attended his Yiddish school in Bershad:

> There were some non-Jews who knew Yiddish better than me. There was Valik—he knew Yiddish as well as you and I are speaking it. Even better! . . . He was older than me. He was one of our friends. There was Zuzhia.

There was Ivanov [who] spoke [Yiddish] just as we're speaking it now. In Berkhivka there were non-Jews who spoke Yiddish better than a Jew. . . . They lived among the Jews. They lived and they learned. . . . There was a Jewish school in Bershad. Non-Jews went to the Jewish school. That's how they learned it.

But non-Jews in the Yiddish schools were an anomaly, and probably come up so often in our interviews precisely because they stood out so much.

Jewish children in Ukrainian schools, though, were much more common than the other way around. The majority of Jewish schoolchildren in Ukraine were always enrolled in Ukrainian- or Russian-language schools; Yiddish-language schools never managed to attract even half of the Jewish schoolchildren. In Pyatka, Binyomin Geller attended a Ukrainian-language school where "in one class there were three Jewish children and twenty or eighteen non-Jews, together." He agreed, though, that in the town "there were many non-Jews who spoke Yiddish better than a Jew." He remembered, in particular, a furniture-maker who worked with Jewish carpenters and spoke Yiddish. Tseytl Kislinskaia remembered, "There across the river there was this one Ivan Bilohano; he spoke Yiddish just like I do." Despite separate schools, there was a good deal of mixing between Jews and Ukrainians in the small towns of the region.

Dora Yatskova, speaking in Russian, told us of her childhood in Kopayhorod in the 1930s, where she moved from Murafa in 1931 at the age of seven: "Those were good times, but it was difficult . . . among us there were good people in the shtetl, who lived together in friendship. Not like now." Kislinskaia echoed this sentiment: "before the war nobody would bother us. We all lived together in friendship. My daughter worked in the village. They really didn't know if she was a Jew or a non-Jew." Arkadii Burshtein went to a Yiddish school for the first four years of his education, where "in the shtetl, people spoke in Yiddish. My friends spoke in Yiddish, but the main administration was in Ukrainian." For his fifth year of schooling, though, he switched into a Ukrainian-language school, where "I had Jewish friends and I had Christian friends. In the fifth grade, there were Jewish children and Ukrainian children. Everybody spoke Ukrainian."

Shloyme Skliarskii told us of the warm relations between Jews and non-Jews in the shtetl of Zhornishche, but he characterized the nearby village of Ivanka, where his family was killed in a trench during the Second World War, as "a town of bandits where everyone was killed" and where you could see "guys grazing their cows." After he related a story about how once, as a child, when he was passing through Ivanka, some villagers threw a stone at him, we asked if there was much anti-semitism before the war. There was none, he insisted. But what about the stone, wasn't that antisemitic? "Well! That was Ivanka!" he replied. "The village where they killed everyone in the trench, in that village." Although Ivanka was located only 18 kilometers from Zhornishche, and Skliarksii regularly passed through it on his way to his native Lypovets, he regarded it as a completely different world. Whereas his own world had no antisemitism and Jews had friendly relations with their neighbors, 18 kilometers away on a well-traveled route sat the village where the antisemites lived. Jewish and non-Jewish relations were often remembered as being friendly and close in the immediate proximity, but the world beyond the shtetl was sometimes remembered as hostile and wild.

Adults were often wary of the close friendships their children formed with children of a different faith, particularly as those children approached marriageable age. Elizaveta Bershadskaia told us that her parents uprooted the family from the village of Chernyatka, where she was born, to prevent her from forming too close ties with the Christian villagers. Bershadskaia's playmates were mostly non-Jews, she told us, and young Jews of marriageable age were mixing with the Christian villagers. When she was in the seventh grade, her family moved to Bershad, her mother's hometown. "My mother moved us away from there because she didn't want her little girls marrying non-Jews. That's why they moved before the war to Bershad. Because she was afraid that it [intermarriage] would happen. . . . There were very few Jews there, so we moved to a Jewish town."

Although children had an easier time traversing ethnic boundaries than their parents, Jewish adults also befriended their Christian neighbors in casual interactions. Close and intimate friendships between Christian and Jewish adults, though, seem to have been rare. Only in exceptional circumstances, such as during periods of military service, did such friendships coalesce. Arkadii Burshtein remembered that in Sobolivka his grandfather was friendly with a local priest who had served with him during the First World War:

> When he served in the Caucasus there was also a non-Jew from Sobolivka in one division. But [he] was a priest's son. . . . During the eight years of duty they became friends. They remained life-long friends in Sobolivka. The priest would celebrate in the chapel and my grandfather would go to synagogue. Above all they stayed friends. The priest would tell him to eat nonkosher food and my grandfather would tell him it's forbidden to eat nonkosher food.

Yet even this friendship seems to have been a formal one, lacking the familiarity common to more intimate relations between Jews. The family carefully maintained an unusual decorum when the priest visited, treating him as a respected guest. As Burshtein explains: "Whenever the priest came to our house, everybody would stop working, cover the table with a cloth, put on a samovar and treat the priest to tea."

"WE WOULD DANCE AND PLAY THE BALALAIKA"

Notably, few of those we interviewed spoke about the Zionist movement. Yet according to the archival record, much of the Jewish Section's propaganda efforts were focused on combating the rise of Zionism. Jewish Section reports are full of warnings that "secret agents occupied with the organization of the emigration of Jewish workers to Palestine" are taking root in the shtetls of Podolia.[33] At a meeting of the main office of the Ukrainian Jewish Sections in June 1925, a report on Podolia stated bluntly: "In Podolia the Zionist movement is very strong, particularly among the youth. There is a noticeable emigration movement to Palestine."[34] On July 25, 1925, the head of the Secret Police (GPU) reported to the Central Committee of the Communist Party in Ukraine that "in Podolia, the number of members in the Zionist youth organization has reached 600. On 1 May, Zionist groups in several shtetls in Vinnytsya organized mass gatherings that involved a great number of Jewish youths. These mass gatherings were conducted almost openly. These groups were directed by leaders with white and blue banners."[35] Reports from Kiev Province warned that "the Zionist movement has a particularly mass character in the shtetls."[36] The archival record makes it clear that

Zionism remained the major threat to Bolshevism among the youth, particularly in Podolia and primarily in the smaller towns of the region. It was in part in an attempt to combat Zionism that the Jewish Sections put so much emphasis on building cultural alternatives for the youth. The silence of those we spoke to on this issue can be attributed to several factors. First was the apparent success that the Jewish Sections achieved in stamping out overt Zionist activities. By the late 1920s, Zionist clubs and organizations were no longer a part of Podolian shtetls. Second, the people we interviewed represented that portion of the population who remained in the region after the collapse of the Soviet Union. It seems reasonable to assume, therefore, that they had less interest in Zionism than the general population, many of whom had emigrated to Israel in the preceding two decades.

Although the Jewish Sections and Yiddishist intellectuals in Moscow, Kiev, Minsk, and Kharkiv hoped to rebuild Jewish life through revolutionary culture, the impact of these movements on the shtetl was far from complete. Few spoke to us about their dreams for a communist future—even if they had such dreams in their youth, the idea of a Soviet Utopia had clearly gone out of style by the time we conducted our interviews, a decade and more after the collapse of the Soviet Union. In contrast to the decades before the Revolution, when a visiting theater troupe would inspire local amateurs to establish their own theater, the Soviet period produced few such grassroots initiatives. Tatiana Marinina was one of the few who spoke of her communist past. Marinina had joined the Komsomol when she returned to Teplyk from the Crimean farm to which her family had been expelled for conducting private trade through her father's butcher shop: "There was a group of us, five or ten people, I don't remember. We were elected. There was a general meeting of the Komsomol. People told about their autobiographies. They told about their family history, they told about their politics. When we were admitted into the district committee—our meeting was part of the district committee—it was a great honor. We received a Komsomol card, and we were so happy, we celebrated." For Marinina, membership in the Komsomol represented rehabilitation for her and her family and offered the possibility of a new beginning.

Even in a larger city like Berdichev many insist that there was little professionally performed entertainment. Isaak Vaisman does not remember much entertainment at all: "Before the war!? No such thing would have occurred to us. We didn't even have a single piece of bread. How could we possibly have concerts? What kind of theater could we have had?" Vaisman denies experiencing even simple domestic celebrations: "We had a very difficult life before the war. It was unthinkable to have Yiddish songs on our minds. Thank God we had a piece of bread!"

Others have fonder memories of leisure activity. For most, a local klezmer group, or *kapelye,* was always a great source of pride to the community. Maria Yakuta told us, "There were many klezmers in Teplyk. There was never anything so magnificent." Teplyk, she continued, was famous for its klezmers, who would travel throughout the region entertaining at Jewish weddings. Indeed, in his memorial book on Teplyk, Tshernovetski also writes of the famous Teplyk klezmers:

> Who hasn't heard of the Teplyk klezmers? I am not exaggerating when I point out that the Teplyk klezmers are famous in the entire region. As a child I used to hear my father, may he rest in peace, boasting more than once about "his" Teplyk klezmers. Later, when I became a bit older and I would go out to nearby shtetls, like Ternivke, Khashchuvate, Holovanivsk, Lidvinke, Kiblych, Bershad, Obodivke, Zhabokrich, or even Haysyn and Uman, I would still hear about what a good reputation the Teplyk klezmers had.[37]

But Teplyk was not alone in its regional pride. "The Sharhorod *kapelye,*" Mordechai Cooper wrote in his memorial book to the city, "had a name throughout the entire world. Even Sholem Aleichem, in his novel *Stempenyu,* cites it as one of the most popular."[38] In fact, every town seems to have been famous for its klezmers.

One of the most opportune times to catch a performance by a klezmer *kapelye* was at a wedding. Weddings were also one of the few opportunities that people had to feast, particularly when a wealthier member of the community was celebrating. In Tulchyn, Yente Kolodenker fondly recalled, "the klezmers would lead the in-laws. The entire night they would lead the in-laws around. And then they would lead them home, with music. And the children would watch from the windows to see them eat. We were jealous . . . we would watch from the windows how they ate. We would watch until our mother came to bring us back some ginger bread or strudel. We would watch all night until our mother came."

A few enjoyed the simple pleasures of reading. For many, reading was still a collective experience. Yakuta paints a picture of a shtetl population intensely interested in the world around them:

> My father subscribed to a newspaper, *Der shtern,* a Yiddish newspaper, and all of Teplyk would come to him to hear about what's going on in the world. He would read it to them. He couldn't write [in Yiddish]. He could read and count money. . . . My father would read it to them, to the people. He was the only subscriber. There was no one else. In heder he was taught to read the Torah, but he didn't know how to read a newspaper. So he had to teach himself to read. The Jews would look at him expectantly: "Arke, read more! Read more! What's going on in the world?" . . . There was no radio. Nobody had seen a television and people didn't read books.

In each shtetl, the "remnants of the old" competed with newer officially sponsored forms of cultural enlightenment: drama circles, libraries, wall newspapers, political circles, cooperative circles, reading houses, and communist clubs. In Kryzhopil, there was, in addition to the seven-year state Yiddish school, a kindergarten, a Yiddish artisans' club, a Yiddish workers' club, a Komsomol "liquidation point" geared toward the liquidation of illiteracy, and a Yiddish drama circle. In Sharhorod there was a seven-year school, a liquidation point, a Yiddish workers' club and a Yiddish drama circle.[39] In a 1938 article he published in the Moscow Yiddish paper, *Der emes,* L. Feldblium of Teplyk painted a rosy picture of his town at the time. After writing about how the town used to be dominated by the Potocki family of Polish noblemen who once owned the town and oppressed the working class, Feldblium continued:

> Today Teplyk is unrecognizable: all the streets are paved, it is spotlessly clean; the houses are whitewashed; and the vast majority of the workers live in orderly houses. Here they are building a new electrical station. The shtetl has radio. In 1937, a bath was built along with a movie theater. There is a magnificent square. There is a full Ukrainian middle school and a partial Yiddish middle school. In the evenings, the shtetl population comes out to the movies, to the park; they go around on bicycles; many houses have gramophones. The worker's life is cultural and rich.[40]

Reflecting on the varieties of entertainment available to them in their youth, few of the people we spoke with brought up organized cultural activities, like the communist clubs, liquidation points, and drama circles that were so often cited in contemporary newspaper reports. Instead they tended to cherish the simpler pleasures of life. Moyshe Vanshelboim remembered, "My father liked flowers very much. We had a little garden and he would grow flowers. My father played a mandolin and a balalaika and he could also play the fiddle. He was very musical. I remember in the evening the whole street of boys and girls would come and he would play and they would dance." He told the Shoah Foundation that he remembered skating and skiing in the winter, and playing soccer in the summer: "I loved flowers and plants like my father. We had a little spot of earth and I helped Dad take care of it."

Those who did recall the communist clubs remember the comradely atmosphere more than the ideological lessons. Avrom Furer told us, "There were all kinds of things. There was a Jewish club in which they did all types of things. . . . It was a club just to gather together Jewish boys and girls. We would dance and play the balalaika." Naum Gaiviker, who also enjoyed jazz, leaned forward on his cane as a broad smile lightened his face when he told us that "as a young lad, I loved going for walks." When young men and women recalled their youthful evenings out, they remembered the simple pleasures of sitting on the steps and playing the balalaika, or sharing a good book, rather than the avant-garde revolutionary culture imported from the big cities.

5

—ᗰ—

The Sanctuary of the Synagogue

The Jewish women's choir of Vinnytsya meets regularly in the Jewish community center not far from the center of town. In 2002, Liudmila Shor invited us to the community center where this group of fifteen elderly and energetic ladies sings together. We were served a brunch of black bread and cheese, after which Shor began to gather the women together for a special performance just for us. As they rose from their tables, an elderly woman with large round turtle-shell glasses approached the camera. Speaking directly into the lens, a bit too close to the camera, she announced: "I was in the war. I am an invalid of the second group. I received the order of bravery." Ignoring Shor's calls to assemble in the auditorium, she continued her monologue in clipped sentences: "I go to synagogue. Every Sabbath I go to synagogue. My last name is Katz, Nesye Sulimanovna. I was born in Brailiv. I was left an orphan without any parents. And my uncle raised me. We sing Yiddish songs. We gather together, we sing, we dance, and we are joyous. My parents were all killed here by the Germans."

Katz's deliberate speech to the camera, juxtaposing her youth as both a war orphan and a war hero onto her current life of singing, dancing, and joy is an inspiring statement of perseverance. She spoke without conjunctions, but nevertheless powerfully asserted that despite what she has suffered—despite what the Germans did to her and her family—she comes here, to this community center, to sing Yiddish songs, to dance, to be merry, and to socialize with other Jewish women. Despite everything, she has maintained her community. Buried within her barrage of assertions, was her divulgence that she goes to synagogue every Saturday. For Katz and so many others, synagogue attendance remains a defining element of Jewish identity.

Once Shor managed to assemble the women to the stage, we took our seats in the last of about five rows of stackable aluminum frame chairs. The choir performed some of the best-known Yiddish songs, including the drinking song, "Lomir ale in eynem," (Let us all together) and "Shabes zol zayn," (Let there be Sabbath). The women seemed to be competing with each other to sing the loudest, but amidst the shouting a few vibrant voices emerged. When the drinking songs ended, the divas among the group took turns taking breakout solos. With the light glimmering off the purple highlights in her hair, Asya Barshteyn began in a sonorous and commanding voice:

> Oy, oy, oy
> Rebbe, Reb Shneyer
> S'hot mir getrofn
> Zeyer a groyser zeyer
> Di shkheyne iz a shiksl
> Nit vaksn zol zi greser
> Z'hot opgeshnitn di puter
> Mit'n fleyshikdikn meser.
> Bin ikh gekumen tsu dir rebbenyu
> Rebbe, Reb Shneyer
> Ir zolt mir paskenen
> Di dozike deye.
> Hot der rebbe ofgehoybn di oygn tsum himl
> Un hot ongemakht a rash mit a timl.
> Shat, shat, vaybele, nisht veyn
> Shik dos shiksele tsu mir aleyn.
>
> Un vus zol ikh tun mit'n meser?
>
> Nemt a bisele ash
> Un git dos meserl a vash.
> Un tut zikh gornisht foyln.

A typical "Jewish" house in Tomashpil, 2007. Residents commonly ascribed ethnicity to the houses in the shtetl. *Photo by Artur Frątczak.*

A typical "Jewish" house in Sharhorod, 2002.
Photo by Jeffrey Veidlinger.

A view down Karl Marx Street from the main square of Sharhorod, 2002.

After services in the synagogue of Berdichev. Isaak Vaisman leans forward second from left. Moyshe Vanshelboim stands at far right. *Photo by Artur Frątczak.*

(ABOVE) "We are Jews and we must thank God and believe in God and one must not forget God." Pesia Kolodenker and Nisen Kiselman, 2009. *Photo by Artur Frątczak.*

(RIGHT) "There were woodchoppers, there was a little synagogue for goose butchers, every trade had its own synagogue." Nisen Yurkovetsky, 2007. *Photo by Artur Frątczak.*

Alexei Futiran showed us where his name is tattooed on his arm: "During the war, before battle," he explained, "in case we were killed, so that our name would be known," 2007. *Photo by Artur Frątczak.*

"When they set up the ghetto, goyim immediately took our house. Immediately." Klara Katsman, 2009. *Photo by Artur Frątczak.*

(ABOVE) Dov-Ber Kerler and I interview Nukhim Gvinter in 2005 in his Bershad home and workshop. Partially finished leather boots that Gvinter makes are visible behind him to his left.

(BELOW) The research team in 2009 interviewing Alexei Futiran on the streets of Tomashpil. Artur Frątczak is videotaping Dov-Ber's conversation with Futiran. Pearl Gluck films Artur. Our graduate student Anya Quilitzsch stands to the side with me. Four of us are wearing hats that we had just purchased from Futiran's home workshop. *Photo by Margot Valles.*

(RIGHT) "There will come a time when all the Jews will be free, and then we will sing a new song." Yosl Kogan reading from his poetry notebook, 2009. *Photo by Artur Frątczak.*

(BELOW) "The more I studied the more I learned. And the deeper I studied, the more I was drawn into it." Aba Kaviner in his Khmelnytskyy home, 2007. *Photo by Artur Frątczak.*

(ABOVE) "The war began and the Jewish boys left. Then very many of them were killed." Klara Sapozhnik in Tomashpil, 2007. *Photo by Artur Frątczak.*

(LEFT) Frida Pecherskaia in her Tulchyn home, 2009. *Photo by Artur Frątczak.*

Shloyme Skliarskii reads from the note he wrote to remember the Messiah's message to him. He credits his life-saving decision to hide in the field instead of the forest during the war to a mysterious voice from the Messiah. *Photo by Artur Frątczak, 2009.*

"Our children's children's children's children must know!"
Moyshe Kupershmidt in 2002. *Photo by Pawel Figurski.*

Sasha Kolodenker and Rita Shveibish in the forest clearing by the site
of the mass grave near Pechera in 2009. *Photo by Artur Frątczak.*

(ABOVE)
"They forced my father to
bury the dead people."
Yente Kolodenker in 2009.
Photo by Artur Frątczak.

(RIGHT)
"My mother didn't sing. She
would cry. She would cry over the
world she had lost so young."
Khayke Gvinter in 2005.

"I remember in the evening the whole street of boys and girls would come and he would play and they would dance." Moyshe Vanshelboim in 2007. *Photo by Artur Frątczak.*

"We lived in the same courtyard. Now he complains to me. Why? Because before the war, I didn't support him: 'You lived well, so why didn't you?'" Beyle Vaisman and her husband Isaak in 2009. *Photo by Artur Frątczak.*

Un brut es up af koyln.
Tif in der'erd zolt ir es araynshtekn
Nemt a bisele shtroy, zolt ir es tsudekn
In tsvey sho arim vet es kosher vern.

Oy, oy, oy, oy
Rebbe, Reb Shneyer
A very great [sorrow]
Happened to me.
My neighbor is a *shiksa* [gentile woman]
She shouldn't grow anymore
She cut her butter
With a meat knife.

I am coming to you, Rebbe
Rebbe, Reb Shneyer
You must pass judgment
On this matter.

The Rebbe raised his eyes toward heaven
And made a great big stir
"Sh, sh, dear, don't cry
Send the *shiksa* to me alone."

—and what should I do with the knife?
—Take a little ash
and give the knife a wash
And don't be lazy
Roast it over coals.
You must put it deep into the earth
Cover it with a little bit of straw.
And in two hours it will be kosher!

The other women seemed displeased at the song; they probably felt that Barshteyn was stealing the show. Perhaps they were also embarrassed by the content of the sacrilegious song, which suggests that the rebbe had little concern for the ritually unclean knife, but was more interested in having his way with the *shiksa*. As Aba Kaviner, who also remembered this song from his childhood noted, "It makes fun of the rebbe."[1]

The song was one of the few remnants of the antireligious campaigns that Barshteyn had been subjected to in her youth. As part of its campaign to rout out religious belief—"the opiate of the masses" in Marx's terminology—the Soviet state, in a January 23, 1918 decree, nationalized all property belonging to religious organizations.[2] Although the brunt of the Soviet antireligious policy in the early years of the revolution was directed against the Orthodox Church and its landholdings, the decree applied as well to other churches, mosques, and synagogues. But worship was not outlawed. The Soviet government permitted prayer in religious buildings so long as the worshippers did not linger to socialize. People attended services, the government contended, not to worship, but to be among friends and form a community. If they could deprive the faithful of the community, the faithful would lose their faith. Thus, an August 24, 1918 decree allowed for a group of twenty or more individuals to manage buildings formerly held by official religious organizations, if the sites were used solely for the purpose of worship and were not turned into social or community buildings. These groups of twenty, or *dvatsatki,* retained control of Jewish synagogues in Ukraine for most of the next decade. The pious were permitted to enter the synagogue for prayer, so long as they left promptly after services and did not linger to gossip, socialize, enjoy each other's company, or establish a sense of community.[3] This policy was encoded in the Law on Religious Associations of April 8, 1929. The *dvatsatki,* however, were forced to contend with barrages of antireligious propaganda aimed at young Jewish workers.[4] In the mid-1920s, the Party mocked religious organizations and beliefs, and used propaganda tools to persuade the faithful to abandon their modes of worship. The League of Militant Atheists, established in 1925, coordinated antireligious campaigns and published newspapers and journals to promote secularism, predominantly with the Orthodox Church in mind.

The Jewish Sections of the Communist Party took the lead in stimulating antireligious propaganda among the Jewish population. While unwilling for the most part to seize synagogues and arrest Jewish communal leaders in small towns, the Jewish Sections directed their antireligious propaganda at Jewish workers and children, most of whom were already drifting away from the traditions of their parents. To combat the surge of religious sentiment that tended to accompany the High Holidays, or "Fall Holidays" in the terminology of the Jewish Sections, the Jewish Sections in July 1925 proposed a campaign of "brochures, slogans, placards, etc.," and the publication of "antireligious propaganda" in Yiddish language newspapers. They sought in particular to target

workers, craftsmen, and their wives, particularly in the shtetls and colonies.[5] Newspapers and magazines were full of stories seeking to "expose"
religious practice as backwards and useless. Books of anticlerical jokes
were published in Yiddish, and schoolchildren were taught songs that
mocked Judaic religious practice.[6] The Jewish Sections established mock
courts to put the Jewish religion "on trial," and published "Red Haggadahs" retelling the biblical Exodus as a story of deliverance from capi-
talist oppression. While these efforts had some success among the local
intelligentsia, who regularly read newspapers and magazines and were
already growing distant from the religious traditions of their parents, the
effectiveness of this propaganda among the small town craftsmen—their
primary audience—was less obvious.[7]

These campaigns had limited successes. Reports in *Apikoyres* (The
Heretic) and other organs of the Soviet Yiddish press from the late 1920s
complained of a resurgence in synagogue attendance. Many Jews were
rejecting Soviet atheism, particularly in the shtetls of Ukraine and Belarus, and were clinging to their religious traditions. Numerous Jewish Section internal reports also warned that the poverty of the Jewish
working class was too great to allow for utopian reeducation projects.
One book intended as a textbook for use in Soviet Yiddish schools states
as follows:

> In the daily life of the contemporary Jew, religious superstition still plays
> an important part . . . even now many Jews on the Sabbath become simply
> slaves of religious dogmas . . . . . . Like in the ancient times the Jews still
> observe the Passover, with its matzos. The rabbis especially see to it that
> the holidays should be observed. The reason is simple: because the main
> thing in religion is not faith, but its practical aspects, to observe the laws,
> fulfill the commandments, to fast and to participate in all the ceremonies
> that are connected with religion.[8]

The Jewish Sections understood that rituals lead to faith rather than vice
versa. If they could prevent the performance of ritual, they believed, the
faith that follows would soon wither away.

The Jewish Sections complained that in the poverty-stricken back-
waters of Vinnytsya Province agitational programming seemed distant
and irrelevant to the working poor, who were unresponsive to their
propaganda, and too preoccupied with obtaining basic foodstuff to be

swayed by political lectures.[9] One secret Agitprop report directed to the Vinnytsya Jewish Section from 1925 concluded that whereas Jews in large cities had responded positively to antireligious campaigns as evidenced by their lack of synagogue attendance and continued appearance at work on Jewish holidays, the Jews of small towns "have not comprehended the antireligious campaigns of the past. To this day, these groups of Jewish workers for the most part faithfully observe all Jewish rituals and holidays." The report urged a renewal of antireligious propaganda directed toward small-town Jews: "All papers, lectures, dramatizations, etc. among this segment of workers must be immediately directed against religious holidays, elucidating their origin and meaning and refuting their connection to legends and prejudices." The Jewish Sections were convinced that more lectures on antireligious themes would lead to a final elimination of Jewish religious practices.[10]

The techniques of agitation employed by the Jewish Sections included public disputations that were designed to embarrass religious functionaries. Such disputations had been one of the hallmarks of medieval Christianity's weapons against the Jewish religion and became a favorite technique of the show trials under the new communist government.[11] In Bershad, the *shoykhet* (kosher butcher) Eli Marchak was forced to participate in one such disputation. According to Marchak's son, as quoted by Binyomin Lukin, "In the shtetl they told stories for a long time about the erudition and cleverness of my father, about his deep knowledge of the subject of the debate and about how he crushed the organizers of the disputation."[12] Another common tactic adopted by the Jewish Section of Vinnytsya was to urge workers to labor extra hard on Yom Kippur as a visible violation of this solemn day of rest.

Yet, at least in the early 1920s, progress was slow and the faithful were reluctant to give up their customs and rituals. As one report from the region that appeared in the Moscow-based *Der emes* put it:

> There is no serious systematic cultural and political enlightenment work being conducted among craftsmen in either Bershad or Tulchyn. . . . The Zionists and rabbis have broken through the front and have started to work seriously among the children. A significant number of children are taken twice a day to synagogue to pray. This situation demands a completely different approach: more careful and active work among Jewish children of all classes. Otherwise we will create a large contingent for the rabbis and the Zionists.[13]

This Soviet report accords with the narratives that émigrés recorded about life in the prewar Soviet shtetl. In the memorial book he wrote for the town of Bershad, Nahman Huberman tells of the Jewish Section's confiscation of the Great Synagogue of Bershad:

> Within days, the members of the Jewish Section came and confiscated the great synagogue by order of the authorities to turn it into a club for the Party. The Jews did not go to ask for mercy because they understood that any request would be interpreted as counterrevolutionary and would bring about a death sentence. "It was an enormous blow for us," they wrote in private letters, "when we saw the holy ark being emptied of its contents and converted into a buffet. We tore our clothing and sat on the earth as mourners." On Yom Kippur, people prayed in private homes. Their cries and weeping pierced the air. They cried over the terrible past and the unknown future.[14]

The people we spoke with harked back to childhoods in the shtetl where the synagogue was the center of the community. Asya Barshteyn, who sang the antireligious song for us in the women's choir, was born in Sharhorod in 1928 and lived there until she left for Vinnytsya in 1938. In her interview, she eulogized the Jewish community of her hometown:

> There were ten synagogues in Sharhorod: nine synagogues and the Great Synagogue. And the Great Synagogue still stands today. They took away all the synagogues, but the great one still stands. They turned it into a factory, but they didn't touch it. . . . Sharhorod was a Jewish city. There were 3,000 families in the town, plus children. Every occupation had its own synagogue. The tailors had their synagogue; the coopers had their synagogue. In general, all the occupations had their own synagogues. And on holidays, from Zhytomyr or somewhere, they would invite a cantor who would lead services. . . . And they sold only kosher meat—no lard at all. All the Jews bought only kosher meat. . . . My mother only went to the kosher butcher shop to get meat. . . . Life was good. There were wealthy Jews in Sharhorod. People had very beautiful weddings. It was a very Jewish city. But now nobody is left.

"EVERY TRADE HAD ITS OWN SYNAGOGUE"

Barshteyn's recollections of prewar Sharhorod are shrouded in nostalgia for a world that has disappeared. In her account, she switched freely from the general to the particular—everybody bought kosher meat; my mother bought kosher meat—indicating a desire to universalize

Standing in front of the still-functioning tailors' synagogue
of Bershad in 2002. From left to right: Zhenye (the wife of the
synagogue beadle), Jeffrey Veidlinger, Evgeniia Kozak, Dov-
Ber Kerler, Lyova (the synagogue beadle), and Efim Vygodner
(the head of the Jewish community of Bershad).

The sixteenth-century fortress synagogue of Sharhorod,
which had been functioning as a juice-bottling factory.

her own experience. The phrase, "every trade had its own synagogue"
is a recurring phrase that we heard in our interviews in virtually every
city and town. When asked to describe Berdichev before the war, for
instance, Moyshe Vanshelboim started by listing trades, but quickly
slid into a list of synagogues, as he counted the trades by their houses
of worship: "There were woodchoppers, there was a little synagogue for
goose butchers, every trade had its own synagogue." Nisen Yurkovetsky
began counting the number of synagogues in Tulchyn on his fingers,
listing them as he went along: "The cobblers had a synagogue, and the
tailors had a synagogue, and the barbers had a synagogue, and the porters had a synagogue, and the water carriers had a synagogue." Maria
Yakuta told us that in the interwar period Teplyk was full of synagogues:
"There were many synagogues. There was a cobblers' synagogue, and
there was a tailors' synagogue, and there was a synagogue for poor folk,
and a synagogue for klezmers [musicians]." Avrom Furer recalled of his
native Kryzhopil, "It was like this: there was a synagogue for the wealthy.
There was a synagogue for the artisans, like coopers and cobblers, and
there was a synagogue for the poor folk." The repeated references to
the number of synagogues not only represents a reality of Jewish life in

small towns, but also serves as a synecdoche for Jewish life in the prewar period; it allows those we interview to speak of both the diversity of Jewish life (there were tailors, coopers, cobblers, woodchoppers, etc.) as well as of the key factor that united the community (they each had a synagogue) in one breath. It is shorthand for the entire shtetl experience. The synagogue building represents much more than a religious identity, and serves as the focal point of the community.

Barshteyn remembered the synagogue as the center of Jewish communal and cultural life in the shtetl. She, like so many others we interviewed, recalled the excitement of hearing visiting cantors who would occasionally tour and perform there. For Barshteyn, with a continued love of music and song, the cantor was the highpoint of religious life:

> There was a cantor, Cantor Gaz was his name. He lived here. He has since passed away and is in the cemetery. During holidays, back when there was a cantor, there were wealthy Jews, who had money and wanted to dance. When there was a Jewish wedding, they would invite musicians from Bessarabia and they would play Jewish melodies and lead [a procession] of all the relatives. And they would put up a chuppah. This was about fifty years ago. . . . I used to go to synagogue with my parents. I was interested in the synagogue. We had a synagogue that they have since taken away where my father would pray. And there on the second floor, through the windows, we would see them praying. And Cantor Gaz would pray. And even better, they would invite cantors. From Zhytomyr, from Moldova.

Numerous residents fondly remembered the practice of inviting guest cantors from neighboring cities. Beyle Vaisman, for instance, told us that in Berdichev, the elderly attended the synagogue on a regular basis, but when a visiting cantor came, so many people would show up that "you couldn't even enter the courtyard."

In 1925 the Jewish Sections began to supplement their propaganda with more aggressive measures to close synagogues. The faithful would be forced out of this sacred space, and the buildings would instead be converted into Yiddish clubs, schools, cinemas, or other communal buildings geared toward the Jewish population. Confiscated synagogues were almost always reserved for use by the Jewish community, but strictly for secular purposes. The insistence on keeping "Jewish spaces" Jewish can be seen as a cynical ploy to avoid accusations of antisemitism.

Certainly, the Jewish Sections were conscious of this possibility, but there is no evidence in the protocols or reports of the Jewish Sections that this was the primary motivation for keeping the buildings open for Jewish cultural purposes. The Jewish Sections spent most of their time in the late 1920s considering ways to expand Jewish cultural, educational, and social activity, and to provide more space for Jewish party cells, meetings, and political agitation. Synagogue buildings, with their central locations and welcoming atmosphere, were simply too valuable real estate to take away from the community. Smaller prayer houses (*besemedresh*) could be confiscated and turned into bakeries, but—at least in the 1920s—the Jewish Sections were adamant that synagogues remain Jewish spaces. The Jewish Sections argued that they were merely consolidating resources: after all, did every town really need a synagogue for each occupation in times of dwindling synagogue attendance and economic need? The buildings, they maintained, could be used more efficiently for clubs and schools.

The Jewish Sections closed some 650 synagogues throughout the entire Soviet Union in the 1920s, but in 1926 there were still more than 1,000 functioning in Ukraine alone, with more than 800 rabbis; most small towns in Ukraine were still left with houses of worship until the late 1930s.[15] These included not only official synagogues established by *dvatsatki*, but also numerous other prayer quorums (minyans) that met officially as "associations," for which a permanent building was not required, and many more that met unofficially in private homes or places of business, often changing locations every day in order to avoid detection.

With the end of the New Economic Policy and the dissolution of the Jewish Sections in 1929, the futures of synagogues and Jewish communal property were placed under the auspices of the All-Ukrainian Central Executive Committee of National Minorities, based in Kharkiv. At a single meeting, on March 14, 1929, the Committee affirmed the closure of some twenty-five synagogues in various provinces across Ukraine, including Tulchyn's Great Synagogue and New Market Synagogue, both of which were to be utilized instead for cultural purposes. The same meeting also affirmed the closure of nine churches, and, indeed, official attitudes toward the Jewish religion were paralleled at every stage by official attitudes toward Christian Orthodoxy.[16]

The means of closing synagogues was virtually identical in each town. The situation in Kopayhorod was typical. There had been four synagogues, two of which were closed between 1925 and 1927, one of which was closed in 1932, and the last of which was closed in 1936. Grigorii Shor remembered that even into the 1930s the town "was a completely Jewish shtetl with all of the Jewish traditions. There was a rabbi, several kosher butchers. . . . I remember when there were only two synagogues left because the others had been closed. . . . Later they closed the *besmedresh* and they built a bakery there." He and his wife, Liudmila, explained that even after the Great Synagogue was closed in 1932 and converted into a school, people still called the school "the synagogue" and would say, "He lives on the synagogue street, near the synagogue." Grigorii had attended the school that was built in the structure of the former Great Synagogue. The synagogue, therefore, remained a Jewish space, but the smaller *besmedresh* was turned into a bakery.

Grigorii had distinct memories of attending the wooden two-storied synagogue in Kopayhorod with his father until it was closed in 1936:

> There was a ladder so that the women could get up to the second floor [where] the women would sit and pray . . . and on the first floor was all the praying. . . . I remember that beautiful benches were next to the wall and everybody would pay for a spot and they would write on it: "this spot is reserved," "this spot is reserved," "this spot is reserved" . . . and the dais was in the middle . . . and there was a big cupboard where the Torah was—it would be closed. My father used to take me to synagogue on the holidays and they would take out the Torah and carry it around and everybody would kiss it, the Torah, and they would read a few words from the Torah in the Holy Tongue. . . . There were Stars of David and menorahs [painted] there and . . . many words were written in the Holy Tongue. It was so beautiful. It was tall. It was probably four or five meters up to the women's section and then the women's section was another three or four meters [tall]. And the roof was made of wooden boards. . . . This synagogue stood, as far as I can remember, as long as I was going to the Yiddish school. . . . And we would go there and look and pray. And it was closed in '35 or '36. . . . The last synagogue, the wooden one, was closed in '36.

Dora Yatskova, who was born in Murafa in 1924, also remembered the Kopayhorod synagogue. Since she had only moved to the town in 1931, her recollections can be definitively dated to the 1930s. Speaking in

Russian, she told us: "Next to the school there was a Jewish synagogue: it was two stories. On the first floor the men prayed and on the second floor the women. I used to go there because it was interesting for me to hear how they prayed."

Parents came to understand that while their own synagogue attendance was tolerated by the state, sending their children to services was a risky endeavor.[17] "The young folks didn't go to synagogue," explained Arkadii Burshtein of his native Sobolivka, "only the elderly." Children who followed the ways of their parents were mercilessly mocked in school. Their teachers, hired by the revolutionary iconoclasts of the Jewish Sections, encouraged the ridicule, and taught texts that reinforced antireligious feelings. Binyomin Geller, who was born in 1923 in the village of Pyatka, about 5 kilometers outside of Berdichev, remembered "one day, during Kol Nidre, when the synagogue was full of people praying, the director of the Ukrainian school, who was a Jew, gathered together the Pioneers to throw stones." Grigorii Shor explained that after 1936, the faithful were afraid of being assessed huge fines or imprisoned for illegally praying, so they would send the children out of the room first.

Those who held leadership roles within the Jewish community also became victims of state sanctions. When internal passports were issued in 1933, for instance, clerics and rabbis were denied passports, thereby becoming *lishchentsy* (disenfranchised): they lost their right to housing and their access to state handouts. Rabbis who had been employed in large cities, where housing demands were tight, were often forced out into the villages; the fortunate few were able to migrate out of the country altogether. In small towns, where housing was in less demand, the issuance of internal passports had less of an impact, but still sent a clear message that spiritual work would be less tolerated. The authorities sent people who were connected to religious traditions to work in villages and collective farms, thereby decapitating the religious community.

For instance, Grigorii Shor continued: "The rabbi, the *shoykhet*, the one who writes the Torah—the *soyfer*, the cantor, were dismissed from their religious positions. In the district newspaper it was announced that they had been dismissed from their positions. Whoever said anything was sent away from there. Many of them were harassed. Quietly, incognito, they were taken away."

The wave of synagogue closures and mass arrests of most of the remaining rabbis during the Great Terror of the late 1930s was far more severe than that of the late 1920s.[18] The closures of the 1930s, while still conducted under the guise of a democratic reallocation of resources for the Jewish community, were blatantly designed to destroy religious practice. In Kiev and other large cities, schoolchildren and Pioneers demonstrated against the faithful during the High Holidays in an effort to intimidate the pious. In some cities, municipalities cut off electricity to the synagogues. Archival documents provide insight into some of the procedures by which synagogues were shut down during this wave of closures. In Dzhuryn, for instance, a general meeting of Jewish workers requested the use of one synagogue for a workers' club. The town council responded by conducting a referendum among the Jewish population in the summer of 1938, which resulted in 397 of the 519 participants (76 percent) voting in favor of closure. By October the synagogue was closed.[19] Similarly, in Yampil, members of the Jewish community brought a request before a plenary session of the local government to utilize the *besmedresh* as a workers' club. A few days later "a general gathering of voters of the Jewish population of the settlement" was held to vote on the future of the synagogue building: 227 of the 239 people present (95 percent) voted in favor of closure. The decision was conveyed to the Yampil Regional Central Committee in July 1937 and then to the Central Committee of the Vinnytsya Province of Soviet Workers' Deputies, eventually making its way to the Supreme Soviet for final approval in 1940.[20] In Sharhorod, the Skverer synagogue was closed in the summer of 1938 after 94 percent of the nearly one hundred voters opted for closure. According to the report given to the Supreme Soviet, the synagogue was already largely abandoned; the faithful had not been attending for the last four years.[21] In Bershad, Khayke Gvinter told us that one synagogue was converted into a movie theater and another into a store where "you can buy things for a buck." Only one synagogue in Bershad survived.

"THEY USED TO GATHER TOGETHER"

The confiscation of synagogues failed to completely eradicate Jewish religious practice. As Burshtein explained, with reference to the liquidation of the synagogue in Sobolivka in 1935 or 1936:

> There was only one synagogue, and when they liquidated the synagogue, my grandfather had nowhere to pray. Although my grandfather was a cobbler and illiterate in Russian, he could read Yiddish. He used to read the Torah and the *gemore* [Talmud] and such things. And he used to pray every day. He would pray both at night and during the day. He would put on tefillin and nobody could bother him when he was praying. So, when they closed the synagogue he had nowhere to go.

But Burshtein's grandfather was not deterred. The congregation simply moved the services from the public space of the synagogue into private homes: "They used to gather together in a house. Nobody could know! And people would pray no matter what. And whenever there was a holiday he also wouldn't go to work. A holiday was a holiday for him." Dora Yatskova also told us that her father stopped attending the synagogue in the 1930s because "it was forbidden then to go. But at home—at home—my father prayed."

Indeed, many Jewish prayer quorums, or minyans, simply moved underground.[22] There are no rites or rituals in Judaism that can only be performed inside a synagogue; it is the community, as manifested in the minyan, that is sacred, not the structure it meets in. The presence of a minyan and a Torah scroll renders any building sacred, allowing for complete fulfillment of all rituals. Thus, when a synagogue was transformed into a sports complex or a movie theater, the faithful could simply migrate elsewhere. This flexibility and mobility are factors that have helped the Jewish religion survive innumerable persecutions and transformations. By contrast, although the Christian Orthodox majority was also able to reconstitute portions of their belief underground, in the absence of priests and churches major religious accommodations needed to be made.[23]

When we asked Maria Yakuta how the Jewish community felt when the synagogues were closed in Teplyk she replied: "Nothing. They didn't protest. They said it must be what God wants. When they were closed, people would gather in a house to pray. A minyan. Ten Jews used to gather together and then they would quickly disperse." Yosl Kogan told us that even after they closed the synagogues in Bershad: "I was part of a minyan. . . . They closed them [the synagogues] but then we went to pray in secret. . . . Before the war, I used to go pray. We used to go on Passover. Everyone would gather together in a house and we would pray in the house. Because back then they would take away and lock up the synagogue. So we came together in a house to pray. We would say *yizkor* [the memorial service for the dead]. We would blow the shofar." Grigorii Shor recalled that "after '36, they would rent a house and they would always hide so that the government wouldn't know where they were praying. And there on holidays, and so on, in the morning they would go to pray. They would say *kaddish* [the memorial prayer for the dead] there." Shor and Kogan both cite only exceptional instances in which they would attend synagogue services—for the *yizkor* service, on occasion of a *yortsayt* (anniversary of a death), for Passover, or for the High Holidays. But they all emphasize the clandestine nature of the services, a factor that likely rendered them more meaningful and memorable than they would otherwise have been. These clandestine minyans sometimes acted without official knowledge, sometimes with the knowledge of local authorities who chose to look the other way, and sometimes perhaps even with local authorities praying alongside the devout.

"THERE WAS A *MOYEL* BUT IT WAS STRICTLY FORBIDDEN"

The covenant of circumcision has long been regarded as a defining rite of male membership in the Jewish community. According to the biblical book of Genesis, God promised Abraham that he would make of his seed a great nation in return for which Abraham and every child in his "generations" would circumcise their male children as a token of the everlasting covenant. When in 1870 a Jewish physician from Hanover refused to circumcise his son, the event launched a wrenching debate within the German Jewish community over whether one could be accepted as a Jew without being circumcised.[24] Although circumcision in the USSR was never officially prohibited, Soviet Yiddish propaganda viciously attacked circumcision as a barbaric rite unbecoming of communist behavior. Nevertheless, the journalist David Meckler, who traveled to Soviet Russia and Ukraine in the mid-1930s, was surprised to find Party members still circumcising their children. Party members were able to excuse themselves from punishment by insisting that their wives had carried out the deed without their consent.[25] It was only later in the decade that circumcising a son became grounds for expulsion. Non-Party members, however, were not subject to the same restrictions and often managed to continue to circumcise their sons until the war.

Trained *moyels* (ritual circumcisers) still practiced in most small towns legally until 1937. Even after the 1937 crackdown and arrest of most of the professional *moyels*, Jewish physicians could still be counted on to perform the procedure quietly and without witnesses. [26] Isaak Vaisman explained that before the war in Berdichev, "It was strictly forbidden. People circumcised, but nobody could know. There was a *moyel* but it was strictly forbidden. I am circumcised and my son is circumcised." His wife, Bella Vaisman, however, recalled publicly celebrating a *bris* to welcome a baby boy into the covenant. Her father, she told us, "played the fiddle. He would never play in front of strangers, except in the court-yard, when a boy was born, they would hold a *bris* and he would go out and play." Aba Kaviner remembered the rabbi of Derazhnya, who also served the community as a *moyel:* "Until '39 people would put up wedding canopies, and there was a *moyel,* and the *rov* [rabbi] was a good *moyel,* may his memory be a blessing. What a rabbi we had! His name was Mikhl Rozhansky. He played the fiddle—you should have heard him! As beautiful as the world! A treasure."

Sime Geller remembered that when her brother was circumcised in Bratslav "they organized a *krishmeleyenen* [ceremony in honor of a newborn] and had cookies, and in the evening people came and had a celebration [*s'iz geven a simkhe*]." [27] Sime laughed about how she would bring home extra cookies for her other siblings, and about how other children would bring an extra hat to the *krishmeleyenen* that they would fill up with cookies. In Tulchyn, the residents still remember the custom of *krishmeleyenen,* during which they would put a cat in the cradle along with ginger bread and other sweets so that the child would grow up to be successful and healthy. [28] They would rock the cradle and children would gather the candy and sweets that fell out of it.

Nisen Yurkovetsky spoke extensively about circumcising his youngest son on the eve of the war:

On the third of May, I circumcised my youngest son. On the third of May. A *moyel* came to us with a white pillow and all that. I remember, it was still in his first year when we circumcised him. And on the fourth of May, they brought me a notification to go to Odessa to enroll in the Naval Academy reserves. . . . My youngest son, on the third of May, I brought a *moyel* from Bratslav to Tulchyn . . . in Tulchyn there weren't any. And he sat him on a white cushion.

The coincidence of the timing provides the story with a parallel structure. Yurkovetsky first fulfilled his duties as a Jew by circumcising his
child, and then fulfilled his duties as a Soviet citizen by joining the Red
Army. The two moments coincided, but rather than colliding they dove-
tailed, allowing Yurkovetsky to express his dual identity. With these two
duties fulfilled, he was able to leave behind his difficult youth and enter
a new phase of his life as a Soviet Jew.

All the Jews circumcised their children, he continued. Only Party
members failed to do so because "they would throw them out of the
Party!" He later justified his decision: "It was a great shame when a child
wasn't circumcised, a Jewish child. And it was the communists who were
afraid. I wasn't afraid at all. They couldn't take anything away from me.
So, I circumcised the children. Why shouldn't I have? Why should I
let them be like a *goy*. I circumcised the kid so that he would be a Jew
even if he didn't go to the synagogue." Dovid Geller also proudly shared
with us that he was properly inducted into the Jewish community. His
father, however, paid the price of Party membership for this breach of
discipline: "One has to be made Jewish. When I was already eight days
old—my father was a communist—so my mother and my grandmother
took me to the *synagogue* and they did the job. In short, my father was
excluded from the Party. He said: 'How am I guilty? My wife and the
grandmother took him.' In short, I am a Jew."

The term for circumcision that most of those we spoke with employed—the German-component term *yidishn* rather than the He-
brew-component *mole zayn* (circumcise)—alludes to a familiarity and
intimacy with the ceremony. Its usage as a verb—literally, to make Jewish—also indicates the crucial importance attached to the ceremony as
a fulfillment of one's identity. As Yurkovetsky explained, his son became
Jewish by the act of circumcision even if he would never step foot in a
synagogue. As Geller put it, circumcision was common "before the war,
when a Jew became a Jew."

"AND THEY WENT TO UMAN AND BRATSLAV"

In 1810, having contracted tuberculosis at the tender age of thirty-eight,
the Hasidic Rebbe Nahman of Bratslav journeyed from Bratslav to Uman
so that he could die and be buried alongside the martyrs of the 1768 Hai-

damak massacre that had left thousands of Jews dead in the city. Before he died he declared that anybody who traveled to his grave and recited the ten psalms he had designated as a general cure would be protected by his soul. Nahman urged his followers, in particular, to visit during Rosh Hashanah, the Jewish New Year. With no heir to continue the dynasty, Nahman's followers felt they had little choice but to continue to look toward their deceased leader for inspiration, believing that his spirit still hovered over his grave. Since the year after his death, Nahman's followers have accepted the Rebbe's deathbed invitation to celebrate the new year with him by making a pilgrimage to his grave in Uman. Their reverence for their deceased leader has earned them the nickname, "Di toyte khsidim" (the Deceased Hasids). The Rebbe's grave has attracted not only his followers, but also other common folk seeking solace and hope. Largely neglected in the immediate postwar period, the graves of Hasidic rebbes have once again become popular sites of pilgrimage both for Hasidic Jews from around the world and for the local Ukrainian population—Jewish and Christian—who sometimes ascribe supernatural properties to the graves.[29]

Most of the Hasidic traditions in the region have been forgotten by the locals, but many residents do still recall their parents embarking upon pilgrimages to the graves of Hasidic rebbes in the 1920s and 1930s. Maria Yakuta's father would make regular pilgrimages on holidays to the graves of Nahman in Uman and Natan Sternharz in Bratslav. The pilgrimages continued, according to Yakuta, until the war. Her mother, who was born in Teplyk in 1897, would "go to synagogue in Uman. She would go to the *mikveh* [ritual bath] in Uman with the women." Until the war, her father continued to travel to Uman "when it was someone's *yortsayt* [anniversary of a death], when it was a holiday." Yakuta's father, she told us, "used to secretly, secretly, go to pray every Friday, to greet the moon. And that was forbidden, and yet they would secretly gather quietly. . . . And they went to Uman and Bratslav. . . . And he would travel in a wagon. They would collect money and the Jews with talliths and tefillin would go . . . there was a prayer house, well—a grave, a pious Jew was there . . . Nahman. . . . was it Uman? Sternhartz?" Breslov sources claim that even during the 1930s, the pious would continue to make pilgrimages to the grave, particularly during Rosh Hashanah.[30] Eli Marchak, the *shoykhet* of Bershad and an ardent follower of Breslov

Hasidism, had moved to Bershad from Poland just to be closer to the grave of Nahman of Bratslav in nearby Uman. In Bershad he organized a community of Breslov Hasidim that met in their own prayer house near the Main Synagogue. Among those who met there was Pinya Shor, the father of Naftoli Shor.[31] Breslov Hasidim continued to meet together for prayer, learning, and pilgrimage until at least 1935–1936 in towns like Teplyk, Tulchyn, and Bershad. There are even reports of non-Jewish neighbors participating in pilgrimages to the graves.[32] The activities of Breslov Hasidim are noted in official documents as well. The interim head of the Ukrainian Commissariat for Internal Affairs noted in a report to the Deputy Head of the Ukrainian NKVD that "an underground sect" of "so-called Breslov Hasidim," admirers of their saint rabbi from the shtetl of Bratslav," was liquidated in 1939.[33] Hasidic rebbes served as alternative power structures that posed a threat to the growing soviets, providing mutual aid and spiritual support for Jews (and sometimes non-Jews) that contradicted the official government line. Because the movement was strictly hierarchical, it was also easier to decapitate the social structure of Hasidism. Thus, whereas some contemporary Ukrainian Jews recall features of the tradition—perhaps a few tales of Hasidic *tsadiks*—the twenty-first century Hasidic revival in Ukraine has for the most part been imported by foreigners rather than revived by locals.

"A LITTLE WINDOW"

Women had important roles to play in preparing the synagogue for the holidays and the Sabbath.[34] Tseytl Kislinskaia told us that her grandmother, Reyzl, was a *shameste,* a synagogue caretaker: "She had to bring water to those who were praying, and she would have to make sure the benches were clean. There were no tables, but there was a place where they would read the Torahs and she would keep that tidy. And this was before holidays. And she would pluck and clean the geese and chickens and help out there."

Women played auxiliary roles in the synagogue service; they did not participate directly in the men's service, which took place downstairs in the main sanctuary of the synagogue. As a result, they were not commonly taught the Hebrew language in which prayers were recited. Only a few Jewish women from the pre-revolutionary generation had acquired some reading knowledge of Hebrew, which remained a source of great pride for them. Chaim Rubin told us, "My mother was an observant Jew. She would pray. All the women would gather—she could read the sacred language [Hebrew]. She had studied it. She was born in 1900." Brukhe Gammer also told us: "None of the wealthy Jewish women could pray. My mother had a little table in the wealthy synagogue. Everybody would gather across from her and repeat after her. She understood, but they, the wealthy women, didn't. And my mother was a tailor's wife." Her father, by contrast, didn't pray at all: "He was a Soviet boy."

Rakhil Shames, who studied Hebrew as a child in the early 1920s with a tutor, told us she remembers how strangers would point out how fluently she could read prayer-book Hebrew when she attended synagogue with her mother. Women with bookish knowledge learned to say their prayers according to the canonical version, in Hebrew, the Holy Tongue. Sime Geller, for instance, explained:

> I remember that my mother prayed. My mother used to go to synagogue. . . . At home my mother used to tell me everything. In Yiddish she was very learned. If she had prayed in Yiddish, I would have understood. But I used to ask her, "Mama, what are you saying? I can't understand anything." She would say, "When you grow up you'll understand that we speak in Yiddish but we pray in another language." Now I understand that my mother prayed in Hebrew.

Those who couldn't read cherished their status as observers in the women's section of the synagogue, and remembered with pride how their mothers were able to follow along in the Hebrew text. In Tomashpil, Klara Sapozhnik recalled fondly watching her father pray downstairs in the synagogue, holding his *siddur,* his prayer book, while the women watched from above through the window. The women who were able to read would follow along in the prayer book, she says, and the others would weep entreaties.

Maria Yakuta recalled the women's section of her synagogue, a structure, she told us, that was made of clay, lime, straw, and wood:

> So there weren't any pretty doors or windows. But there was, up above, near the ceiling, a little window to see into the men's section. And when they would pray down there the women could hear. And when the cantor would sing down there, it could be heard up here. They used to open the window and listen to everything. . . . I myself remember how I used to

look on as the men danced with the Torahs. They would dance around.
. . . And there was a cupboard [ark] where they kept the Torah and the
books. It was by the wall. That's how it was. And there in the middle was
the dais. . . . We could hear everything. . . . You could peek in and see
everything. And they didn't let girls, even little ones, go to where the
dais was.

Yakuta told us her mother "used to pray. She had a *khimesh* [Pentateuch],
a large *siddur* and a small . . . *khimesh*. . . . My mother used to read and
weep. She read and she read until . . . she would cry and then afterwards
she would tell us what was written there."

The image of women weeping as they prayed recurs frequently in
descriptions of women's piety. We were repeatedly told that women's
prayers were accompanied by genuine tears. Liudmila Shor, for instance,
told us that "my mother used to gather all the women on holidays—in
the shtetl people couldn't read in Yiddish, but she knew how; she had
learned when she was a little child—the women would come, they would
sit down and my mother would put on a kerchief, and she would open
the *siddur* . . . and begin to read and they would weep. Reading and
weeping." Her husband, Grigorii, chimed in: "They would read in Yiddish because the prayer book had Yiddish commentary underneath."
Liudmila continued, "When they began to pray, my mother would read
and they would weep and they would send me out of the room." Klara
Sapozhnik also remembered how her mother would take her to the
women's section on the upper level of the synagogue, where they would
peer through the window at the men praying with their books, their *sid-
durs*. She recalled several people actively praying in the women's section,
while others just watched the action down below. Still others, she told us,
just wept. When asked if her mother would pray during the High Holidays, Khayke Gvinter replied simply, "My mother didn't sing. She cried.
She cried over the world she had lost at such a young age." Gvinter's
older sister died of smallpox as a child and her father perished during
the famine, leaving her mother alone with the two young children. Like
so many others of her generation, she had reason to weep and pray.

Women wept their prayers in part because they viewed prayer as a
personalized appeal to God rather than as an abstract recitation required
as a religious obligation. Their prayers were more similar to the *tkhines*
(supplicatory prayers) recited by women for generations as a parallel

to the formal Hebrew liturgy.[35] Asya Barshteyn remembered that her mother would recite prayers in simple Yiddish, the common spoken language, rather than in the lofty Hebrew of the prayer book. Indeed, for generations Yiddish had been derogatorily considered a women's language, whereas Hebrew erudition was for the most part restricted to men. Arkadii Gelman remembered his mother praying extemporaneously in Yiddish and in her own heartfelt words for the health of the family, as she welcomed in the Sabbath: "Every Friday night she would bless the candles. I used to hear what she would say when she was thanking God: that He should provide, that the children should be healthy." These prayers were more personal than the abstract prayers that were printed in the canonized prayer book; rather, they were composed spontaneously as genuine expressions of needs and desires. Even many women who claimed to know the canonized prayer still reported that they personalized the prayer for themselves rather than strictly adhere to the authoritative text.[36]

Bella Chirkova, born in Krosne in 1912, discussed with us in detail how she would pray and what meaning she ascribed to it. Chirkova was one of the women we met at the Vinnytsya women's choir performance. She was wearing a purple and red patterned smock dress with a yellow flowered kerchief covering her head and knotted tightly under her chin. She was the oldest woman in the choir, but the other women knew she could dance like no one else. As the choir erupted into a rousing Yiddish classic, some of the women cajoled Chirkova into showing off her moves. As the rest of the women sat around the table singing, Chirkova, who was ninety years old at the time, hopped up and began to dance, her outstretched arms swinging, her body swaying, her feet tapping, and her voice ringing out in harmony. Later in her home, she demonstrated for us the type of homespun prayer that she would say over the lighting of the candles. Eschewing the canonized liturgy, she spoke simply, holding a candle, as her voice wavered in supplication. Using simple Yiddish words, she entreated God for help in a conversational tone: "Dear God, I beg of you, help me. You have helped me all the time up until now, I beg of you. Dear God, help me. As you have helped me all the time, help me now as well. Help my children so that they will be healthy." Utilizing the Yiddish word for blessing, she continued, "That's *bentshing*. And you say Amen."

Chirkova's piety was a personal one, derived not from the rabbinical learning of her father, the rabbi of Krosne, nor from her grandfather the cantor, but rather from her own personal faith in God, and from the lessons she had learned from the American and Israeli emissaries sent to Vinnytsya in recent decades. "Whatever God says," she told us, "you are supposed to do. And when the time draws near for you to die, God will take your soul and you should thank Him. I thank God for everything. I thank God wherever I go." Many of the people we interviewed who reported that they observed Jewish customs specified that they did so because "one is supposed to." When asked why they ate matzo on Passover, for instance, few would tell us that they did so in commemoration of the ancient Israelites who fled Egypt and did not have time to let their bread rise. Rather, they followed the commandment "because you are supposed to." Their faith did not demand rational or historical explanation; it was more firmly rooted in a personal and domestic setting, where rituals were followed simply because they were supposed to be followed.

Chirkova believed that suffering and endurance were part of what made her Jewish:

> One should endure anything. One should not fight that. One should deal with all the troubles. If you don't, then you can't call yourself a Jew. That's how it works, my children. If you want to be a Jew, then you need to preserve your Jewishness. And then you will be a Jew the way it's supposed to be. And God will protect you, and God will take notice and remember that you are devoted Jews for the sake of the world, humanity and yourself. That's how it is.

Her confidence that the righteous are rewarded in the afterlife and the wicked are punished was unshakable: "With God . . . with us, God is One. Everything a Jew does is recorded by God—the good and the bad. If you do good things then you will go to [heaven]." Her beliefs were derived from a mixture of Jewish and Christian doctrine, as evidenced by her report of her religious rituals: "There are non-Jews who speak Yiddish and go to the Jewish prayer houses. I also go to services at non-Jewish prayer houses, to the Polish, Ukrainian, and Russian ones." She showed us some literature that she had acquired from Jews for Jesus, the Christian evangelical sect that actively proselytizes among Jews in the Former Soviet Union. Chirkova sought the religion of her father and grandfather wherever she could. When there were no longer any synagogues to attend, she sought God instead in the Polish, Ukrainian, and Russian churches of her Vinnytsya neighborhood. But her God was a personal God, who intervened in the world, protected her, and could be counted on for sustenance in times of need. Her religion knew of no doubt but was also largely devoid of dogma.

Pesia Kolodenker expressed similar sentiments in her interview in 2010. When asked what advice she would give to the younger generation of Jewish women, she spoke of the importance of belief in God and Jewishness:

> We are Jews and we must thank God and believe in God and one must not forget God. One should always remember Him when you go to bed, when you get up, and when you eat. My husband used to say that back then they would say the *moyde [ani]*. When I was a child I asked what *moyde* is. They told me that upon waking up and washing you go to the door, where there is a mezuzah, you kiss it and say that you believe in God and you tell God "thank you."

Growing up in the Soviet Ukraine, where she was unable to acquire a formal Jewish education, Maria Yakuta derived her faith and religious identity from a variety of seemingly conflicting sources. Like many people we spoke to, she drew lessons from biblical stories, but she knew these stories from sources other than the canonical text. The names and life stories of the biblical patriarchs had receded from her memory, but the lessons remained relevant to her daily life. For instance, she summarized what it means to be a Jew by telling us the story of *Akeydes Yitskhok* (the near-sacrifice of Isaac), but she could not recall the names of Abraham or Isaac or even the origins of the story:

> My mother told us how they used to have to make sacrifices. How he, a Jew, had brought his son . . . he had brought his son, and his son asked him, "Father, why do we come to this fire? What shall I do here?" And he explained to him that he was going to lay him out on the fire. But an angel came down from heaven and took him and saved him. . . . He said, "This is enough for God, he believes that you are faithful because you didn't hold back your son." . . . Yes, indeed. She used to say that a Jew needs to be faithful until death. Until the end she must be pious and she must have a good conscience.

Yakuta didn't treat this central story in the Bible as part of a textual tradition, but rather viewed it as an element of folk wisdom. Like many

women, and men as well, she knew her biblical stories not from reading the Pentateuch, but rather from retellings of the stories designed to
emphasize their moral lessons. This moral essence—that a Jew must
be faithful and endure whatever hardships God has in store for him or
her—was a staple of popular Jewish belief in the region, as articulated
by Chirkova, Kolodenker, and Yakuta.[37]

—⁓—

Prior to the opening of archival collections, specific evidence about
Jewish religious life in the Soviet Union came predominantly from
the Soviet Yiddish press, sporadic comments made by Soviet officials,
and anecdotes collected by contemporary foreign news sources. These
sources tended to report on change rather than persistence: it was certainly more newsworthy to report on the closure of a synagogue than on
another synagogue's continued existence. Western observers also sought
to sound alarms to world Jewry about the tragic fate of their coreligionists in the Soviet Union in the hopes that the Jews of Israel and America
would be propelled to take action in support of Soviet Jewry. This data
was centered overwhelmingly on the major cities of the Soviet Union,
particularly Moscow, Leningrad, Kiev, and Odessa. Recent scholarship
on Jewish religious practice in Vitebsk Province, Minsk, and the Crimea
have provided an increasingly complex and detailed picture of religious
life in the provinces. These studies have utilized extensive archival evidence to demonstrate the persistence of institutional religious practice
throughout the 1920s and into the 1930s.[38]

Indeed, in a variety of ways, religious observance persisted in those
decades. A conference of rabbis was held in Korosten in October 1926;
the Lubavitcher Rebbe actively and openly promoted Jewish religious
practice until his arrest in 1927; a yeshiva openly functioned in Nevel
until 1928; and heders were not uncommon into the early 1930s.[39] The
secret police also followed these activities closely, usually ascribing any
religious activity in the Soviet Union to the meddling of foreign agitators. As late as February 1939, the director of the Ukrainian Commissariat of Nationalities Affairs complained about "the high concentration
of leading clerical elements in Ukraine, and their significant organiza-
tional role among former merchants, tsadiks, rabbis, butchers, and other
synagogue employees." The directive singled out in particular the orga-

nization of underground schools and prayer circles that met in private homes. This directive led to the arrest over the following months of several Jewish community leaders, including two in the Tulchyn district.[40]

In the 1937 census, only 17 percent of adult Jews reported that they were "believers," a number that contrasts sharply with the much larger percentages of Muslims and Christians who declared themselves to be so, 66 percent and 55 percent respectively.[41] Were Jews so much less likely to be believers, or were they simply better prepared to answer the census-takers' questions with the desired answer? Certainly, the fits and starts that characterize reports on Jewish religious practice in the Soviet Union reflect a broader ambiguity in Soviet Jewish understandings of religious practice.[42] As Tsolik Groysman put it, "In Tarashche, there were many Jews. There were those who strongly believed in God and there were those who didn't."

6

Religion of the Home

FOOD AND FAITH

When Mendl Osherowitch visited a Ukrainian shtetl in 1932, he lamented that the Sabbath was barely distinguishable from any other day:

> In the street . . . it does not feel like Sabbath. Rarely does a Jew do anything different on this day than any other day of the week. There is simply nothing to do. And in the home, there is also no sign of Sabbath food or white challah. People have already forgotten the taste of challah.
>
> The synagogue, the old synagogue, which is locked for almost the entire week, is opened on this day. It is opened by the caretaker, an elderly, beaten-down Jew, in whose heart beats not a single shard of hope. And people say that every time he takes down the lock of the synagogue, tears flow. When he closes the synagogue up again, he cries even more.
>
> Jews come into the synagogue, they pray quickly and leave for home quietly. And at home they catch a little rest from their hard work—and in the shtetl it is hard to find a Jew who doesn't have to work hard: either they are in a *kolkhoz* [collective farm] or in an artel, and if they are not in an artel, they work so hard in order to earn a piece of bread. They rest a little from their hard work, and this they call observing the Sabbath.[1]

But many of the residents we interviewed a decade or more after the collapse of the Soviet Union remembered the Sabbaths of the 1930s dif-

ferently: they visualized a pious life full of Jewish ritual. They themselves
were often unable to articulate the precise meaning of the rituals they
recalled, but these acts continued to inform their identity in important
ways. Osherowitch was searching for "The Great Tradition" of religious
observance as expressed publicly in a formal institutional setting.[2] But
Soviet restrictions on the public expression of religious faith had, in
many cases, forced religious ritual into the domestic sphere, where it
continued to be recognized as a family affair.

Maria Yakuta, who was born into a family she described as very pious,
told us that on Sabbath "My mother would light candles and my father
wouldn't let us go to the movies or anywhere like that. We had to sit
there and listen to him make the seder or the Sabbath, and we'd finish
our food and take a nap. No movies or anything like that." Sime Geller
remembered, "My father was a wagon driver, a serious workhorse. My
mother was a typical Jewess. She raised the children, she stayed at home.
Every Sabbath she made the blessing over the candles. On Rosh Hashanah and on every holiday she would observe the holidays, because that's
the way it was with *yidishkayt* [Jewishness]." Moyshe Kupershmidt, born
in Bratslav in 1914, told us, "My mother would light candles. . . . The
older women made the benediction over the candles and everyone kept
the Sabbath." Nisen Kiselman said of Tomashpil, "The old times were so
interesting. There was Sabbath. There were prayer houses. People prayed,
they would lay out the Torah on the table and people would kiss it. If
someone had a *yortsayt* they would bring a bottle of beer and they would
bake ginger cakes and distribute them. And the cantor sang so well the
entire town would hear." Pesia Kolodenker, born in Tulchyn in 1927,
remembered how her family would welcome the Sabbath by smearing
clay over the dirt floor in order to beautify the house. "Even the poorest
believed in God and celebrated the Sabbath," she insisted.

Etia Shvartzbroit remembered that she would put on a beautiful kerchief on Sabbath to cover her head, and that her mother would wear a
kerchief over her wig. "Every Friday she would light the candles. Every
Friday. And on Sabbath one didn't work." But, Shvartzbroit continued,
"During the Soviet times they didn't teach this to children." Her mother
never taught her to pray. By the mid 1930s, when Shvartzbroit was becoming old enough to perform religious rituals on her own, it was already too dangerous for children to be seen performing them. The chil-

dren nevertheless could watch their parents and integrate their parents'
piety into their own life stories.

Many of those who were born in the 1920s and 1930s recall their
parents attending synagogue over Sabbath as part of a regular routine.
"When we came to Bershad, my father would go to synagogue. He would
go there all the time. Every Sabbath and every holiday. And my mother
went too. The synagogue was still there," recalled Elizaveta Bershadskaia, who arrived there from the village of Chernyatka in 1938. In the
1930s, she continued, the few Jews in Chernyatka practiced their religion
without a synagogue or religious functionaries: they prayed together
in a private home "just like a synagogue." They read from a communal
Torah scroll, lit Sabbath candles, cooked *cholent* for the Sabbath, and
imported kosher meat from Bershad. Grigorii Shor, born in Kopayhorod
in 1925, implied that religious life for his parents' generation continued
much as it had in pre-Soviet times: "On Friday evening, my father would
go to synagogue and my mother would stay at home, where she would
get candles and bless them. . . . When my father came home from synagogue, he would greet us and tell us about the good angel that will come
to us so that we will have a good Sabbath."

"GEFILTE FISH, *CHOLENT* AND LATKES"

Minutes after we first met her on the streets of Bershad in 2002, Khayke
Gvinter told us about the gefilte fish her mother had taught her to
make. It was so tasty, she crooned, as she abandoned us on the street,
rushed across the yard into her kitchen, and brought us some of her fish,
wrapped in paper. She made gefilte fish just like her mother did, even
pulling up carrots from the very same garden.

Many Jewish homemakers in Ukraine today emphasize in particular
that they learned their recipes from their mothers, and that they make
their dishes—gefilte fish or challah—exactly as their mothers made it.
During the interwar period in Soviet Ukraine, so much of the old world
that the elder generation knew was rendered unrecognizable. Parents
were deprived of the pleasures of passing many of their most cherished
traditions on to their children. Schools and clubs taught children to
reject their elders' prayers, religious rituals, and customs. Traditional

modes of healing and of curing the evil eye were mercilessly mocked as harmful superstitions. Even their work-ways could not be passed on, as the state eschewed traditional artisanal skills in favor of factory work, and interpreted business acumen as hostile "anti-government" activity.

Yet Soviet ideologues not only tolerated ethnic food customs, but even encouraged them as part of the ethnic kaleidoscope that constituted the Soviet Union. National minorities were encouraged to retain visible markers of ethnic difference, such as dress and food, provided that they were emptied of any national sentiment. The Soviet government often showcased the colorful peasant dresses and exotic spices of its national minorities as a means of asserting the ethnic diversity of the Soviet Union. Foodways, along with language, were the most tangible traditions that could safely be passed from generation to generation. Food came to represent the last link with the older generation. A gefilte fish recipe could become a cherished family heirloom. Private remembrance was the predominant means of evoking the past, and the kitchen was as close to the private sphere as was possible. The eating of a gefilte fish made in accordance with a traditional recipe was a literal imbibing of the past and a means of merging with one's ancestors by sharing a meal with them across time.

In the Soviet Union, where public expressions of faith were taboo, piety and religious expression were relegated to the domestic sphere, and to the kitchen in particular. For a population whose everyday meals varied little from day to day, the sudden change in cuisine for a festival meal left an indelible mark in memory. Prior to the advent of refrigeration, supermarkets, and takeout items, the preparation of food was a time-consuming activity for everyone the world over, and even more so for those not living in urban centers and with little disposable income for delicacies. Preparing meals was an important part of the daily routine and it comes as little surprise that the elderly remember with such consistency how to prepare certain meals. For many women the holiday *was* the meal preparation.

Food is also a major stimulant to memory. Taste and smell can work synesthetically, evoking seemingly unrelated memories. Indeed, urban Russian Jews have also looked toward food in an effort to reclaim their Jewish identities.[3] In immigrant communities, food often becomes a metonym for a wider cultural context, for the lost world of the Old Country.[4] Much of the scholarship that has been conducted on foodways focuses on immigrants and diasporic nostalgia, a longing for the tastes and smells of a world that immigrants can no longer access, where cooking is part of an attempt to reconstruct and remember another world.[5] Numerous immigrant memoirs speak of a single dish that is unavailable in the new country as a symbol for all that has been lost of the abandoned cultural world. Elements of this nostalgia can certainly be found today in Ukraine. In fact, this diasporic evocation was exacerbated in the Soviet Union, where foodways provided one of the few means of expressing ethnic identity and memory. The example of Jews in the small towns of Ukraine demonstrates that this same phenomenon can be observed in communities that remained in place, but had their old customs torn asunder in political violence. For them, food provided a means of memorializing and commemorating a past that could not be publicly expressed.

Food was also strongly associated with religious festivals and practice, a phenomenon by no means unique to Soviet Jewry.[6] Sabbath foods—challah, gefilte fish, *cholent,* and latkes—feature prominently in memories of the Sabbath. *Cholent,* in particular, a slow-cooked stew, usually consisting of meat, barley, beans, potato, and whatever else could be found around the house, symbolizes the Sabbath for many. The Sabbath rest prohibits cooking from Friday evening through Saturday sunset, but does allow the consumption of a hot meal provided that the fire was lit before the onset of the Sabbath. It is traditional, therefore, to place the stew in the oven prior to the start of the Sabbath, on Friday evening, and remove it, fully cooked, for lunch on Saturday.

Elizaveta Bershadskaia remembered sealing the oven with clay in order to prevent heat from escaping (and to stop anybody from violating the Sabbath by rekindling the oven) as the *cholent* cooked overnight: "Well, we would cook everything inside and afterwards knead some clay, and you would go like this with the clay [she demonstrates "smearing" with her hands]. . . . We would put in a pot of *cholent* and then afterwards we would smear it with clay. I still remember that." On Saturdays, she continued, they would open the oven and take out the *cholent.* Using the term *cholent* to refer to the oven itself, Etia Shvartzbroit also remembered that "On Friday they would smear the *cholent,* the oven [with clay], and on Saturday they would open it up and take it out."

Donia Presler of Tulchyn described how her family would shield the oven door with a tin cover to prevent heat from escaping after putting in the *cholent* on Friday afternoon. Sometimes, she continued, the non-Jewish neighbors, who were not bound by the religious strictures of the Jews, would bring over some hot tea for them to drink on Saturday afternoon. For Moyshe Kupershmidt, the *cholent* was also an important part of the Sabbath meal: "What can I tell you? Piety was everywhere. My mother would *kasher* [make kosher] the chicken. We had an oven . . . on Sabbath we had *cholent*."

Evgeniia Kozak, who was born in Bershad in 1926 and continued to live in the town her entire life, told us in detail about her family's weekly Sabbath preparation:

> Well, there would be a *cholent* in our oven that was prepared in advance. Everything would be cooked already. The *cholent* was so delicious, goodness me! And everything was prepared, cooked and baked with a cooking board. Oy, what more was there? There was a tasty soup, good chopped fish, a stew made of beans and ground chickpeas.

At the mention of chopped fish, her thoughts became nostalgic, "It's been a long time since I've eaten chopped fish," she mused.

Beyle Vaisman of Berdichev told us about Sabbath in her relatively wealthy family's home:

> There was an oven. There was no gas. There was a [wood burning] oven in the kitchen. On Friday we would bake latkes and challah on the oven. . . . We would make *cholent* for Sabbath. My mother would throw wood into the oven. When the oven was lit, we would cook for Sabbath. We did not have gas, it was a [wood-burning] oven. . . . In front of the oven there was a *pripetshek* [stove]. It would stand on three feet. It was called a *trinotshke*. We would bake latkes until the wood burned. And we would be standing and running around: "Yay, yay, latkes, latkes." . . . Everything was delicious. Everything. Since it was for Sabbath, whatever we cooked was good. . . . I remember that after the wood burned, coal would remain left over from the wood. My mother, may she rest in peace, would put pots on it. She would make a *cholent* from meat and potatoes. She would shut the oven, and on Sabbath take it out. . . . My mother was such a great homemaker. . . . Sabbath was Sabbath. But my father, may he rest in peace, he would work on Sabbath. In those days, he had to.

In Vaisman's recollection, the memory of food evokes visceral emotions that beautify the moment: "Since it was Sabbath everything was good." Sabbath time was sacred, rendering even the profane good. For those who formally welcomed the Sabbath with prayer on Friday evenings, lighting Sabbath candles and eating traditional challah bread was an important part of the custom. Asya Barshteyn recalled her family's Sabbath preparation in Sharhorod, emphasizing that her family did everything "like you were supposed to do:"

> At home, on Sabbath. We had an oven. You could bake bread, you could bake challah. During the week, you would eat bread, but on Sabbath it was challah, as though God had baked it, like you were supposed to. Cooked and baked with all types of cookies and baked goods that my mother cooked. Everything like you were supposed to do. And on Sabbath we would light candles. I light candles. Every Sabbath I light candles.

Barshteyn's insistence that she did everything "like you were supposed to do" was echoed by many of those we interviewed, who insisted that they followed religious strictures "just as they were supposed to," or occasionally described how they performed a custom even though "you are supposed to do it differently."[7] These phrases indicate the people's strong sense that the performance of religious ritual was a requirement that they had agreed to fulfill in accordance with established guidelines and customs. In their narratives, religious obligations trumped the expected behavior of a Soviet citizen, for whom religious performance was not an obligation, but rather an infringement. In Soviet Ukraine in the 1930s, one was certainly not "supposed to" light Sabbath candles and bake challah bread.[8]

Another popular Sabbath dish was gefilte fish, which could be served either Friday evening during the welcoming of the Sabbath, or consumed cold on Saturday afternoon. Naftoli Shor's family would cook gefilte fish, meat, a broth, and bean *tsimes* on Sabbath. Sofia Palatnikova of Teplyk also remembered the Sabbath gefilte fish, which she continued to cook from the recipe her mother taught her:

> I take off the skin. That's right, and I take out the bones. And then I put the fillet through a meat grinder. My mother did it with a chopping knife. She used to say that when you use the grinder it doesn't taste as good. But I use the meat grinder. Then I add raw grated onion, then fried onion—just fried a little. Pepper. Salt to taste. Eggs. . . . And if there's matzo meal—I have matzo meal almost all year round. I take matzo—it's good for fish. I also sometimes use little biscuits, nonsweet ones, "croquettes." I had taken off the skin, so the place where I had cut it, that's where I stuff

it. Then I set it out on a plate, with the head, the tails and then the middle part, you get a whole fish. And after that I stuff it, I put it in a pan and fry it a little. And to the bottom of the pan I add carrots and raw onions and fried onions and a bay leaf and pepper and salt and let it cook over a low flame for two hours. And it comes out just right. . . . My mother made it like that. They say my fish is good. I give some to the non-Jews . . . they don't know how to make fish.

In this description, Palatnikova subtly turned what seemed to be a straightforward recipe for gefilte fish into a value-laden identity marker. She concluded her recipe by vouching for its authenticity—"my mother made it like that." She established the recipe as esoteric knowledge, available only to her exclusive group—"they [non-Jews] don't know how to make it like that." The use of matzo in the recipe further marked it as Jewish. On the other hand, she also asserted the universal appeal of the dish by insisting that the non-Jews, although they were incapable of making it, still acknowledged its supremacy. In some respects, the gefilte fish recipe Palatnikova shared is reminiscent of kabbalistic knowledge— it is esoteric and can only be created by the initiated, but has a potency recognizable to all. A good gefilte fish transcends ethnic boundaries.

Evgeniia Kozak also marked gefilte fish as distinctly Jewish. Her recipe had been passed down from generation to generation, but was modernized through the use of a meat grinder. Indeed, whether or not one uses a meat grinder or a cutting board was often represented as an integral marker of modernization, or alternatively as a corruption of an ancestral heritage, or even as blasphemy. Donia Presler exhorted: "Some people make the fish with a meat grinder. No, no, no. Only with a chopping knife!"

Grigorii Shor remembered the food items associated with the Sabbath: "And then we would pray and eat a chicken noodle soup with *mandlen* [soup nuts]. . . . There was a challah. We would pray over the challah. And there was wine. . . . The Jews didn't make the wine in the shtetl. The wine was from the vineyards in Yaruga, near Mohyliv-Podilskyy, and from there they would bring big barrels of wine. There were collective farms there that made wine and sold it. They had special wine cellars and they sold wine from there." The image of Soviet workers in collective farms producing wine from the vineyards of Yaruga that was blessed and served with challah over Sabbath dinner in nearby Kopayhorod provides a perfect example of the ways in which Soviet products could be retooled and appropriated for spiritual purposes.

In addition to the role that special dishes and food preparation play in the annual holiday cycle, food practices, particularly observance of the laws of kashrut, have traditionally served as a major boundary marker for Jews. Whereas kosher meat remained readily available in the 1920s, its acquisition became increasingly difficult throughout the Soviet Union during the 1930s. It was almost impossible to obtain kosher beef, as cows were confiscated by the state and the slaughter of cows was heavily regulated. Chickens, however, were more easily obtained, and legal kosher butchers continued to exist in certain locales; in 1935 there were twenty-one kosher butchers in the city of Kiev alone. Kosher butchers were targeted during the Great Terror of 1937, but in small towns some continued to practice clandestinely through the war.[9] In her book, *Soviet and Kosher*, Anna Shternshis notes that while retaining the idea of kashrut as an ethnic marker, Soviet Jews largely eschewed halakhic (legal) dietary requirements.[10] While most of the people we spoke to had also overcome Jewish taboos against mixing milk and meat and eating pork products, many continued to associate their Jewish identity with specific food customs. In her recollections of Sharhorod, Asya Barstheyn told us that "they sold only kosher meat—no lard at all. All the Jews bought only kosher meat. My mother only went to the kosher butcher shop to get meat." Sofia Palatnikova's father, who owned a butcher shop in Teplyk until 1930, also remembered that if the meat was not kosher, nobody would buy it. The Jews ate only kosher meat, and the non-Jews, she explained, did not eat meat at all. When we asked why, she ventured, "Why? I should know? They didn't have anything to buy it with. My father explained that there were a lot of fast days . . . for a month and a half they don't eat meat."

But such stark divisions between kosher and nonkosher meat were rare. More commonly, kashrut, when it was thought about at all, was considered an ideal rather than a reality. Evgeniia Kozak was familiar with the custom of separating milk and meat, but saw this particular practice as a local custom that she observed when visiting relatives who lived in Khust, a town in the Carpathian Mountains that had been a part of Czechoslovakia and Hungary before its occupation by the Soviet Union in 1944. Since Khust was only subjected to Soviet antireligious campaigns in the postwar period, the surviving Jewish population retained Jewish traditions for a longer period of time. "In the Carpathians, for example," she told us, "if you would cook a soup in a pot, you then couldn't put any dairy in it. You are not permitted to mix milk and meat. That's how it is for the Jews." She recognized this custom as a Jewish practice, but despite her own strong sense of Jewish identity, excluded herself from this stricter community of observers.

Others saw kashrut not as a principle ordering and regulating daily life, but rather as an extraordinary activity, performed only periodically and typically during the week of Passover. Elizaveta Bershadskaia, for instance, told of her house and her father's role in rendering it Jewish: "Yes, it was a Jewish home. He taught us everything Jewish that one must know." When asked if it was possible to keep kosher in her home, she insisted that everybody owned kosher dishes; her family would bring these down from the attic for Passover, implying that it was only during the week of Passover that kashrut was observed. Similarly, Chaim Rubin remembered Passovers in Buki: "They would make it kosher, they would bring down the Passover dishes from the attic." When it became difficult to observe the dietary restrictions year round, many Soviet Jews made do with observing them at specific appointed periods of time. Jewish dietary restrictions were turned into an extraordinary ritual observed only during the week of Passover, rather than as a daily routine.

"PASSOVER IS PASSOVER"

Of all the Jewish festivals and holidays, Passover is the one most Soviet Jews remember.[11] Many imagine Passover as the defining Jewish holiday, and it is the food of Passover—the matzo—that most represents the holiday itself. Tatiana Marinina of Teplyk, who spent much of the 1930s living on the Lunacharskii collective farm in Crimea with her sister Sofia Palatnikova, recalled how Passover brought the whole collective farm together:

> All the children and grandchildren would come to the seder. They used to come . . . my father had friends and they would come. My mother would cook up a wonderful chicken soup with matzo meal. She would make Passover pancakes from potatoes and beetroots. We used to pickle, I'm not sure you know this, but Jews also pickle borscht.

Once again the holiday is associated primarily with food. Certainly the matzo serves as an identity marker, distinguishing Jews from their neighbors, but in Tatiana's memory, it was also the custom of pickling borsht—that most Ukrainian of dishes—that defined what it means to be a Jew during Passover.

The ritual of *bdikes khomets* (search for unleavened bread), in which on the night before Passover the pious search through their homes for grains prohibited during the holiday, was and remains an important part of the Passover ritual. Elizaveta Bershadskaia told us that in her childhood village of Chernyatka, the Jews celebrated Passover together throughout the 1920s and 1930s. She recalled that her family took out the separate dishes they kept in their attic, brought in matzo from Bershad, and celebrated seders together with the other Jewish families in the village. Evgeniia Kozak told us, "On Passover we took down the dishes from the attic. And when Passover was over we would bring them back up to the attic." Etia Shvartzbroit told us, "My grandfather was a rabbi. We had separate kosher dishes in the attic."

Women were predominantly responsible for *bdikes khomets* and Passover cleaning. Accordingly, these traditions tended to be one of the first things that women recalled about the holiday.

Sofia Palatnikova recalled:

> My mother was truly religious. My father was really not. . . . Nothing could be in the house during Passover according to my mother. She took out the flour and everything. And she had special plates and pots and everything in the attic. Everything. There was another set of utensils for Passover. . . . Yes, that's how it was. I remember how Passover was observed. But, we still used to gather in houses. There were a lot of these. . . . But by then they were prohibited. I don't remember the earlier years. But before the war, well, we used to celebrate. The Jews used to celebrate Passover.

Several noted the custom of throwing a hot stone into a pot in order to render certain utensils kosher for use during Passover. Evgeniia Krasner of Shpykiv told us, "In the oven we would heat stones to make them glow and we would throw these stones and prepare all of the pots and pans—earthenware pots—and we would put the stones in and pour water over them, and steam would rise up over everything." Tatiana

Marinina told us that her mother "would take down the dishes from the attic, and throw a stone in the oven. There wouldn't be a crumb of bread in the whole house." When we spoke with her, she explained that she had revived these practices for herself, but regretted that she has not been able to pass them down to her own children:

> I do the same now. We also have matzo here. I buy matzos—you're supposed to do it differently—but I buy them all year round. And I make latkes and matzo bry. I make a Passover pancake from sour beetroots and potatoes. In my book, Passover is Passover! No bread comes in my house! I am alone. When I had children, I couldn't do it. Now that I'm alone, though, why shouldn't I do it when it is such a pleasure?

There is a wistfulness in her implication that during that period of her life when she was bringing up children to whom she could pass on these traditions, she was unable to fulfill her wish. Only now, when she is alone in a new democratic Ukraine, is she able to perform them. But her children have grown up without learning the customs, and will likely never have these rituals embedded in the fabric of their lives.

Her insistence that she buys matzo all year round is also indicative of the degree to which matzo has become associated with Judaism. Even though the ritual eating of matzo is only required for eight days of the year—and it is precisely the extraordinary nature of the diet that renders the ritual significant, as symbolized by the question "Why is this night different than all other nights?"—the display of matzo and occasional eating of it is a year-round activity for many Jews in Ukraine today. Ukrainian Jews use matzo not only as an essential ingredient in their gefilte fish, but also a means of expressing their identity publicly. Although we conducted our interviews either during the summer or the winter season, months away from the Passover festival, countless homes we visited proudly displayed a box of matzo on the mantelpiece. The boxes distributed annually by the Federation of Jewish Communities in Ukraine are even designed as keepsakes: they are colorfully illustrated and include a list of useful phone numbers for Jewish organizations throughout Ukraine. The Federation suggests that the matzo has a shelf life of one year. Matzo boxes are clearly intended not just to hold the matzo for consumption during Passover, but are also to be displayed year round and kept as visible identity markers. No longer used exclusively for ritual purposes in accordance with the periodic calendar of festivals, matzo continues to have a deep symbolic value as a public expression of ethnic identity.[12]

Whereas today matzo is distributed by the Federation of Jewish Communities and is readily available for pickup in Jewish community centers and synagogues throughout the region, acquiring matzo—or more commonly, the flour used to bake it—in prewar Soviet Union was difficult. Preparations for the Passover holiday often began months before the beginning of the festival, thereby lengthening the sacred time associated with it. Passover was transformed from an eight-day festival into a full season of preparation, culminating in the celebration of the holiday itself. Most people baked matzo themselves at home from flour obtained either in the marketplace, when flour was still available for purchase in the 1920s and early 1930s, or from state stores. Often foreign currency sent to them by relatives abroad helped smooth the purchase of flour. Others obtained it in November, when it was distributed in commemoration of the October Revolution, and stored it until needed for Passover four or five months later.[13]

Memoirs from the period and reports from foreign visitors often noted the importance Soviet Jews ascribed to obtaining matzo for the holiday. Rabbis in the Soviet Union made numerous appeals to Jews abroad in the 1920s requesting that they send matzo to the USSR, and in 1929 the government responded to popular pressure by briefly permitting its importation. David Soyfer recalled, "It was forbidden to bake matzo. That I remember. Before Passover, there was this Jew, and the Jews—the poor Jews—would give him flour and money and he would give them matzo." Others baked matzo in their homes. Sime Geller remembered how in Bratslav her mother would bake it in the family kitchen: "On Passover, my mother would bake three *poods* of matzo. Do you know what a *pood* is? It's 16 kilos! My mother had six children. We were forbidden bread. We would remove all the bread from the house." Chaim Rubin told us:

> we would make matzos ourselves. In those days there wasn't anywhere to get them from. A few women and men would gather together and they would help, and with a roller they would make the sheets. They would eat the matzos. They would make matzos. There were also egg matzos. We would mix the matzo with egg, make *farfel* (egg-noodle pasta) from matzo, make matzo meal, and bake latkes.

Raisa Teplitskaia told us that when she was a child in Ternivke:

> My mother would bake matzos. She would gather together three to five
> neighbors and they would bake. I remember that my father had a rolling
> pin. He would use the rolling pin and my mother would bake. We had
> an oven and they used to put the matzos on top of the oven to dry. Three
> or four neighbors would gather together and would bake matzos and
> celebrate Passover. My mother would get everything down from the attic.

Grigorii Shor recalled the preparations that took place in Kopayhorod:

> Until 1936 they sold matzo made from a machine. But then they confis-
> cated everything and in Kopayhorod there was no machine left, so we
> brought matzo in from Mohyliv-Podilskyy or Vinnytsya. And then there
> was nowhere to buy from, so several families would gather together, I
> remember, with us in our home. They would bring out all of the kosher
> utensils that you need and lay them all out with the dishes. They would
> kosher the oven and the cooking utensils. They would roll it out with a
> rolling pin . . . I myself would roll, help roll it. And then they would put
> it on the cooking utensil and stick it in the oven.

Dora Yatskova also had recollections of importing matzo to Kopayhorod
from Mohyliv-Podilskyy: "We observed [holidays] at home. It was forbidden, but we observed them. We bought matzo . . . we bought it from
Mohyliv. They baked it there and brought it here," she told us.

After the dishes were cleaned and the Passover utensils were brought
down from the attic, the cooking began. Donia Presler recalled a favorite
recipe:

> For Passover we would make farfel from matzo meal. You would break
> up the matzo, not too much. You would brush it with two eggs. And you
> would fry it up. You pour in a little water, you crumble it in the mixture.
> And then you add potatoes and you already have a *kugel* [casserole]. . . .
> My mother used to make a potato *kugel*. . . . You grate in the potatoes,
> maybe five. You grate the potatoes into water. Then you squeeze the
> potatoes through a cheesecloth and beat some eggs with a little salt and
> pepper. You put in a little oil and you bake a cheese in a casserole dish.
> You are left with some starch in the water, which you drain out. . . . You
> take four, five eggs and beat them with a little water. You dilute it with the
> starch and you make noodles. These are Passover noodles. . . . Then you
> cut it up. You let it cool and you cut it just like noodles. For a Passover
> soup this is the best. There is nothing in the world like it!

Evgeniia Kozak remembered: "On Passover we would make great
casseroles from matzo meal, latkes from matzo meal, horseradish, a

good chicken." When asked specifically how her family used to observe Passover, she added more details:

> Well, listen, we had an oven. We would bake the casseroles. And we would make gefilte fish and good chickens and we had everything. And horseradish. It was good. Potato latkes and gefilte fish from pike perch. . . . On Passover we would also make gefilte fish in school. . . . My mother taught me to make them. My mother [also taught me that] for a good broth you stuff a neck with chicken fat, with flour and the neck will be just so. A neck from a chicken. For a good broth you stuff the neck. And you boil it with homemade noodles. Or else you can eat it with matzo and horseradish. . . . Fish and horseradish is very good. So, we used to also have horseradish for the holidays then. And we had gefilte fish and cheese and we had matzo.

Kozak cherished these foodways all her life, and the memories they instilled were an integral component of her heritage, valued both for gastronomical satisfaction and as a family birthright.

Evgeniia Krasner remembered that during the seder, the central event in the holiday tradition, her father would sit on a cushion, an *esebet,* and read the Haggadah to the family. Nekha Vainer Shpak, who was born in Vinnytsya in 1921, told us, "on Passover we used to find the *afikoymen* [matzo hidden during the seder as part of a game]. My father would put it out [hide it] and since we were small children we would see where he put it. And so we would find it." Maria Yakuta placed particular attention on the custom of reclining during the seder meal:

> There was a matzo plate, it was called a matzo bag, beautifully embroidered silk. We used to put matzos in there and then lay it aside. . . . My father would sit on a cushion. It was a cushion, and the table was moved up and we sat all around. And he sat himself on a cushion like this and he asked questions. People asked questions. And he prayed. And we spent the whole night there like that.

She does not remember any Passover songs, though, because "we didn't sing songs in our family. Those who had a large family with a lot of people did. But with us, it was just . . . four children and our mother and father."

Most of the people we interviewed remembered that asking the Four Questions was a central part of the seder meal, but few could recall either the specific content of the questions or even who was supposed to ask them. These questions, traditionally posed by the youngest male child at the seder table, introduce the central component of the seder, in which the leader retells the story of the Israelite exodus from Egypt. It is noteworthy that many of the people we interviewed told us that their father asked the questions himself because the children had not learned them. According to Bella Chirkova, the women's role in the ritual was purely observatory:

> During the celebration of the seder one asks the questions of the father. I didn't ask the questions because I am a girl—not a boy. . . . So my father asked the questions of the children, of the boys. . . . The table was set, and my father, grandfather, and the other men would sit down. The women would sit on the other side. And my father would ask the children, the boys, the questions.

One of the primary purposes of the seder—to pass the story of the Exodus down from one generation to the next—was not fulfilled. In the absence of the Exodus story as an heirloom, children adopted the foodways of their parents, which they savored as a central part of the tradition.

The Passover holiday is a domestic affair and is intricately bound up with memories of family and loved ones. For Beyle Vaisman, memories of the Passover seder provided a concrete and specific memory she could attach to the family she lost during the war:

> I remember Passover, with the four questions. . . . And the plates. We were daughters, three daughters. There were no brothers, so there was nobody to ask the four questions, but I remember we would open the door . . . for Elijah the Prophet. We had separate dishes. Everything would be koshered. . . . We had a very religious family and that's why I remember the laws. A very religious family. My father would keep Passover and we would have a seder. And we kept kosher. There was a *shoykhet*. He would slaughter a cow that people took to him. And there was a *shoykhet* for poultry. . . . We led a very religious life, a religious family. And in addition to this, my father was very learned. We had a big family with cousins, aunts, uncles. All of them would celebrate Passover with us, and Sabbath back then. It was so interesting. My father was so learned. He would tell such interesting stories. We children never wanted to go because we just wanted to hear these Jewish stories. They were so interesting. And Hitler took and murdered these people.

The last sentence of her description—"And Hitler took and murdered these people"—seems at first to be out of place in her memory of Passover. But the phrase reveals that the memory is not really about Passover—it is about her loved ones and her loss. The holiday's significance does not lie in the commemoration of the biblical exodus from Egypt. Rather, it is given meaning because the seder meal is tied to so much else that has disappeared, most importantly loved ones and familial heritage.

Passover was the most observed Jewish holiday in the interwar Soviet Union, as well as the one most condemned by the government. The Jewish Sections of the Communist Party also recognized the popularity of Passover celebrations, and so concentrated much of their propaganda on combating its observance through the use of "Red Haggadahs" and mock trials of Passover. Some have suggested that the nationalist connotations of the holiday also angered Soviet officials—and inspired worshippers.[14] Stalin could easily be imagined as a second (or third, or fourth . . .) Pharaoh, and the dream of liberation from slavery could be applied to modern times. However, I encountered no awareness of the subversive potential of the Passover liberation story among those to whom we spoke. In fact, few seemed even aware that the Passover holiday tells the story of the Exodus. Passover, like the Sabbath, is remembered today primarily because it evokes memories of family, food, and domestic harmony. Passover's central rituals—eating matzo, cleaning the house of bread products, and the seder meal—are focused on the home rather than on the synagogue, just as the Sabbath meal and rest are domestic rituals. Both holidays can be observed in private, inconspicuously, and with few resources. Although both also have a synagogue component, it is the home rituals that define the holiday. Passover was and remains a cherished holiday neither because of its universalist message of liberation nor because of its centrality as one of the three pilgrimage festivals in the Jewish religious tradition, but rather because the unique tastes and smells associated with its specific dietary restrictions evoke a nostalgic longing for childhood. This nostalgia was perhaps best expressed by Pesia and Yente Kolodenker of Tulchyn. After discussing the Passover meals, Pesia remarked: "Everything we ate, everything we baked back then was very tasty," to which Yente added, "now it's not good."

"WHEN GOD HIMSELF CAME"

The memories many have of Passover and Sabbath contrast sharply with those of the High Holidays—Rosh Hashanah and Yom Kippur. While some remembered aspects of these holidays and regarded them with reverence, few spoke of them with the same level of affection and intimacy they reserved for the domestic rites affiliated with Passover or the Sabbath. The High Holidays represent "the Great Tradition," the formal dimension of Jewish religion as practiced in the synagogue and formally led by a trained professional rabbinate, in contrast to the Sabbath and Passover, the traditions of which are celebrated in the intimacy of the home and passed down informally within the family. The Kol Nidre ceremony, which ushers in the solemn Day of Atonement, is a public nullification of oaths that must be performed in a highly ritualized public setting, designed to emulate a rabbinical court. In the Soviet context, the observance of these holidays required a deliberate and visible violation of Soviet norms, which eschewed the synagogue and the great traditions of religious observance. Pious Jews continued to observe these holidays for as long as possible, but spoke of them without the intimacy they reserved for the domestic rituals. Beyle Vaisman, who came from a relatively wealthy family in the city of Berdichev, is one of the few who recalls the meaning attached to the Days of Awe. She told us that "on Yom Kippur, when God himself came, the entire city knew. . . . They would sit in *shul* for the entire day. The entire day."

Unable to share in the domestic rituals affiliated with the Sabbath, outsiders commented mostly on synagogue attendance during the holidays. In his memorial book to Bershad, Nahman Huberman writes of the Jews of Bershad during the 1930s: "In obstinacy they observed the holidays of the people of Israel—Passover, Rosh Hashanah, and Yom Kippur, and observed the commandments and the customs."[15] Reports from the Jewish Sections attest to continued synagogue attendance during the High Holidays among elderly members of the community. But most adults seem to have heeded the warnings and kept their children away out of fear. Schoolchildren were influenced by extensive social and political pressure to stay away, and often embraced such antireligious sentiments as their own. In any case, these holidays are adult-centered: their focus on forgiveness of sin has little to offer innocent children. Children are exempt from the Yom Kippur fast, and there are none of the holiday games—hiding of the *afikoymen,* gift giving, dressing up—that appeal to younger children. But some still recalled the rituals associated with these holidays. Arkadii Burshtein told us about *tashlikh,* in which it is customary to empty one's pockets into a flowing river as a symbolic gesture of casting out one's sins: "On Yom Kippur we would go to the river and we would empty out our pockets." Others recall the sweet foods and honey cakes customarily eaten on Rosh Hashanah, when food takes on a literal meaning and a sweet or honey cake is said to bring about a sweet year. Sime Geller remembered preparing for the Yom Kippur fast with fish and soup and that "after the fast we also would have honey cake, sugar cake, sweets. There would be jam, tea of course. As you left the synagogue, breaking the fast." But none recall even the words to the Kol Nidre or Unesane Tokef prayers, among the most powerful of Jewish prayers from the High Holiday liturgy. Once again, foodways remain in the memory longer than abstract principles of faith, or rote ritual drawn from the Great Tradition.

"EVERY DAY THERE WAS A PRESENT"

The annual eight days of Passover and the weekly Sabbath meal evoke the greatest amount of nostalgia today and were probably the most important religious identifiers in the Soviet shtetl of the 1920s and 1930s. But many people we interviewed also remembered some of the other holidays that fill the annual ritual calendar. Yakuta recalled that during the festival of Succoth her father would put up a sukkah, the temporary booth in which it is traditional to eat meals and sometimes sleep, and "all our neighbors would come over to sit in the sukkah. And we used to sing songs like 'The small Sukele, with pretty little panels, Jews, it's made for you and me.'" In the Lunacharskii collective farm, according to the Palatnikova sisters, sukkahs transformed the skyline during the week of the holiday. But elsewhere in the region, the custom was less common. The building of booths during Succoth was already declining in Russia by the time of the revolution, particularly in large towns. Whereas Passover could easily be observed inconspicuously in the home, the construction of a sukkah created a physical landmark, a structure visible to neighbors and government officials. As a result, the pious devised means of following the commandment as best they could without drawing outside attention. Many houses in Soviet shtetls, for instance, had partially enclosed verandas that were commonly used as sukkahs during the festival holiday.[16] Others had lofts with windows whose shutters could be opened to create a sukkah. Avrom Furer's grandfather "had a loft. You could open a door on the ceiling and [it led to the loft]. He put in a table. We were children. We would run here and there. But my grandfather would pray there.... He couldn't sleep there—it was a small loft. But he would eat there."

Many also remembered Tishah b'Av, the fast day that commemorates the destruction of the Temple. Few, however, could tell us what the holiday actually commemorates. Instead, they remembered the now largely forgotten custom of throwing burrs. During the mournful day, as the men fasted and wore torn clothing, children would collect burrs and throw them at each other and into the beards of their elders. Yakuta remembered: "Oy there was such a clamor, an outcry, chatter and a lament. People cried. The girls ran away, ran away from the boys. On Tishah b'Av we wouldn't leave the house. We were so afraid of the burrs." Evgenia Kozak added that children would throw "burrs, these little burrs. And they would stick to them [the adults]. Around us the burrs really grew. They would stick to your coat.... It was a great game to throw the burrs."[17]

Recollections about Hanukkah, although not as prominently celebrated in the Soviet shtetl, came up often in interviews. Yakuta recalled: "On Hanukkah we would get Hanukkah *gelt* [money]. Everybody had a little bag for holding it. My uncle would give us five kopeks. Somebody else would come and bring twenty kopeks and would put them in little bags. Hanukkah *gelt*. Every day there was another present of money or gifts." Evgenia Kozak had vague recollections of the holiday: "Hanukkah is also a joyous holiday," she told us. "My grandmother would give Hanukkah *gelt*." Tatiana Marinina, too, recalled, "And our father would always give us Hanukkah *gelt*." Donia Presler remembered the jelly donuts and sweet latkes of Hanukkah. Many others remember baking potato latkes: Tatiana Marinina told us, "On Hanukkah we would make potato latkes, from potatoes. And we would prepare everything like for a holiday." A few people we spoke with remembered lighting menorah candles: Nekha Vainer-Shpak vaguely remembered "eight candles— eight or seven? . . . We had a menorah. Hanukkah was a joyous holiday." In Haysyn, Arkadii Burshtein remembered, "On Hanukkah, the kids would get Hanukkah *gelt*. My grandfather used to give us all Hanukkah *gelt.* The candles were lit and we would celebrate Hanukkah, but not as we celebrate it today." Only a few people we spoke to could recall the custom of playing games of chance, often while spinning a dreydl. Avrom Furer remembered playing games of chance with nuts.

Writing back in 1937, Berl Botvinik described the celebration of Hanukkah during his childhood in the prerevolutionary era: "Only the truly pious Jews would light Hanukkah lights silently and nonchalantly. And here and there a cantor in a synagogue would utter a prayer in honor of Hanukkah before a small gathering of pious people."[18] Indeed, the growing importance of Hanukkah in the modern era was largely an innovation of secular Zionists, who first embraced the holiday, viewing the Hasmonean State that Hanukkah celebrates as an early manifestation of the Jewish State they hoped to establish. The Hasmonean victory provided a concrete example of Jews asserting their sovereignty over the land. Jewish socialist youth organizations of the early twentieth century also looked favorably upon the holiday, viewing the Maccabean revolt as a victory for the lower classes against the Hellenized aristocracy. Since the holiday has no restrictions on work and few specific religious obligations, it was a usable festival for secularists seeking a national holiday to replace the major religious holy days of Judaism. During the pogroms in the early twentieth century, some interpreted the Seleucid oppressors as precursors to modern pogrom perpetrators, allowing for the historical contextualization of contemporary problems. The coincidental timing of Hanukkah with the Christmas holiday further elevated the Jewish holiday to a major festival in some traditions. Today those who remember its celebration in their childhood shtetl are probably prompted to think of it because of the high importance it has in the post-Soviet Jewish ritual calendar, as well as their reminisces of Hanukkah *gelt.*

—⁓—

Writing about post-Soviet Jewry based on 3,300 interviews conducted in major cities in Ukraine and Russia, Zvi Gitelman argues that Jewish identity in the Soviet Union was based on "thin culture"—cultural identity without any tangible manifestations (language, customs, foods, clothing).[19] In contrast to the majority in Gitelman's much larger urban sample, the elderly small-town Jews we interviewed retained a deeper sense of religious sentiment. Their recollections and knowledge of aspects of Jewish religious ritual and culture indicate that in small towns in the Ukrainian hinterland, Jewish religious life persisted well into the 1930s.

The older men we were able to interview focused their piety on institutionalized forms of religious expression, the synagogue and the heder from which they learned a consciously cultivated religious tradition. For the most part, the antireligious policies of the state pushed religious life out of the public synagogue and into the domestic sphere, where it was more resistant to public censure, and where it was seamlessly integrated into the routines of everyday life. The result was an amalgamated faith, rooted in Jewish tradition but transplanted to a Soviet garden, where it cross-fertilized with a host of adjacent beliefs and practices. In addition to venerating the synagogue as the most salient expression of Jewish life, many experienced their religious lives in the form of "domestic religion," the informal inculcation of religious identity through home ritual rather than through formal public practice and dogmatic education.[20] Among Jews, domestic religion is commonly associated with women because women were traditionally excluded from public rituals in the synagogue—they were not permitted to read from the Torah and were relegated to their own section of the synagogue, usually behind a wall or curtains in the balcony, where they were hidden from the gaze of the men conducting the service below. But in the prewar Soviet shtetl, Jewish men and women alike expressed their Judaism primarily in the home.

Recent scholarship on the role of religion in identity has shifted focus from public demonstrations of prescribed ceremony—in the church, mosque, or synagogue—to expressions of faith and spirituality in the home, and to constant and routinized domestic observances, which in the case of the Jewish religion includes such practices as Sabbath observance and the display of religious artifacts, such as mezuzahs. Many of the periodic Jewish holidays that mark the calendar, like Passover and Hanukkah, are more commonly celebrated in a domestic setting than in the public synagogue. Among scholars of the Soviet Union, in particular, interest in domestic or "popular religion" has helped us understand the impact of the formal attacks on institutional religion.[21] Due to the political and social constraints on the public observance of Judaism in the Soviet context, even men shied away from synagogue attendance and public displays of religiosity. As a result, male as well as female religious expression, activity, and ritual were largely moved into the domestic sphere, the private home. Domestic religiosity, which folklorists looking at Jewish religious practice in Israel and America have identified as a female space, was, in the Soviet context of the 1920s and 1930s, the primary means of religious expression for both men and women. It also contributed to the perseverance of Jewish religious practice and faith under the Soviet government.

The oral histories examined here tell us more than the institutional history of religious organizations. They also tell stories about the role that religion played in the home, and about the role that personal faith played in the hearts and minds of ordinary individuals. They paint a picture of a shtetl population in Ukraine, whose lives were still steeped in Jewish religious belief and ritual in the interwar period. Their patterns of belief mirror those that Glennys Young observed for the Russian Orthodox peasantry during this same period: they were characterized by "the delicate integration of behavior, beliefs, and institutional loyalties that we would assume to be incompatible."[22]

Synagogues were a regular part of the elder generation's life, and continued to serve as important symbolic landmarks for children, whose lives incorporated both Soviet and Judaic rituals. Jewish holidays were routinely celebrated in domestic settings with special food and family time. The generations that grew up in the 1920s and 1930s—at least those who speak Yiddish and continue to reside in the region—still recall their childhoods as pious and insist they grew up in a deeply religious environment. From their perspective, they did. They may not recall all the words to the *moyde ani* or the *Shema*—two of the most important prayers in the Jewish liturgy—but their piety and faith was, and remains, genuine. They acted out the rituals "as it should be done" and followed the rules "as you are supposed to do" to the best of their knowledge and ability. This faith, which sustained many people through the turbulent revolutionary era, the famine, collectivization, and the Great Terror, was about to be put to a test that would fundamentally demarcate the lives of Soviet Jews along with the rest of the world, between "before the war," "during the war," and "after the war."

Indeed, many Soviet Jews, when asked when they stopped going to synagogue, responded simply "when there were no more Jews." Ultimately it was not the Jewish Sections and their successors that dealt the death blow to Jewish religious observance in the Soviet Union, but the Second World War. As Nekha Vainer-Shpak put it: "Before the war, Jews were Jews. And then the war—Hitler took everyone away."

7

—ɱ—

Life and Death in Reichskommissariat Ukraine

On June 22, 1941, as the first light of the second longest day of the year appeared in the east, over three million German troops stormed across the Soviet border along a line that stretched from the Baltic Sea in the north to the Black Sea in the south. Having ignored the German troops amassing on the border, the Red Army was taken largely by surprise; despite the paranoia that had led Stalin to order the murder of many of his top generals on the eve of the war, the Soviet leader had displayed an unwavering trust toward, of all people, Adolf Hitler. All references to the barbarism of fascist Germany had been purged from public discourse after the conclusion of the Soviet–German Nonaggression Pact of 1939, by which the two states had divided Poland between themselves, with the Soviet Union adding significantly to the Ukrainian Soviet Socialist Republic through its annexation of what had been eastern Poland. This pact provided the green light for Germany to invade Poland on September 1st, occupying the country up to a line roughly following the rivers Narva, Vistula, and San. Seventeen days later, the Soviet Union easily secured its half of Poland. As a result of the 1939 pact between the two states, when Germany launched its invasion in 1941, neither the military nor the citizens of the Soviet Union had sufficient warning of the coming cataclysm.

Word of the invasion spread quickly, as the news was broadcast on radio and over loudspeakers throughout the country. The Soviet media and propaganda machine rapidly began covering German atrocities in gruesome detail; on June 25, 1941, in its first issue after the invasion began, the Russian-language photojournalism magazine, *Ogonek*, published a photograph of Polish prisoners being forced to dig their own graves. German armed forces, known as the Wehrmacht, with their Blitzkrieg tactics swept through the Ukrainian and Belarusian countryside at lightning speed, arriving in many towns before any preparations had been made. Within the first six days of the war the Germans had already captured the Belarusian capital of Minsk and would soon control all the territories that Hitler had ceded to Stalin in 1939. When Stalin, who remained conspicuously silent during the early days of war, finally addressed the nation on July 3rd—twelve days after hostilities began—his tone was grave, but the information he conveyed was misleading, and overly optimistic: "The best German divisions and air force units had already been smashed and had found their grave on the fields of battle,"[1] he claimed. Radio announcements continued desperately to downplay the extent of Red Army losses, and the enemy's advances were hidden from the public eye. It was only when working-age men were mobilized that the impact of the war became apparent on a local level.

The murder of Jews was an integral part of the war from its first hours. Among the first units of the Wehrmacht to reach a populated town was Paul Ludwig Ewald von Kleist's First Panzer Group, which captured the border town of Sokal on the morning of June 22nd. That same day, German soldiers shot eleven Jewish men suspected of being communists. As German tanks rolled across the Ukrainian plains in the first weeks of the invasion, they were followed by Einsatzgruppen, divisions of the security police entrusted by Reinhard Heydrich to "carry out certain special security-police duties which are outside the army's domain." These units secured the rear, provided logistical support to the army, stamped out potential resistance, and massacred Jewish civilians. Less than one week after the first executions in Sokal, Einsatzkommando 4a, a division of the Einsatzgruppen that was responsible for establishing civil order in Sokal, executed 17 townsfolk they labeled as "communist functionaries, agents and snipers." The next day, they found "with the help of the Ukrainian militia" another 117 people they deemed "active Communists and agents of the NKVD," all of whom were promptly shot. Again, the next day Einsatzkommando 4a shot another 183 individuals as "Jewish Communists." Similar massacres took place in dozens of locales during the first weeks of the war; an Einsatgruppen operational report dated July 16th boasts of 7,000 executions within these first three weeks. In the initial killing operations, the Einsatzgruppen concentrated on rounding up communists and Jews, but years of Nazi propaganda had taught Germans to equate the two. On July 22nd, one month after the invasion began, the Einsatzgruppen were apparently given instructions to murder not only suspected communists and potential threats to Nazi rule, but to kill Jewish women and children as well.[2]

On August 26, 1941, Einsatzgruppen and local collaborators began perpetrating the largest single massacre to date, when in the fortress town of Kamyanets-Podilskyy, just across the border of Vinnytsya Province, they murdered 23,600 Jews over the course of forty-eight hours. The following month, the Einsatzgruppen perpetrated the largest mass murder in Ukraine. During the Days of Awe, the ten days that mark the time between Rosh Hashanah when God opens the Book of Life, and Yom Kippur, the Day of Atonement when God seals it, Einsatzgruppen and local collaborators murdered 33,000 Jews in Babi Yar, a ravine on the outskirts of Kiev. Over the next several months, they killed another 70,000 individuals, most of them Jews, at the site. Babi Yar was the largest single killing site in Ukraine, but there are hundreds of other *yary* (ravines, in Russian) that hold the bones, dreams, and aspirations, of more than a million victims of Nazi atrocities.[3]

—⁓—

When the war began, there were approximately 3.7 million Jews living within the territories of the Soviet Union that would come under occupation. About 1 million fled in advance of the front and others were mobilized into the army, leaving about 2.7 million Jews under occupation.[4] Within the borders of modern Ukraine, approximately 1.55 million Jews were murdered during the course of the war; another 50,000 Jews from the region were killed outside the borders of Ukraine. In sum, two-thirds of the prewar Jewish population of Ukraine as a whole was

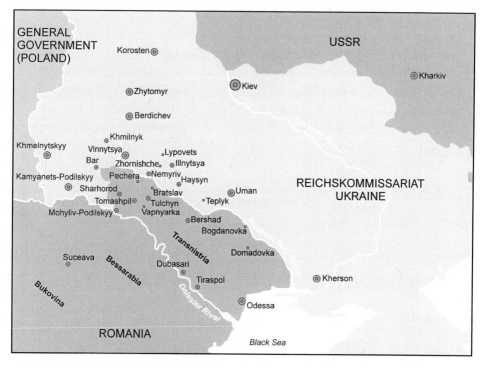

Ukraine during the Second World War

murdered. In Vinnytsya Province, a total of about 150,000 Jews were killed between 1941 and 1943, including 45,000 Bessarabian and Buko-vinian Jews, expelled to the region from Romania. By the end of the war, the Jewish population of Vinnytsya Province was only 35 percent of its prewar size.[5] More than half of those remaining in the province survived in Transnistria, the slice of territory between the Southern Bug and the Dniester rivers that was under Romanian control, and which will be discussed in the next chapter. Only in Transnistria were Jewish communities able to survive the war, albeit under brutal conditions and with significant loss of life. In Reichskommissariat Ukraine, the official new name for the part of Ukraine that came under direct Ger-man rule, no Jewish communities survived intact. The individuals from the Reichskommissariat who managed to survive—those whose stories this chapter tells—did so either by hiding out, most commonly with the help of Christian neighbors; by disguising their Jewish identities; or by surviving in labor camps before eventually fleeing across the border into Transnistria. The only means of survival for Jews in the Reichskommissariat—in contrast to the Jews who evacuated or were drafted into the Red Army prior to the occupation of their town and therefore escaped German rule—was to do so as solitary individuals rather than as part of a community. It therefore becomes impossible during this period to continue telling a communal story, and the narrative must switch to individual stories of survival, occurring in isolation and each with its own distinct horrors.

"HE PACKED WHATEVER HE COULD"

Most able-bodied men were drafted in the first days of the war. Lev Kolodenker, Pesia's brother, was sixteen at the time, too young to be sent to the front but not too young to be sent for training:

> I was sixteen when the war began and immediately in Tulchyn they gathered all the young folks of sixteen and fifteen years of age and sent them to the rear. And in two years, they became soldiers. They sent them to Voroshilovgrad Province in Ukraine and then to the Urals. We had to work. There were a lot of evacuees—women with children. They took all the men into the army. Here in Tulchyn, there were women with little children crying, but all the men were taken into the military. . . . When I turned eighteen, they took me into the army. I ended up being trained in an artillery school. They awarded me a stripe and I became a sergeant. They immediately sent us by night to the front. I ended up in the First Belarusian Front under Zhukov.

In addition to drafting young able men, the government began making provisions for utilizing other Soviet citizens who could serve the war effort in the rear. In the first days of the war, the Soviet government in Moscow established an Evacuation Council, initially headed by Lazar Kaganovich, the Commissar of Transportation who himself had been born and raised in a small shtetl near Kiev. The Council was responsible for coordinating the orderly relocation of critical industrial and consumer infrastructure from the warzone to the Russian interior, where it was imagined industrial output could be preserved with limited interruption. The Council privileged the evacuation of people and entities that were crucial for the military and industrial needs of the state, singling out engineers, workers in factories critical for industrial and military output, youth fit for military service, and state and party elites. Family members of those individuals fitting into these categories were later added to the list. No specific provisions were made for the evacuation of the rest of the civilian population, and at no point was the evacuation of the Jewish population prioritized, despite the mortal danger Jews who fell under German rule faced. The Council also adopted a scorched earth policy, ordering the destruction of all valuable resources that could not be evacuated, so that the enemy—not to mention the civilians caught under enemy rule—would be deprived of even the most basic necessities.[6]

The lack of official sanction and governmental assistance in preparing for evacuation, though, did not stop hundreds of thousands of Jews from fleeing in advance of the German army. Many Jews were able to evacuate as part of the official evacuation because they were represented among the state and party elite or other categories scheduled for evacuation. These chosen evacuees were often able to bring along family members and even friends on the special trains allocated for this purpose. As word of the atrocities being committed to the west spread, though, most Jews recognized the necessity of flight and took desperate measures to flee. Those who did not make the official list took what they could and headed east.

Dovid Geller was fortunate that his father was among those privileged to be included in the official evacuation list. As a result, he was able to leave in an orderly fashion from his native Zhmerynka:

> When the war broke out . . . my father was a communist. He worked as a barber, but he was a communist. They led all the Jews and all the communists out of Zhmerynka. Wherever the train went, that's where they went. We—my father and my mother, and all my brothers—left Zhmerynka in August or July. . . . Then they loaded us onto train cars . . . there weren't any passenger cars. They were heated freight cars, small cars. There were many families inside. Quite a few trains loaded with people departed from Zhmerynka mainly with Jews and communists. Why? Because they knew that when the Germans came they would shoot both the Jews and the communists. So we left and we were en route for one month.

As his comments indicate, Geller believed that the evacuation list included not only communists, but also all the town's Jews. Despite this common perception that all Jews were scheduled for evacuation, there is no documentary evidence that any government official had a policy to evacuate all Jews.

In fact, the experience of the woman who would become Geller's wife after the war—Sime-Leye Dikkerman—demonstrates that many Jews had to use their own initiative to evacuate without government assistance. Sime-Leye's father was a coachman, and so was able to transport his family out of Bratslav in his wagon:

> When the war broke out in 1941, I was twelve, just like my husband, we didn't have any freight wagons. My father had a carriage with two horses. So, he packed up whatever he could and whatever we needed. Across the street, over there, was the house we lived in and next to it was another house where he [my father] worked. Although he was a coachman he worked very hard. . . . He got up in the morning. It was July 20th. The war had already been going on for a month. He put us onto the carriage— myself, two sisters, two brothers, and my mother, who, may she rest in peace, is in the other world with my father. And also my brother's wife with their child. And we drove all the way from Bratslav to the Donbas, to Lugansk. We traveled with the horses for six weeks, day and night.

Outside of immediate danger, those with specialized training were placed in factories to serve the military or industrial mission of the state. Those without industrial or military training were usually put to work on collective farms. The Dikkermans worked initially in a *kolkhoz* in Lugansk:

> The police stopped us and told us to rest a little before we should go and work in a *kolkhoz*, planting grain, potatoes, and whatever they needed. They led us into a village. They provided a house and so we became homeowners [*balebatim*]. My mother, my brothers, my sisters and I all went into the fields to work. . . . So we worked in the *kolkhoz* and my father and brother would transport bread from the grain elevator to the station. We lived there for a while, and then it was already December.

When the Germans approached Lugansk, the family was forced to evacuate further, traveling in freight trains to Tashkent, and eventually to a town by the Iranian border, where they worked on a *kolkhoz* for the remainder of the war:

They approached us to tell us that the Germans were coming closer to the Donbas and that we should leave. They led us out, and gave us money and bread. They put us in freight cars. We traveled for a month and five days all the way to Tashkent. We arrived in Tashkent on December 25, 1941. There, they transferred us to another train and took us to the Kamashi station [in Kaskadarya Province, Uzbekistan], two stops from the Iranian border. Over there, we worked in a *kolkhoz*. . . . We went hungry. We sold whatever we had.

Dovid Geller also traveled to Uzbekistan, first to Tashkent, and then to a collective farm in Samarkand:

Over there [in Tashkent] was the evacuation point, where they admitted all the refugees. So, we came to Tashkent, but Tashkent couldn't admit everybody. Hence, people were sent further. I left with my parents toward Samarkand. . . . There was also an evacuation point in Samarkand. They sent us to work in a *kolkhoz* in the Samarkand Province. They sent us a kind of bullock cart with those particular wheels. In short, we were sent to Samarkand. In Samarkand, they sent us on the cart to the Panjakent district [Tajikistan] to work in a *kolkhoz*. When we arrived there, they told us that we should live in a storeroom full of cotton. . . . There was cotton. They collected the cotton and brought it there, so it wouldn't get rained on. They told us to stay there, and we slept on the ground. There weren't any windows or doors; it was a storeroom with cotton.

Geller's father was drafted soon thereafter and his mother, who gave birth en route in Dzhambul (Kazakhstan), died in Samarkand, leaving the two older boys with their newborn brother to fend for themselves. Dovid learned how to become a lathe operator and eventually made it to Krasnovodsk (Turkmenistan), on the Caspian Sea. He worked first as a lathe operator, and then, thanks to the intervention of friends of his father, managed to secure work for himself in a cafeteria, where the labor was less physically demanding and where he knew he would have access to food.

But the Gellers were among the fortunate few. About two-thirds of those Jews who lived in the territories that eventually came under German rule were unable to evacuate in time. Sofia Palatnikova of Teplyk told us: "We wanted to evacuate, to flee from the Germans. We went on a horse-drawn wagon, but they—the Germans—overtook us. As soon as they invaded the Soviet Union, they were already here. The border [the front] was already close by. We were overtaken and forced to return home." When Teplyk fell to the Germans on July 26, 1941, there were about a thousand Jews still residing there, including Sofia Palatnikova and her sister Tatiana.[7]

Those who were unable to evacuate before the Germans arrived remember the bombing that usually preceded the entry of German troops into town. Nesye Katz, who was living in Vinnytsya at the time, remembers the first bombs falling on the city: "They gathered us in a tower near the military command, on the second floor. It was after ten o'clock at night; it was already dark. I heard the thunder of the plane; it was so strong. It flew past our building, past the military command, to the old city. The first bomb fell. They descended and the shooting began. The war had started."

"WE JEWS BUILT IT"

The first memory that most of those we interviewed have from after the Germans arrived is of being sent to work. Sofia Palatnikova explained: "We returned [from their attempt to evacuate] home and the Germans came and took us to work. They made us scrub the floors and do their laundry. They made us do everything. Then came winter and they would force us into the snow—it was really cold and there was a lot of snow—and they would take the Jews, and also some Christians, and make us clear the snow off the road." Arkadii Burshtein and his family were also not able to evacuate and were still in Sobolivka, about 20 kilometers from Teplyk, when the Germans arrived on July 28th: "One day they took the Jews—children, women, and men—to work. They had to scrub the floors so that people could sleep there in the school. They had to dig potatoes, they had to sweep. They only took Jews; not Christians."

The Germans, though, were not there for long; they soon left the town in the hands of the local Ukrainian police. The local police continued to force the Jews to work in the fields, digging potatoes in the fall and clearing the railways of snow in the winter. Only now instead of laboring for a foreign invader, the Jews were laboring for their former neighbors. The hardships of labor and occupation were compounded by the indignity of being oppressed by one's own townsmen.

Toward the end of the year, the Germans established ghettos in most towns, restricting Jewish residence to one or two streets. Sometimes these streets were surrounded by barbed wire, but more commonly—as in Teplyk—they were open ghettos with no physical boundaries demarcating them from the rest of the town.[8] Thus, in December 1941, Sofia Palatnikova continued, "they resettled all the Jews into two streets. They were required to live on two streets and they didn't have the right to leave. They had to wear an armband with a Star of David so that they would be noticed if they went outside."

As the winter of 1941 began to thaw, the Germans initiated a new round of selections, taking able-bodied men to labor camps that were hastily established in the region. Most of the Jews from Teplyk district were taken to a camp in Raygorod, a town on the German side of the Southern Bug about midway between Nemyriv and Haysyn, where they worked on the Thoroughfare IV road project that would link Vinnytsya to Uman as a military supply route. The project was subcontracted to a private German firm, run by Dr. Fritz Todt, and therefore was commonly called Todt. Todt hoped to construct a massive supply line by turning small country roads into a major thoroughfare stretching over 2,000 kilometers from Lviv in the west to Taganrog in the east.[9] The thoroughfare remains a major highway, since renamed M12: "You know that road you took from Uman that goes through Ivanhorod and then through Oratov [Oradevka]?" Tatiana Palatnikova (Marinina) asked us, "We Jews built it!"

Burshtein was among the one hundred Jews selected for labor from Sobolivka in April 1942, and taken to Raygorod: "There we worked breaking stones to build the roads." Tatiana Palatnikova who was also taken from Teplyk to work on the thoroughfare, recalled how the German and Ukrainian police treated the laborers: "They would stand on both sides: the Germans or the [Ukrainian] police. But the police were a hundred times worse than the Germans. They wouldn't even let us bend down, they would beat us and that's that." The police, she explained, were "ours, Russians." When we asked her to clarify if she meant Russian or Ukrainian, she replied "Ukrainian or Russian—what's the difference. They were all the same." "They would beat us and not give us any food," she continued. Again, she cites the experience of being tortured by "one's own" as a particularly disturbing feature of the time, combining physical pain and degradation with a profound sense of betrayal.

After three months in Raygorod, Tatiana was taken to another camp in Bratslav, on the Romanian side of the border. In 1943, though, she fled the Bratslav camp back to Teplyk in the Reichskommissariat, where her father was still working as a slave laborer in a German hotel. She was ultimately saved thanks to two Germans, Johann Koch from Czechoslovakia, and an Oberleutnant named Schweisser from Cologne, both of whom worked at the hotel and helped her escape to Bershad, providing the family with food and money. "He was a very good man. He was an engineer. He saved many people. He brought a covered truck and took people to Chernivtsi and to Bershad." In Chernivtsi and Bershad, both of which were in Transnistria, they would be relatively safe. Sofia and Tatiana Palatnikova were placed in an orphanage in Bershad, where they survived the war.

Those Jews who were not taken for labor in the towns of the Reichskommissariat Ukraine were usually shot in one of the Aktions—or "pogroms" as the locals still call them—that the Germans perpetrated in the spring of 1942. The rest of Burshtein's family remained in Sobolivka, and were among the three hundred victims of the May 27, 1942 shooting there: "They killed my mother and sister and brother. They killed my grandmother. They killed all my relatives in Sobolivka."[10] Palatnikova also told us about a shooting that occurred in Teplyk on May 27, 1942, in which all the Jews in the town who had not yet been taken to the labor camp in Raygorod—1,289 Jews in all, according to subsequent reports—were shot.[11] Only about forty artisans with specialized skills were spared: "a cobbler, a tinsmith, a saddlemaker," as well as "one woman who would cook for them." That same day, German security police together with Ukrainian police murdered approximately 1,400 people in Ilnytsya, 270 in Voronovitse, and several hundred in Ternivke.[12] Burshtein continued to tell us about the massacre that annihilated the Jewish population of the region, leaving only him and a few others alive. He had earlier explained that he could speak some German from school. This is probably one of the reasons he was spared and permitted to continue working:

> That was in April. In the month of June, they gathered everybody from the region, from Nemyriv, from Bratslav, from Raygorod, they gathered all the women and children and shot them all. Six hundred people. I stayed alive, because the Germans wanted me to stay alive. He left four of us. And they didn't shoot us. We worked. Two of us worked in a foundry, and two of us worked on a compressor.

Having survived the massacre of six hundred residents of his native town, Burshtein and the three other survivors were taken first to a camp in Bratslav and then to Mikhailovka, about which he cynically commented, "It was also really delightful there; they gave us food once a day and made us work the entire day." He was subsequently taken to Haysyn, where he survived a pogrom on May 13, 1943, during which "they shot the entire ghetto." He fled to Bershad, where he remained until he was liberated on March 14, 1944 by the "Russian army." "God wanted me to survive," he concluded.

"LOOK AT THE SILLY JEW DIGGING HIS OWN GRAVE"

Moyshe Kupershmidt was twenty-seven years old when the war started in 1941. He was born in Bratslav in 1914; his father was a coachman and his father's father had been a horse trader. Kupershmidt had trained as a driver. As far back as he knew, his paternal ancestors had lived in Bratslav. His mother was from a small village about 12 kilometers away, where her father ran a mill. His father's family was poor, but his mother's family was wealthy enough to have their own cow. When the Soviet Union attacked Finland on November 30, 1939, beginning the Winter War, the Red Army quickly realized its need for more drivers; Kupershmidt was drafted to the northern front. When he returned home in 1940, he had already been hardened in battle. He sought to return to the driving school at which he had been employed before the war, but found that it had closed in the interim. His record in uniform and reliability, though, impressed the chairman of the executive committee of the local Communist Party branch, who hired Kupershmidt to become his personal chauffeur.

Kupershmidt was still serving in that capacity on June 22, 1941. Within days able-bodied men were mobilized into the army, and Kupershmidt expected to serve as well. Instead, he received instructions to remain in his position as chauffeur to the chairman of the executive committee. During the second week of July, as the Wehrmacht conquered the southern banks of the Southern Bug River in a southeastwardly direction toward Bratslav, the chairman decided to evacuate his wife and daughter. He ordered Kupershmidt to drive the two to a village in the district of

Byshev, near Kiev, east of the encroaching front. The chairman hoped that from Byshev his family could escape into the Russian interior where his brother ran a factory. But by the time Kupershmidt reached Uman, the Germans had already encircled the city. The Battle of Uman would end with the city falling to the Germans. One month later, during the festival of Succoth, German Police Battalion 304 massacred six thousand Jewish men, women, and children in the city.

In Uman, Kupershmidt was captured. The Germans confiscated his car and documents and took him as a prisoner to a nearby village. When they inspected his identification papers, they discovered that he was a Jew; nationality, an identity the Soviet bureaucracy kept distinct from citizenship, was clearly marked on Soviet identification papers. Kupershmidt described what happened next:

> They led me to an orchard with trees. And behind the orchard was a garden, a clearing, with covered trucks. And the German gave me a shovel to dig. There were non-Jewish prisoners standing there and the German was shouting "quickly, quickly." They were saying, "Look at the silly Jew digging his own grave." After I started to dig, a plane came and it started to bomb. So, the plane came and the Germans ran into the orchard, and I fled for who knows how long, into the night.

He covered himself with dirt, digging himself his second grave of the day, and hid beneath the ground until he felt the coast was clear. But this story of how he "ran away from death" was only the beginning of his remarkable story of survival. "Wherever we turned, death was behind us," he recalled.

After emerging from the forest, Kupershmidt was captured again, but was able to blend in with some Christian prisoners. The Germans loaded all the prisoners into the back of a captured Russian truck and then turned to the prisoners and asked if any of them could drive. Kupershmidt volunteered, and drove the truck through the night. In the early hours of the morning, they reached a prisoner-of-war camp in the city of Zhytomyr, where the German SS (Schutzstaffel) maintained its Ukrainian headquarters. The SS, which controlled the camp, first separated out Jews and Communist Party members from the general camp population.[13] The guards used all types of treachery in order to ascertain who among their new prisoners were Jews, including making false promises to release any non-Jew able to identify a Jew. Once they were singled out, Jews and Communists were assigned the most difficult work, were fed only once every three days, and were subjected to a variety of tortures. According to an inmate of another camp, "Every evening the Gestapo would enter the barracks with dogs. The dogs would fall upon the prisoners, biting them and injuring them. After extensive taunting, the prisoners would be taken out of the city and shot."[14] When Kupershmidt arrived in Zhytomyr, he too was subjected to a selection. He was separated from the rest of the prisoners and taken to the Jewish section of the camp, where he was stripped naked and told to sit and wait with about a hundred other Jewish men, women, and children. He reported to us that he waited for two days without food, while a German stood guard.

Kupershmidt had already witnessed what the Germans did to Jews in the orchard outside of Uman; he was determined not to allow himself to be taken out to another forest clearing. He managed to hide in the communal lavatory and then in an attic at the camp. Through a peephole, he watched from above as his fellow prisoners were forced into horse carriages in groups and taken away to be shot.

Since his mother had been born in a small village where she was the only Jew, Kupershmidt explained, he knew how to act like a non-Jew and blend in. He grew a moustache that made him look Georgian or Armenian, and he managed to mix in with a group of ethnic minorities, who were being held in a separate section of the camp. He stayed with the ethnic minorities and worked in their labor battalion for about a month and a half.

Later in the fall, Kupershmidt was taken to another camp in Rivne (Rovno), the new capital of Reichskommissariat Ukraine, where he spent three and a half months. In this camp, he found a former colleague of his from the driving school, Janik, a Polish communist. "You're out of your mind," Janik told him, "You look like a *goy*, you should say you're a *goy*." So Kupershmidt took on the identity of Aleksei Kharitonovich, a Polish friend with whom he had served in Finland, and whose personal details Kupershmidt could freely recite from memory. Janik and Kupershmidt each shared a secret about the other: Janik knew Kupershmidt was a Jew and Kupershmidt knew Janik was a communist. Their mutual trust was put to a severe test on one occasion during roll call, when as the camp prisoners stood together in a line, the Germans demanded to be told who among the prisoners was a Jew or a communist. The prisoners were warned that anybody concealing one or the other would be shot together with the one they sought to protect. Kupershmidt glanced at Janik and took in the Pole's dark complexion—"like a gypsy," in Kupershmidt's words. He could take this opportunity to remove the only threat to his new identity simply by pointing to Janik. The Pole looked more like a Jew than Kupershmidt did; the Germans would readily take Kupershmidt's word over Janik's. He realized that Janik was likely thinking similar thoughts about betraying him. Both knew that the other posed a mortal threat, and both realized that whoever spoke first would be saved. They stood silently for five excruciatingly long minutes, eying each other suspiciously, as the guard counted down the time. But when it was over, they had both been given another lease on life. Neither had succumbed to the terrible temptation.

Kupershmidt was taken out of the camp as part of a labor battalion, where he worked on road construction with another group of prisoners, each of whom, he recalls, was swollen from hunger. Worried that his identity would eventually be revealed, Kupershmidt fled in the middle of the night through the forests back toward Bratslav. He had already left Rivne by November 6, 1941, when Security Police together with German Order Police Battalion 320 and local Ukrainian gendarmes murdered more than fifteen thousand Jews in the city.[15] By this time, though, Bratslav had been cut off from the Reichskommissariat Ukraine, as it had already been incorporated into the territory of Transnistria, and was under Romanian rather than German control.

As a result, Kupershmidt was not able to make it to Bratslav, but found his way instead to a village where he had Christian acquaintances. These villagers helped him establish contact with a German soldier who was looking for a driver. "You can take the Jew," one friendly villager told the soldier, inadvertently revealing Kupershmidt's identity. But this time, the German was sympathetic, "a kind man," as Kupershmidt explained. "You will be safe as a Jew driving a German soldier," the German assured him. He secured a ten-day pass for Kupershmidt that would allow him to drive to the nearby town of Nemyriv and suggested that Kupershmidt turn himself in at the ghetto there, where he believed he would have a better chance of surviving than out in the open. He made it to the ghetto, which was really just three narrow streets opposite the main highway, cordoned off by barbed wire, and secured by a guard stationed by the single gate leading past the barbed wire. Kupershmidt put on a white armband with a six-sided Jewish star on it, in accordance with the rules of the ghetto, and settled into ghetto life. He worked during the days on the construction of Thoroughfare IV and returned to the ghetto at night.[16]

In early 1942, Kupershmidt received the opportunity he had been hoping for: a driver was needed to bring a few barrels of petrol across the river to Bratslav. Kupershmidt was assigned the task and given a pass that would allow him to cross into Transnistria and reach his family. When he arrived in Bratslav, though, he discovered that he was too late. His father, he learned, had been shot in the initial days of the occupation. His mother, wife, and two sisters had survived the initial onslaught and been confined to the ghetto along with about 750 other Jews, but in December 1941, when most of the ghetto was liquidated, they had been sent to nearby Pechera, where a concentration camp had been established on the grounds of a former Soviet sanatorium. Eventually, as the Germans began to retreat in late 1943, Kupershmidt managed to escape deep into Transnistria, to the town of Dzhuryn. There he found a Red Army field recruitment center and volunteered to join on the long journey west. Kupershmidt's wife survived the war in Pechera, but succumbed soon after, in 1947.

Before we bade farewell to Kupershmidt in Bratslav, we asked if he could take us to the Jewish cemetery so we could visit the grave of Natan Sternhartz, Rebbe Nahman's disciple. Kupershmidt led us outside onto the cobblestone street. As we stood in his garden, looking at the street that led down to the river outside his house, a fisherman strolled past carrying a pole with a piece of string tied to it, much like the kind of rod Huck Finn would have used. We hopped into our van and turned off Kupershmidt's side street onto the two-lane paved road that had been Lenin Street and served as the city's main thoroughfare. We turned a corner, driving slowly down a dirt road toward the river. Kupershmidt pointed excitedly out the window: "This is where the synagogue was . . . just behind there. These were all Jewish houses." We looked out the window—only an empty lot and an automobile repair shop remained. Suddenly, about a quarter of a mile from his home, Kupershmidt turned to face us with an agitated tone of voice: "I want to show you. From that place, over there, during the war they threw the Jews down, drowning them in the Southern Bug River." His voice quivered as he pointed out the window while the vertical wall of a magnificent cliff came into view, scenically overlooking the dirt road on one side and the pristine sparkling waters of the river ahead on the other. "Since I had a pass," he continued as his voice trembled, "I saw everything they did here." "Children, living children, they were throwing over." When we visited him again three years later, he broke down in tears upon recalling this same episode, shaking and clutching his head in sheer agony. Dozens, perhaps hundreds, of children from the Jewish orphanage were thrown off the cliff into the waters below to be drowned.

Ukraine's rivers are full of stories of such massacres. It is even said that some rivers are cursed from the days of the Haidamaks and Khmelnitsky, who also drowned elderly Jews and children in the river. In Bershad, it is said that the Baal Shem Tov himself cursed the river when he was told about the atrocities that had taken place there in the eighteenth-century.[17] The massacre Kupershmidt described took place after the surface of the river had begun to freeze, creating a thin layer of ice that easily gave way to the force of the bodies plummeting from above.[18]

When we reached the cemetery, which is located on a plateau overlooking the river, we could see children and young couples splashing and frolicking in the waters below, while older men in Speedo bathing suits basked in the sun on the riverbank, all seemingly oblivious to the history of the waters. We were able to interview Kupershmidt twice, in 2002 and 2003. He died before we returned next in 2005. His grave now lies in the cemetery eternally guarding the bend in the Southern Bug River.

"WE LIVED IN THE PIT"

When we first arrived at Shloyme Skliarskii's house in 2009, he was standing outside on the sidewalk, waiting for us by the green picket fence that enclosed his modest yard. He was wearing a leather spitfire cap, a gray blazer, and suspenders over his dress shirt. He lived on Lenin Street, Bershad's main thoroughfare, across the street from the Center of Culture and a few short blocks from the synagogue and the site of the former ghetto. Buses and trucks were speeding by behind him, noisily thumping over potholes and spewing diesel exhaust our way. Skliaeskii was anxious to share his story and began to do so immediately upon our approach. We were still walking toward him and hadn't even introduced ourselves when he began, shouting over the din of the street:

> At the age of seven I became an orphan. I was three years old when my mother died. I was seven, in the first grade, when my father died. So I was taken in by my aunt who lived in a shtetl of about two thousand people called Zhornishche, in Ilnytsya district. But they were all shot. My mother had a sister with two children, another sister with two children, and a third sister with two children. Only one girl survived the war. She lives now in Kaliningrad. I was fourteen years old when the war began. She stayed alive. My half-brother also survived [under occupation], but he died at the front as a volunteer. So only I remained alive. Twice I was shot. The first time was on May 27, 1942. They gathered together all the people. The police were standing there. There were few Germans; it was mostly the local police. They had two wagons led by horses, and they were throwing the children into the wagon. Those who could walk walked; the others were thrown into the wagon. My aunts were watching from an attic up above. I ran away, out of the line, and was shot.

He struggled to take off his blazer, and rolled up his sleeves to show us the scar from the bullet wound.

The war began in the village of Zhornishche on July 16, 1941, when the German Sixth Army occupied the village on its way from Vinnytsya to Uman. The Germans quickly turned the administration of the village over to a headman, a chairman of the village council, and two Ukrainian policemen.[19] A few weeks later, the local Ukrainian police led a group of about a dozen Jewish men, including one thirteen-year-old boy, to a clubhouse, and shot them.[20] Soon thereafter all the Jews of Zhornishche were required to wear a Jewish star on their arm and back, and were put to work, carrying stones for the construction of roads. Just as in every other town in the region, a small ghetto was established.[21]

Word reached Zhornishche the night of May 26, 1942 that pits had been dug in the nearby town of Ilnytsya. That night, the village elder's son, who had seen the pits and understood their purpose, ran the 8 kilometers from Ilnytsya to Zhornishche to warn the Jews of what was to come. He had many friends among the Jewish children of Zhornishche and hoped to save them. He ran in circles around the village warning anyone he could find, but Ukrainian police had already surrounded the village. Skliarskii's three aunts together with their children managed to hide, but Skliarskii was left outside. Even his half-brother, Yasha, who was a mere three months younger than Skliarskii managed to hide in the attic with the rest of the family.

The next morning, all the Jews of Zhornishche, with the exception of a few who had specialized skills, were ordered to march together under guard to Ilnytsya. "Two tailors, two cobblers, and two glaziers were left behind," Skliarskii explained. "I mean the tailor and his wife—each one and his wife were left so that the non-Jews could learn how to work. So these ones weren't taken, at least not immediately." A Noah's Ark of survivors was to remain, not to repopulate the village, but only to train replacements among Christian apprentices after which they too would be eliminated. The massacre, Skliarskii recalled, was led by Police Captain Zavalinsky, a local Ukrainian who had been a stable boy before the war; since he had ethnic German roots, the new authorities had promoted him to police captain soon after the town's occupation. It was Zavalinsky, Skliarskii told us, who pulled the trigger, sending a bullet into Skliarskii's upper left arm as he fled the column marching down the road.[22] According to testimony taken by a Soviet Extraordinary Commission in Ilnytsya immediately after the war, "The Germans arrested more than 800 civilians, put them in a building that had been a Jewish school, where the arrested were subjected to inhuman suffering and tortures; they were all taken to the field and shot."[23] According to another witness, Shloyme Yablonsky, who testified before the Extraordinary Commission in April 1945:

> On April 24, 1942, while it was still morning in the village of Ilnytsya, regulars from the German army, along with police, conducted a round-up and caught nearly a thousand civilians, mostly Jews. They were taken under guarded convoy near the forest about 2 km. from Ilnytsya to a previously prepared grave. Before execution they were terribly humiliated and forced to undress. Then they were all executed; among them were many women and small children. The Germans did not shoot the children but threw them into the pits alive. On May 27, 1942 more than 800 civilians were also arrested and taken to the premises of a Jewish school. They were held there for one day and were not given food or water. After this, they were executed in the same manner as those who had been executed before and in the same place.[24]

Liudmila Koroteska also testified to the Extraordinary Commission about both the April and May incidents and added the gruesome detail that after the massacre "the clothes they [the victims] were wearing were brought back to Ilnytsya and sold here."[25]

Skliarskii told us that he continued running as blood poured from his wound. He leaped over a fence and fled through the wheat fields that mark the Ukrainian countryside. These fields are normally planted with winter wheat in the fall to be harvested in July and August of the following year. In a good year, at the end of May, the fields would be a brilliant gold and green with stocks rising waist-high, perfect for hiding. But the 1941–1942 harvest was anything but good—the prime seeding season from mid-August to mid-September had been disrupted as tanks rolled across the fields instead of tractors, and the winter had been one of the coldest in memory, with temperatures reaching minus 40 degrees (where Celsius and Fahrenheit meet), rotting the roots and crowns of the wheat and spreading infectious diseases. In the spring of 1942, when so many people sought protection in the fields, they had little to offer in the way of camouflage or nourishment; the stalks were knee high at best and muddy bare spots were visible from afar. Skliarskii's route was even more discernible as a bright red trail of blood followed him wherever he ran.

The blood trail lasted for several kilometers, until it, along with Skliarskii, reached a river near the village of Luhova. As Skliarskii was cleaning his wound in the fresh river water, he saw a former classmate of his, a shepherd who for many years had traveled across the fields each day to attend school in Zhornishche. His classmate looked at the wound and cried out: "Oh, Solomon, you would have been better off if you were killed on the spot." Skliarskii soon returned to Zhornishche, where the non-Jews told him about the massacre. Everyone knew. He was reunited with his three aunts, Rive, Rukhl, and Reyze, and his six younger relatives, including his half-brother Yasha. They spent the remainder of the summer hiding out wherever they could find shelter, in a quarry or in the forests. Although the mass shootings of Jews had died down, dangers still lurked throughout the region. Not even the Christians were safe. In June 1942, for instance, the Germans arrested en masse the youth of Ilnytsya, and sent them in convoys to Germany where they would be employed as slave labor.[26] As the weather turned colder, Skliarskii and his family realized they would need a warmer hiding spot for the winter; a Christian peasant friend agreed to help. They conferred about how best to survive, and concluded the family would be safest beneath the wheat fields. Under the ground, together, they could keep warm.

Their Christian friend knit them clothes for the winter and helped them dig a bunker in the middle of one of his fields, near the village of Ivanka. In early winter the three women, together with the six children, climbed down into the earth and settled in for the winter, hiding from the fate that awaited those who ventured above the earth. Not far from their underground bunker was another grave, this one located on the outskirts of the town of Ilnytsya. It held the bullet-ridden corpses of about eight hundred people, including the rest of the Jewish community of Zhornishche, the town in which Skliarskii was raised.

Skliarskii is unsure how many months they spent in this pit. When we first visited him, he reckoned they had been hiding for six months. On another occasion, he estimated, "we lived in the pit for about two or three months, for as long as it was cold outside." When asked for clarification, he explained that they were consistently in the pit for the harshest winter months, but used it as a sporadic hiding place for a longer period of time. When their supplies would run low, Shloyme and Yasha would wait for sunset and climb out of the grave into the icy night in search of food. Among trustworthy peasants they knew in the village, they could trade their few possessions—mostly clothes—for a bit of food, a potato, or a crust of bread, to bring back to the family crypt. For months the only respite from the darkness of the earth beneath the field was the occasional moonlit winter night. Emerging out of the wooden trapdoor, which was covered with straw and snow, Shloyme and Yasha would make their way to Ivanka. "When I ran out of the field," he told us, "I made it to a neighbor's attic and waited there several days. My throat was so dry. I wanted to drink. There was such hunger." In order to avoid leaving footprints in the snow that could be traced back to reveal the site of their hideout, they would walk in circles, first in one direction, and then they would reverse back the way they came, zigzagging through the vast expanse of frozen fields to confuse potential predators. In the winter, when the trees that encircle the fields are bare, the sight line across the snow-covered plains can stretch to the horizon. Even natural hills are seemingly ironed out as snow fills in the crevices. It is hard to imagine a landscape less conducive to concealment.

Skliarskii and his family were not the only Soviet citizens living beneath the ground that winter. From the extreme western frontlines of the war, where Red Army soldiers fought together in trenches, to the far

A frozen wheat field in Ukraine, much like the one that
Shloyme Skliarskii hid in during the winter of 1942.

eastern labor camps of Siberia, where convicts survived the grueling arctic tundra in makeshift dugouts, thousands of Soviet citizens, refugees, soldiers, and convicts sought sanctuary beneath the ground. As one veteran, David Barksy from Bershad, recalled in an interview with the Blavatnik Archive Foundation, when he first arrived at the front and lay down on the grass, he received the following advice from a more experienced soldier: "The first thing you have to do is dig yourself a trench. That's your lifesaver. If you don't have a shovel, dig with your bayonet, with your nails, with your teeth, just dig into the earth. This lesson I remembered for the rest of my life and it truly saved me many times."[27] In Russian these foxholes are called *zemlyanki,* from the Russian word for earth. The Yiddish term, *grib,* by which Skliarskii refers to his home that winter, is perhaps more evocative: it means both pit and grave.[28]

As the earth began to thaw in early March 1943, the family considered where they would go next. The talk became more urgent when one night, as they huddled in the ground, they heard footsteps above them. The next day, March 8, Skliarskii, Yasha, and Zhenya, one of his cousins, left the hole in search of food and alternative hiding spots. They had hardly traveled more than 500 or 600 meters when they heard shooting from the direction of the field. Skliarskii immediately understood that they had been betrayed—one of the peasants had revealed their hiding spot. Skliarskii realized that the murderers would have expected to find all nine Jews hidden in the ground; a hunt had likely already begun for the remaining three. Shloyme, Yasha, and Zhenya traveled the 3 kilometers back to Zhornishche, where they hoped to find refuge with Christian friends. Word soon reached Zhornishche that six of the Jews hiding in the ground, including three children, had been killed. Skliarskii explained: "The youngest, Mitya, he was nine years old, in the second grade. They wounded him. This they told me, those who witnessed it. He was shot. They had taken his clothing. They started covering him with dirt. They forced him into the grave. Alive. They buried the injured child alive. The rest were dead, but he was only injured and was buried alive. He started to yell, 'Mister, get me out.' But they forced him in alive." Mitya's clothes probably found their way into the market in Zhornishche or some other nearby town.

Shloyme and Yasha spent much of the spring hiding out in Zhornishche. It was there that a girl, about twelve or thirteen years of age, convinced them to follow her in a quest to seek out and join the partisan fighters they had heard were seizing control of the forests, working with Moscow to disable the enemy from the rear. The girl's father, a glazier, had gathered together a group of about a dozen people, all of whom were to head out together into the forests. On the appointed day in the summer of 1943, they secured food supplies and set off south from Zhornishche toward the village of Krasnenke.

On one of the first nights, a Friday evening, as they rested on the edge of the forest, Skliarskii had a vision: "It was five or six in the morning, I thought at first it was God Himself who had come to me, but later understood it was the Messiah who had come. He said, 'you must not go into the forest. There will be a fire. Run into the field.' He repeated it several times, two or three times: 'Don't go into the forest; go into the field. Don't go into the forest; go into the field.'" Suddenly, two Don Cossacks fell upon the group. Everyone scattered, running into the forest, except for Skliarskii who found refuge instead, as the Messiah had instructed him, in the fields. In the open field, he ran down a hill and into a water-filled gulley. He splashed through the stream and managed to elude the

Cossacks. The other members of his party, those who ran into the forest, were overcome. The glazier's daughter was shot in the leg, violated, and then killed. Yasha survived by climbing a tree where he hid as the shots rang out below. As Skliarskii was telling us this story, he pulled out of his pocket a piece of paper onto which, after the war, he had inscribed the words of the Messiah so that he would forever remember how his life had been saved. Some may consider that it was not the Messiah, but rather some type of angel who saved Skliarskii. Or perhaps it was simply the vast wheat fields of Ukraine that once again provided him shelter in his time of need. In his interview with the Shoah Foundation, Skliarskii confided that the experience turned him into a believer.

Skliarskii succeeded in joining the partisans after he and Yasha stole rifles from some drunken Germans. By this time, the partisan movement, which began as an ad hoc group of fighters in the early days of the war, had come under the command of the General Staff for the Partisan Movement. By the spring of 1943, there were nearly 100,000 partisans active behind enemy lines, mostly in the forests around Minsk and western Belarus, southeastern Lithuania, and western Ukraine, with smaller pockets active in Vinnytsya Province.[29] Without weapons, though, it was difficult for Jews to be accepted as partisans. Because of intense German reprisal attacks against villagers caught assisting Jews, it was also difficult for Jews to survive in the forests. Many of the Jews who did fight as partisans, therefore, did so as all-Jewish brigades, in violation of Soviet policy that prohibited the formation of brigades along national lines. Although it is difficult to determine the total number of Jewish partisans accurately, the best guesses are that the figure was about 20,000, of whom only a few hundred were active in Vinnytsya Province. Probably another 12,000 Jews throughout the German-occupied regions of the Soviet Union lived in the forests in family camps, hiding out but not fighting.[30]

Skliarskii told us he first met up with members of the Lenin Brigade, but was soon transferred to a Jewish brigade under the command of David Mudrik. Mudrik was one of many Jewish partisan leaders who saved thousands of lives by turning the forests into safe havens and arming Jews to fight, only to fade into obscurity when the war ended. Mudrik would spend most of his postwar years in the Department of Finance of the government of Ilnytsya, his days of heroism long forgotten and barely acknowledged. His entry in the Yad Vashem Shoah Resource Centre amounts to two sentences: "(1913–1987) Commander of a Jewish partisan unit of about 250 persons, part of them armed and others old women and children. They operated in the Vinnitisa [*sic*] district of the Ukraine as part of the second Stalin brigade." One of the few memorials to Mudrik can be found in the small immigrant town of Dimona, deep in the Negev Desert of Israel, where the Museum of Fighting Glory includes an exhibit devoted to "the Jewish guerilla group over which David Mudrik supervised." Skliarskii only spent a couple of months with Mudrik's unit, but his gratitude is never-ending. Skliarskii was shot once again in 1944, landing himself in a field hospital in Germany, where he was when the war ended. Yasha, for his part, died fighting in the Red Army. We interviewed Skliarskii twice, first in the summer and then in the winter of 2009. The USC Shoah Foundation also recorded his testimony. When we knocked on his door again in the summer of 2010, his son, Yasha, answered. Shloyme, he was sorry to inform us, had passed away.

—๛—

Kupershmidt understood that his life had been spared numerous times by sheer chance. "When I tell you what I lived through during the war," he told us early in the interview, "you simply won't believe it." It was difficult for him to relate his experiences in a coherent narrative and he understood that he could not recount his whole war experience for us: "We would need three days for me to tell you everything," he confessed. Three years later, he told us "it would take two weeks for me to tell you all that I have lived through." His narrative—he spoke for hours virtually uninterrupted on both occasions—was punctuated with phrases indicating his frustration that he simply did not have the strength to tell us everything: "In a word," he would say, or "so, in short." His story seemed to be unrehearsed, as though he had never before tried to put it all together. Yet this same quality, that of telling the story for the first time, could be discerned the second time we interviewed him as well. He felt a primal need to tell his story, to ensure that it is not lost to history, but there was simply too much to tell, and it came spilling out quicker than he could organize it for external consumption. "In my life I will never forget," he repeated. His narrative jumped from episode to episode, allowing his memory to take him to its darkest recesses. Events seemed to unfold about them with no reference to the wider world; he seemed reluctant to place his own personal experiences into a historical narrative. These difficulties all stem in part from the ways in which the Jewish experience during the war was dealt with in the postwar Soviet Union; survivors like Kupershmidt never had their wartime experiences reinforced with public memorials, testimonies, or even acknowledgment.[31]

The iconic symbols of the Holocaust—sealed railway cars, gas chambers, and crematoria—were largely absent from the experiences of the survivors we interviewed. The Holocaust, as it is told in its canonical memoirs and diaries—Elie Wiesel's *Night* or *The Diary of Anne Frank,* for instance—is simply not recognizable to many Soviet survivors. Those like Kupershmidt and Skliarksii who survived the war in Vinnytsya Province did so in isolation, as individuals or in small family groups. The common Holocaust trope of losing one's identity in massive camps, of becoming atomized, merely a number among a vast collective, has little resonance for them. They did not ride in trains with thousands of other Jews who shared their fate, nor did they live in barracks with hundreds of other Jewish inmates. Skliarskii lived in a pit in the ground with only his family. Kupershmidt moved among numerous camps and ghettos, but was rarely with other Jews, and was often by himself. Palatnikova and Burshtein spent a few months in labor camps, but ultimately survived because they escaped into Transnistria early enough.

Ukraine lacks the architectural remnants of the Holocaust that have become sacred sites of memory in places like Poland and Germany. There are no slogans forged in iron promising that work is liberation, nor are there brick furnaces and barracks marking places of concentration and death. Only in a few communities were private memorials erected. The roads, rivers, cliffs, ravines, fields, palaces, and parks of the Ukrainian countryside are the sites of the Holocaust in Ukraine. The places in which Kupershmidt spent the war—Nemyriv, Uman, and Zhytomyr—fail to evoke the type of universal recognition equivalent to that of the major killing sites of the Holocaust. Nemyriv may be famous for its vodka and Uman for its gardens and Hasidic pilgrimages, but for the most part they are simply neighboring towns. To the end of his days, Kupershmidt lived a short walk from the cliffs and rivers that haunted his sleep; he is buried today in the Jewish cemetery atop the very cliff from which he witnessed the drowning of the Jewish children. Many years after emerging from the ground, Skliarskii would return with his son, Yasha, to the fields of Ivanka, a few short kilometers from his home in Bershad.

Survivors in the region lived for sixty years amidst the physical sites of atrocities they had witnessed, and among people who had collaborated or stood by. After the war, they found their way back to their hometowns and returned to complete devastation, where the impact of the war was truly universal. They knew that Jews bore a distinct fate under the Nazis, but returning home after the war, they must have also noticed that their neighbors had suffered terribly as well. Kupershmidt saw thousands of individuals returning from prisons and camps across the Soviet Union; some were freed from German concentration camps, others returned from the Soviet GULAG. Hundreds of thousands had found themselves in both, and millions never returned from either. But in the Soviet Union, internment was regarded by many as a part of life, and the experience of being in a concentration camp was shared by millions of Jews and non-Jews alike. Population displacement was also a common experience. Wartime Ukraine was a region on the move, as millions of people were displaced; more than 1.5 million Ukrainians were rounded up and deported to Germany to work as laborers, millions more fled as refugees into the Russian interior, and still millions more were driven from their homes as internal refugees.[32]

Kupershmidt witnessed Jewish children being murdered and lost his family because they were Jews, but he also saw Ukrainian and Polish friends die of hunger, disease, and violence. Similarly, Skliarskii saw the suffering of the non-Jewish neighbors among whom he lived, some of whom risked their lives to save him and others who betrayed him. Some did both. Skliarskii returned to live with the local stable boys who had become executioners and saw the partisan hero David Mudrik take a desk job in the local Department of Finance. Had he left Zhornishche forever on May 27th, his last memory would have been of violence and hatred. Had Kupershmidt left Bratslav after the massacre on the cliff, his indelible memory of the shtetl would have been of its worst day. Neither would have been there when Jews and Ukrainians together began the long process of rebuilding. They would never have prayed with the few returning Jews in the storehouse that became the postwar synagogues.

They would never have witnessed a return to normalcy. For sixty years, Kupershmidt, Skliarskii, and others like them worked alongside their Ukrainian neighbors, shopped in the marketplace with them, and relied upon them for assistance in their old age. There has been little reconciliation, but sixty years of cohabitation have helped bring about appeasement. As Jewish survivors reintegrated themselves into Soviet society, their wartime memories were conflated with those of their non-Jewish neighbors, and their own personal memories were submerged into the collective memory of the now predominantly non-Jewish town. It is this ability, or need, to integrate the war into their larger life and into the community as a whole, that makes it possible for survivors in the shtetl to live among the mass graves and the collective memories, to walk along the Southern Bug at sunset with their wives, and to stroll through the frozen wheat fields with their children.

8

Life beyond the River

TRANSNISTRIA

An American immigrant originally from Tulchyn, Manya Ganiyevva, wrote down her recollection of her wartime experiences in Transnistria and deposited that memoir through the Jewish Family Service of Cincinnati with the United States Holocaust Memorial Museum in Washington, D.C. She begins her memoir with the lament that "after the war I often happened to read about the camps in the territories of Poland and Germany: Buchenwald, Maidanek, Ravensbruck, Auschwitz, Dachau, Treblinka, Sachsenhausen, Mauthausen and many others, where many thousands of Jews were exterminated and cremated. But in all these years, I have never read about those German concentration camps in which I was held, in which many thousands of Jews from all of Ukraine, Bessarabia and Northern Bukovina were detained."[1] Her memoir is remarkable in that in all the interviews we conducted with former inmates of camps and ghettos in Transnistria, we never heard such references made to the notorious extermination and concentration camps of Germany and Poland. When survivors relocate—usually to America, Israel or one of the larger cities of Ukraine or Russia—as Ganiyevva did, they come to understand their experiences within a wider context, and begin to compare their own fates with those from other regions. They come to understand their wartime memories in relation to a prevailing narrative of the Holocaust. They become aware that their own experiences in Transnistria do not fit comfortably into the Holocaust as it is commonly understood in the West. In the previous chapter I noted that many of the most recognized symbols of Holocaust experiences were largely absent from the Soviet experience. Instead, Soviet Jewish victims of the Holocaust tended to be killed closer to home, in ravines and cemeteries on the outskirts of their towns. However, the experiences of the local Jews in Transnistria also do not fit this model. With few exceptions—such as the murder of 150 Jews in Tomashpil on August 11, 1941—Jewish communities of Transnistria were spared such massacres. Even the "Holocaust by bullets" was largely foreign to the experiences of Transnistrian Jews.

Second World War Transnistria—not to be confused with the current breakaway republic of contemporary Moldova—was established on August 19, 1941 when German military officials ceded the area between the Dniester and Southern Bug rivers to Romania in return for Romania's continued cooperation in Operation Barbarossa.[2] This territory had no political history as a united region and was a completely arbitrary creation. Some 300,000 Jews lived in the region that became Transnistria before the war, 180,000 of whom lived in Odessa, the only major metropolis.[3] The rest of the Jewish population was scattered across various towns and villages in what had been the Moldavian Autonomous Soviet Socialist Republic and the southern portions of Vinnytsya Province. The largest of these towns—among them Tiraspol, Dubosar, Mohyliv-Podilskyy, Zhmerynka, Balta, and Ribnitsa—had Jewish populations of 3,000–7,000, and total populations of 10,000–30,000. The region also included numerous smaller shtetls, including Tulchyn, Sharhorod, Tomashpil, and Kopayhorod, each of which had prewar Jewish populations of 2,000–5,000, and in which Jews often constituted up to three-quarters of the total population of the town.

The Romanian authorities who seized control of Transnistria hoped to use it as a dumping ground for the Jews they were expelling from Bessarabia and Northern Bukovina—the provinces that Romania had acquired from Russia and Austria in the aftermath of the First World War, which were then seized by the Soviet Union in 1940 before being recaptured by Romania the following year. Romanian authorities sought

to expel the Jews ostensibly in retaliation for the alleged Jewish support
of the Soviet occupation. In reality, the Jews were victims of an extensive
Romanian ethnic purification campaign. The little that has been written
on Transnistria has focused on the fate of these approximately 150,000
Jewish deportees.[4] The deportations began in late July 1941, when about
20,000 Jews arrived in Mohyliv-Podilskyy, a town that became the main
transit point across the Dniester River. Many among the initial wave of
deportees were subsequently returned to Bessarabia, where they were
imprisoned in several camps and ghettos, but about 700 were either
shot or died during the journey.[5] Between October 13 and November
15, 1941 another 46,000 Jews were deported across the river, this time
mostly from Czernowitz in Northern Bukovina and several southern
Bukovinian towns, including Suceava, Radauti, and Vatra Dornei. On
November 7, 1941, about 9,000 Jews from Dorohoi were added to the deportees. For the initial deportees, Transnistria was only a transit point in
their journey across the Southern Bug into German occupied territory,
the Reichskommissariat Ukraine. But in November 1941 the Germans
began to fear the spread of disease across the border and halted the
deportations across the Southern Bug, resulting in the establishment of
"colonies" of Romanian Jews between the two rivers. During the course
of the war, about two-thirds of the Romanian deportees perished either
during the forced marches across the Dniester, at the hands of German
soldiers in Reichskommissariat Ukraine, or from starvation or disease
in Transnistria. Local Ukrainian Jews, though, who were not subjected
to deportation but rather were confined to ghettos in their towns of
residence or nearby camps, were more likely to survive. Since few of
these survivors were able to emigrate out of the Soviet Union until the
1990s, their stories were late in being told, and it was often assumed that
they had suffered the same fate of the Jews in German-occupied regions
of Europe.[6]

Tulchyn, though, had a prewar Jewish population of 5,600 and a postwar 1959 Jewish population of about 2,500. Bershad, similarly, had a
prewar Jewish population of 4,300 and a postwar Jewish population of
2,200. In smaller shtetls, off the beaten track, survival rates were higher.
Tomashpil, for instance, had a prewar Jewish population of 1,800 and
a postwar Jewish population of 1,400. Each of these towns suffered un-
speakable tragedy during the war, with between a quarter and a half of

the Jewish population perishing, mostly of starvation or typhus. But the discrepancy between the death rates in these towns and those in German-occupied territory across the Southern Bug are noteworthy, particularly since the border was arbitrarily drawn; it had never before served as a political boundary, and did not mark any significant cultural, demographic, or historical division. Yet the fate of those on either side was drastically different. In Nemyriv, for instance, the Jewish community ceased to exist in any meaningful way after the war. Yet Bratslav, a mere 20 kilometers across the river, retained a functioning Jewish community for decades.

"BUT OUR SOLDIERS WERE POOR FOLK"

By the time the Germans arrived in Tulchyn on July 23, 1941, most of the able-bodied men had been drafted into the Red Army. It was a city of mostly women, children, and the elderly. The military and technological superiority of the Germans was instantaneously apparent. As Yente Kolodenker told us, "They were all on motorcycles and with cars, but our soldiers were poor folk, poverty-stricken. And they were rich." This same theme was repeated by many others, including Manya Ganiyevva, who spent the first few weeks of the war fleeing from town to town, traveling eastward almost to Kirovohrad, before deciding it would be safest to return to Tulchyn. She writes, "Not a single German soldier was going on foot. They all traveled in cars and motorcycles, some on bikes. But our soldiers retreated by foot, worn out, dirty, injured with filthy carts."[7] Numerous people remember the German trucks, which contrasted sharply with the horse-drawn carts that locals still commonly used for transportation in the district.

The first thing Pinia Golfeld remembered the Germans doing in Tulchyn was marking each of the Jewish houses with a Jewish star: "They would mark it with a Jewish Star of David and then go on to the next one." Many recall the chaos and lawlessness during the first month of joint German and Romanian occupation of the city. But unlike the situation in most towns on the other side of the Bug, there were no mass killings of the civilian Jewish population in Tulchyn during this period.

For those who remained in Tulchyn, the first month of the war was a time of great confusion. One witness writes: "The Red Army retreated.

Before the entrance of the Germans, the residents began to rob stores and Jewish homes. They dragged their things and food in bags. The roads were clogged with refugees. Few succeeded in evacuating. They believed the propaganda that the war would last for a month or two. Many could not leave behind their ailing elders. They evacuated with carts, behind which the elderly, women and children walked. Planes bombed columns of refugees."[8] Manya Ganiyevva writes that she headed toward the train station in Zhuravlivka, about 15 kilometers from Tulchyn, but seeing that it was clogged with soldiers, and after hearing warnings that other stations were also closed, she returned to Tulchyn. All the roads were clogged with refugees and carts, everybody fleeing in all directions. At one point, she made it as far as Demkovka station, where the situation was chaotic: "It was impossible to obtain tickets for the train. Whoever was alone, without children, without luggage would jump up onto the foot of the train and squeeze into the vestibule. And those who remained, among them our family, could not get on the train. In the station, there was a din, shouting, children crying. The radio announced that everybody needs to leave the station in order not to be killed because this type of place was often bombed."[9]

"EVERY DAY WE WAITED TO DIE"

Bershad fell to the Germans on July 29, 1941. Yosl Kogan was not able to get out in time:

> We didn't manage to evacuate ourselves, so we lived under occupation. And every day we waited to die. They were supposed to send us out somewhere. It says in the Bible: "We are witnesses because we survived."[10] We look heavenwards and must say "Thank God." We need to tell the youngsters how they tortured the Jews. Well, we wanted to evacuate ourselves, but they didn't allow it anymore. They came in right away. Before anything else could happen, they bombed Bershad. They threw two bombs next to the bridge.... I ran into a grocery store. They dropped a bomb on a Jewish house and the house burned down all the way to its roof.

Khayke Gvinter told us it was her house that was first bombed in Bershad, although she had fled the city by that time: "The first bomb fell on our house.... There was a big square there. It was such a nice house with a fence and trees. . . . When we returned, it was just a pit. We took what we could out of the house." Another time she told us, "I remember the war well, how the bombs were flying. We evacuated, and then the Germans were here. When we returned, our home was no longer there. It had been a beautiful house. People thought of it as a palace." Gvinter spent much of the next twenty years living in the basement of the synagogue, a space that had been utilized over the years by the forlorn and the homeless.

As soon as the Germans took over Bershad, they prohibited Jews from having contact with Christians, ordered the Jewish community to elect a council that was responsible for collecting valuables to be turned over to the Germans, and organized labor brigades. The kosher butcher, Eli Marchak, who had hosted the clandestine Breslov Hasidic group before the war, became the leader of the Jewish community and later of the ghetto. All Jews were required to wear a white Star of David badge on their chests and back.[11]

In nearby Tomashpil, German soldiers rounded up and murdered about 150 Jews when they first came into the city. Klara Sapozhnik was living in the nearby Gigant *kolkhoz*. During the first days of August, the Germans gathered all of the Jews from Tomashpil and the surrounding villages, including Gigant, together into two streets that were designated as the ghetto. Sapozhnik explained that a group of Ukrainians were taken to the outskirts of town, by the Polish cemetery, to dig several large pits. Several days later, she saw Romanian gendarmes and German soldiers start taking groups of Jews outside of the town to the cemetery, where they were executed. "The Germans came in and immediately, on the 4th of August, they started to execute them." Nisen Kiselman, who we interviewed in 2009, managed to flee the killing, but not before the Germans took his mother and sister. He recalled that "the Germans invaded Tomashpil in August 1941. They gathered 250 people and killed them. My mother was also in this pack and my sister was in that pack. And they took them all and killed them. I barely escaped."[12] He later explained that "the German thought that I was a non-Jewish boy, a Ukrainian boy," as a result of which he was able to evade the massacre.

The Germans remained in the town for eight days before Romanian gendarmes moved in to take over control. When the Germans left, Kiselman told us how the surviving Jews buried the bodies of those who had been massacred. He sifted through the corpses in the hopes of finding the bodies of his mother and sister, but the bodies were already decomposing in the hot humid summer heat and were recognizable only from the clothing: "And then, as soon as the Germans left that ravine, they collected all the old Jews. They carried the people [corpses] to the field and lay them all down. People looked for their parents. I recognized my mother. I couldn't find my sister. I don't know why. I couldn't recognize her clothes. I remembered what my mother was wearing." As a result, he told us, "Leyke is buried in the mass grave, but I buried my mother separately." Sapozhnik, who attributed the murder to the Romanians rather than the Germans who, she told us, only moved in later, also described how she went to the site of the mass grave a few days after the massacre. She took with her a child whose parents and siblings had been murdered in order to help him identify his family from among the corpses. In her interview with the Shoah Foundation, she described how "the ground moved for three days, spouting a fountain of blood."

There are differing recollections and inconsistencies on some specifics of the massacre: the exact day on which it occurred, whether Romanian gendarmes took part in addition to the Germans who directed it, and how long it took before the survivors were able to bury the dead. Sometimes the same informant gave varying details during different interviews, or even in the same interview. In Tomashpil today, where there is a small Jewish community without a strong leader, narratives have not been standardized, and recollections are fluid, subject to the fluctuations and vicissitudes of human memory—the dates and details of this massacre have yet to become ingrained in the town's collective history, but the general contours of that terrible day remain etched in the minds of those who witnessed it.

Tomashpil was not an isolated incident. Although the pace and death toll of massacres south of the Southern Bug was not as great as that on the northern shores, there were still many innocent victims of German atrocities. On Saturday, July 19th, in Ozaryntsi, Germans on motorcycles gathered all the Jews in the old synagogue and selected forty-three men whom they executed in a field near the town. Romanian soldiers killed another twenty-eight Jews in the town the next Saturday. German security police executed fourteen Jews in Kryzhopil on July 22nd and Sonderkommando 10a executed ten Jews in Pishchanka on August 3rd.

Between July 24th and July 27th, German and Romanian soldiers executed and drowned twenty-five Jews in Chernivtsi (Vinnytsya Province). The largest single recorded massacre in the part of Vinnytsya Province that became Transnistria took place between July 27 and July 29, when German and Romanian soldiers killed 435 Jews in Zhabokrich, a small village near Kryzhopil with a prewar Jewish population of around seven hundred.[13]

Yosl Kogan's wife was one of the few survivors of the Zhabokrich massacre. We have interviewed Yosl Kogan on many occasions over nearly a decade, but his wife finds the experience too painful to talk about directly. She has on occasion sat in on our interviews, but she cannot bring herself to speak of the horrors she endured. When we first met the couple, Yosl summarized his wife's experience for us, while she sat beside him nodding assent and groaning in anguish: "She was born in Zhabokrich. . . . In Zhabokrich they gathered the Jews together in five cellars and they massacred the entire city. And nobody has documented it. . . . They rounded up all the Jews and forced them into cellars. And she was the only one who survived from her cellar." "It's a major story and nobody is documenting it," he lamented. Indeed, the scale of murder and the number of individual acts of atrocities is so large that it is difficult to account for each one.

After the conquest of the area, the Germans immediately moved on, eastward across the Southern Bug River, leaving Romanian gendarmes and local police to guard the west bank, while the Germans themselves guarded the east bank. Manya Ganiyevva, upon returning from German territory to Tulchyn, wrote of her encounter with a German soldier on the river embankment: "In Ladyzhyn, on the bridge over the Bug, there was already a guard. A single German was standing with an automatic gun, and a policeman. They wouldn't allow anybody to cross the Bug." But when the German came to understand that they were from Tulchyn, he allowed them to pass "The German was not a member of the SS, and didn't look at our passports."[14]

Once Romanian authorities took control of the territory they established ghettos in each town, to which Jewish residence was restricted. In Romanian terminology, the space of Jewish residence was called a "colony," whether it was located within a distinct quarter of a city, as in a ghetto, or outside the city, as in a camp. As a result, residents today

often conflate the terms *ghetto* and *camp*, making little distinction between the two spaces of forced Jewish concentration. The fact that no
towns in Ukraine had ever before had areas to which Jewish residence
was restricted—in contrast to Central European towns, for instance,
which had had ghettos in the medieval and early modern periods—also
render the terminology of *ghetto* problematic.[15] Romanian authorities
established about two hundred of these concentration points, most of
them with only a few dozen residents, throughout Transnistria. Of the
fifty-three ghettos in Mohyliv district, for instance, twenty-six had fewer
than one hundred and fifty people in them, and only two imprisoned
more than one thousand people.[16] The first ghetto to be set up in the
region was probably in Mohyliv-Podilskyy, which was established on
August 15th, and held 3,733 local Jews as well as another 15,000 from
Bukovina and Bessarabia in December 1941.[17]

According to documentation from the Odessa State Archive, a formal
order to establish a ghetto in Tulchyn was issued on September 22, 1941,[18]
and the ghetto was established on October 1st, which corresponded to
Yom Kippur in the Jewish calendar.[19] In accordance with the general
order for the Jews of Romania issued on September 3rd, all Jews were
required to wear a black circle with a yellow star on their chests. Sasha
Kolodenker recalled the construction of the Tulchyn ghetto: "They drove
everybody out of their houses, destroyed the houses, and threw everybody into the ghetto. They stuck them there, surrounded by a fence."
Yente Kolodenker added that when the Jews left their homes and moved
into the area of the ghetto, non-Jews would tear apart the wood of the
abandoned Jewish homes and use it for firewood. Her own house, she
told us, was used for kindling. Klara Katsman of Tulchyn now lives
across the street from her former house: "When they set up the ghetto,
goyim immediately destroyed our house. Immediately."

The Romanian gendarmes instructed the Jews to assemble in the town
square, and allocated them a segment of "Beggars' street" in what had
been a poor Jewish neighborhood in the city. Barbed wire was strung
around the area. The Romanian authorities established a Jewish communal authority and appointed some of the wealthier members of the
community to lead it. All able-bodied workers were required to report to
the Jewish community office by the bus station every morning for work,

which usually entailed cleaning the streets or clearing rubble from the German bombs.

In Tomashpil, Romanian gendarmes established a ghetto by string-ing barbed wire around two streets and ordering the Jews to stay within the confines of the wire. Those, like Dora Guzman, who already lived within the cordoned-off area were able to stay in their own homes, and thus had access to some familiar comforts. Nisen Kiselman explained: "They drove out all the Jews from every street and made one single street. They spanned it with barbed wire." Romanian gendarmes and Ukrai-nian policemen guarded the street. Jews from the neighboring collective farm Gigant were also brought into the ghetto and forced to find shelter for themselves among the other residents. "Wherever you were able to sleep you slept, in a basement, on an oven. We suffered such torture," continued Kiselman. Within the ghetto, starvation was a constant threat and conditions were exceedingly difficult. Kiselman's wife filled in some details as Kiselman nodded along: "They sewed pants out of bags. That's what they wore. They didn't have anything to heat, but there was a sugar factory, where they discarded the coals. They would go up the hill, rags wrapped around their feet, and collect coal for themselves. And they heated the oven." Ghetto life in Tomashpil was characterized by slow suffering. When we asked Manya Gingold, who was born in Tomashpil in 1927, if people went into the synagogue or observed any holidays in the ghetto—Passover or Rosh Hashanah—she shook her head and replied, "If you went in there, they would beat you and kill you. They would take you to work . . . paving, clearing snow."

The establishment of the Bershad ghetto followed a similar pattern, but in contrast to the Tomashpil ghetto, which held mostly locals, the Bershad ghetto would become a major congregation point for Jewish refugees from Northern Bukovina and Bessarabia. The ghetto was es-tablished in September 1941 when Romanian gendarmes prohibited the Jews from leaving the ghetto district on pain of death, and ordered them to wear a Star of David on their chest and back as well as a white band on their arm.

The lack of a physical barrier in ghettos like Tulchyn and Bershad, or the semi-porous barriers of barbed wire that surrounded the Tomashpil ghetto, allowed for continued interaction between the Jewish and the non-Jewish world throughout the war. Although Jews were prohibited from leaving the ghetto except for work, those inside could receive assistance from non-Jews outside the ghetto, or could trade what little they had for food. Dora Guzman explained, "If you had to go out to buy things, you couldn't. It was difficult enough already, and you couldn't even go out anywhere. It was good that we had Christian acquaintances, who would come and bring us milk or potatoes. Such wonderful people." Most surviving Jews therefore were never wholly cut off from the surrounding communities; at most, they were sealed behind barbed wire rather than concrete walls. The world outside was still visible to the ghetto inmates, and those outside could still see in. This arrangement facilitated some empathy from those on the other side, who remained in regular contact with their imprisoned former neighbors. Residents of the ghettos also worked alongside Russian and Ukrainian prisoners of war, suspected communists, and other prisoners as slaves in the massive labor projects the Germans undertook.

"AND THEN REFUGEES STARTED TO COME IN"

During the fall of 1941, large convoys of deported Jews from Bessarabia and Northern Bukovina were being relocated into several towns selected to receive the deportees, including Mohyliv-Podilskyy, Sharhorod, and Bershad. The influx of tens of thousands of individuals from Romania into the already congested ghettos led to massive overcrowding: by late 1941, the population of Mohyliv-Podilskyy swelled to 19,000, Shagorod to 7,000, and Bershad to more than 25,000.[20] Khayke Gvinter remembered: "And then refugees started to come in.... There were ones from Edinet, Chernivtsi, Moldova, Mohyliv-Podilskyy, and from other districts. So many people." Yosl Kogan remembered how his mother fed the Bessarabian and Bukovinian Jews with soup. Many of the Romanian Jews who were herded into the ghettos arrived already sick and tired after enduring forced marches across the Dniester River, and living in stables and other temporary dwellings along the way.

The refugees, who tended to come from wealthier and more urban communities than those of Vinnytsya Province, brought with them valuables and money they had managed to salvage when they were forced out of their homes. Many of those without material assets came with spiritual sustenance—a resilient faith in God and intimate familiarity with religious ritual. In her interview with the Shoah Foundation, Clara Grinberg of Chechelnyk told of religious life in the Chechelnyk ghetto under the Romanians. Speaking in broken English, she explained, "The people who came from Moldovia. They was religious. They make in a small house like a synagogue. And it was when the holidays we went all to these people, they pray and it was out and see and hear what they did."[21] The revival of spiritual life helped sustain some whose faith had been repressed by twenty years of Soviet rule.

In Bershad, the Romanian gendarme Lieutenant Colonel Gheorghe Petrescu protected the Jews in the ghetto from excessive violence and allowed for the functioning of a market in the ghetto, at least until his dismissal in August 1942. Yosl Kogan remembered that when the Jews from Bessarabia and Bukovina came into Bershad, they set up a *piata*, a square in the town next to the well, where they sold bread and other food. Bershadskaia also recalled: "There was nothing to eat. There was a Jewish bazaar in which you could buy a potato pancake *[totch]*. Jews would go around and sell a hot polenta from cornmeal. And that's how they earned a kopek. My father worked for the proprietor of the house we lived in and Benchik [her younger brother] sold the wood; they would chop the wood, and he would sell it in the marketplace. They would sell it for a few kopeks." Gvinter told us, "I gathered potatoes under the Romanians. I dressed like a non-Jew and I would sell them there in the Jewish market. And that's how I lived." After Petrescu's dismissal, the new gendarmerie further restricted the importation of food into the ghetto. By 1943, nevertheless, some semblance of institutional functionality had been achieved in the Bershad ghetto with the establishment of a hospital, an orphanage, and schools, much of which was made possible with the assistance of aid from the Jewish community of Bucharest.[22]

"HOMEWARD, BROTHERS, HOMEWARD"

Yosl Kogan styled himself as a type of bard of the Bershad ghetto. He recorded his experiences in the Bershad ghetto in the songs he wrote during and immediately after the war. He explained to us once that he wrote poetry both as a protest and as a mnemonic device to preserve the memory of what happened in the ghetto during those terrible years: "I wrote the first song because I was afraid that they would kill me. Someone would find a Jew and would go around telling people that he wrote Yiddish songs against Hitler." He had notebooks full of poetry that he kept by his bed and recited to us whenever we visited. He told us that he wrote the poems during the occupation and kept the books hidden until the town's liberation. Most of the pieces in his notebook were songs circulating in the region that he had copied down, but a few were compositions he had created, often by stringing together stanzas and phrases he had picked up from other sources. He told us that after the war, he stopped writing his own pieces. When he sung the songs for the Bukovinian Jews who remained after the war, he continued, they all applauded, chanting his name and honoring him. These versified memories draw motifs from other poems and well-known songs, which Kogan adapted to the circumstances of the Bershad ghetto, freely combining tunes and stanzas to create poetic tributes and memorials. Most of Kogan's poetry—written in conditions of unimaginable despair—contain hints of optimism, reflecting the hope that the suffering will soon end and that the Jewish people will one day be free in a land of their own. Even his most bitterly satirical comments on the Jewish predicament in the Soviet Union are tempered with a kernel of optimism. These songs seem a reflection of Kogan's personality: he spoke freely of the most terrible atrocities he had witnessed and endured, but did so with the firm conviction that bearing witness will bring about a better world. One of Kogan's favorites is a song called "Aheym" (Homeward), which he has sung for us in several variants over the years. The poem's opening verse laments the sorry state of Jewish life in the ghetto, in which Jews are disdained and disgraced simply on account of their names—for being Jews—and ends with a fervent declaration, issued in almost messianic terms, that "there will come a time when all Jews will be free."

Nem farzets dos letste hemd
Abi nit zayn do in der fremd.
Aheym, briderlekh, aheym.

Mit dayn nomen yeder shemt zikh, yid,
Mit dayn nomen yeder krimt zikh, yid,
Un af der velt bistu gor na-venad.
Aheym, briderlekh, aheym.

Dayn mokem, dayn menukhe
Dayn eygene melukhe,
Vu du host, Yisroylikl, farbrakht.

Mit dayn nomen yeder shemt zikh, yid,
Mit dayn nomen yeder krimt zikh, yid,
Un af der velt bistu gor na-venad.
Aheym, briderlekh aheym.

Es vet kumen nokh a tsayt,
Ven ale yidn veln zayn bafrayt
Un demlt veln mir zingen a nay lid.

Af der fon der mogn-dovid
Un ale yidn hobn koved
Mit dem nomen: pintele yid.

Take and pawn your last shirt
Only don't stay here in a strange land.
Homeward, brothers, homeward.

You are disgraced for your name, Jew,
You are disdained for your name, Jew,
And you are homeless in this world.
Homeward, brothers, homeward.

Your own place, your own repose,
Your very own state,
Where you, dear Israel, once dwelled.

You are disgraced for your name, Jew,
You are disdained for your name, Jew,
And you are homeless in this world,
Homeward, brothers, homeward.

There will come a time,
When all the Jews will be free
And then we will sing a new song.

The star of David on the flag
And Jews will have pride
In the name of the Jewish spirit.

The piece is cobbled together from various songs and poems that Kogan likely heard in the ghetto, probably from the Romanian deportees who knew of the Yiddish source tunes, which were popular in interwar America. The opening lines of "Aheym"—"Homeward, brothers, homeward" and "Take and pawn your last shirt / Only don't live here in a stranger's land," as well as the phrase "Your own place, your own repose, your very own state," for instance, were derived from David Meyerowitz's song "Aheym, briderlekh aheym," which was written in 1918 for Jacob Adler's New York Yiddish theater and appeared in the operetta *Di kraft fun natur* (The Power of Nature).[23] It is doubtful, but not impossible, that Kogan would have known of this Zionist song from his time in prewar Bershad; he more likely learned it from the Romanian Jews who populated the ghetto. Other motifs can be found in Louis Gilrod's lyrics for the song "Dos pintele yid" from the 1909 operetta of the same name. But the sentiments are those of Kogan and others who may have sung the song together with him in the Bershad ghetto.

Another one of Kogan's songs is a sardonic satire of the well-known Soviet song, "Zhankoye," an upbeat propaganda piece about Jews building farms and new lives for themselves in the collective farms of Crimea. The original song begins with the famous lines: "As you travel to Sevastopol / Not too far from Simferopol / There's a railroad station" and continues to celebrate how former shtetl Jews with typical shtetl names—Abrasha, Leye, Beyle—are now working on collective farms as productive Soviet workers, as reapers, threshers, and tractor drivers. Kogan took the basic melody of "Zhankoye," but sung it at a slower, more somber pace, and altered the lyrics to deride the optimistic life promised by the original song. Rather than the open fields of the Crimean countryside, Kogan situated his song in the overcrowded Bershad ghetto, which he calls a camp.

> *Az me fort keyn Balonvike*
> *Iz nit vayt fun Obodivke—Bershad*
> *Dortn iz a lagerl faran.*
> *Yidn lign op meslesn*
> *Nit getrunken, nit gegesn*
> *Gitler, merder, zogt azoy darf es zayn.*
>
> *Oy-vey, tsores, tsores*
> *Toygn yidn af kapores*
> *Hoft men afn mazldikn tog.*
>
> *In a vinkl khropet Dvoyre*
> *Reb Gedalye halt di toyre*
> *Un bet got er zol shoyn tun dem nes.*

Oy-vey, tsores, tsores
Toygn yidn af kapores
Hoft men afn mazldikn tog.

Avrom-Iche fort af dem vogn
Es iz a kharpe im tsu groyln
Er makht shoyn skhakl shoyn dem zektsn tur.

Di obshchine hot im geheysn
Im farnemen ale meysim
Groyen im far veytik azh di hor.

Oy-vey, tsores, tsores
Toygn yidn af kapores
Hoft men afn mazldikn tog.

Inem shtetl, Bershad, der besoylem
Prinimayet yenem oylem
Griber shtaygn poshet nit farshit.
Es lign yidn un zey foyln
Azh dos harts heybt on tsu groyln
Akh farvos darf opkumen der yid.

Oy-vey, tsores, tsores
Toygn yidn af kapores
Hoft men afn mazldikn tog.

As you travel to Balonivke
Not too far from Obadivke, Bershad
There you will find a little camp.
Jews lie dying,
Not eating, not drinking.
Hitler—murderer—says
It must be so.

Oy, vey, sorrow, sorrow
Jews are left for rubble
Hoping for a more fortunate day.
In a corner Dvoyre snores,
Reb Gedalya holds the Torah,
And pleads to God for a miracle.

Oy, vey, sorrow, sorrow
Jews are left for rubble
Hoping for a more fortunate day.

Avrom-Itshe leads the wagon
It is a disgrace to speak to him,
He is already doing his sixth round.
The community appointed him
To take all the bodies.
His hair is gray from grief.

Oy vey, sorrow, sorrow
Jews are left for rubble
Hoping for a more fortunate day.

In a shtetl—Bershad—the cemetery
Is receiving the entire community.
Graves pile up not yet covered,
Jews are lying and they rot.
The heart shudders.
Why does the Jews have to suffer.

Oy vey, sorrow, sorrow
Jews are left for rubble
Hoping for a more fortunate day.

Instead of the railroad station found at the end of the road in the original song, Kogan finds a concentration camp. Instead of Abrasha, whose tractor races through the field, Kogan inserts Avrom-Itshe, who hauls a wagon full of corpses. Leye the reaper is replaced with Dvoyre who snores, and Beyle the thresher becomes Reb Gedalya, who holds the Torah. Each of the characters in Kogan's song is based on a real individual he knew from the ghetto: Avrom-Itshe Lekhetser, he told us, "was given a wagon with a horse. He would collect the corpses six times a day—no less. They were falling like flies." Gedalya, he continued, "was one of our *shoykhets*," and Dvoyre was his wife. When the Germans came through the town on their retreat in 1944, Kogan explained, they executed Gedalya on charges that he had been assisting the partisans in the forests outside the town. Kogan honored the murdered Gedalya as the one who "holds the Torah and pleads to God for a miracle." Kogan vacillates between referring to Hitler as a "murderer" and a "thief." In the several variants of the song that he sung for us over the years, he sometimes sung the verse, "Hitler—murderer—says it must be so," and sometimes "Hitler—thief—says it must be so."

Another one of Kogan's songs from the Bershad ghetto, "What Have You Given Us, Hitler," describes in verse the horrors he witnessed, as

he watched refugees from Romania forge across the river with their belongings on their backs. In "What Have You Given Us, Hitler?" Kogan
accuses Hitler of placing thieves on the throne. The poem again borrows
phrases, rhymes, and motifs from other sources: the phrase "scattered
and dispersed," for instance, is often used as a general reference to the
state of Diaspora Jews, but was employed specifically in songs of Transnistrian ghettos to refer to the Jewish deportees from Bessarabia. The
Yiddish writer Szmerke Kaczerginski, for instance, published a song that
parallels the variant sung by Kogan, which Kaczerginski obtained from
a source who was in the Sharhorod ghetto.[24] Kogan ends his song with a
verse of hope, drawing from the same themes he employed in "Aheym."
Once again, the Jews will wait for a time when all the Jews in the world
will be free, they will fly a flag emblazoned with the star of David, and
will have respect for the Jewish Spirit. In Kogan's variant the song drifts
into recitative mode, as he parenthetically comments on the suffering
he witnessed.

Vos hostu Gitler—merder—mir azoy gegibn
Akhuts a numerl af geln karton,
A hoykhn zabor arum dem shtetl?
Un di gazlonim hostu geshtelt afn tron.

Tsezeyt un tseshpreyt,
Vu ir zeyt, vu ir geyt.
Yidelekh fun yener zayt brik
Mit di pekelekh in di hent,
Kleyne kinder af di hent.
Me traybt undz, me shlogt undz,
Nit farvos.

Itstert vil ikh, az ir zolt zen dos.
Dos harts heybt on tsu flakern,
Zen tsukukndik af di kinder,
Vi-zoy zey mutshen zikh.

Tsukukndik af zey
Rayst zikh op dos harts.
Tsukukndik af di kinder un af di mentshn.

Yidelekh fun yener zayt brik,
Farshvoln, hungerik in kelt
Aroysgetribn hot men undz fun yener zayt,
Fun undzer shtub.

Brider, shvester, fraynt.
Zey hobn dertseylt di yidn, azoy.

A sakh undzere brider un fraynt
Zenen geblibn af di felder, af di felder.
S'iz take emes, take azoy.

Un me shlogt undz un me traybt undz un me pakt.
Me zogt azoy: mir hofn, mit gots hilf
Az s'vet kumen di mazldike sho
Ven ale yidn fun der gorer velt veln besholem zayn.
Mit gots hilf zayn bafrayt,
Un demlt ver s'vet blaybn lebn
Veln mir ale undzere zingen a naye lid.
Af der fon—dem mogn-Dovid.
Ale yidn fun der gorer velt veln hobn koved.
Mid dem nomen pintele yid.

What have you given me, Hitler—murderer,
Aside from a number on a yellow badge,
A high fence around the shtetl?
And you put the thieves on the throne.

Scattered and dispersed,
Wherever you look, wherever you go,
Jews from the other side of the bridge
With packs in their arms
And little children in their arms
They goad us, they beat us
For nothing!

Now I want you to see this:
The heart begins to flutter
Looking at the children
How they torture them,
Looking at them,
It tears your heart,
Looking at the children and at the men.

Jews from the other side of the bridge,
Swollen, hungry, and cold,
They forced us from the other side, from our home.
Brothers, sisters, friends.
That's how the Jews explained it.

Many of our brothers and friends
Were left in the fields, in the fields.

It's completely true, just like that.

And they beat us, and goad us, and grab us
They say "we hope, with God's help, a better hour will come,
When all the Jews in the entire world will be at peace.
With God's help, they will be free.
And then, those who remain alive,
Will sing a new song, all of us together."
On the flag—the star of David!
All the Jews from the entire world will have respect
For the name, "the Jewish Spirit."

"LIFE WAS A LITTLE BETTER FOR US LOCALS"

In Sharhorod today, there remains a myth that those who survived in the town did so thanks to the spirits of the two holy men buried in the cemetery. When we visited, the gravestones of Naftali-Herts ben Aaron and Avrom ben Meir were singled out for special honor—their trim had been painted blue and a blue fence surrounded them. In the years since, Hasidic pilgrims from Israel have erected a chapel around the graves to better shelter them from the elements and protect them from marauders. Asya Barshteyn told us that people used to come from all over the world to visit the cemetery and seek protection from the righteous ones buried there. She told us that the government had wanted to remove the graves of the *tsadik*s. "Go ahead," the Jews said, "we won't stop you." But the officials were too frightened of the spirits, and left the graves in place. Most of the residents we spoke to dismissed the role the *tsadik*s played in protecting the town as a fairy tale, but all agreed that with respect to the types of mass killings that took place in hundreds of Ukrainian towns during the Second World War, in the words of Feyge Rivelis—"there was none of that here."

Abram Vaisman does not know why neither the Germans nor the Romanians killed the Jews en masse. Many believe, he told us dismissively, that the city was spared because of the holy men buried in the cemetery, but he insisted they were saved because of the kindness of their Ukrainian neighbors: the "Ukrainian people" (Ukraynishe mentshn) or the "uncircumcised," he tells us using the Yiddish *areylim* rather than the more familiar *goyim* (nations). Although *goyim* had long been the normative term used by Jews to refer to Ukrainians, some of those in the younger generation had come to regard it as pejorative. Born in

1940, Vaisman was among the younger of those we interviewed, and was more sensitive to the term's usage. As a result, he sought other terms to describe the Christians who helped Jews during the war. One woman in particular—Ksenia Vasilovna Loyanich—helped Jews by bringing them food every day. He repeated her name again for us, very slowly, to be sure that we recorded it accurately. Certainly, he told us, many Romanian Jews deported into Sharhorod died of hunger during the war, but the Romanians did not kill the Jews in Sharhorod: "Life was a little better for us locals."

The Sharhorod ghetto was established in September 1941 and immediately became a refugee center for approximately 3,000 Bukovinian Jews, mostly from Suceava and Dorohoi, who were transferred into the city in October. The Jews of Suceava, led by Dr. Meir Teich, had arrived in Sharhorod in better condition than many other deportees, as they had managed to bribe Romanian officials at the crossing into Mohyliv-Podilskyy to take them the rest of the way in a truck and wagons rather than by foot.[25] The influx of refugees swelled the Jewish community of Sharhorod from the 1,800 people who had originally lived there to a high of 7,000 in December 1941. The community developed a reputation for being relatively welcoming to the new refugees. According to witness testimonies, when Jews from Dorohoi were passing through the city, the Jewish community appealed to the Praetor to allow the Dorohoi Jews to stay rather than be sent further north to an unknown fate. The community even took in Jews who had fled across the Bug from the Reichskommissariat Ukraine, despite the knowledge that the entire community would be at risk if these refugees were discovered. When searches took place, those in hiding were concealed in the catacombs underneath the city. Remarkably, even local Ukrainian peasant women interceded on behalf of the refugees from Dorohoi: "Many of the Ukrainian peasant women who had come to the market crowded around the deportees and gave them food for the journey. Arriving in front of the Praetor's office, the women knelt down and blocked the road ... the peasant women cried and screamed, raised their fists against him [the Praetor] and shouted: '... How can you be so hard against human beings?'"[26] In the end the Dorohoi Jews were permitted to stay. Seven thousand people huddled into 337 houses and settled down for what was to be an exceptionally cold and disease-ridden winter.

The Romanian Jews who had been transplanted into the ghetto brought with them their religious traditions, leading to a revival of spiritual life. Asya Barshteyn explained, "During the time of occupation, people came from Romania and from Poland, who were sent here. They were sent here from their towns. Among them were people—a *rebbe* and a *rov*—who prayed in the Great Synagogue." The Great Synagogue of Sharhorod, which had been closed by the Soviet government before the war, was reopened for the High Holy Days of 1942 and remained open for the duration of the occupation.[27]

The Romanian Jews also brought money and valuables that they used for bribing Romanian occupation authorities, saving individuals from forced labor and deportation to concentration camps. Klara Kurman remembered, in particular, Meir Teich. He died, as she put it, in "Yiddishland, or what do they call it—Palestine." According to Teich, who published his own version of events after the war, "In the case of lighter local labor service we allowed people to buy themselves off. We thereby created a fund with which we provided well-paid jobs for volunteers. But no buying off or furnishing of substitutes was allowed under any circumstances for heavy labor, especially when it involved working outside the area."[28]

The Romanian deportees, who had arrived after enduring forced marches and living in squalor along the way, also often brought disease with them into the ghettos. Within these towns, a massive typhus epidemic began to spread as the winter of 1941 set in. Epidemic typhus was always a threat in overcrowded conditions; the disease ran rampant in Nazi concentration camps, claiming the lives of thousands of prisoners, including famously Anne Frank and her sister Margot. The disease is caused by the *Rickettsia prowazekii* organism that spreads through lice. As the louse feeds on the human who carries the bacillus, the bacillus grows in the louse's stomach and is excreted in its feces. When an infected louse bites another human, the disease is spread when the bite victim itches, releasing the feces into the wound. The disease begins as a rash on the chest that spreads to the trunk and extremities, accompanied by a high fever. In its late stages, victims often become delirious. Inadequate hygiene thereby contributed to the typhus outbreak in Sharhorod: the small town's population had quadrupled in six months: there was inadequate sanitation and overcrowding, and the ground was too frozen for the dead to be buried properly. About a quarter of the inhabitants of Sharhorod—1,449 people, according to official figures—perished, mostly of typhus, during the winter of 1941–1942.[29] Similarly, about ten thousand people—half the ghetto population—perished in the Bershad ghetto during the winter of 1941–1942, mostly from hunger and typhus. Asya Barshteyn remembered that there were so many people dying in the ghetto that a man would come around once or twice a day with a horse-drawn cart to collect the frozen bodies that had been laid outside the houses.

The disease was finally brought under control with the spring thaw. In Sharhorod, a Jewish burial society buried the victims of the winter epidemic. In addition, the Jewish community set up a hygiene and delousing service and a soap factory; they also cleaned the wells and distributed antibiotics that arrived from Jewish aid organizations in Bucharest.[30] Thereafter, the death toll in the Sharhorod ghetto declined significantly. During this time, the overcrowding in the ghetto was brought under control as about 1,000 people were relocated to neighboring settlements in June 1942, and in May 1943 another 175 Jews were taken to work camps near Mykolaiv. In September 1943, a total of 2,971 Romanian Jews remained in the city, in addition to the local Jews.[31]

"NO ONE KNEW WHERE TO, WHERE WE WERE GOING"

Romanian authorities panicked at the typhus epidemic of late 1941, and, in some regions where the epidemic was already rampant, responded with extreme violence: in the last weeks of 1941 and first months of 1942, some 48,000 Jewish prisoners, mostly deportees from Bessarabia and Bukovina, were massacred in camps set up in Bogdanovka and Domanevka, in the Golta region of the southeastern part of Transnistria. The authorities justified the massacre as a means of preventing the spread of the disease and of protecting supply lines to the north. The massacre was also the culmination of a eugenics and purification mentality that had pervaded Romanian political and social thought.[32]

In northwestern Transnistria, the Romanian authorities sought to protect their soldiers and supply lines from the spread of the disease, and so decided to isolate the Jews, whom they believed were its carriers. In December 1941, the Jews of Tulchyn, who had been languishing in the city's ghetto for the first months of the war, were ordered to report for disinfection and relocation. Pinia Golfeld explained: "On December 7, 1941,[33] they gathered everyone on one street and took them into a school and said that the Jews were carrying disease." They were kept there for three days. Yente Kolodenker described the situation in the school:

> When we were brought into the school—what can I say? There was no-where to stand. Imagine fitting all of Tulchyn into one courtyard, is that possible?! But they were pushing everyone inside. People wanted to drink something. It was raining then, and between the puddles there were little streams. We went outside the school, because they allowed people to walk around. We scooped up the water from the puddle and drank it. And the children were whining because they wanted to eat. There was such a tumult and screaming. The Romanians would shoot every minute.

Sasha Kolodenker described the experience as having been like sardines packed together, one lying on top of the other: "They gathered everyone in the Ukrainian school. They threw us out of our homes and stuck us into different streets in Tulchyn. Then they took us in into the school. [Then] they needed to bathe us, to disinfect us. Some people escaped; some stayed in the bath. From there they drove us into the camp." Others told of how the Jews were counted and their names were recorded before they were forced into the school. One eyewitness wrote that before they were put into the school, the Jews were forced to hand over their valuables as a "redemption."[34] Nisen Yurkovetsky told us that some of the men of means were able to hide their valuables in cellars and then left for the camps in rags.

After they were gathered together and counted in the school, 3,005 Jews from Tulchyn were taken to the city's baths to be disinfected.[35] According to Golfeld, "There they gave us injections. There was this doctor, Biletsky, a Christian, and he said to the Germans that the Jews were all carrying infections. They gave us injections in the bath and then led us again into the school." Pesia Kolodenker added:

> They set up a clothes boiler. They made everyone undress, naked. There were no men because they were all in the army. But there were children of thirteen, fourteen years, very old people, and women. They stood there and they were embarrassed in front of each other. So, they covered each other up so that nobody saw their nakedness. The Romanians and the police stood there and laughed at the Jews. . . . Afterward they took

out their clothes and they were left entirely in rags. They didn't have anything to wear. They [The Romanians] had burned them [the clothes]. . . . Whatever they could get, they put on; otherwise they would have been left entirely naked.

Rita Shveibish, a child survivor herself and local amateur historian, attributed the typhus epidemic that later spread through the region to the injections: "They made it so that we would become sick with typhus," she told us, alluding to a theory that the Romanians purposely infected the Jews with typhus.[36] In fact, the Romanian authorities were alarmed by the typhus epidemic and were adamant in their desire to create a typhus-free corridor through Transnistria as a military supply line. It was, in part, out of fear of the spread of typhus that the decision was made to further isolate the Jews from general society and therefore to liquidate the ghetto of Tulchyn. A group of 118 artisans—bakers, tailors, cobblers, and others with specialized skills—were kept in the ghetto while the rest of the Jews were driven out.[37]

Gerhard Schreiber, a deportee from Chernivtsi, arrived in Tulchyn sometime after the liquidation of the ghetto and in a written memoir described what the largely emptied town looked like:

> The Jewish ghetto, as it was called, comprised one street with small in-dividual houses, about 250–300 yards long. Our group, about 100–120 people, found shelter in either empty houses with windows and doors, or with the local Jewish families. These were the few remnants of a larger Jewish community, who had survived the mass killings, which occurred when the Germans occupied the city.[38] They were retained by the Romanian authorities, because of their skills, since most skilled craftsmen had left with the retreating Soviet troops. There was a dentist, a dyer, a watchmaker, a capmaker and a few others. The dyer was the most prosperous of them, his business extended over two houses, one could see the colored fabric being hanged out to dry from afar.[39]

By 1943, the community in Tulchyn began to receive some aid from the Central Jewish Board in Bucharest and, according to Schreiber,

> With some help from the authorities, an empty schoolhouse, located at the end of the street the ghetto was located on, was transformed into a crafts center. There were workshops for various trades, such as locksmith and metalworking, tailor, watchmaker, capmaker, dyer, housepainter, carpenter, and a few others. When the center was officially opened,

the Romanian civilian authorities brought along all the German and Romanian military brass, who apparently were quite impressed. Many of them later patronized these shops.[40]

After the majority of the Jews of Tulchyn had been taken into the baths and counted in the school, they were forcibly marched through the town along the village road—"no one knew where to, where we were going," recalled Pinia Golfeld. "Whoever wasn't able to continue walking, was shot right away," Pesia Kolodenker added. Rita Shveibish told us that there were policemen with large dogs guarding them on motorcycles and horses. They marched for two days, spending the night in the village of Torkiv. Golfeld remembered "they drove us into a *kolkhoz* where there had once been cows and horses, into a stable, and we spent the night there. And in the morning, there was a tumult. The first people already died there. It was also cold and wet. They passed away. In a word, they buried them there on the road."

The three thousand Jews of Tulchyn eventually arrived in the town of Pechera, where, set on a cliff overlooking the Southern Bug River and surrounded by parkland was a three-story Romanesque palace that had once belonged to the Potocki noble family, but had been used as a sanatorium for tuberculosis patients by the Soviet government. It was an ideal isolation ward for quarantine purposes. Pinia Golfeld explained, "They led us to a place. They opened a gate, there was an iron gate. And there had been a sanatorium there in Pechera, a tuberculosis hospital. They forced us through the gate, and the Jews ran like mice into the hospital wards. They didn't heat the wards. And they lay down on the floor; that's how the people slept."

The Jews of Tulchyn and surrounding towns were dumped in the building and left to their own devices. This was not a labor camp nor technically a death camp—although death rates were exceedingly high. Rather, it was simply a de facto concentration camp, a place where the Romanians could quarantine Jews to prevent the typhus epidemic from spreading. Over the course of the next months, additional shipments of Jews were brought into the camp, including about 750 Jews from Bratslav who were brought to the camp in January 1942, and several hundred more who arrived over the next few days from Ladyzhyn and Vapnyarka. Sporadic deportations into Pechera continued over the summer and fall: about 3,500 Jews from the Mohyliv-Podilskyy ghetto were deported to

The sanatorium that was used as the Pechera concentration
camp during the war as it looked in 2009. The building is
back in use as a sanatorium. *Photo by Artur Frątczak.*

Pechera in two waves in July and October–November 1942. Many inmates of the camp were Bessarabian and Bukovinian Jews, whose long
forced exodus from their homes in Romania finally ended here. In total
about 9,000 Jews were held in Pechera.[41]

"SHE WAS STILL TWITCHING"

Frida Pecherskaia, together with her mother and two sisters, was brought
to Pechera from her native Bratslav. Her brother and father had both
been drafted into the army before the Germans arrived in town. Her
brother died at the front at the age of seventeen; her father survived. Her
youngest sister, who was only six months old when they were taken to
Pechera, died within a week of their arrival in the camp. Her other sister,
Rivele, was also dying of hunger but had not yet succumbed when she
was taken to be buried. The Jewish inmates charged with collecting the
dead took her alive and threw her onto the cart of corpses: "They took
her—she was still alive—our people, the Jews, they took her by the hand

and threw her onto a pile of corpses. My mother and I were screaming so loudly. She was still twitching. They closed it [the cart] and there was nothing we could do."

The Bessarabian and Bukovinian Jews who sometimes arrived with valuables were initially better off and able to trade their jewels for food. This created resentment between the two communities, some of which persists to this day. Rita Shveibish told us, "The Bessarabian Jews and the Bukovinian Jews were a little better off than us, and so they supported the people. People shared. There was a Judenrat, but they were not good at all. They were only for themselves. They didn't treat the people well at all. The only people who saved us were the elderly non-Jews." Sasha Kolodenker has a kinder interpretation of the Romanian Jews who worked with the Germans, recognizing that they were working under compulsion: "They were forced to. They were taken to work and killed as well."

Once the Romanian Jews ran out of valuables, the local Jewish communities had the advantage of knowing the terrain and the local language. Pesia Kolodenker cited her memory of a particularly beautiful young Bukovinian girl she encountered in Pechera:

> A very beautiful girl came into the chamber. She was no more than sixteen years old. What a beautiful girl and so well dressed. It was obvious that she belonged to a wealthy family. But she didn't speak any Yiddish, only Russian. She said to us: "Have mercy on me. Give me some bread. I don't know if I can even eat any bread, but I just want to try once. Give it to me please."
> Nobody gave.
> "Where's your mother?"
> "My mother already died of hunger," she said.

When they went looking for the girl sometime later, she had already died. Those without family to protect them and to share the little bread and potatoes they could acquire were condemned to starvation. The wealthier Bukovinian Jews may have had the advantage of having something to trade, but once that ran out, they were worse off than the locals, who had more "of their own" to rely upon and were more accustomed to living with starvation.

Throughout 1942–1943, the death rate in Pechera rose. Yente Kolodenker's father was forced to work as a gravedigger: "They forced my father to bury the dead people. They gathered people to work as grave-diggers; he would go out to the field where they had to bury people. The non-Jews brought him food. He would bring it home." She paused at the irony of calling the camp home: "'home'—to the camp," she spat out. Pesia Kolodenker told us, "They transported the corpses in a hay cart to the place where they were buried. They threw in the corpses. Somebody's hands or somebody's hair would fall through the slats. The wheels rolled and the corpses moved back and forth."

Thousands succumbed to hunger and disease: "There was no food, nothing to drink. Nothing. I don't know how we survived," recalled Pinia Golfeld. Pesia Kolodenker remembered one time when the potato peels she had painstakingly foraged were stolen from her: "We suffered from such hunger. We were so proud and really looked forward to having those peels fried," she lamented. Yente Kolodenker told us that her father had three sisters and seventeen nieces and nephews with him in the camp—"What a joke!" she said, "How could he possibly have given food to everyone?" She described how they would fight over how to divide a potato between them. Once, her sister managed to get two potatoes: "She wanted to eat it herself, but she shared it." She divided it not only among the family but also with a stranger, a "woman with a coat," who approached, begging for a bite.

Stories of cannibalism recur throughout testimonies of Pechera. Pesia confided: "A woman was lying there [next to] a dead person. She was holding something—I thought maybe a small child. I went closer. She was right next to the dead person. She ran after me like a dog, so I escaped. She was eating him." She told us that when a verification commission came to take testimonies after the war, the officials refused to believe that the hunger had reached such levels.

One great irony of the camp was that it was so scenically situated, on a cliff overlooking the river as it flowed past rapids around a bend. The sound of the water rushing past the rocky bend could be heard above in the barracks. The river taunted those in the camp with an abundant source of fresh water and fish, which were denied to the prisoners. The river divided Romanian Transnistria from the German Reichskommissariat, and German soldiers stood watch on the other side of the river, well within bullet range. Donia Presler told us about how difficult it was to obtain water, about how people would scour the camp for any type

The Southern Bug River at the base of the Pechera concentration camp. The camp was on the right bank, which was under Romanian rule, and the Germans were stationed on the left bank, opposite the camp. The starving and thirsty inmates of the camp were not permitted to drink from the river. Today, it is a site of leisure for bathers. *Photo by Artur Frątczak.*

of container—a jar, a can, a broken pot—and sidle down the cliffs to the water in the darkness of night. German search lights from the village of Sokilets across the river, would watch the prisoners. The Germans shot at anyone they saw on the Romanian side. Pinia Golfeld told us "people would go down to the Bug to get a bit of water, but the German police stood on the other side and shot. Whoever they saw, they shot." Pesia Kolodenker told us of one woman who had somehow obtained a piece of bread from the German side for her two starving children and was trying to cross back over. From the hill above, Kolodenker and the other prisoners could see the woman's body floating in the water. "Her white undershirt was full of blood—she had been shot in the heart." A gendarme came and told them to get the body out of the water and bury her. Kolodenker told us that the woman's children survived two more days before dying. "I saw it myself," she concluded.

Some Ukrainians collaborated willingly and stood out among the inmates for their cruelty. A Dr. Biletsky, who oversaw the initial deportations from Tulchyn, is remembered as being particularly callous. Yente Kolodenker told us about one episode: "a doctor came, Biletsky, and he asked how many people died. They told him . . . and he said 'that's not very many.' It was the big frost. We didn't have heat. That year it went down perhaps to forty degrees below zero. He took a stick and broke the windowpanes so that more people would freeze to death. He was that kind of bandit." Sasha Kolodenker remembered the same story, but added that the death rate before he broke the window was about three hundred people per day. In her telling of this act of cruelty, Yente was particularly enraged that the doctor "was one of ours," a Soviet citizen, who was working for the Germans. After the war, though, she was consoled that he was tried and imprisoned for his collaboration.

Donia Presler told us that at one point her older sister, Tsirl, who was about eighteen at the time, managed to get out of the camp and make it all the way back to her native Tulchyn. Presler and her sisters would occasionally sneak out at night and beg for food in the village. She told us that Tsirl didn't look Jewish and when she put on a Ukrainian scarf could pass for a Christian. Once, sometime in 1942, her sister decided to flee together with another girl, Roza, back to Tulchyn, where they figured they could obtain some alms from the better-off Jews in the ghetto. Presler told us that when Tsirl and Roza arrived in Tulchyn, "they [the Jews in the ghetto] didn't even want to let them through the door." Tsirl and Roza could see milk and bread on the table, but the Jews in the ghetto were not willing to help the girls other than give them some pocket change—"50 kopeks, a half mark." Nobody was willing to take them in: "They'll kill us because of you. Why did you come here? Go, go, go!" was all they heard. Reflecting upon this episode in her interview with the Shoah Foundation, Presler commented that "those who lived in the ghetto didn't know the camp. They didn't suffer like we did." Tsirl decided to turn instead to an ethnic German, Zhenya Malina, who had been a close friend of the family's before the war: she was "with the Jews," in Presler's words. Malina took the girls in, washed them, and fed them. Presler related to us that Malina went to the ghetto to rebuke the Jews, telling them they should be ashamed of themselves for failing to help the girls from the camp. In the end, Malina helped the girls collect some more money from the Jews in the ghetto, and led them to the village of Tarasivka, on the way to Pechera, where she left them on their own. The girls started to make their way back to the camp, but were captured by a Romanian brigade of police in the village of Bortnyky. According to other testimonies, the police officer stationed in Bortnyky, a man by the name of Mukha, was particularly evil.[42] The police, who had also captured some Romanian Jewish men who had escaped from Pechera, executed the men, but took the girls back to the camp.

At this point, Presler continued the story as an eyewitness. She remembered the police coming into the camp and gathering all the prisoners to tell them that the next day there would be a "show trial:"

> We saw how they brought in my Tsirl and Roza and led them into the camp. This is how they brought them: they took a horse from [the village of] Bortnyky. And they tied both of them to the horse. The horse went off at a gallop and they ran after the horse. The Romanians drove. One or two Romanians in a horse-drawn machine gun platform, and the police were on the horse. And the horse stepped on Roza's foot and her entire leg was ripped open up to her shin. And she was running in the sand like this and the blood was spurting out like a fountain into the mud. They brought them into the camp. She quickly collapsed. After two hours, she died. And they interrogated my Tsirl. They asked her who her mother and her sister were. . . . They didn't bother with me. I was only twelve years old, but I could pass for five. . . . They took my mother and they laid her down. And they began to whip her. One whipped from one side; another whipped from the other side. Blood was running from her mouth, from her body. Blood was gushing from everywhere. Then they took my older sister. My older sister became a little [crazy] from the camp. . . . They beat my older sister as much as they could. Then they took out coals and forced her onto her knees. . . . And they gave her a stool that she had to hold up like this. And then they pummeled her. . . . They forced her onto her knees and poured out coarse sand with pebbles, and then they forced her onto her knees. And Tsirl was no more: no face, no head, no hands, no feet. . . . She was spurting blood for a half-year. And that was her ordeal.

"THE KINDLY UNCIRCUMCISED"

Those who survived often managed to do so by begging or trading for food with Ukrainians in nearby villages. Pesia Kolodenker told us she would occasionally sneak out of the camp in order to beg for bread and sugar from the villagers, the *latishe areylem,* literally the "kindly uncir-cumcised." She would walk barefoot with rags on her feet in the freezing cold, and villagers would give her a bowl of noodles, some milk, and some clothes to wrap herself in. Rita Shveibish told us, "I would stand where there was a big, tall fence, and I would stand and beg. Non-Jews would come and people would give them a golden ring or whatever they had for a bit of bread or beetroot or a piece of potato. I didn't have anything, so I would just stand there and beg. Elderly non-Jews came up to me, would have pity on me, and would give me what little they had." Pinia Golfeld also attributed his survival to the kindness of the Ukrainian locals, who would toss beetroot over the fence. "Thankfully, we had food. There were Ukrainians, very devoted people . . . they would throw food over to the Jews." He remembered how difficult it was to eat the frozen beetroot: "They were frozen, and my teeth would remain in the beetroot." He remembered licking the icicles and drinking the snow that would fall from the roof, in order to assuage his fever.

Whereas some attribute the occasional willingness of neighbors to help to kindness and empathy, others emphasize the motive of greed. Certainly, everybody remembers what a bit of gold could be traded for. Those without gold, traded their skills for food: Nisen Yurkovetsky ex-plained how his uncle would give the Romanian gendarmes haircuts in return for food. Yente Kolodenker's mother was able to bribe the police with a bottle of moonshine, and traded clothing for food with the peas-ants. In her written memoirs, Manya Ganiyevva also wrote of individual acts of kindness by some peasants: "I remember one particular peasant woman who approached the stone fence of the camp in order to trade for bread. She had a bag of bread, but when she saw these starving, worn-out prisoners and children who looked like skeletons, she threw the bag of bread over the fence, cried and left never to return."[43] The extent of the need inside the camp was so great that even the kindly villagers were sometimes overwhelmed to the point of inaction. Despite her initial compulsion to throw the bag of bread over the fence, this peasant woman never returned, and presumably lived through the war with full knowl-edge of the suffering in her own backyard. She was likely discouraged by what she thought was the minimal impact her own actions could have, unaware that even her crusts could have meant survival for those imprisoned inside.

Initially, the inmates relied upon the nearby residents of the town of Pechera for sustenance, but eventually the town residents tired of giving alms, and the inmates who managed to get out were forced to go begging in more distant villages, in Vishkivtsi and Bortnyky. Some even forged across the Southern Bug to Sokilets, where the Germans were stationed. A few former inmates spoke of escaping the camp for multiple days at a time, traveling from village to village in search of food, before returning to the relative safety of the camp. Donia Presler remembered once "during their Passover," she said of Easter,

> When we came to Pechera, people had already stopped giving out food, and they sent us further, so we walked further. If the herdsmen—young boys of ten years old with cows in the fields—got hold of you they would immediately kill you. It was worse being caught by them than by the police. They would cut you to pieces. So we hid behind the haystacks. When they took away the cows for the night, we showed up in the village. The older people would take pity on us. We would come and say "Christ has risen" and they would reply, "Truly, He is risen." People would give us a piece of bread, or two potatoes, or beetroot.

Frida Pecherskaia was also able to escape the camp in search of food. She recalled bundling her feet with rags and running through the snow from village to village. Once, sometime in the fall, she persuaded her mother to join her: "We left the camp through a fence. I was only a child and my mother was twenty-eight years old. She didn't manage to get over the fence." Frida was caught by a police officer who beat her and brought her back. She managed to escape again and made it back to Bratslav: "In Bratslav there was a camp, a German camp. I was caught there and imprisoned in the German camp. We received a piece of bread once a week." At one point in the spring or summer, German covered trucks arrived to take prisoners into the woods, where they would be killed. Frida managed to escape by hiding in a lavatory hole. When the operation was over, she was pulled out of the hole by a Polish Jew—"the elder," she called him—who pulled her out by her hair. She remembered that he was weeping because his daughter had been taken in the roundup. The covered trucks came again. This time, she was caught and tossed into the car, but managed to escape by throwing herself out of the truck into a ravine below: "I was fated to live," she philosophized. She was saved by non-Jews who found her lying in the ditch, covered in blood with a broken hand. They took her to their home, and helped hide her in the stable, where she spent two weeks. When she left, she found herself once again in a German camp. There she spent about a month, before being sent back, once again, to Pechera, from where she was eventually liberated.

Individual Ukrainian villagers and townspeople saved Jews throughout Transnistria. Outside the barbed wire of the Tomashpil ghetto, Nisen Kiselman explained, "There were good Christians who helped us during the war. They brought us food to eat. There was a ghetto and one couldn't get out, so they would come and give food. . . . Non-Jews passed by the barbed wire and threw in potatoes. Potatoes; there was bread—whatever they could salvage." In Sharhorod, many survivors comment on the kindness of the Ukrainian peasants who lived in the vicinity of the town, and even of the Romanian gendarmes who guarded the town. Dr. Felicia (Steigman) Carmelly wrote in her memoirs of a Romanian officer who brought her food and medication on a regular basis: "He told us that he had been married to a Jewish girl, and that they had a four-year-old son. His wife and son had been taken away to a concentration camp, and he did not know of their whereabouts. He spoke with sadness in his voice and with a sincere desire to help us. His name was Peter, a truly good human being."[44] Asya Barshteyn remembered a German who worked as an engineer at the mill before the war, where he had befriended many Jews. She credits him with saving the community from a potential massacre when the Germans first came into the town and gathered the Jewish community together in the monastery. She told us that he pleaded with the Germans, trying to convince them that not all Jews were communists: "He felt they were simply people, not Party people, so he saved them."

In another act of humanity, Khayke Gvinter told us of one German soldier who turned his weapon on his comrade-in-arms in order to save a child: "There was a German who couldn't shoot the child. As long I live I won't forget. That's when the other German realized he could fire. He overcame him. . . . Yes, one [shot] the other. He said, 'I also have a child. I can't! I can't!' There were also good ones among them." Even in the midst of a massacre, perpetrators were capable of small acts of humanity. But far too rarely.

Others who fled the camp managed to obtain help from the Jewish communities still in the ghettos. Yosl Kogan, who spent most of the occupation in the Bershad ghetto, remembers that many people who had escaped from Pechera, sought refuge in town. Pinia Golfeld, who had been imprisoned in Pechera, told us he would walk 40 to 50 kilometers a day, from village to village in search of food. At one point he ran into someone on the road who suggested he could get help from the rebbe in Chechelnyk, Yosef Pinhasovich. The Jewish community in the ghetto of Chechelnyk had managed to bribe the gendarme in order to allow them greater freedoms, and had set up a system of mutual assistance within the ghetto, a situation similar to that which prevailed in Sharhorod.[45] Golfeld made it to Chechelnyk and received help from the rebbe: "At night they would pray and put out a plate to collect alms. . . . people prayed with him. Every day there was a minyan . . . he had a courtyard and a house and they would pray there," he told us.

Golfeld eventually left Chechelnyk and continued to flee, relying on help from Ukrainian peasants, Romanian gendarmes, and even German soldiers. He recounted to us how he once reached a house, from which he could smell the aroma of *varenikes*. A Polish Catholic priest answered the door and asked if he was a Jew. When he responded truthfully, the priest chastised him for killing Jesus, but then took him in and fed him: "The priest was also a good guy," Golfeld concluded. Later, Golfeld made it back to Tulchyn, where he endured the rest of the occupation in the ghetto. Sometime in the winter of 1942–1943, as the Battle of Stalingrad was deciding the future of the war some thousands of miles from Tulchyn, he became acquainted with a Russian-speaking German soldier who was passing through the town on his way to join the battle. The soldier gave Golfeld cookies and bread in exchange for washing his car. "Petia," the soldier confided, using the diminutive of Golfeld's name, "I am going to Stalingrad. I will be killed there." By this time, the war had already turned against the Germans, and the soldier knew his likely fate, as he traveled east to sacrifice himself in the battle. His kindness to the little Jewish boy may have been an early capitulation—an admission that the ideology for which he was fighting was depraved—or else it was just an all-too-rare moment of compassion.

Local Ukrainians sometimes also provided spiritual support. Yurkovetsky and Golfeld both remember one Christian, whom they called Misha the Russki (literally Misha Katsop), who smuggled a Torah scroll into Pechera for the Jewish inmates. Misha had lived in the Jewish quarter of Tulchyn prior to the war, spoke Yiddish, and was friendly with many of the Jews in the town. Yurkovetsky had been close to Misha's daughter before the war. Thanks to Misha's Torah scroll, the camp inmates were able to pray in a part of the building they called the synagogue. The influx of religious Romanian refugees also contributed to a spiritual revival among the Soviet Jews, who had been more distant from organized religious life. "There were people learned in Judaism who knew all types of things," explained Yurkovetsky, and these people would lead services in the camp.

Clearly, relations between Jews, Ukrainians, Romanians, and Germans were highly complex affairs in Transnistria, where the power structure was nebulous and constantly being negotiated and revised. Survivors tell many stories of Romanian gendarmes, Ukrainian peasants, and Jewish prisoners risking their own safety in order to protect life. That is how they survived. Those who did not survive have no such stories to tell.

We interviewed only people who chose to remain in Ukraine after the collapse of the Soviet Union. They likely have a greater affinity toward their Ukrainian neighbors than those who left and a more conciliatory attitude toward Ukraine than that held by many émigrés. These individuals may feel a need to justify their decision to remain in Ukraine and can do so by forgiving their neighbors for their wartime conduct, or by downplaying the callousness that surrounded them in favor of the individual acts of kindness that kept them alive. Memories and judgments of wartime conduct have been informed by half a century of postwar life.

"THEY CAME IN BIG CARS, WITH THE IRON CROSS"

Beginning in August 1942—once the typhus epidemic in Transnistria began to reside—the Germans started making incursions into Romanian-controlled Transnistria in order to seize individuals for labor.[46] A clause in the Tighina Treaty had allowed for the presence of German units on Romanian territory in order to perform special tasks. Most of those taken prisoner were put to work on the construction of the German supply thoroughfare that was being built to traverse Ukraine, particularly on the segment of the road between Haysyn and Nemyriv.

In total, about 15,000 Jews were deported from Transnistria into Reichs-kommissariat Ukraine between spring 1942 and early 1944, at least 4,800 of whom came from the Tulchyn district.[47] In Bershad, the Gestapo, which had established a unit in the city in the spring of 1943, took about 1,200 residents into the Reichskommissariat for work, where most perished.[48] In the Reichskommissariat, the Germans worked the prisoners to death on starvation rations, or shot them when they became too sick to continue laboring. In a final statement, toward the end of the occupation as the Red Army approached, the retreating Germans murdered many of those Jews who had survived the labor brigades and remained relatively strong.

About 2,500 prisoners from Pechera were seized for work in the Reichskommissariat. Pinia Golfeld remembered:

> In Pechera, the Germans would come and take people to work. Big cars came with the iron cross, with SS officers, and they would take women to work, men and women. . . . There were some mothers who had little children in their arms. They would rip the child from the mother's arms and throw it against a tree. They killed the child, and threw her [the mother] into the car and took her to work somewhere. She was taken to work, moving stones to build a road for the Germans.

Presler remembered how the Germans would conduct a selection, separating the healthy from the elderly and sick:

> Suddenly we see, the gate is opening, and a bunch of cars with SS officers wearing those emblems drive in. And they force us all out of the camp. Anybody who could make it got out; those who couldn't—the elderly—were immediately shot. There was such a shooting. . . . They forced everyone out of the camp. And there were large cars, and they set up a table with Germans on one side and Germans on the other. And we had to go in the path between them. The young and healthy were taken into the cars. The sick were thrown off to the other side.

According to several testimonies, the Romanian gendarmes guarding the camp sometimes sought to protect the inmates or at least the most vulnerable among them. Presler recalled one episode in which the Germans arrived in Pechera and started loading their trucks with prisoners: "Just then a Romanian brigade arrived. . . . The Romanians stood there with rifles and wouldn't let the German cars drive out. There was a

Romanian commandant with us, but the chief prefect was in Tulchyn. A bunch of Romanians came from Tulchyn. They began to talk, they began to fight. And the Germans drove out and left us behind."

"END THE BONDAGE! AND LET IT BE ENOUGH!"

Khayke Gvinter told us about one time in 1943 when a German punitive brigade crossed over in black trucks from the other side of the Bug, and massacred a group of Jews. She was among those shot and left for dead in a mass grave:

> I endured all the hardships. I was in the concentration camp. They killed everyone. But they didn't [shoot] me in the heart or head—I was lying like that [she shows how she was lying on her side]. They wounded me [she points at her shoulder and her lower back]. They killed men, women. Oy! There was this Max from Chernivtsi. As long as I live I won't forget him. The wife was pregnant and they stuck a knife in her, cut off her breast. The hands with fingers! And the child they choked with the cord. God—what I have seen! . . . She was pregnant, and had another child . . . a six-year-old boy. What a beautiful little boy, a pale boy. I can still see him before my eyes . . . he was shouting "Mama! Mama!" The German stabbed and ordered him to go. They gave him a candy or something. I remember! I saw it ! I ran away before they could kill me. I saw how they were laying them down. They were putting them down face first. They began to shoot from behind. They were running. From there they fell immediately into the grave. . . . Then they went to liquor it up in the forest. They went into the forest and they left behind some type of hole, a pit. Somebody—I don't know who, I don't know, I can't tell, maybe it was Jesus, Who knows?—But he gave me a hand. He pulled me out. And I came back to the camp. The gate, it was called the portal. And I was terrified. Blood was pouring from me. Oy. . . . It was in '43. It was when I was in Pechera.

She told us the story again on another occasion, this time adding the song she remembers Max singing, which has been seared into her memory:

> In the camp . . . there was this Max and he had a wife, a beautiful pale wife, a real beauty, and a child. They killed him [Max] first. They turned him around toward the grave, threw him into the grave and shot him. Then the wife began to shout: "Max! Max!" Then they killed her too. And

this little child, five years old with blue eyes, he stood before me—such a beautiful child. . . . "Mama! Mama! Where are they taking you? Mama!" And they turned his little head away and gave him a candy or something, I don't remember—I was a child. And they took him to his mother and killed him too. All three of them. But before that, he would sing this song—Max would. I will never forget it as long as I live. It goes like this:

Afn yidishn beys-oylem iz a shreklekher vint,
Dort lign di yidn azoy vi di hint.
Funem himl a blik,
Af di idelekh gib a kik,
Leshn shoyn op dos fayer,
Un loz shoyn zayn genig!

Vey adonoy,
Farvos shlogt undz der nyemets azoy?
Lesh shoyn op dos fayer,
Un loz shoyn zayn genig!

Altitshke yidn mit di grove berd,
Me hakt zey, me brakt zey, me varft zey tsu der erd.
Funem himl a blik,
Af dayne yidelekh gib a kik,
Lesh shoyn op dos fayer,
Un loz shoyn zayn genig.

Kleyntshike kinder fun der muters brist,
Me hakt zey, me brokt zey, me varft zey afn mist.

In a Jewish cemetery there is a terrible wind,
There the Jews lie like dogs.
From the heavens take a look,
Cast a glance at the little Jews:
Blow out the fire already,
And let it be enough!

Oh God,
Why do the Germans beat us like this?
Blow out the fire,
And let it be done!

Elderly Jews with gray beards,
They hack them, they break them, they throw them to the ground.
From the heavens take a look,
Cast a glance at your little Jews:

Blow out the fire already,
And let it be enough!

Little children taken from their mothers' breasts,
They hack them, they break them, they throw them in the rubbish.

She broke down in tears, unable to continue: "And this I lived through!"
she groaned, shaking her head. Gvinter preserved the song, as though
to hold onto the memory of Max and his family. She knew he would
have no other memorial. Gvinter's memory of that terrible episode is
embedded within this song, which she sang for us on two occasions.
Unable to fully articulate the trauma of the moment in words or in a
coherent narrative, Gvinter resorted to song to communicate her suffering, as though to distance herself from the moment. At the same time,
the tune is a mnemonic device transporting her back to that moment.
Her voice quivered and she broke down into tears when she sang it, each
time reliving the horror.

The song itself is derived from another Yiddish song from Bessarabia and Bukovina that laments the anti-Jewish atrocities committed
by Ukrainian brigands during the 1919–1921 pogroms. The song likely
entered Transnistria with the deportees, and was reworked to refer to
Nazi atrocities. Thus, Gvinter learned it from Max, the deportee from
Chernivtsi. In the earlier version, the singer alludes to *Eicha*, the biblical Lamentations, and includes the same refrain, begging the heavens
to "cast a glance" and "let it be enough" as well as several lines from the
verses, including "little children taken from their mother's breast" who
are "thrown in the rubbish," and "elderly Jews with gray bears," who are
"thrown to the ground." The crucial difference between the two versions,
though, is that the biblical references have been dropped. Gvinter does
not associate her song with *Eicha*, most likely because the biblical book
had no resonance for her, if indeed she had ever heard of it: she no longer
lives in a world in which daily events are measured in accordance with
biblical precedents and archetypes. Other versions of the song that were
recorded in Polish ghettos during the Second World War also include
verses about holy books being torn to pieces and synagogues turned
into stables, both of which are excised from Gvinter's variant. By the
time Nazi atrocities began in Pechera, the holy books had already been
forgotten and many of the synagogues had already been reallocated, if
not to horses, then to communists.[49]

"BUT THE FRONT CAME A LITTLE CLOSER,
SO THE GERMANS DIDN'T SUCCEED"

In early 1944, as the war began to turn in the east and the Red Army slowly rolled westward, liberating eastern Ukraine from occupation, the Romanians retreated from Vinnytsya Province, and the Germans retook control. Many of the specialized artisans who had survived in Tulchyn for most of the war were now forcibly relocated into the Pechera camp. Knowing the war was almost over, the Germans no longer needed their expertise.

Presler told us that during the final days of the occupation in Pechera, SS officers forced all of the camp's inmates inside the sanatorium building, and prohibited them from looking out the window or going toward the door on pain of death. She remembered hearing the Red Army airplanes flying overhead and worrying that the planes would bypass the camp, not realizing that it held prisoners. She told us that a Romanian Jewish inmate who was locked in the camp with them was able to convince a guard to undo the chains that locked the door. When the chains came off, all the prisoners went running out, dodging the soldiers' bullets. She hid underground where the water pipes were located, and waited for several days with some other prisoners. After a couple of days, a little boy who was hiding with them could no longer withstand the claustrophobia, and emerged from their hiding spot. When he surfaced, he saw that the camp had been abandoned except for some Red Army soldiers wandering about. The remaining prisoners emerged from their hiding spots, liberated as "living corpses." The soldiers brought them cookies and kasha.

In many towns, the Germans sought to destroy any evidence of their atrocities before retreating: the most obvious evidence was the testimony of survivors. In Tulchyn, as the Red Army approached in late January 1944, German soldiers surrounded the ghetto with the intention of executing the few remaining Jewish artisans. The Germans were forestalled, however, by the commander of the Romanian gendarme, Fetecau, who refused to allow such a bloodbath. The Red Army liberated Tulchyn on March 15, 1944. In Tomashpil, Nisen Kiselman told us, "When the Germans left to move on, they gathered the entire ghetto, to take them back to the field, to kill. But the front came a little closer, so the Germans didn't succeed."

Anna Tkach, who we interviewed in Yampil, told us that in 1944 the Red Army arrived at Chernivtsi, a town in southern Vinnytsya Province, across a bridge over the River Murafa from the villages of Moyivka and Babchyntsy. She remembered how the Soviet soldiers took revenge on one particular individual who had worked as an informant for the Germans. He had used the little Yiddish he knew and his connections with the Jewish community from before the war to gather information on Jewish resistance and pass it on to the German occupiers: "When the tanks came into Chernivtsi—I remember it was a Friday—he went running out with a bouquet to meet our soldiers, but they shot him immediately and threw him into the river." They knew, she explained, that he had been an informant.

The Germans returned to Bershad after the Romanians fled. Elizaveta Bershadskaia told us, "Before ours entered, the Germans were here and killed so many Jews. . . . they were here about a week and carried out a pogrom." Just before the Red Army arrived, the Germans captured a Jew who had been working for the underground assisting the partisans. Under torture, he revealed where a bottle had been hidden containing a list of the names of those who were active in the underground. The Germans gathered all those on the list together with their families and executed them in early February 1944.[50] As the Red Army grew closer, the Germans carried out additional massacres: among those executed were Eli Marchak, the *shoykhet*, as well Gedalya—who held the Torah in Kogan's song—and other members of the Jewish communal leadership. All the corpses were left under a bridge near the neighboring village of Balonivka. Several people we interviewed remembered seeing the bodies. Kogan told us: "After the Red Army liberated us, I went to look as well. Those who remained alive—the women and whoever else—made caskets, put the bodies in them, and buried them in the Jewish cemetery." These were the artisans whom the Germans had kept alive. After the war, there were no more artisans in Bershad.

Bershadskaia remembered how the Red Army—"ours"—arrived in Bershad: "The tanks came in—the tanks were already on the road—and everyone went running into the streets to meet them. . . . They were still bombing us, planes were flying." When Red Army soldiers liberated Bershad on March 14, 1944, they found approximately ten thousand people in the ghetto.[51]

—◊—

The final bombings and destruction that characterized the last days of the war destroyed much of the infrastructure that had managed to survive the years of occupation. The shtetls that were liberated by the Soviet army were very different from those they had left thirty-two months before: factories had been evacuated or destroyed, houses had been leveled by bombs, electrical networks had been disrupted, and power plants had been demolished. Most importantly, the population had been transformed: what had once been largely Jewish shtetls were now mostly Ukrainian villages.

The worst of the atrocities were over, but the people of the occupied territories—Jews and non-Jews alike—still had a momentous struggle ahead of them. The surviving Jews would begin a process of bereavement that continues to this day. But it was not just the Jews of the shtetl who had suffered during the occupation. Christians and Jews alike shared in the experience of destruction, and would have to work together to rebuild. Jewish residents would have to continue to live with the knowledge that many of their Ukrainian neighbors had stood by and allowed the Jews to be murdered, or had even actively participated in the killing. They sought justice, but knew that it would never come. Those who had survived with the help of Christian villagers knew they would live the rest of their lives in debt to their neighbors. Sometimes the extent of the slaughter made it impossible to repay the debt or even to extend a simple word of thanks. Khayke Gvinter confided that after it became safe to travel again, she left Bershad to find the Christian villager who had saved her from Pechera: "When the Soviets entered, I went with my mother to look for the non-Jewish woman who had saved me. They set fire to the village, Pechera, and her house burned down with everything. And they told us that she had burned to death. Varvara was her name."

—◊—

In many of the lands on which the atrocities themselves were committed, the Holocaust as an entity distinct from the war in which it took place is hardly recognized. Yiddish-speaking Jews in the small towns of Ukraine don't even have a word with which to express the common fate of Jews during the war. When discussing their lives under German occupation, those we have interviewed speak of *di shlekhte,* the bad times, or simply, *di milkhome,* the war. When they speak of massacres and atrocities, they call them *pogroms,* invoking the Russian term for "riot" that had been used to describe anti-Jewish violence in that part of Europe for hundreds of years. The violence they lived through, therefore, is terminologically equated with the same type of violence that their parents and grandparents had survived. The absence of a word to denote collectively the atrocities experienced by Jews during the war is not simply a semantic idiosyncrasy, but is rather part of a broader aspect of how the war is remembered by Jews in the shtetls of the former Soviet Union.

Many elderly Jews in small-town Ukraine, who have not been exposed to the postwar explosion of Holocaust representations in the West or to the more recent rediscovery of the Holocaust among young students and survivors in the larger cities of Eastern Europe, view themselves primarily as survivors—or even victors—of the "Great Patriotic War." For much of the postwar Soviet generation, the Second World War was marked in very specific ways, what historian Nina Tumarkin has called "nothing less than a full-blown cult."[52] But the cult of the Great Patriotic War was radically different than remembrance of the Second World War outside of the Soviet Union, as evidenced not least by the specific names ascribed to the war. Soviet-era historians portrayed the Great Patriotic War as an ideological battle between fascism and communism, a heroic and united struggle of Soviet peoples of all nationalities acting under the unwavering leadership of Joseph Stalin and the Communist Party. The military leadership's tragic unpreparedness for war along with its disastrous military decisions that needlessly sacrificed hundreds of thousands, if not millions, of soldiers to protect strategically insignificant territory, and the collaboration of many Soviet citizens with the German invaders were repressed in the 1950s. Official Soviet histories discussed Nazi crimes against civilians, but glossed over—and at times deliberately denied—the specific German policy of systematic mass murder of the Jewish people. The Soviet refusal to acknowledge the racial dimensions of the war helped detract attention away from the issue of local collaboration, which in turn helped bring about a sense of normalcy—if not reconciliation—in the aftermath of the war. The government did not want returning Jews to be in conflict with their Ukrainian neighbors who may have collaborated with the enemy or stood idly by. The myth that all people suffered equally mitigated the competing claims of victimhood that would have made reconciliation difficult. At the same time, though, it created a false history and prevented victims and survivors from making sense of their experiences.

In the years that followed the war, any attempt to highlight the suffering of one particular ethnic group over another was branded as national chauvinism, a crime that could result in imprisonment, exile to Siberia, or even a death sentence.[53] Thus, despite the fact that in most of the Soviet Union the Holocaust took place in plain sight, memory of the event has only recently become a part of public discourse. Behind the Iron Curtain, few had access to the standard narrative of the Holocaust that so permeates Israeli, Western European, and American culture; books, poems, and films that dealt with the war were sanitized of the unique Jewish experience. Remembrance was often restricted to the private domain. In some towns, like Tulchyn, groups of Jewish survivors would meet, share their experiences, and bond over their common fate. In other towns, like Korsun-Shevchenkivskyy, the director of the Jewish community told us that it was only after the fall of the Soviet Union that a group of Jews met to plan a memorial museum and realized that it was the first time they had been in a room together since before the war. The lack of a public discourse about the fate of Jews meant that there was a great deal of regional variation in modes of remembrance. Many of those residing in provincial small towns do not embed their stories of survival within the context of the Holocaust, but rather Soviet survivors can integrate their memories into the wider Soviet narrative of "The Great Patriotic War."

9

A Kind of Victory

Throughout March 1944, the Red Army slowly inched westward across Ukraine, liberating the lands of Vinnytsya Province from German occupation. In Transnistria, Soviet soldiers found pockets of surviving Jewish communities: they liberated 12,000 indigenous Jews and another 40,000 Romanian Jews who had been deported to the region from their homes.[1] In the Reichskommissariat the Red Army found no intact Jewish communities; there were only individuals who had managed to survive the occupation in hiding, usually in isolation.

The occupation was over, but the war was not. Young men throughout the region were immediately drafted into the military, scooped up by the war machine, and joined the historic journey westward toward Berlin. They would end the war not as victims, but as victors. "As soon as the Red Army came, they took me. I was only seventeen years old," recalled Yosl Kogan of his liberation. "They took me to the draft office and asked: 'Were you under occupation?' I answered, 'Yes, I was under occupation.' So they took me to the draft office and the Reds enlisted me in military training." After a truncated training in Rzhev, some 1,200 kilometers to the east, Kogan was placed in the first reserve rifle regiment and sent into the bloodiest front in human history.

Kogan's own narrative of his journey to Berlin is framed as a story of peripeteia, a sudden reversal of fortune, from what seemed like certain death to a spectacular victory. Kogan, who had briefly been imprisoned in Pechera, escaped, weakened, with swollen legs, and near death, back to Bershad, where he hid from the Romanian gendarmes in a chimney. In his telling, he emerged from his hiding spot to join the Red Army and fight all the way to Berlin, where he was able to inscribe his name on the Reichstag as a victor. Like his songs, which always end with a glimmer of hope, Kogan framed his own life as a journey from victimhood to victory, a realization of the optimism promised in his song:

> I went inside a chimney, where I could hardly breathe. I almost suffocated there. I had to hold my nose. At night, I would go out because my nose was bleeding. . . . When my mother, may she rest in peace, was already gone, I went to a non-Jewish woman. The woman took me in and I went up to the attic. And I spent a week lying in the attic. They couldn't give me any food. Telling you about such things, I can't fully describe to you what I lived through. And afterwards, the Red Army came and drafted me into the army. At the age of seventeen, I was off and in the army for seven years. I served at the front for two months. I went all the way to Berlin.

The peripeteia, though, does not end here. Kogan even frames his moment of victory as a struggle for survival ending in triumph. As the Soviet troops celebrated their victory outside the Reichstag, a sniper began firing on them from above. "I can tell you about an episode I lived through: upon arriving in Berlin, there was someone up on the fifth or sixth floor of a high building. Berlin was burning. He cried: 'Surrender, Russian! Down with the Jews!' How could anyone surrender to them? And he began to shoot. He killed so many people. Such terror." The Red Army soldiers, Kogan bitterly revealed on another occasion, "dropped like flies."

> He started to fire and he shot, perhaps, fifty people. They started to fall, perhaps fifty or sixty people. And this was victory? We had to fight for every house. I looked over at a cinema, and there on the fourth floor was a sniper. He wanted to kill me. I ducked, and the bullet flew right past me. Then they took the entire building. They flooded it with water.

Many of our soldiers were drowned in the bunkers. It was May '45. They were shouting, "Victory!" They were already shouting "Victory!" But what kind of victory was it? Victory. It wasn't yet victory; they only said it was. I remember there was a second soldier, a little soldier, holding up a red flag. They had already raised it. It was already over. We had won.

Lev Kolodenker was also in Berlin during the liberation. He had been drafted from Tulchyn in the first days of the war and was put in charge of seven soldiers, with whom he helped liberate "all of Western Ukraine" as well as Poland. "I took Berlin. The Reichstag was right next to me," he proudly declared. The military, which largely privileged skill over social status, provided unprecedented opportunities for the advancement of poor Jews from the shtetl.

Those who had served in the military before the war were drafted immediately without additional training and were sent to the front, if not as fighters, then at least as auxiliary staff. Moyshe Kupershmidt arrived in the Mohyliv-Podilskyy ghetto just days before it was liberated: "It was my luck that I had already served in the army," he told us. Kupershmidt, who only months before was forced to dig what was supposed to have been his own grave as German soldiers mocked him, was now drafted at the Red Army's field office as a driver. Nisen Yurkovetsky, who had already served in the Black Sea Fleet in Odessa, where he had defended the city in the early days of the war before being injured and ending up in Pechera, was also drafted as a chauffeur; he traveled with his unit through Bucharest, Budapest, Prague, and Vienna. Like many Red Army soldiers exposed to the West for the first time during the Soviet campaigns, Yurkovetsky was impressed with what he naively regarded as the West's ability to keep up with the cultural developments of the Soviet Union: "In Vienna, there was an opera house. It felt just like being in Odessa!" he told us. Yurkovetsky soon realized though that "They lived better than us. They were wealthier than us. The people were cultured."

For those who had grown up in places like Bershad or Tulchyn, where they were surrounded predominantly by other Jews, the military provided an introduction to non-Jewish life and served as a force of assimilation: "In the army, they filled my head with Russian," remarked Kogan, "You didn't hear one word in Yiddish. There were a number of Jews in the army, but they would speak Russian." Many Jewish veterans have memories of the Second World War that are so intertwined with the

Isaak Vaisman of Berdichev served in an elite military
intelligence unit during the Second World War.

mythology of the "Great Patriotic War" that they have trouble asserting their wartime stories in the Yiddish that flows so naturally when they discuss the prewar period. In many interviews, our interviewees switch seamlessly into Russian when the topic of the war comes up. Sometimes they utilize Russian root words, which they Yiddishize in describing how they fought. "Ikh hob zashchishchaet Stalingrad" (I defended Stalingrad) says one proudly, combining the Yiddish and Russian. The war, for many Jewish Red Army veterans, was a Russian experience, not a Jewish one.

There are few indications that the army was overtly antisemitic during the height of the war. Sime Geller summarized a sentiment that many felt: "During the war, there was less antisemitism than today. If antisemitism during the war had been as strong as today, not a single Jew would have survived," she asserted. Jewish soldiers earned medals in numbers disproportionately higher than their overall percentage of the population and were promoted to senior officer at a higher rate than that of the general population. A recent study of 220 Soviet Jewish veterans found that only 16 experienced any overt antisemitism. Individual Jews also served in highly visible positions within the military throughout the war, including Lieutenant Colonel Leonid Vinokur, who, as second in command of the 38th Brigade of the 64th Army, accepted the surrender of Friedrich Paulus and the German 6th Army at Stalingrad. Another highly visible Jew was David Ortenberg, who served as editor in chief of the influential military newspaper *Red Star,* at least until his abrupt dismissal in July 1943, a change of fortune that heralded the beginning of discrimination against Jews in the military. Many people we spoke with recalled antisemitism in the army after the war, but those who served during the war, served with pride as Jews.[2]

"I CUT THEM TO PIECES"

In a familiar scene to anybody who has interviewed survivors of the Holocaust, Alexei Futiran, who standing at his full height of 4' 10" filled his Tomashpil home with energy, pulled up his sleeve during our interview to show us the tattoo that will forever remind him of those terrible days. But Futiran's tattoo is not the iconic number that scars so many survivors' flesh, reminding them of their prisoner status in the extermination camps. Rather, his tattoo, crudely engraved on his arm by his comrades-in-arms, spells his name—Alexei: "During the war, before battle," he explained, the soldiers tattooed their names on each other, "in case we were killed, so that our name would be known." The tattoo, which has become to many Holocaust survivors a representation of dehumanization and atomization, from a time in which the Nazis tried to reduce them to a number, is instead for Futiran a potent and proud declaration of his valor in battle fighting the Nazis. It is a powerful symbol of how the war is remembered by the many Jews who fought in the Red Army.

Despite the role of the army as a force of integration, many Jews had their Jewish identity strengthened in service. Even as a loyal communist, Avrom Furer, who commanded an anti-aircraft unit, made a clear distinction between those serving with him who were Jewish and those who weren't: "A lot of Jews served with me. There were thirty-six comrades who served with me, and eight of them were Jewish: Misha Pinyok, Zaltsman, Comrad Shuk, Furman, and my commander Kotlik; there were several Jews. Of the six Jewish comrades who went with us, only three remained of the Jews. And of the thirty-six, perhaps eleven remained. The rest fell. That was the war." Jewish soldiers knew that they were fighting for much more than just territory or ideology; those who were drafted after the occupation had witnessed first-hand the atrocities the Germans committed against innocent Jews. They recognized that defeat at the hands of the Germans would mean certain death for themselves and any surviving family members. They had seen their loved ones murdered and had been forced to endure the horrors of the ghettos and camps. Even those who had not been under occupation, but joined the military in the first weeks of the war or from points of evacuation, still heard of the fate of those left behind. Jewish soldiers knew what their fate would be if the Red Army lost the war.

As the war turned in the Soviets' favor and the Red Army became more confident of eventual victory, Jews also started to demand vengeance. Chaim Skoblitsky of Berdichev put it best to us when he told us: "The Germans killed my mother, my father and [my little brother] Motele. But I reckoned with them. I killed more of them than they killed of mine. I cut them to pieces." A diary collected by the Blavatnik Archive Foundation records a Jewish soldier whom the diarist encountered; the soldier, too, spoke of revenge: "We drank their blood. I got plenty of revenge for my family," he tells the diarist after explaining how the Germans murdered thirty-five members of his family.[3] Many Jews were motivated not only by patriotism, but also by revenge. After testifying in disturbing detail to a wrenching experience fighting with the Red Army, Aba Kaviner summed up the war: "It was difficult, bitter, desolate, and dark." He paused for a few seconds before taking a deep breath and continuing in a somber and decisive tone, "but we beat them." This theme was echoed and reinforced by Yiddish-language newspapers and political speeches, which urged Jews to fight for vengeance. The famed war correspondent, Ilya Ehrenburg, who came to identify more and more with his Jewish roots throughout the war, famously wrote articles screaming for vengeance to motivate the troops: "We will die, but we will destroy the hated butchers," he vowed in one article.[4]

Many believed that the war had cleansed the world of oppression, and that the postwar period would usher in a new world of tolerance. It was an era of great optimism. Like all Soviet citizens, the Jews of the Soviet Union were exalted at the victory and shared in the general euphoria that defined the immediate postwar period. Avrom Furer served seven years in the military before being demobilized in 1947: "After the war, I was already a communist. In the army, I was accepted as a communist," he explained when asked what kind of work he did after the war. This feeling was replicated among the survivors in the shtetls: "If it weren't for Stalin, I wouldn't be alive," mused Elizaveta Bershadskaia in her interview with the Shoah Foundation. "I was upset," she said of her reaction to Stalin's death in 1953, "because Stalin won the war."

At least initially, the Jews of the shtetl came out of the war convinced that the Soviet Union was capable of greatness. They had fought hard for their victory, overcome enormous obstacles, and witnessed unimaginable atrocities. They imagined now that the Soviet state they so valiantly defended would reward them for their service. But Soviet veterans, Jewish and non-Jewish alike, were disappointed: the benefits they expected to be bestowed upon them for defending the country in its time of need were not forthcoming. They received orders, medals, and the gratitude of a nation, but were then sent on their way. At least in the immediate postwar period, as the state struggled to bring itself to its feet again by fostering its youth, returning veterans were largely neglected.[5]

Jewish veterans fared even worse than their non-Jewish comrades-in-arms. Whereas other returning veterans could, albeit with great difficulty, reintegrate themselves into their families and prewar communities, Jewish veterans returned to find that their families had been killed. There were few communities left in their hometowns to welcome them. Most had discovered the fate of their families while they were fighting. The few who retained some semblance of hope were crestfallen when they found their prewar homes empty, leveled by the bombing, or inhabited by Christian neighbors. They had been sustained at the front by the thought of eventually walking through the door to the embrace of their loved ones, a reward bestowed upon returning soldiers the world over since antiquity. But this time, there were few spouses, children, or parents eagerly awaiting. "When I returned home, I couldn't find anybody I knew," David Furman told us of his return to Berdichev after heroically fighting at Stalingrad and Kalinin (Tver). Decorated veterans, particularly those who were members of the Party, were given favorable treatment upon their return, but their struggle forward was still great. Avrom Furer was lucky: "Since I was a communist they provided me with a [job in a] shop." This gave Furer access to foodstuffs, a luxury in the postwar environment. The shop grew, and he eventually became the manager of the store.

With no home to return to, many Jews simply remained in the military. Jews were more likely than other nationalities to continue their service after the war as a career choice, both because of the heightened sense of patriotism the war instilled in them, and because upon returning home, they found that they had few other options. Their prewar community and support system had been destroyed, and many found that the only community they now had was the military.[6] Alexei Futiran, for instance, was drafted in 1943 and remained in the military until 1950.

Some veterans had their faith in God fortified: Tsolik Groysman explained, "My parents believed in God, but us youngsters were Pioneers and members of Komsomol. But when I was injured during the war, I started to believe in God." Groysman can only attribute his survival to divine intervention:

I will tell you why. We had to attack. As we moved forward, 50 or 60 meters toward the village, we all had to lie down. There was such heavy shooting where we were that we couldn't even lift our heads. They started to yell "Forward!" and we got up to attack. That's when the tanks started coming at us. The tanks were approaching one after another every 5 meters. . . . They started to scream that everybody should save themselves however they can. We simply ran and the tanks followed us. . . . The tanks passed and it became quiet. There was this tank that would start to follow me, I was running and the tank followed me. . . . I threw myself to the ground and spread out my arms as though I had been killed. I stood up, and didn't understand how I was still standing on the ground. The tanks had crushed everyone and I was still standing.

Approximately 500,000 Jews served in the Red Army during the war. Only 300,000 of those who served survived to bear witness.[7]

"I DIDN'T HAVE A HOUSE; I DIDN'T HAVE ANYWHERE TO SLEEP"

In addition to soldiers returning from battle and Holocaust survivors returning from hiding or camps, evacuees began to return from the east. Although we don't have specific numbers for those who returned from evacuation, it has been estimated that a "large majority" of evacuees returned to their previous place of residence.[8] The return was arduous both physically and bureaucratically. Demobilized soldiers shared the hardships of return with those returning from evacuation, many of whom had to fight for seats on the few trains heading west.[9] When they returned home, they found that housing was scarce; entire housing blocs had been bombed into ruins, and retreating Germans had employed a scorched earth policy, destroying buildings as well as sewage and water systems, along with other essential urban infrastructure in their flight.[10] Local officials were having difficulty providing basic shelter to those who had remained under occupation and were in no position to accommodate an influx of new homeless people. Factories that had been evacuated feared the loss of their workforce as workers dispersed to their hometowns, leaving abandoned industrial plants in Tashkent. In an effort to stem the tide of people seeking to return to recently liberated cities and towns, larger cities, with the support of the State Defense Committee, began to restrict the number of people permitted to return.[11] It was particularly difficult for Jews to return. Although no official decree has been identified that discriminated against Jewish returnees, anecdotal evidence strongly suggests that numerous officials made it difficult for Jewish evacuees, particularly those who held leading intellectual positions, to return to their hometowns.[12]

Upon returning home, whether from evacuation, the army, a ghetto, or a camp, the first challenge that met most returnees was simply finding shelter. Many returned to find only ruins where their houses had once stood. Those whose houses had been spared the bombs, found that in their absence their homes had been occupied by neighbors or others in search of shelter. Invariably, their property had been plundered. Those who remained in town, Jew and non-Jew alike, had assumed that the evacuees would never return and that their property was available on a first-come, first-served basis. The law was ambiguous on ownership rights, as a 1937 edict had deprived those absent for more than six months of any claims to abandoned residences. City officials had no means of determining which of the evacuated families were ever going to return, and so assigned abandoned houses to newcomers in need of shelter. If the prewar owners returned, their claims of ownership conflicted with those of the newer residents who had been allocated the property by civil authorities.[13] Frida Pecherskaia told us, "When I returned to Bratslav after the war I didn't have a house. I didn't have anywhere to sleep. I stayed with a non-Jew and carried water for him and did his laundry. I was only sixteen years old. I couldn't work because you had to be eighteen to work." Donia Presler returned to Tulchyn after her liberation from Pechera: "Our house had been destroyed. We didn't have anywhere to go. Where the ghetto had been, there were two broken-down houses [and we moved into them], because in my mother's brother's house—it was a good house—Christians were living." Her family appealed to the authorities, but the city council told them that they should return to her uncle's house. When they tried to reclaim her uncle's house, the non-Jews occupying it refused to leave. A fight ensued, during which her mother was beaten. In the end they moved into her uncle's house: "it had no windows, no doors, no roof." They fixed it up and lived there for two or three years, until her cousin, her uncle's son whom they thought was dead, returned asking for the house back. Her mother summoned witnesses to testify to how much improvement they had made to the house and how much they had invested in it. In the end, her cousin obtained the house and offered to rent them a room.

Alexei Futiran recalled that during the war he encountered a fortune-teller, "a Gypsy" in his words, who prophesized that when he returned to his home, he would find his house burned to the ground with only a single wall standing. She was right. Futiran continued in tears: he returned home to Tomashpil to find his house burned down except for a single wall. He moved in with his parents and rebuilt his life. Although he had worked as a carpenter before the war, he now trained as a leather-worker in order to work in his new father-in-law's artel. As was often the case, he was able to secure a position there through familial connections. Sofia Palatnikova was liberated from Bershad, but returned to Teplyk soon thereafter to find her house completely ransacked: "Our house was in ruins, it was an empty house. The non-Jews came and brought food, a pillow, a bed, and dishes. My father had good non-Jewish friends."

Some were able to reclaim their belongings with little effort. Elizaveta Bershadskaia told us she had little difficulty returning to her home in Bershad; the non-Jews who had moved in during the war simply left when the occupation ended: "Non-Jews were living there, but when ours [the Soviet authorities] returned, they left on their own. They understood how it would end." She told us the house was still standing, but was in need of repairs: "We made a little renovation. It's better than living among strangers." Nekha Vainer-Shpak also returned to her native Zh-merynka after the war and found Ukrainians living in her apartment. She moved in with a neighbor in the same courtyard, and later returned with the neighbor and her husband to reclaim her prewar residence.

There were new faces in cities and towns as well, as individuals unable to return to their own homes settled in with their new spouses or wherever they could get a job. Klara Vaynman was born in Vinnytsya, but had been brought up in Lviv before the war. She evacuated during the war to Samara (Kuibyshev), and sought to return to Lviv as soon as the hostilities ended. However, since her birthplace was recorded as Vinnytsya, she was only permitted to travel that far: "They wouldn't let us go further. Only as far as Vinnytsya. Since the Germans had already left, we wanted to go to Lviv because there we had a house and everything. But they wouldn't let us. Since I was born in Vinnytsya we could go only to Vinnytsya. And then when it became possible to go further, we didn't." She explained that the rumors of antisemitism in western Ukraine convinced her mother that they would be better off abandoning their home and starting a new life in the Vinnytsya region: "My mother had written there and received an answer that our house was intact and everything was there, but that in Lviv, there were many bandits—Banderists—perhaps you've heard of them. They would kill Jews and cut off their heads. I didn't have a father and I was a small child, so my mother was afraid." She considered some of the difficulties of starting a new life:

My mother came to Vinnytsya, but there was nowhere to live, no one knew us. Nothing. She needed to get work until we could go to Lviv. She had a little child and she was alone with nowhere to live. They told her there was a shtetl, Bar: "Go there! They need to set up a kindergarten. There is nothing there. Go there for a while, get children and go to work, and then when you get a pass to Lviv, you can leave." So my mother went there and there was a sugar factory. There were several sugar factories. We went there and said we had been sent from Vinnytsya and the director said, "Good." . . . So she worked there, got married, and we ended up staying in Bar.

Rather than return to his native Sobolivka, where his entire family had been killed and no community remained, Arkadii Burshtein moved to Haysyn. His father had been a tailor in Sobolivka, and Burshtein became chief engineer of the garment factory in Haysyn. Occupational skills were still largely passed down from generation to generation, but after the war the youth needed to adapt to the new way of life in the postwar industrialized Soviet towns.

Dovid Geller returned from evacuation in Baku to Zhmerynka, where he lived with his aunts for a few years. He moved to Kiev in 1947 to continue his training as a lathe operator. However, he was drafted into the military in 1950, and served for three years in Vladivostok. When he finally returned to Zhmerynka again, now five years after the end of the war, he found that there was no life for him in the city; he left instead for Bratslav, where he moved in with his brother.

Numerous Jews and non-Jews alike were on the move after the war, seeking a means of building a new life. Many Jews who survived in evacuation or the military never even returned to their hometowns, settling instead in Moscow or St. Petersburg. Others sought to make a new life for themselves in urban metropolises closer to home: about 110,000 Jews arrived in Kiev between November 1943 and January 1946, many of whom were newcomers to the city.[14]

"WE CAME BACK FROM THE EVACUATION SO POOR"

Even for those who managed to acquire their former houses with little struggle, the first few years after liberation were difficult. Bershadskaia remembered that "when ours [the Red Army] entered there was nothing at all. There was a hunger." She had to buy soap and powder in town and go out into the villages to trade these items for food. Since the bridges had been destroyed, she would cross the river to neighboring villages on a barge. Evgeniia Kozak also remembered the poverty of the postwar period:

> When we first came after the war, we were very poor. They suggested that they would give us some charity to get us through the holidays. You know what that is? So, my mother came home and said, "No, it would be an indignity." And we didn't want to take it. We came back from the evacuation so poor, naked, and barefoot . . . we went to synagogue. It was Yom Kippur then and they had collected money for us. They wanted to give it to us. But we didn't want to take it.

But charity was an important means of sustaining the community and providing for the sustenance of its members. Groysman told us: "After the war, we, the injured, came back individually. Widows would come . . . older children whose parents were killed would come. We would collect money. We would collect the money in a way that nobody knew whose money it was. They would give, and we wouldn't say who the donor was. Not everybody was in the same situation. There were people in our midst who starved to death. They wouldn't want anyone to know that they needed money." But along with the feeling of community came competition among the victims over who had suffered most, feelings that persist to this day. Donia Presler complained in her interview with the Shoah Foundation that the specialized artisans who remained in the Tulchyn ghetto "didn't suffer like we did. They lived just like they live now." In Haysyn, Arkadii Burshtein, who survived a genocidal massacre in the Reichskommissariat, belittled the experiences of those who survived in Transnistrian towns: "In Bershad nobody was bothered. Whoever died there, died of hunger, and the rest lived."

The year 1946–1947 was the most dire—just as the long process of rebuilding got underway, the region was plagued with a devastating harvest that combined with counter-productive government procurement demands to create an all-out famine. Brukhe Feldman returned to Bershad after the war, and remembered the famine most of all, as her family was forced to seek sustenance in a soup kitchen:

I still remember the hunger on October Street, where I lived with my mother. There was a woman who used to make borsht. She would give me the rinds of the beets and potato peels. It was a little. I used to cook. My mother used to cook the rinds with anything. She used to cook it up and that's how we ate. And we lived through it. And I remembered also that there was some type of canteen. They would give us some type of token, I remember. I went myself. I used to take a jug of borsht with a little bread, black bread. There was no white bread. Black bread. With this we had a dinner. I would sit with my mother and we would eat it up.

Yurkovetsky, still working as a driver, used to transport food supplies, mostly booze, in his American Studebaker during the 1947 famine. The end of wartime rationing in 1947 did little to alleviate the demand for food, and, in fact, made foodstuffs less accessible to the poor of the provinces.[15]

"AND THE *GOYIM* SAY THAT JEWS DIDN'T FIGHT!"

Returning evacuees were often met with antisemitism.[16] The influence of years of Nazi propaganda in the occupied territories was palpable, and was seen in the unleashing of latent anti-Jewish sentiments that had been repressed in the interwar Soviet Union, and the invention of new forms of racial hatred that had been largely foreign to the region. Even those who neglected to buy into Nazi antisemitism still resented the Jews, believing that they were at least partially responsible for bringing the wrath of the Germans upon the territory. Anti-Jewish sentiments were further exacerbated by the common misperception that the Jews had been protected from the worst atrocities, a notion that many spread maliciously. Many were simply ignorant—or in denial—of the existence of camps, ghettos, and mass killing sites. Christian townspeople had endured immense suffering during the war, and simply knew that the Jews had not been around. The Jews, they contended, had abandoned the town during the occupation when the going got tough. Many refused to believe the reports of mass killing sites, finding more credible the rumors that the Jews had fled the front for Tashkent, where they had lived in the relative safety of evacuation, leaving the Christian townspeople to the mercy of the Germans. As they saw Jewish evacuees begin to return to town after the war, they believed their suspicions were confirmed. Many chose not to ponder where the rest of the Jews had gone.

Anti-Jewish hostility was further exacerbated when the returning Jews sought to reclaim their property and real estate. Those residents who had looted "abandoned" Jewish property during the war came to resent the returning former owners. Even those who had innocently benefited materially from the Jewish absence, believing in fairness that the property was freely available for the taking, came to begrudge the new claimants, seeing the Jews' return as a reproach to their own wartime conduct.[17] The theme of anti-Jewish sentiment was probably best summarized by the Ukrainian writer Ostap Vishnia, who published a story in the newspaper *Radianska Ukraina* (Soviet Ukraine) which contained the line "It was already clear to a certain extent, who fought at the front, and who in Ferghana and Tashkent, who returned as rebuilders and restorers, and who to trade in beer and soft drinks and win back apartments."[18]

The accusations that Jews sat out the war in Tashkent continue to haunt Jewish veterans to this day. After concluding his story of the liberation of Berlin, Kogan mused acerbically, "and the *goyim* say that Jews didn't fight. *Vey, vey, vey, vey!*" David Soyfer, who reenlisted in the military in 1950 after having served during the war, told us how things had changed during his second stint in the service: "They ridiculed Jews. They wouldn't beat us, but they would make fun of Jews, saying, 'A Jew can't be in the military,' 'a Jew can't serve.' That's how it was." He later added, "There were antisemitic officers; it wasn't just the soldiers."

Indeed, sporadic reports of antisemitic incidents became all too common over the summer and fall of 1945, as Jewish residents began to trickle back from evacuation, to come out of hiding, or to return from their military service. In Kiev, an anti-Jewish riot erupted in September 1945. On September 4th, Lieutenant Joseph Rozenshtyen, an elderly NKVD officer of Jewish background, was taunted and beaten by two drunken soldiers, who called him by the derogatory term for a Jew, a "Zhid," and a "Tashkent rebel," as he returned to his apartment from the bakery dressed in civilian clothes. Rozenshteyn noticed which apartment the two aggressors ducked into, and returned later with a pistol, allegedly with the intention of forcing the two to turn themselves in to the police. After an altercation inside the apartment, though, Rozenshteyn shot the two soldiers, killing them both. At the funeral three days later, about three hundred people gathered to accompany the caskets from the hospital to the cemetery. According to the police report, at the corner of Shevchenko and Pushkin streets, two participants in the procession "inflicted blows upon two citizens of Jewish nationality, walking towards the funeral procession." As the procession passed the Galitsky bazaar, "a group of individuals inflicted blows upon a clerk." The mob continued marching through the streets for several hours, attacking Jews along the way and shouting antisemitic remarks. Three dozen people ended up in the hospital and five were killed. Rozenshteyn was sentenced to death by a military tribunal on October 1st.[19] Interestingly, one of the soldiers was at the time of the attack living with his mother in an apartment that had belonged to a Jewish family before the war.[20] The Kiev riot was particularly blatant, but was just one of numerous documented cases of violence and intimidation perpetrated against returning Jews.[21]

As a result of attacks like this, combined with a more subtle discrimination against Jews, many became ashamed of their Jewishness and tried to camouflage it, usually by changing their names. Raisa Rusakovskaia confided: "After the war there were fewer Jews. . . . At work I had to work among non-Jews and among Jews. For instance, after the war I worked in a bank and there was only one Jew in the bank and the rest were non-Jews, and I had to mix in with them. I said I was Raisa Isaakovna, not Rukhl. I stopped being Rukhl Isaakovna, but Raisa because they were all Russian." In her interview with the Shoah Foundation, Asya Barshteyn also spoke about how all of her family members changed their names after the war—Asya herself abandoned the more Jewish sounding Ite for Asya, and her sister changed her name from Khone to Anya. Her father, she explained, also changed his name from Kolman to Konstantin so that his daughters could change their patronymics from Kolmanovna to Konstantinovna. In each case, they needed to pay the passport officials and use their influence with friends to have the record changed officially. Donia Presler told us that when she returned, the Christians of the city had already become hostile to the Jews—"people had already begun to say 'Sarochke, Abramchik' [derogatory terms for Jewish women and men]. And to this day, they don't like Jews."

In addition to changing their names, many consciously chose not to speak Yiddish any longer in public, so as not to stand out obviously as

Jews. Arkadii Burshtein told us that when he returned to Haysyn after the war,

> There were about one thousand Jews more or less who came back to Haysyn from evacuation, and they did speak Yiddish. We were ashamed to speak Yiddish. You understand, we were ashamed to speak Yiddish in the street and in the shop. But among ourselves—I worked with another Jew who was two years older than me—we always spoke Yiddish, but we made sure that nobody heard us.

Many responded to the climate of unspoken antisemitism that surrounded them by becoming embarrassed and even ashamed of being seen as Jews. Others saw it as just part of being Jewish. Aba Kaviner waxed philosophically about the persistence of antisemitism: "Antisemitism there was, there is, and there will be. As long as there is a Jew, there will be antisemitism [*antisemitizm iz geven, un s'iz do, un se vet zayn. Biz vanet se vet zayn a yid, vet zayn antisemitizm*]." Kaviner, who had received a deep Jewish education, was likely paraphrasing the Adon Olam prayer's invocation of God: "He was and He is and He will be." The replacement of God with antisemitism can be seen as an sardonic aspersion on Jewish life in postwar Ukraine.

"IT WAS DIFFICULT, BUT I DID REBUILD"

In the late 1940s, the Yiddish newspaper *Eynikayt* (Unity) was full of stories about the revival of life in the postwar shtetls of Ukraine. Although none of these articles explicitly mentioned the fate of the murdered Jews, they framed their story of communal rebuilding around a narrative of resurrection. One article about Bershad introduced Dr. Moyshe Hofman and the pharmacist Rafail Furman: "If you walk into the Bershad regional pharmacy, you would hardly believe that during the German–Romanian occupation this bright spacious building was a ghetto hospital where tens of thousands of people perished from the typhus epidemic. . . . On the streets of Bershad one sees step by step a revival and improvement: new artels are opening, and there are other undertakings, workshops, and tea houses. You encounter old artisans and young apprentices."[22]

Another article celebrated one local man, who valiantly rose to heroism when duty called: "Before the war he was a porter. When the German fascists attacked the Soviet Union, he went to the front. He can tell a lot of stories about the atrocious war days: about the destruction of the Romanian forces in the village of Banderovke, about the battle in the environs of Zhmerynka and Shpykiv. He fought for victory. Now he builds. He was the first chairman of the Bershad city soviet, immediately after the liberation of the city." The paper also lionized simple working folk: "The artel members speak with a special attention about the sixty-four-year-old tailor, Chaim Sikor, a father of two partisan daughters who participated in the underground movement in Bershad under the Romanian occupation. Both of them died a heroic death." Another article concluded by pointing to the success of Bershad's revival:

> The years of the Romanian occupation remain in everyone's memory as a terrible nightmare. But the shtetl did not remain silent—it fought. Hundreds of Bershad men and women fought at the front and those who remained in the shtetl actively participated in partisan brigades. After its liberation, the shtetl again began to come into its own. People returned from the front and began to rebuild life in the city soviet, in the artels, in the pharmacy and hospital, in the schools—everywhere you meet people in overcoats, yesterday's warriors, today's happy builders. . . . Bershad is now a shtetl of workers and artisans, a shtetl with an entire intelligentsia. Aside from the aforementioned artels, in which the majority of the population works, there are many inhabitants who participate in state undertakings—in the furniture factory, in the mill, in the oil factory, in the sugar factory.[23]

In an article in *Eynikayt* in December 1946, Hershl Polyanker featured the story of Avrom Gorshteyn, who was born in Litin and was seventeen when the war started. He had wanted to learn a trade, but ended up as a soldier. When he returned to Litin after the war "with a military order of bravery shining on his breast and a medal for courage and several other honors, earned in battle," he discovered the city destroyed: "He earnestly served the Soviet people and returned home full of glory, but in place of his home he found a pile of rubble. He traveled around neighboring shtetls in hopes of finding out about his family, but everywhere he saw ruins, destroyed and half-destroyed buildings. He thought about how much work there is to do and at that moment he decided to become a builder."[24] In a June 1947 article, Sh. Zinger wrote about Yashe Nayhorg of Sharhorod: "When Yashe Nayhorg was designated chairman of the soviet, the shtetl was in ruins. Today it is hardly recognizable: squares and parks, a movie theater and clubs, a library and schools, a polyclinic and hospital. . . . A gentle spring evening. Electric light shines in the houses and on the streets. The squares are full of people. The club and movie theater are particularly lively and joyous."[25]

"THE BEST TIMES WERE WHEN I
RETURNED TO MY FAMILY"

These triumphant portraits of postwar Soviet life in the shtetls of Ukraine are more the fodder of newspaper sensationalism than of human experience. But echoes of the public portrayal of these years can be found in some of our oral histories. Recognizing the hardships and difficulties that returning soldiers and evacuees encountered, many of the people we spoke with remember the postwar years as the best years of their lives. It was a time of rebuilding and renewal, both literally and metaphorically. Yurkovetsky told us that "the best times were when I returned from the war. I was reunited with my children. What could be better? When I went to war, I left behind my children. When I came back from the war they had already gone to school. The best times were when I returned to my family. Then I started to rebuild. It was difficult but I did rebuild. I worked as a chauffeur. Those were my best years."

Many of those born in the 1920s married and started their families right after the war. Tsolik Groysman waited only days after Victory Day to register his marriage: "My son was born after the war, of course. We waited until the war was over on May 9, 1945, and on May 26 we registered. And a year later, on May 28th, my son was born." Those who had lost their families, in particular, had a profound need for companionship to help overcome the trauma of the war years. They wanted, more than anything else, to reestablish loving families and stable homes. When they returned from the front or evacuation alone, marriage provided a vital opportunity to reintegrate into civilian life and to begin anew. Frida Pecherskaia was working in a brewery when she met her husband two years after the war ended; they registered their marriage soon after: "My husband had returned from the war, and was also injured in his hand. He thought I was a *shiksa* [non-Jewish girl]. We chatted and it was fate." "I was outside, washing the windows with a pink apron, and he saw me, he saw that I was Jewish. . . . He was homely, and I was a beauty, but it was fate." The young couple moved to his hometown of Tulchyn, but had no home and no means of support: "We were poor, but it was good." As a reward for her exceptional work performance at the factory, Pecherskaia received a bonus of two piglets. She used the prize of piglets to partake in the fruits of Soviet socialism, selling the animals to buy some bedding, pillows stuffed with hay, and broken military cots that they propped up with bricks. It became their home.

Most of those who married in these years did so with little ceremony, simply registering their marriage with the municipal authorities. Only a very few managed to celebrate their matrimony in accordance with Jewish law under a chuppah. Molke Sobol told us, "We were liberated in '44 and on the 19th of December we married according to Jewish custom [*farshribn af yidish*] and put up a chuppah." She was able to get a rabbi, "an older man," to perform the service, but the festivity was subdued: "We put a chuppah up in our house because after the war we were poor. We invited relatives and we set up a chuppah, but they told us we had to hide." Her husband's whole family had been killed during the war, so the newlyweds moved into the house that had belonged to her deceased husband's family. In Shpykiv, Evgeniia Krasner boasted that in 1948 her brother got married in Kiev under a chuppah. "In 1948," she repeated with emphasis, shaking her finger in recognition of how rare such a feat was. She herself, she told us, never managed to find true love. With so many men killed in the fighting and under occupation, the postwar Soviet Union was faced with a severe gender imbalance that resulted in a surfeit of women and eventually a disproportionate number of unmarried women, a problem, like so many others, exacerbated in the Jewish population, where Nazi genocidal policies had ensured that few Jewish males survived.[26] As Klara Sapozhnik put it, "Even back then there weren't many Jewish boys. They all left for the war immediately. The war began and the Jewish boys left. Then very many of them were killed."

Some managed to celebrate a "Jewish wedding" without religious sanction or tradition. Dovid Geller, who moved in with his brother in Bratslav after returning from military service in Vladivostok, met his wife, Sime, at that time. Both of them wanted to leave Bratslav for

Sime Geller of Bratslav in 2010. When she married Dovid
Geller after the war, she insisted that they celebrate a Jewish
wedding: "We need to have a wedding! It should be just
the way other people do." *Photo by Anya Quilitzsch.*

a better life in Kiev, but they realized it would be easier to receive an
apartment in the city if they were married. Dovid thought they should
just register the marriage with the city, but Sime insisted: "We need to
have a wedding! It should be just the way other people do. . . . So we
made a wedding of 150 people in [Dovid's] house." It was important to
the couple that they have a Jewish wedding, but they were afraid to put
up a wedding canopy. Instead, they made the wedding Jewish by just
inviting Jewish friends. Although they did not put up a chuppah, they
insisted that "it was a Jewish wedding. We didn't invite anybody from
my work or his work—there were no non-Jews there. Only Jews. It was
a Jewish wedding with Jewish musicians." The wedding would not have
been sanctioned by Jewish law, but retained a distinct Jewish flavor that
provided the couple with the meaningful foundation they craved.

Donia Presler remembered her musician father performing at weddings after the war. She told us he was one of the only people left in
town who could sing traditional Jewish wedding songs and serve as the
wedding marshal:

There weren't any left after the war [who could sing the Yiddish songs].
... Without him there was no wedding. He would congratulate and announce the groom, the bride, the families, bless them ... he would put on a tallith for a Jewish wedding. He would say "mazel tov" to the groom and bride and wish them and their families health, and he would announce the names and he would take out a hat and everyone would throw in a buck or two and then the klezmers would divide it up.

Although Brukhe Feldman did not celebrate a wedding herself, she recalled other weddings from the postwar period:

There was a klezmer musician. I knew him. I was friends with his daughter. His name was Kheskele. He played the clarinet. And he had with him a drummer. They died. They are also buried in the cemetery here in Bershad. There was a clarinetist. There was a trumpeter. In general there were four people who played together. And I remember the Jewish weddings. There were Jewish weddings. They played so beautifully. I used to go back then. I would watch the weddings, and they played. . . . They would play music and everyone would dance together.

Newly married couples produced a baby boom after the war.[27] Parents of Jewish boys were confronted with the question of whether or not to circumcise their sons. Frida Pecherskaia, who moved to Tulchyn after she got married in 1945, had her first son when she was nineteen years old, in 1946. But she did not have him circumcised: "I was afraid. I had nobody, and I had pity on the child." But she did remember that there was a traveling *shoykhet,* Yosl from Bratslav, who would also act as a *moyel* and circumcise children in the region. Nukhim Gvinter also told us that the *shoykhet* in Bershad would circumcise children. Others, like Tsolik Groysman, made sure to circumcise their children, even traveling to nearby cities where the ritual could be performed: "We did what Jews are supposed to do, we circumcised him. We brought him to Kiev, and they did what Jews are supposed to do. Even though I was young, I've kept Jewishness throughout the years." Sonia Yarmulnik in Khmelnytskyy, as well, had her son circumcised in a private ceremony in her house: "Why should we have been afraid? I was not a Party member, my husband was not a Party member," she defiantly asserted. Klara Katsman had her son circumcised. When we asked if she was afraid, she told us she was afraid of the blood, but she had no fear of repercussions from the government: "My father provided vodka and cakes, and then we did the circumcision."

"I USED TO CRY WHEN I HEARD THE *YIZKOR*"

Inasmuch as the Christian majority turned toward time-honored religious rituals in search of solace, the Jewish community was in even greater need of consolation. Jews sought to rebuild synagogues and Jewish life both for pious reflection and for psychological comfort; with their families annihilated, Jews looked toward wider kinship networks and the Jewish community at large for support. The community was plagued by trauma, shellshock, desolation, and survivor guilt, and so looked to faith and community as the only sources of relief from the unbearable anguish. The most pressing need that religious communities filled for Jews was allowing them to say *kaddish,* the prayer for the dead. There were an unprecedented number of mourners, and even those who had abandoned other aspects of Jewish religious tradition continued to feel the need to say this prayer, if not for themselves then for the souls of their murdered relatives. The *kaddish,* in distinction from almost all other Jewish religious rituals, requires a prayer quorum, traditionally a community of ten men, to complete the ritual. Jewish law recognizes that mourning cannot be done in isolation; the bereaved demand communal support. In their grief, individual surviving Jews turned to the community for solace and to age-old religious traditions for comfort.

Brukhe Feldman, who was born in 1939, was just a child after the war. She doesn't remember her father, who was drafted when she was only three years old and was killed fighting at the front, but she diligently insisted she honored his memory with the *yizkor* memorial prayer: "I also remember that my mother would say to me 'you must say *yikzor.*' I would say *yizkor* after my father. My mother would also say *yizkor* after my grandmother and after my grandfather. In the synagogue, the women were above and the men were below. I could hear the *yizkor.* I used to cry. I used to cry when I heard the *yizkor.*" Remembering the death of her mother, she told us:

> I didn't even have money for a gravestone. I had nothing. There was a Jew, Noyekh was his name. He was a window-maker. He made windows and fixed windows. We lived together on the same street. He said: "Let me

take it. I will do it." He said: "The Jews will collect money to make a fence for your mother." He made my mother a fence [to protect the gravestone]. He has since also died and his children are in Israel. He made me a fence and he made me a gravestone. That's how the Jew helped me. How could my mother lie without a stone, without a fence when I have nobody?

The Germans vandalized many Jewish cemeteries during the war, stealing gravestones and using them for paving and construction. Once the Red Army arrived, the vandalism continued, as locals made up for the shortage in building supplies by raiding what remained of the Jewish cemeteries. In the years after the war, local Jewish communities tended to what was left of the cemetery; they sought out toppled gravestones and replanted them on the ground as close to the grave they marked as possible. They carved new gravestones, marking the hundreds—sometimes thousands—who lay in mass graves. Since many of these mass graves lay deep in the woods or in unknown locations, often the Jewish cemetery served as the only available memorial site. In cemeteries like Teplyk, where only a few stones remained, the community established a new cemetery adjacent to the old.

To this day, Jewish cemeteries in Ukraine appear neglected. They tend to be overgrown and poorly maintained, a stark contrast to Ukrainian Christian cemeteries, which receive visitors weekly on Sunday and are blossoming with flowers. Jewish taboos about visiting cemeteries remain strong in Ukraine: according to local custom, it is not proper to visit a cemetery more than once per year. It is expected that one visit the graves of one's parents only during the month of Elul, which precedes the Jewish New Year. In special circumstances, such as a family sickness, it is permitted to make an exception to visit the cemetery to ask for intervention from the spirits of one's predecessors. Orphans are also permitted to visit the graves of their parents before they wed. Those whose parents are alive, though, are generally not expected to ever visit a cemetery. Thus, cemeteries are generally not well-trod sites and so are often allowed to remain in a state of disrepair.

Notable exceptions are the graves of *tsadiks*. At least into the 1960s, the pious continued to visit the graves of Hasidic rebbes and to leave written petitions for them. Ethnographer Valery Dymshits, who has conducted extensive interviews with Jewish informants from the Podolian region, recorded one testimony in which the informant remembered a large group of Jews appealing to the graves of the *tsadik*s in Sharhorod for help during the 1947 drought: after the gathering in the cemetery, the informant concluded, the drought ended with a rainstorm.[28] Aba Kaviner told us that his first pilgrimage to the grave of the Baal Shem Tov in Miedzyboz occurred in 1946: "When I was demobilized, I went around from grave to grave, to all of the graves of the holy ones (*kedoyshim*), and then I went to Miedzyboz."

In addition to cemetery visits, Jews in the postwar period struggled with how best to remember the war dead, and particularly the Jewish victims of Nazi atrocities. In the aftermath of the war, the Soviet government downplayed the racial character of Nazi genocide, instead attributing German atrocities to the ideological differences between Nazism and communism. According to the state-sanctioned narrative, the Nazis and their war machine targeted all "Soviet citizens." The war memorials that officials erected throughout the Soviet Union spoke of "peaceful Soviet citizens" who were murdered; the Jewish character of the victims was obscured. Victims who had been shot in the early days of the war, in the forests and ravines outside the towns, usually remained in unmarked graves, identifiable only by the intensely lush vegetation that grew around the well-fertilized soil. Those who were shot in the last days of the war by retreating Germans were more often reburied by Jewish survivors in what remained of the Jewish cemeteries.

When evacuees began returning to their hometowns after the war, many sought to erect memorials for their murdered townsfolk. When they petitioned authorities for permission to establish a memorial, the petitions were usually refused. On July 3, 1948, for instance, the Jewish community of Kamyanets-Podilskyy, where 23,600 Jews were killed on August 26–28, 1941—the first major massacre of the Holocaust—complained to the Supreme Soviet of the USSR that local authorities refused to permit the establishment of either a synagogue or a memorial site for the surviving Jewish community to mourn their dead. The supplicants protested that the Jewish community's "repeated requests to the local authorities and particularly to the chairman of the town council regarding the restitution of the synagogue to us in accordance with the laws of the Great Stalin Constitution, remain unsatisfied to this day." The community noted in particular the town council's refusal in 1946 to allow Jews to commemorate "the tragic day of mourning when our mothers, fathers, and innocent children were executed and tormented in mass order." Most poignantly, the town council was even refusing to allow the community to preserve and mark the ground of the mass grave where their "fathers, mothers, and little children were buried alive in the earth by the German barbarians, and for three days the earth shuddered from the dying convulsions of the innocent victims." The community's repeated requests to mark and preserve the area of the mass grave were denied. The letter concluded with the following appeals:

> Numerous requests to receive permission to modestly fix up the mass grave, where our fathers are buried and where tens of thousands of our parents, brothers, sisters, and children were buried alive, where the earth trembles from fear and terror—in the passing of another year it will be impossible to identify the place: the pit is overgrowing with weeds and grass, gradually erasing traces and memory—the submitted request has to this day not been decided.
>
> In the name of all the innocent victims who fell at the front in the Great Patriotic War, in the name of our fathers, mothers, brothers, and sisters, who were tormented and executed by the German butchers, we elderly men and women, with great pain in our hearts, with tears in our eyes, turn our voices to you—to the symbol of fairness, to give us the possibility and to permit us elderly people, to offer up a prayer to the Lord our God in honor of the savior of the Jewish nation—the great Stalin.[29]

Most towns remained without any official monument or even a plaque marking the site of the mass grave. Those that were able to erect a memorial usually shied away from acknowledging the specific fate of the Jews during the war. The memorial in the new Jewish cemetery in Tomashpil, for instance, stated only in Ukrainian: "To the Citizens of Tomashpil, who were brutally murdered by the German-Fascist Aggressors on August 4, 1941."[30] A crudely etched *mogen dovid,* which looks more like a Christmas tree than the double triangle of the Star of David, was the only indication that those citizens were Jewish. When we visited him in 2010, Nisen Kiselman revealed to us that a new monument had just been erected in Tomashpil, marking the site where the Germans had killed around 250 people, including his mother and sister: "They made a fence and on one side in Yiddish and the other side in Russian. Because before that there was nothing. I go there a lot." Kiselman apparently did not recognize the preexisting monument, without its mention of Jewish victims, as a memorial to his family. Similarly, a monument on the road between Haysyn and Uman, marking the site where thousands of prisoners were murdered was erected only in the 1970s and referred to the victims simply as "Soviet citizens."[31]

In Tulchyn, the Jewish community took upon itself the obligation to visit and tend to both the old cemetery in the city and the mass graves that lay in the forest near Pechera. According to Klara Katsman, "soon after the war" several survivors started to return to Pechera regularly, in the month of Elul that marks the weeks before Yom Kippur, to mourn at the graves of their family members. They sought assistance from the villagers who surround the forest to tend the grave, but the villagers were resistant: "Everybody knew—the entire village knew—but nobody wanted to tell," remarked Pesia Kolodenker accusatorily. She, like many other survivors in Tulchyn, was adamant that "everybody should know that there are many people lying there in that ravine!" Some years after the war—local historian and survivor of the camp, Rita Shveibish, dated it to 1949 or 1950; others have cited the year 1945—the community succeeded in erecting a memorial by the mass grave, deep in the woods along overgrown paths. There was no marker on the road, though, and since the graves and memorial were located far inside the forest, they could be found only by those who knew of their location. These makeshift memorials remain to this day, a poignant tribute to the tenacity of the community and the call to remember.

In 2009, we traveled from Tulchyn to Pechera, to the site of the grave with Shveibish. The site itself was located deep in the forest; our van was only able to navigate part of the way along a path overgrown with weeds. As the undergrowth thickened, our driver stopped the van, and we walked the rest of the way. Shveibish had not been to the site in a few months and was disturbed at the condition of the path. On our way out of the thicket, she approached a few villagers whose homes abutted the forest: "Do you want to mow the grass and make some money?" she pleaded. "We don't need it. We have too much work already to do," shot back one villager. The others, as well, were unwilling to commit. The mass graves in their backyards were not their problem.

In front of the mass grave is a large obelisk topped by a bust of a weeping mother looking down into the grave. One arm rests over her chest, as though she is holding an absent child; her other arm is raised to her chin. Two photos adorn the obelisk: one is an image of Nathan Rapoport's famous Warsaw Ghetto Monument, which was unveiled in Warsaw in 1948 and portrays a group of heroic-looking proletarian figures rising up in defiant rebellion. A caption underneath the photo states *poslednii boi* (the last battle). The second photo is more abstract than the socialist realism of Rapoport's relief; it depicts Bronislaw Wojciech Linke's painting, *El Mole Rachamim* of 1956. In this haunting painting, the image of a man in tallith and tefillin emerges out of the ruins of a building, clutching his head in anguish. Both photos are crudely plastered onto the memorial; white paint has dripped onto them from the obelisk. A white stone memorial plaque that appears to have been added onto the monument at a later date calls for revenge in a stilted Hebrew, concluding with a quotation from Psalm 79: "Here lie holy martyrs, who were murdered in all manners, for the sanctification of the name, during 1941–1944, in the town of Pechera, by the fascist murderers, whose hands are full of the blood of some 8,000 thousand [*sic*] men, women, and children. May God remember them for ever. And may the spilled blood of your servants be avenged." Underneath the Hebrew inscription, a black plaque is carved with gold Russian lettering. The Russian inscription shies away from such explicit calls for vengeance and instead personalizes the tragedy:

> Ponder, people! Thousands of these unfortunate people did not survive to see victory. The German fascist henchmen and their police bestially cut the breath, the voice, the thoughts, the lives of women, children, and the elderly. Words cannot describe their death. This is your mother, your father, your brothers, and your sisters, who were murdered, and to whom you owe your new happy lives. Do not suffer, but internalize the hatred, and swear that you will never allow a repeat of such sacrifice. Keep alive the bright memory of them in your offspring. Do not forget. This is their bequest.

A few kilometers from the mass graves in the forest, the sanatorium that became the site of the Pechera concentration camp has now been reestablished as a sanatorium. When we visited in 2009, nurses were walking patients up and down the grounds, helping them recuperate in the serene parks. Down by the river, where parched Jews were shot as they sought to quench their thirst with the clean flowing waters, children and young lovers were splashing around the rocks. We asked Sasha Kolodenker how it made him feel to see young people enjoying the site, oblivious to its history. It took him a while to understand the question,

ЗДЕСЬ ЗАХОРОНЕНЫ ТЫСЯЧИ
БЕЗВИННО ПОГИБШИХ ЕВРЕЕВ,
РАССТРЕЛЯННЫХ И ЗАМУЧЕННЫХ
ГОЛОДОМ, ХОЛОДОМ И БОЛЕЗНЯ-
МИ В ПЕРИОД НАХОЖДЕНИЯ ИХ В
ФАШИСТСКОМ КОНЦЛАГЕРЕ СЕ-
ЛА ПЕЧЕРА В 1941 - 1944 г.г.

A plaque by the Pechera mass grave reads, "Here are buried thousands of innocent murdered Jews, who were shot and tortured by hunger, cold and disease in the period of their confinement in the fascist concentration camp of the village, Pechera in 1941–1944."

before he replied, "Let them! Of course!" Kolodenker, like many others of the region, understood the need to move on. If all the killing sites of Ukraine were cordoned off, there would be almost no riverbanks, forests, cliffs, or ravines left to enjoy.

Other communities also did their best to commemorate the murdered Jews and to mark the mass graves that tarnish the landscape. In Bershad, Sofia Palatnikova told us that on March 14, 1944, "When ours [the Red Army] liberated us, some invalids and others returned from the army, and when they came back, there were these pits that had not been fully covered. There were children's shoes and clothing lying around, so some of those who had been saved from the camps and I took shovels and covered them and made a grave." They later erected a stone to mark the spot. Palatnikova then returned to her native Teplyk, where she helped gather together the invalids and other young folk who were passing through town in order to fix up the mass graves there. A captain passing through the town on his way back from evacuation helped the

A memorial deep in the woods by the Pechera mass grave
reads in Yiddish and Russian: "Sleep peacefully innocent
people. The memory is hard as stone. We will not forget
the way to you. We come here with flowers."

Memorial in the woods by the Pechera mass grave. The inscription in Yiddish quotes from Psalm 79: "May the spilled blood of your servants be avenged." The Russian text states in part: "This is your mother, your father, your brothers, and your sisters, who were murdered and to whom you owe your new happy lives. Do not suffer, but internalize the hatred, and swear that you will never allow a repeat of such a sacrifice."

community by traveling to Odessa to raise funds. "There were three graves: the first for those who were killed first, then a grave for those who had been in hiding and were found, and the third for those who were working, which also includes some non-Jews like partisans. They were not properly covered. So we youngsters gathered together, with the help of a few adults, and put things in order." Klara Vaynman told us about the memorial in Bar: "Even today, one still can't drive there. There is no road. You have to have someone take you to where the Jews are lying.... Those who remained . . . put up a stone. Many of them lived in Kiev and used their own money. They asked those who lived in the forest to take them there and they came and put up a stone. But there is no road to get there. My mother has been there. Everybody is lying there."

Without communal markers and modes of remembrance, individual survivors took it upon themselves to remember alone. Arkadii Burshtein told us that every year he travels with his family from his home in Haysyn to Sobolivka to visit: "My mother together with my sisters and brothers and my grandmother were killed. All my relatives were killed, there in Sobolivka. Every year I go there with my whole family to Sobolivka. There is a memorial. Three hundred and seventy Jews are buried there."

With most cemeteries destroyed, new cemeteries needed to be constructed. In Bershad during the war, the Jewish community dug a mass grave in the southeast corner of the city for those who had died in the ghetto of typhus and hunger. After the war, a new cemetery was added adjacent to the site; the war dead would be accompanied by the postwar dead. Jews continued, for the most part, to be buried in separate cemeteries from non-Jews. Coexistence between Jews and Christians in the Ukrainian shtetls is thereby marked as a temporary respite; when they are laid to eternal rest, Jews and Christians sleep in separate quarters, the Christians in the *tsvinter* (Ukrainian cemetery) and the Jews in the *feld* (Jewish cemetery). Throughout the Soviet era, Jews even continued to carve Hebrew names and inscriptions into the gravestones, or even occasionally a Star of David. Prohibitions on the use of Hebrew and Jewish symbols seem to have been relaxed for those who were no longer capable of laboring for the communist future. The grave of one David Chaimovich Bondar in Bershad, for instance, includes a Star of David and the Hebrew characters *pe* and *nun* (an abbreviation for "here lies"), and the Russian-language inscription: "Shot by the fascists, March 7,

1944." Some traditional Jewish taboos, such as the display of human figures on gravestones, were abandoned, as Jews emulated their Christian neighbors in placing photos of their loved ones on the stones, or even, for those who had the means, in engraving images directly into the granite, a practice that had already begun before the war. Even the grave of Yankl Lipman, the last rabbi of Bershad, who died in 1958, includes a photograph of the bearded rabbi. Sometimes the names of those killed during the war who were not properly buried were added to a family member's gravestone.

Surviving Jews continued to mourn the dead in the Jewish fashion, and visited the graves of loved ones regularly, at least on the anniversary of their death. Feldman recalls the practice of burial: "Back then I remember that when a Jew or a Jewess died, they didn't carry him with an automobile or a bus or anything. They carried him with their hands. I remember that four men would carry the stretcher . . . and they would take the body to the cemetery and when they returned they would go to the river to wash hands." She remembered that the non-Jews would ask: "'What are you running for here and there!?' We would say 'one has to wash one's hands. So we go over there.' What could we do? I remember also that when a Jewish woman or man died they dressed him or her in a shroud [*takhrikhim*]. The shroud would be made of linen. They would fasten it. Bind the face. Now when someone dies, they do to him like the *goyim*, covering the face. And that's that." Feldman was referring to the practice of *avnet*, in which a sash is wrapped around the shroud and tied in the form of the Hebrew letter *shin*. She mentioned that the non-Jews would comment on Jews "running" with the body, likely viewing the custom of carrying the body by hand as bizarre.

Feldman continued:

When a Jewish woman or a Jewish man died, they say that it is forbidden to wear the shoes that he or she wore. It is forbidden. One must burn them. New shoes can't be used and those shoes must be burned . . . put in the oven and burned. . . . Back then when my mother, when my mother died they explained to me that I had to sit shiva. I put on stockings and I would sit on the floor. I would sit for eight days and when the shiva ended I would stand up. And if there was a man they said for a month you may not shave . . . the shoes that he went in you had to burn, do you understand, burn? It was forbidden to walk in them, you understand. They would say you are walking on the dead. It's true.[32]

Moyshe Vanshelboim of Berdichev told us that he commemorates the dead by baking bread. In the early days of the war, he explained, there was nowhere to buy bread, so his mother would gather flour and bake it herself. One early morning in September, as his mother was baking the bread, there was a knock on the windowpane. The police had come to take his mother "to work." She turned to Moyshe, and told him to watch the bread and take it out in an hour. He never saw her again: "And so I bake bread at home, and on Friday I bake a bread. Why do I bake bread? Because my mother left me with the bread, and I survived." He invited us to wash our hands, and offered us some bread: "Everybody who tries it, licks their fingers," he boasted. In the absence of an officially sanctioned means of public commemoration, individuals devised their own means of remembrance.

In 2009, after breaking bread with Vanshelboim, we asked him to take us to the site of the mass grave on the outskirts of Berdichev, where more than 18,000 Jews—including his family—were killed and lay buried. We had visited the former airfield—now an empty field—previously without a guide, and had found a plaque by the side of the road commemorating the "18,640 peaceful Soviet citizens" who were brutally murdered on the spot in what came to be known as the Bloody Monday massacre of September 15, 1941. Vanshelboim told us that he had escaped another massacre across the road. He and his father, who as a specialized artisan was spared during the Bloody Monday massacre that killed the rest of his family, had already undressed and were awaiting execution when his father urged him to flee: "Moyshe, run away! I will stay and join your mother and your siblings. But you are still young. You can run. Perhaps you will survive and tell the truth."

On our visit to the site, Vanshelboim stepped out of the van and marched purposefully straight into the brush through the vast empty field, muttering along the way about how abandoned and desolate the site is. It was early spring and the fields had not yet blossomed. In the middle of the vast pasture were two visible mounds: "They made two mass graves; one wasn't enough for them," Vanshelboim remarked bitterly. The first mound, the larger of the two, was covered with growth. Weeds—fed by the rich nutrients the grave continued to supply—grew much higher over the mound than elsewhere. A plaque in Ukrainian again declared itself an "eternal monument" to the "peaceful Soviet citizens." Only a Star of David hinted at the nationality of the victims. Van-shelboim's attention, though, was turned to the second smaller grave, a short walk away: it had no growth, and only earth was exposed. As we approached, we saw that the surface of the grave, a mound of earth, was littered with bones: a collarbone caught my eye. Vanshelboim had earlier divulged that marauders occasionally come by, digging for gold. Vanshelboim's eyes fell upon a child's skull, still screaming at the heavens seventy years after its burial. He bent down and lovingly wrested his hands into the fertile soil to bury the skull: "Who knows?" he muttered, "This could be the skull of my little brother. He was just five years old."

"THEY PAID A LOT OF MONEY TO KEEP THE SYNAGOGUE OPEN"

Rebuilding family lives—marrying, having children, and mourning deceased kin—was a priority for most Jews in the postwar period. At the same time, there was a sense that Jewish communal and religious life should be rebuilt as well.[33] In order to rouse the population during the war, the state had made concessions to most religious organizations, recognizing the Russian Orthodox Metropolitan and permitting Muslim pilgrimages to Mecca, for instance. Religious belief provided comfort to those facing loss during the war and gave incentives to fighters to continue the battle. In the immediate postwar period, the state continued its more relaxed attitude toward religious belief and institutions, particularly on a local level. Jews in the shtetls assumed that just as their Christian neighbors were being permitted to return to a semblance of religious life, so would they.[34]

In addition to providing spiritual sustenance, synagogues, like churches and mosques, also supplied some of the essential material needs of veterans and returning evacuees. With the state overwhelmed and unable to provide basic necessities for its citizens, faith-based organizations could help fill in the gap, providing welfare and commemorative functions.[35] It was in recognition of the beneficial role that faith-based organizations could serve in the postwar climate that in May 1944 the Council of People's Ministers established the Council for the Affairs of Religious Cults, with the task of regulating religious activity.

We can get an idea of the rapid growth of Jewish religious organizations in Ukraine from the regular reports issued by the Council: in 1945, the Plenipotentiary of the Ukrainian division of the Council counted sixty Jewish religious communities in Ukraine and thirty-seven rabbis. Later that same year, fifty-nine additional synagogues were added to the account, meaning that the number of synagogues had virtually doubled within the year. The Plenipotentiary reported that only five of these had received the permission required from the Council. Clearly the needs of the community could not wait for the state bureaucracy to catch up. The brazen disregard for the regulations is also indicative of a general feeling of urgency that beset those who reclaimed the synagogues. By the end of 1947, seventy-nine synagogues were legally functioning in Ukraine, representing more than 40 percent of the 190 legal synagogues in the entire Soviet Union.[36]

Aba Kaviner explained that "after the war when I came back home here, there were two synagogues: the big synagogue became the big sports hall and the butcher's synagogue is the one functioning today." With his pipe in hand, he leaned forward as if to bring us into an exciting conspiracy, and shared with us the story of the rebuilding of the synagogue and Jewish life in the city:

> When the Jews came back from evacuation, they realized that they couldn't rebuild the big synagogue. They would have to make significant repairs. The butcher's synagogue is small. The butcher's synagogue was given over to the Jews. It had a roof riddled with holes, no ceiling, no floor; only four walls, the holy ark, and a part of the women's section. Although the times were difficult and the hunger was great, the Jews gave their last kopek and more or less fixed the roof, made a ceiling, made a floor. There were a lot of Jews. And they prayed.

David Soyfer remembered that when he was demobilized and returned to Berdichev immediately after the war, the pious prayed outside in the empty courtyard against the synagogue wall:

> After the war, Jewish officers came and requested that a synagogue be opened for their parents, the synagogue that still stands. There was a broken wall and they said, "Make it a synagogue." The Jews were naked and had nowhere to live. It was difficult; they had nothing to wear. There were no sponsors [aid workers]. So they made a synagogue—not as nice

as you know it today, but I remember that in '45, on Yom Kippur, people prayed by the wall, but in '46, on Yom Kippur, they already prayed in the synagogue and it was a holiday for the Jews.

At times, the needs of the community conflicted with the needs of individuals for shelter and basic necessities. Some sought to rebuild communal life and religious institutions first, whereas others prioritized private housing. Similar debates beset the Soviet reconstruction effort at all levels: most famously, the central government ordered the reconstruction of the tsarist palaces surrounding Leningrad before the population of the city had been provided with adequate housing and hospitals. On a smaller scale in each and every town that had been destroyed by the war, the local population argued about whether resources would be best allocated toward restoring large symbolic buildings or meeting the more mundane needs of the population. Yente Kolodenker told us about the conflict in Tulchyn between those who sought to use the precious few bricks that could be found around town to rebuild the synagogue, and those who prioritized the construction of homes for the homeless:

> We didn't have a home. We didn't even have a corner to sleep in. We didn't even have rags on us. We didn't have even a fragment of a house. So we started to build. There was a synagogue. It was a big synagogue—two-stories. But it wasn't finished. So when ours [the Soviet authorities] came in, they started to take the leftover bricks. They would take the bricks and build houses with them.

She complained that the patricians, "the *balebatim*," chastised the poor for taking the bricks, asking, "How will we ever finish building the synagogue if you keep taking the bricks?" Kolodenker framed the debate in Tulchyn as one between the haves and have-nots, between the leadership of the town, who sought the reconstruction of communal institutions, and the common folk who simply wanted to rebuild their homes. Donia Presler also remembered the Jewish leadership privileging the rebuilding of communal institutions over private residences. She told us about how some communal leaders purchased a house and remade it into a synagogue: "They bought a house and took it apart to make two big rooms: there was one room for the women and one for the men." In Haysyn, where the synagogue had been confiscated in 1932 and was being used to house five families in apartments, the authorities refused to relinquish the building despite a formal request from a group of Jews claiming to represent the community, who sought to restore it to its former purpose.[37] Still, the two uses often coexisted—Khayke Gvinter lived in the basement of the Bershad synagogue for some twenty years, having moved in after her own home was bombed.

Since Soviet law prohibited religious organizations from owning buildings, Jewish prayer groups could either lease a building from the state or municipal authorities free of charge, or rent a building from a private individual. In the immediate postwar period, the easiest means of establishing a synagogue was to rent premises registered to a private individual, usually for a nominal sum. Archival sources tell of a group of Jews in Tulchyn who outfitted a private house as a synagogue, and registered it under the name of a certain Yankl Mikhelkis. However, when Mikhelkis relinquished the house in 1950 and the community sought to register it officially as a synagogue, their request was denied.[38]

The Jews of Bershad were more successful. A religious community was registered on June 25, 1946, consisting of some three hundred members.[39] According to Efim Vygodner, the director of the Jewish community of Bershad, "They say that after the war, the Jews of Bershad went to Moscow where they obtained a permit to open the synagogue." Yosl Kogan recalled a similar story: he attested that the synagogue in Bershad remained open throughout the Soviet period: "They paid a lot of money to keep the synagogue running," he explained. "There was a Jewish city council president. . . . In order to keep the synagogue opened, they paid money, quietly. The Jews would come together and pay the taxes." The synagogue was even protected by several mayors of Bershad. Vygodner continued:

> For several years, the synagogue was closed. During the war, when Bershad was under the Romanians, the Jewish community started to function. But after the war, they closed everything, and then this became a synagogue again. There was a synagogue here, and in Vinnytsya there was a synagogue in a small apartment, and in Kiev on Podol the synagogue also opened the same year. There were some. I remember that about forty years ago, the Soviet government tried to close down the synagogue, but it couldn't. I can tell you that the government wasn't so strong. They said they wanted to close it, but they weren't so strong here. My grandfather was one of the ten Jews who were leaders of the [Jewish

community]. My father said to him, "I am a communist; you must leave the [Jewish community leadership]," so he left and another person took his place.

State and local authorities sought to thwart attempts by believers to reestablish synagogues. Between 1946 and 1947 the Council for Affairs of Religious Cults confiscated or closed ninety-four religious buildings, of which nine were synagogues.⁴⁰ In Sharhorod alone eleven Jewish prayer groups were closed in 1947.⁴¹ In the early 1950s, as official policies of antisemitism intensified, new attempts were made to close down synagogues in even the most out-of-the-way small towns. A notice in 1952 from the Plenipotentiary of the Council for Affairs of Religious Cults for Vinnytsya Province to the district council of Yampil, for instance, noted the existence of an unregistered synagogue in the town of Dzygovke, and ordered its immediate closure:

> According to information available to me, in the town of Dzygovke in your district there is an unregistered Jewish synagogue. The religious community submitted a petition, and the Dzygovke community was denied by the provincial executive committee already on September 22, 1947. I admonished you about this.
>
> I ask for the immediate closure of the Dzygovke synagogue; property remaining in the synagogue is to be removed and transferred to the District Finance Section for implementation, and religious books and Torahs are to be sealed and given for preservation to the District Council local museum. . . .
>
> I ask you to investigate who is to blame in relation to the prayer gatherings and unregistered religious community and to bring to trial those responsible.⁴²

In the city of Khmelnytskyy, Aba Kaviner remembered: "In '51 the entire Jewish community—the caretaker of the synagogue and all of its members—were arrested as German and American spies. To inflame the antisemitism even more, they added that in the synagogue where the holy ark was, a radio transmitter was set up, from where they would broadcast military secrets from the synagogue to America and to England." Kaviner laughed at the idea that these Jews, some of whom could barely communicate in Russian, let alone English, would have been privy to Russian military secrets and capable of transmitting them abroad.

Throughout the early 1950s, citizens repeatedly filed complaints to the local councils and to the supreme court demanding the restitution of synagogue buildings. These requests commonly referred both to the suffering of the Jews under Nazi rule and to the Soviet constitution: "They write one thing in the newspapers and the constitution, but follow different policies in relation to religious organizations. . . . In the provincial center the synagogue is closed because we are Jews. It is like the Beilis Affair," concluded one complaint in Vinnytsya Province, making reference to the notorious 1911–1913 arrest and trial of Mendl Beilis in Kiev on fabricated charges of ritual murder.[43] Despite the refusal of local authorities to turn over synagogue property, Jews continued to attend services even at the risk of censure and punishment.

The case of Uman, although a much larger city than most of the towns discussed here, is instructive and well-documented. The three hundred members of the Jewish community in the city established a synagogue immediately after the city's liberation in March 1944, but only officially registered it in December 1945. Six years later, in 1951, the Council for the Affairs of Religious Cults confiscated it. According to the Council, "From the very beginning of its registration, this community violated the laws of the USSR regarding religious cults." The community was also accused of using the building of a workers' club as its prayer house without having received permission to do so from the city council, and of falsifying names on the petition for official registration they had filed in 1945. Perhaps most seriously, they were accused of using an unregistered cantor, "who recently arrived from Austria. This cantor was detained by the local governmental authority with a full suitcase of nationalist literature." In 1949, the community was allocated a synagogue on the outskirts of town, on Sholem Aleichem Street, but the community refused to use this building, instead insisting upon retaining prayer houses in private apartments in the center of town. The Council believed that at least some of the names on the new petition for a synagogue were also falsified, and concluded that the number of Jewish believers in Uman was insignificant and that they therefore did not warrant a synagogue.[44] By 1953, only four synagogues were officially registered in Vinnytsya Province: Bershad, Zhmerynka, Chernivtsi, and Yampil.

Religious functionaries—where they existed—continued to provide spiritual sustenance and perform rituals for the faithful, although on a far smaller scale than in previous generations. Soviet law permitted—in fact, even required—the appointment of a rabbi in instances where a synagogue had been officially registered.[45] But without yeshivas, there was no means of formally training new clergy. As a result, the postwar rabbinate and other religious functionaries were carry-overs from an earlier age; they had all been trained before the revolutionary era and were already in their sixties and seventies after the war. In Bershad, Rabbi Yankl Lipman, who was born in 1879, was appointed rabbi in 1946. During the interwar period he had taught Hebrew out of his home. Evgeniia Kozak remembered that "he was a very handsome Jew. He had a very nice beard." Similarly, the Jewish community of Zhmerynka appointed L. Sh. Averbukh as their rabbi in 1949. Averbukh was born in 1880 and had graduated from a yeshiva before working as an accountant. P. N. Shmidel, who was born in 1862 and had previously worked as a teacher and trader, became rabbi of Yampil in 1947.[46]

Other religious functionaries were even more rare. In Tulchyn, a kosher butcher after the war also worked as a *moyel;* they called him Moyshe Shoykhet (Moyshe the Butcher). Klara Katsman remembered that he would slaughter poultry, but you couldn't purchase kosher meat in the stores. Shveibish explained, "But there was a *shoykhet* for a while. Until '55, even until '60 there were two *shoykhets.*" Tomashpil had a *shoykhet* until the 1960s: "A stranger [*shoykhet* from another town] came—he was traveling through Tomashpil and stayed because he could work here." Evgeniia Kozak remembered a butcher who worked in Bershad and went by the nickname Gedalya Shoykhet (Gedalya the Butcher); he served as both the butcher and *moyel* in town.

There were also a few cantors working in the region. Tsolik Groysman remembered a cantor who came to town without any money or means of earning a livelihood. Groysman responded by organizing a group of Jews who would get together in an apartment to pray with him: "He was a cantor. I offered him charity, but he didn't want it. He wanted to earn money with his profession. His profession was a cantor; he wanted to sing. So, we gathered Jews together, and he would earn his kopeks singing songs." He later noted, "There was no synagogue, but people had apartments where we would meet." He remembered how fearful they were of being discovered: "In those times we were afraid, but we could not call it off. We would cover the windows."

Jewish music remained popular both for secular and religious purposes. It was common to bring in visiting cantors from neighboring towns, and these visits always attracted a crowd. In 1954, the Jews of Bershad brought back Shoyel Zus Gershkovich, a native Bershader who had since moved to Kharkiv, to lead the High Holiday services: some four hundred people attended the service, up from 186 who had attended two years earlier.[47] Aba Kaviner remembered the cantors who would come to Khmelnytskyy after the war from Romania and Kiev. In the late 1950s, when local authorities began to crack down on synagogue attendance, one of the key practices they sought to discontinue was bringing in a guest cantor, noting that guest cantors tended to draw large crowds to synagogue.[48] Synagogue worship in the postwar era was limited, for the most part, to the elderly. The young had little experience with such customs and were largely ignorant of traditional Jewish religious practice. But even the young enjoyed listening to a talented cantor.

"THE WAR AGAINST MINYANS"

Communities without synagogues continued to meet in private homes for the purpose of prayer. The Council for the Affairs of Religious Cults noted that in Kiev "the believers cannot fit into the sanctuary (hall), they satisfy their religious demands in the synagogue courtyard under the open skies and even organize so-called 'minyans' of which the number of attendees is fifty to one hundred people. The war against 'minyans,' which I have come to conduct, is difficult and almost impossible; that is, one 'min' [*sic*] is closed, and a group of believers migrates to another 'min.'"[49] In the provinces, an even larger percentage of the Jewish community attended private prayer quorums. According to one secret report issued in 1955 by the Council for Affairs of Religious Cults, in Vinnytsya Province alone there were at least thirty-five separate prayer groups, each with at least twenty members, meeting in Bratslav, Tomashpil, Tulchyn, and Vinnytsya. Another report issued later the same year counted eight separate prayer quorums meeting in Bratslav and ten in Tulchyn.[50] Tseytl Kislinskaia told us that in Korsun-Shevchenkivskyy there were at least two prayer quorums, one for women and one for men: "After the war, those synagogues weren't there anymore. There weren't synagogues. There was a Jewish woman and people would go to her to pray. My mother would go to them. She would always go. I was at work." Kislinskaia worked on all the holidays, but she claimed that on Yom Kippur she would fast at work, and then after work go to pick up her mother from the synagogue. In Tulchyn, Pesia Kolodenker told us, "There was a coachman, and when he prayed you could hear in the central street because his voice stretched out so that everyone came to see him."

Many of those we spoke to recalled the fear that permeated the secret prayer quorums, as the devout knew they could be arrested at any time. Pinia Golfeld confided, "It was that kind of time, when people were afraid. I myself was at home and put up a lock so that nobody could get inside the house." He added, "Ten people would pray in a private house. And we paid the landlord maybe thirty, maybe twenty, I don't remember how much we paid. And that's how we prayed. We were afraid." Ron Shoykhetman told us he celebrated a bar mitzvah in Derazhnya after the war:

> We received a package in the mail from Israel. It was, perhaps, in '49 or '48. It was a package from my father's brother. And there was tefillin and a tallith in it. I went with my father and we put it all in this American-made canister, or box, and we hid it underground because it was dangerous in those days. But the Jews would come to us to pray and gather together for a minyan, thirteen or eleven [people], in Derazhnya in our home and other homes.

In Bar, Klara Vaynman told us that since there was no synagogue after the war in the town, all the elderly Jewish women would come to her mother's house to pray, and the men would gather in a separate house. When they could not constitute a minyan, they would go around town gathering people together to make a minyan, which she erroneously recalled as requiring eleven rather than ten men:

> There were very few who could read. They would all come to us in our house. My mother would pray and at all the holidays everybody would come to us in our home. She would pray and they would listen. . . . There were also other houses at which people prayed. There was one at Mittleman's. . . . The men would gather when someone died. They had to have eleven. They would come, just barely eleven people would gather. . . . They would gather together and make a minyan when someone died.

She explained that the minyans continued "as long as the elderly were still around. Until there was nobody left . . . the younger ones didn't know how to pray and didn't go. When the elderly died off, there was nothing left."

"A JEW SHOULD EAT MATZOS"

Passover remained a major holiday, as it had been before the war, and the acquisition of matzo began months in advance. In 1946, matzo was included in the official price list of the Ministry of Trade of the USSR; officially, at least, the Council for Affairs of Religious Cults required state bakeries to stock sufficient amounts to meet demand.[51] The reality, however, was much more complicated. The central organization responsible for supplying bread, Glavkhleb, was caught between the state law, which required the baking of limited amounts of matzo, and local party organs, which opposed its production. As a result, the availability of matzo vacillated from year to year.

By the mid-1950s, official reports were noting the extent to which the Jewish community prepared for Passover. A secret report from Vinnytsya Province, dated April 19, 1955, for instance, noted that "Preparations for the Passover holiday by the Jewish community began already at the end of February and through the entire month of March: there were capital repairs to the inside of the synagogue premises and to the outside. The roofs of practically every synagogue building were repaired. They redecorated the altars, the cupboards in which the "Torah" is kept, the benches, and the place for the rabbi; they made order in the synagogue and in the synagogue courtyard."[52] The report provides an indication of how the authorities made it difficult for the Jewish community to acquire matzo by passing responsibility for making provisions from one department to another: "On the 9th of March of this year, I had a meeting with the president of the Executive Organ of the Jewish Religious Community of the town of Bershad, Bershad district, Yosef Leibovich Rozen, regarding the question of the baking of matzo. I explained to him that I have no relationship with the baking of matzo as matzo is not an object of the religious cult, and I recommended that he take the question of the baking of matzo to the Regional Trade Department."[53] Three years later, the Council continued to express concern about the excitement that surrounded the Passover holiday. A report from April 22, 1958 noted that preparations for the Passover holiday "began already in the month of February 1958 with repairs and whitewashing of the synagogue" and matzo was being baked forty-two days before the holiday, so that it could be distributed to the nearly 1,500 people who would attend services. The same report mentioned that residents of Zhmerynka were receiving packages of matzo from larger towns such as Odessa, Kiev, Vinnytsya, and Haysyn.[54]

Frida Pecherskaia insisted that she always baked matzo. "When I got married, when I already lived in Tulchyn, I would get flour and mix it just with water and roll it. And my husband would help with a rolling pin." Klara Vaynman told us that her mother ensured that the family always observed Passover: "Everything was kosher for us. My mother made sure from one year to the next that we didn't eat that which you shouldn't eat. . . . On Passover I eat only matzo and things made with matzo. And today I follow all of the holidays just as my mother taught me." Etia Shvartzbroit of Mohyliv-Podilskyy told us that, after the war, "People sat around and did nothing. . . . I was a procurement officer in a creamery and then I owned a factory for matzos." She later explained that it was actually a bakery, but people would mockingly call it the matzo factory since it employed some two dozen people, working in shifts to produce enough matzo for the community, beginning a full two months before Passover. Brukhe Fedman also remembered how some members of the community would bake matzo together, utilizing old-fashioned techniques reminiscent of the methods the Ancient Isra-elites used during the exodus the holiday commemorates: "In Bershad there was an oven, a particular oven. . . . And the women would roll [the dough] and the men would lay it inside the oven. We would bake them and then eat them. I also ate that kind. . . . But there weren't the matzos like we eat today. Now they are manufactured. Each one was rolled out, authentic. Just as they were carried out of Israel." She also told us that her family would bake matzo in the home where, "My mother, or whoever it was, had rolled out several little matzos. And we would bake them in baking pans." When asked why she eats matzo on Passover, Feldman theorized, "Why do I eat matzos? Because I am a Jewish woman." Upon further reflection she added, "A Jew should eat matzos, of course, a Jew must eat matzos."

Religious traditions coexisted with the newer customs of communist life. In many cases, parents followed one tradition and children another. Sometimes divisions existed between in-laws, all interacting together. Mire Murovanaia, whom we interviewed in Haysyn, told us how her family celebrated holidays after the war: "After the war, when I got married and my husband became a part of my family, his father was a communist but his mother celebrated all of the holidays. So, on revolutionary holidays they would come to us and on Jewish holidays we would go to them. Passover, Rosh Hashanah, all of the holidays we spent with them." Murovanaia celebrated both Soviet revolutionary holidays and Jewish religious holidays, allowing the two to seamlessly interact and coexist. Soviet and Jewish identities intersected, collided, and merged with each other in a myriad of ways.

—∞—

When we first met David Furman in a Jewish soup kitchen in Berdichev, we began to ask him about his childhood. Rather than dwell on that period of his life, Furman erupted into a monologue about his military service: "I went to *heder*. I was thirteen years old when I went to work. I became a carpenter, a furniture maker. In 1939 I was drafted into the army. I served in the Pacific Navy, in the Far East. When the war began I was sent to the front. I defended the Kalinin front, the Stalingrad front. I was in the 62nd Army. The 8th Guard Unit." At this point, he reached into his shirt pocket and pulled out a color snapshot of him posing outdoors dressed in his military regalia. Furman had no idea that an international team of researchers together with a cameraman would be visiting the soup kitchen that day. But he was still carrying his photo in his shirt pocket, to remind himself of what he had done and his moment of victory. His story continued, "When I came back to Berdichev, I found no one. I arrived already without a leg. I had lost my leg. And that's my autobiography." By the time that the Battle of Stalingrad began, in August 1942, he had already received word that his entire family—his father, Zelig; his mother, Leyke; his sister, Kheyved, and his two brothers, Moyshe and Berl—had been murdered by the Nazis in Berdichev. He knew what he was fighting for, and carries the picture in his pocket to commemorate it.

May 9th marks Victory Day (Den Pobedy) in Russia and most of the former Soviet Union. The holiday commemorates the German surrender to the Soviet Union late in the evening of May 8, 1945. Today many elderly Jews continue to identify with the Red Army and the Soviet Union, under whose hammer and sickle they fought during the war. Preparations for Victory Day begin in April, as veterans clean their uniforms and polish their medals to display on parade. For many who fought valiantly, these are the proudest moments of their lives. The pride they feel in their achievements is palpable; and the respect and admiration they have earned should be limitless.

However, Victory Day celebrations in Ukraine have become contentious. Many veterans seek to memorialize Victory Day by marching under the hammer and sickle—the flag under which they defeated Nazism. Others, mostly younger Ukrainians, view the Soviet period as an occupation, and bristle at the idea of honoring the Red Army, which wiped out their dreams of establishing an independent Ukrainian state. Since it is often the Jewish veterans who feel most strongly and unambiguously about the Red Army victory over Nazi Germany, the scuffles that sometimes break out during Victory Day parades can take on an antisemitic tint. Some Ukrainian nationalists view the hammer and sickle as an offensive symbol, akin to the Nazi swastika. For others, the Soviet flag is precisely the symbol that liberated Europe from the swastika.

The festivities—and controversy—surrounding Victory Day proclaim this date as a turning point, a moment that demarcates forever a "before" and an "after." Certainly, those we have interviewed share this sense of time and chronology. Life was difficult before the war, but they had families, friends, and communities. After the war, most of their friends and families had been murdered and their communities were scattered. Lives were shattered. Over time, they would rebuild, but what was lost would never be recovered. So many memories we have recorded—of family celebrations, youthful affairs, and grand dreams—end with a pause, followed by the dejected remark, "but the Germans killed them all."

But the world did not begin anew on May 10th. The next ten years became a decade of rebuilding and return. Injured soldiers recovered in hospitals for months, and sometimes years; healthy soldiers remained in the service with no other options before them. Hundreds of thousands of refugees began the long trek back from evacuation in Central Asia. Many would travel only as far as Moscow, never again to return to the shtetl. Others emerged from hiding or from concentration camps, and began the long process of reintegration into society. With no beds to return to and no family to welcome them, many literally gathered bricks from among the rubble, laid them on top of each other one by one, and began to construct shelters. People were still returning to their homes and rebuilding when the region was hit again by the famine of 1947. With no infrastructure developed to aid them, the suffering continued.

As Jews worked to integrate themselves into the community again and to come to terms with their neighbors who had failed to help in their time of need, and sometimes even aided the enemy, they found that they were no longer welcome. Too many villagers blamed "the Jews" for the war and remained suspicious about where all the Jews had gone. Could the Germans really have murdered whole towns, they wondered, or did the Jews just manage to escape in time, and live out the war in Uzbekistan? And what of the houses and property they abandoned? Surely, the Jews could not reclaim it and displace those who had settled in what was left behind? These questions were answered in large part by the central authorities in Moscow, which began to question the loyalty of the Jews as well. Newspapers and public announcements began to refer to Jews as "cosmopolitans" and "bourgeois nationalists" unable or unwilling to share in the patriotism of the Soviet people. Jews were suspected as fifth columnists; they were accused of working as agents for the United States or for the newly established State of Israel. When the famed Yiddish actor and public figure Solomon Mikhoels was found dead—murdered by Stalin's agents—in January 1948, the message was clear. Jewish institutions were soon closed, and within a few years, the newspapers announced that a group of doctors, a suspicious number of whom had Jewish-sounding names, had been arrested for plotting to poison Stalin. Rumors spread that these measures presaged a total deportation of Soviet Jews. All these actions served to enhance many Soviet Jews' desire to emigrate, and to join in the struggle to establish and then strengthen the Jewish state in the Land of Israel. When the doctors were released and rehabilitated after Stalin's death in March 1953, a new era began. The intense anti-Jewish campaigns of those postwar years settled down, but a new climate of distrust set in. Those we have interviewed have only vague memories of the cataclysmic events in faraway Moscow: they had lives to live, families to raise, and communities to rebuild. But they do remember the sentiments that trickled down to them: the sense that they were living in shadows.

—〰—

Conclusion

Prior to 1989, our views of the Jewish experience in the Soviet Union were derived primarily from the memoirs of émigrés and published writings that came out of the Soviet Union. Both sources agreed that the shtetl had been destroyed and with it "traditional" Jewish life had been eliminated. Whereas Soviet sources—plays, novels, and newspapers—celebrated the Jews who gave up their petty trade and instead found work among the factory proletariat, and enthused about the Jews who were abandoning their religious superstitions, Western writers bemoaned the loss of "traditional" Jewish livelihoods and the forsaking of time-honored traditions. But the archival record and oral histories reveal a much more complicated story. Even into the 1950s, representatives of the Council for Affairs of Religious Cults were still writing confidential reports expressing concern about the persistence of holiday celebrations and prayer quorums among small-town Jews, and current residents re-member childhoods full of Jewish life and report continued faith and identity with Judaism. Sociological surveys confirm the persistence of faith and Jewish ethnic identity among Jews living in the major cities of Russia and Ukraine.[1] The residents we have interviewed often lack a detailed bookish knowledge of Jewish history and Judaic faith, but they retain an intimacy with many informal modes of Jewish expression, including the Yiddish language, Jewish food customs, and a sense of the Jewish calendar cycle. Jewishness remains an important part of their everyday life.

This book has shown how oral histories contribute to the historical record by offering remembered details of the everyday. Oral histories illuminate the rhythms and textures of daily life, and highlight the habitual. They refocus our emphasis onto what ordinary folk considered important—family, food, stability, recognition, and community. They help us understand how individuals structured their lives, how they constructed narratives to understand the world around them, and how they gave meaning to their experiences.

In many cases, the oral histories provide testimony, filling in details about traumatic moments of violence or other crimes against humanity. These memories, seared into the witnesses' consciousness, are more stable than everyday memories and retrievable even seventy years after the events they describe. In these cases, the oral histories add factual data to the historical record. In many cases, the only written evidence we have of major massacres committed by the Nazis and their accomplices in Ukraine are the records of the Soviet Extraordinary Commissions, which themselves were based on oral testimonies taken in the spring of 1945. These terrifying testimonies are usually no more than a paragraph or two in length and often tell little about the sources for the incidents they describe. The witnesses who provide the sworn testimony are often local officials who are recounting information they have learned during the course of the war, but of which they themselves were not eyewitnesses. Many of the commission reports present compilations of testimony or summaries of incidents with little explanation. One typical report "about the murder and torture by Germans of people in Dankivka" includes only a brief statement testifying to the murder of an entire innocent family: "Losinsky, Ben, born in 1909, was shot in a field in the village of Dankivka. Losinska, Tsima Plotyivna, born in 1910, and her son, Losinsky, Anatoly Benovich, born in 1930, were shot in a field near the village of Paryivko."[2] The oral histories help supplement these vital records, providing coordinating evidence and at times additional details. For the thousands of massacres about which we have only the names of victims, oral testimony—even recorded decades later—can help fill in important missing information.

There are certainly some individual episodes that have remained in human memory but are otherwise inaccessible. But oral history is not about mining the human mind for untainted facts. Rather, its primary goal is to understand how individuals and communities construct their pasts and understand their history. The oral histories we have collected provide context and color for the written record. They remind us that decisions made by officials have an impact on individuals, and that the impact is not always direct or as intended. Further, they show us the long-term impact of governmental policies, how the subjects of official campaigns were faring twenty, thirty, or forty years later.

Whereas the names of common folk occasionally pop up in the archival record, they tend to appear only when the lives of individuals intersect with the state machinery—when they are involved in court cases, when they are the subjects of police reports, or when they are recognized for extraordinary achievements. In other words, they are mentioned when they have experiences that are out of the ordinary. These moments of contact provide just one snapshot. A worker may appear in the historical record when she outperforms her quota and is featured in the local paper, but we are unlikely to hear what became of her twenty years later. Life histories allow us to discover the wider context of life, to explore what these experiences meant to the individuals who lived through them and to hear what role these stories played in their life trajectories. They tell us about the ordinary lives that people lived in the midst of extraordinary times.

One of the themes that emerged in our interviews was the disorganized and haphazard way that government orders—whether Soviet, German, or Romanian—were carried out. Whereas the archival record tends to show a plan, albeit a plan that may not have been fully implemented as originally imagined, the oral histories portray the impact of government officials as largely haphazard. When officials appear, they seem to do so out of the blue with no apparent reason or context. As a young girl, Maria Yakuta, for instance, was not aware of the widespread arrests and deportations of so-called kulaks until officials came for her uncle Khotskl. Those we interviewed often shrug their shoulders when asked why government policies were carried out, or they offer rationalized explanations that cleanse these decisions of any ideology or plan: Yiddish schools were closed because parents thought Russian schools were more practical, and synagogues were closed because people stopped going. Neither is presented as the result of a governmental decision to mold young minds in a particular direction, or as part of a policy to absorb Jews into Ukrainian culture. There is a reluctance to attribute major changes to shifts in the policies of a remote authority, and a desire instead to assert local and populist agency in change. Whereas intellectuals and political activists in Moscow spoke of forging a "new Soviet man," the people we spoke with refuse to see their lives as having been orchestrated from above, and instead attribute change to internal forces within their own community.

In oral histories, the state structure, "the Soviet state," comes across not as a totalitarian entity that infiltrates every aspect of life, atomizing individuals, but rather as an ineffective bureaucracy sporadically interfering with regular activity. It is only in references to the early 1930s, around the time of the famine, that people speak of the advent of Soviet power, seeing the earlier decade as a continuation of the revolutionary and war violence. Occupational structures are presented as having remained the same and religious customs are believed to have continued unabated. Those who grew up during this period imagine the households in which they were reared as similar to the households in which their parents were reared. There is a strong sense of time having been uninterrupted: people lived as they had always lived. These days of childhood are imagined in highly nostalgic terms: everybody helped each other out and everybody knew their place in society. The Jews lived in the town and the non-Jews lived in the surrounding villages, but relations between the two were good.

The generation we interviewed was educated in the late 1920s and 1930s and most attended one of the new state-sponsored Yiddish schools. They are proud of having received a Yiddish education and view it as an integral part of their Jewish identity, but report remembering few details of the school curriculum. Only those, mostly men, who had their education supplemented with a religious heder can isolate specific knowledge they retained from childhood. They remember childhoods full of religious life, albeit focused in the home rather than the synagogue. Only the elderly went to the synagogue, they explain. As children, they stayed away, knowing it wasn't safe. Ironically, when we interview these people today, who as children were warned to stay away from the synagogue, we often find them in the synagogue, where they gather with other elderly folk to worship and to socialize. As was the case in their childhood, there are no children in the synagogues today.

The absence of talk about communism in the oral histories is striking. Few people weave the experience of living under communism into their life stories. Even officially organized leisure clubs, like Pioneers and Young Communists, appear only sporadically and with little comment. There are few movies or books that are presented as being particularly influential, perhaps because theaters came late to the shtetl and few residents had time or inclination to read. Instead, those we have interviewed highlight their informal leisure activities with friends, sitting around with drink and a balalaika. This could be a function of selective remembering, but is also an important indicator of how, looking back, those we have interviewed believe communism had an impact upon them. Most were far from the center of power and tended not to view their lives within a political context. Authority appears as remote.[3] Instead, power rests within individuals—their neighbors who saved them from pogroms, or who simply gave a helping hand in times of need, or their friends and family who sustained them and brought them joy.

Many recall how the war interrupted larger plans and activities— school, vacations, love affairs, and job opportunities. Those on the ground had no notion of what the future held or of what plans external actors had in store for them. In some cases, this allows them to ascribe greater agency to officialdom, as reflected in Dovid Geller's belief that the Soviet government had planned the evacuation of Jewish residents from the war zone. More often, though, the picture that emerges is one of total chaos, as families travel from station to station in the hopes of boarding a train heading east. The chaos of the war years is further elucidated in the testimonies of people like Shloyme Skliarskii and Moyshe Kupershmidt, both of whom emphasize the role of sheer luck in their survival, but also frame their narratives in such a way that their own actions saved them on multiple occasions. The Jews of the Tulchyn and Bershad ghettos also focus on the proactive moves each of them made in order to survive, hiding in a chimney or escaping to neighboring villages in search of food.

Rarely have we heard references to the Holocaust as a distinct event. The survivers we interviewed do not view their wartime experiences within the context of the Holocaust as it is written about in the West. They do not share many of the iconic experiences of that genocide—deportations in sealed railway cars, death camps, and murder by gassings. Instead, they call the mass killings "pogroms," thereby associating these horrific atrocities with the anti-Jewish mob violence that had periodically erupted in these towns for generations. German euphemisms for these mass roundups and killings, like Aktion, have also not infiltrated their vocabulary. They understand genocide within a local context.

Those we have interviewed also embed the victorious narrative of the Great Patriotic War into their life stories. Veterans of the Red Army view themselves as victors, and not just victims. Yosl Kogan's story of how he escaped from the chimney and managed to join up with the Red Army to fight in the battle for the Reichstag is emblematic of this triumphalism. The cult of the war resonated with Soviet Jews, who prided themselves on their role in the victory. Emphasizing their victimhood, on the other hand, brought no material advantage from the state or sympathy from the community. On the contrary, it brought them under suspicion for having lived under German occupation. Survivors struggled to mourn for the dead and took measures to commemorate their losses, but they were more likely to emphasize the disproportionate number of Jews who fought than the disproportionate number of Jews who were murdered.

Those we interviewed were among the minority who moved back to their native towns rather than migrate into one of the large cities after the war. Most don't speak of this decision as a conscious choice: they returned because it was their home, or they followed spouses or work opportunities. Within their new communities they sought to recreate a Jewish communal life, but were hampered now by government intrusion. It is only in the postwar period that they admit to having been afraid. Fear permeated many expressions of Jewish life, and there are numerous stories of authorities getting in the way. But still they persevered. Indeed, the perseverance of those we have interviewed and their continued commitment to retaining some aspect of their Jewish identity in spite of all the hurdles they have overcome is inspiring. The performance of simple acts—gathering for prayer, commemorating the dead, eating matzo for Passover—became a means of carrying on tradition and defying fate.

—⁓—

The Jewish cemetery of Bershad is coming to life again. The few remaining stones from the prewar era have been set upright, and new graves, now in ordered rows and properly labeled, are emerging every year. Most of the people interviewed for this book have since died and are buried in cemeteries just like this. Elizaveta Bershadskaia, Yosl Kogan, Khayke Gvinter, Lev Kolodenker, Chaim Skoblitsky, Naftoli Shor, Moyshe Kupershmidt, Shloyme Skliarskii, and many others have passed away since we spoke. The shtetl landscapes are also rapidly deteriorating, being replaced with more modern gentrified housing, paved roads, commercial development, and cell-phone towers. Although it is hard to fault the locals for wishing to see their towns enjoy the fruits and amenities of the modern world, it is, at the same time, sad to see the final architectural remnants of Jewish life in the region be replaced with convenience stores and cafes. That being said, in my more recent trips to the region, I have fervently enjoyed the espresso and Wi-Fi that now wafts aromatically through the town from the new outdoor cafes.

It is not only Wi-Fi and espresso that have changed the region in the ten years since we began our interviews. The last decade has seen revolutionary change in Ukraine, epitomized by the Orange Revolution of 2004–2005 that brought the Western-oriented Viktor Yushchenko to the presidency after a tight race marred by a poisoning attempt on Yushchenko's life that left his face pockmarked, and which was widely blamed on his opponent, the Russian-backed Viktor Yanukovych. Ironically, Yanukovych succeeded in retaking power in the 2010 presidential election that reversed much of the Orange Revolution. The Jews of the region are torn between their Western orientation and the promising economic opportunities offered by European integration on the one hand, and their identification with Russian culture and apprehensions about the ultranationalism that has fueled some aspects of the Orange Revolution on the other hand. Yushchenko's rehabilitation of Stepan Bandera, for instance, was condemned by the Simon Wiesenthal Center and brought discomfort to many Ukrainian Jews, who recalled Bandera's fascist orientation during the Second World War. But young Jews have largely embraced the change and see a future for Ukraine within a greater Europe. Many have returned from time spent abroad with business expertise, which they have used to import goods into their hometowns, or to open up small businesses in the hopes of contributing to the nation's rebirth. One middle-aged man we met along the way proudly gave us a tour of the McMansion he had built on the outskirts of a Ukrainian town. He explained that he had lived in Israel for several years, but found it too difficult to make a living there. With money he had saved in Israel, though, he was able to live well in Ukraine. He planned on opening up his own business, using the business skills and connections he had obtained abroad.

At the time of the collapse of the Soviet Union, Ukraine hosted the sixth largest Jewish population in the world—the last Soviet census, conducted in 1989, counted 487,300 Jews in Ukraine. Rapid emigration to Israel, America, and Germany in the decades since depleted the Jewish population. The 2001 Ukrainian census counted 104,300 Jews, and one 2012 estimate put the "core" Jewish population at 67,000. The current Jewish population of Ukraine is also an aging population; its mean age is 56.4. Like most world Jewry, Ukrainian Jewry is concentrated in large metropolitan areas.[4] But some continue to live in small towns.

In addition to the Jews who continue to reside permanently in Ukraine, the country has emerged as a site of pilgrimage and tourism for Jews from around the world. The brand new International terminal that El Al Israeli airline uses at Ukraine's Borisopil airport in 2012 has aided these tourists, many of whom come from Israel. On Rosh Hashanah 2012, an estimated 25,000 Hasidic pilgrims visited the grave of Nahman of Bratslav in Uman, and the Pushkina neighborhood around the gravesite retains a Jewish presence—and Israeli style security—year round.

Tensions, however, are always high between the Hasidic population and the locals of Uman. Residents complain that the Jewish pilgrims fail to contribute to the local economy—they eat only imported kosher food and refuse to partake in any other activities around the city. Others cite prostitution as the only local industry that benefits from the annual pilgrimage.[5] Defying a state order, about one hundred right-wing nationalists of the Svoboda (Freedom) Party protested the 2012 pilgrimage, many of whom were arrested by riot police. There have been sporadic antisemitic acts of violence in Ukraine: in April 2012, Ukrainian neo-Nazis severely assaulted Aharon Alexander, a twenty-five-year-old worshipper, near Kiev's central synagogue. The assault came on the heels of vandalism at Lviv's Holocaust memorial and was followed the next month by another act of vandalism at a Jewish cemetery in Rivne. In 2007, Neo-Nazis murdered a yeshiva student, Aryeh Leib Misinzov, in Kiev on April 20th, the anniversary of Hitler's birthday. A Chabad Hasidic school in Kiev has also repeatedly been the target of Neo-Nazi vandals. Several prominent Ukrainian academics have blamed Jews for inflicting the terrors of the twentieth century on Ukraine, in accordance with the myth of "double genocide." Among these are Serhiy Bilokin, who was honored by the Kyiv-Mohyla Academy in 2012 despite the protests of the Association of Jewish Organizations and Communities of Ukraine. In a 2004 article entitled "Twenty Years of Jewish Statehood in Ukraine, 1918–1938," Bilokin referred to interwar Ukraine as the "Judaeo-Bolshevisk" state, and ascribed the "state terrorism" of the era to the Jews.[6] In the parliamentary elections of October 2012, the ultranationalist Svoboda Party, which has often utilized antisemitic rhetoric, won 10 percent of the vote. The future of Jewish life in Ukraine is hard to predict, but there are certainly ominous signs as I write.

Those Jews who remain in the small towns of Vinnytsya Province, many of whom are intermarried and have little connection to the wider Jewish community, generally tell us that they no longer feel as secure as they once did. Many, as nonethnic Ukrainians, have trouble identifying with a Ukrainian state. Only one person we interviewed—Maria Yakuta—voluntarily referred to herself as a Ukrainian; most have a greater affinity to the Russian language than they do to Ukrainian, and tend to use Russian in their daily lives. They remain in Ukraine, as one person we spoke to in 2010 put it, to be buried next to their parents and grandparents. Most of the younger generation, though, has emigrated, to Israel, the United States or Germany. As a result, those who remain have developed new international ties; Brooklyn and Bat Yam have become part of the orbit of the shtetl. Some elderly Jews shuttle back and forth between children living in Netanya and parents buried in Bershad. Jewish life in small-town Ukraine is unlikely to recover from the current wave of emigration. Its future will be in the "Diaspora"—America, Germany, or, if one can call it a diaspora, Israel.

The Second World War and the Nazi genocide against the Jews eviscerated Jewish life in the shtetl, but it did not immediately eliminate it. In contrast to the common perception, Jewish life continued for another generation in some small towns in Ukraine. In Vinnytsya Province, in particular, sizable Jewish communities continued to exist into the twenty-first century. These communities present a powerful counterimage to the stereotype of the Soviet Jewish intellectual in the large urban centers. The ways they construct their collective memories pose an alternative to the mainstream interpretation of the history of Soviet Jews and world Jewry writ large. Despite Soviet efforts to assimilate them and Nazi efforts to annihilate them, Jewish communities persevered into the twenty-first century in the small towns of Ukraine, living in the shadow of the shtetl.

BRIEF BIOGRAPHIES

The Archives of Historical and Ethnographic Memories (AHEYM) team conducted ninety-five full life-story interviews with forty-three men and fifty-two women born in the region covered by this book, as part of a larger project that interviewed nearly four hundred people across Eastern Europe, mostly in Ukraine. Sixteen were born before 1920, twenty were born between 1920 and 1924, thirty-two were born between 1925 and 1929, twenty-one were born in the 1930s, and one was born in the 1940s. Not everyone we interviewed was mentioned by name in this book, but each of their stories informed the content. The brief biographies below provide a guide to the reader in identifying the individuals named in this book. The biographies tell only a snippet of their lives. Each individual lived a life that was too varied and too full to faithfully summarize in a short paragraph.

Recordings of all the interviews we conducted have been deposited at Indiana University's Archives of Traditional Music, and portions of those interviews are available for viewing online at www.aheym.org. I have provided accession and shelf numbers for each interview at the end of the brief biography. In cases where individuals have also been interviewed by the USC Shoah Foundation Visual History Archives, I have provided a reference to their interview number as well.

Barstheyn, Asya Konstantinovna (Ita Kolmanovna) was born in Sharhorod in 1928, where her parents were also born. Her father was a purveyor and her mother was a homemaker. She attended a Yiddish school for six years, until her schooling was interrupted by the war. She survived the war in the Sharhorod ghetto. After the war, she completed her schooling by correspondence. She worked as a telegraph dispatcher and a switchboard operator at the post office, and later as a cashier at a barber shop. In 1983 she moved to Vinnytsya, where she is one of the leaders of the Vinnytsya Jewish Women's Choir. We interviewed her on June 28, 2005 in Vinnytsya and on December 12, 2005 in Vinnytsya and Sharhorod. [AHEYM 09–010.56-F MDV 753, 760–763]

Bershadskaia, Elizaveta Konstantinovna was born in Chernyatka in 1927, where her father, who was also born in Chernyatka, worked as a barber. Her mother was born in Bershad and worked as a seamstress. She had two brothers and a sister. She moved to Bershad at the age of thirteen, and spent much of the war in the Bershad ghetto. We interviewed her on July 18, 2002 in Bershad. [AHEYM 09–010.06-F MDV 369–372] She was also interviewed by the USC Shoah Foundation Visual History Archive. [37797]

Burshtein, Arkadii Lvovich was born in Sobolivka in 1928. His father was a tailor. He attended a Yiddish school for four years, and then finished his education in a Ukrainian school. He survived in labor camps in Reichskommissariat Ukraine before making his way into Transnistria. After the war he returned to Haysyn, where he worked as chief engineer in a garment factory. We interviewed him on July 16, 2002 in Haysyn. [AHEYM 09–010.16-F MDV 439–440, 681] He was also interviewed by the USC Shoah Foundation Visual History Archive. [46564]

Chirkova, Bella Simkhovna (Beyle Kleyman) was born in Krosne in 1912. Her father was a rabbi and her grandfather was a cantor. During the war, she served at the front as a nurse. After the war she moved to Vinnytsya to study at a pedagogical institute, and then worked as a teacher. We met her at the Vinnytsya Jewish Women's Choir, where she was dancing and singing at the age of ninety. We interviewed her the next day, on July 13, 2002 in Vinnytsya. [AHEYM 09–010.56-F MDV 753–757]

Chuk, Raisa Iosifovna (Rukhl Rozenblat) was born in Berdichev in 1919. Her father, who was born in Poland, made and sold colanders, and her mother was the manager of an *artel*. She trained as a nurse before the war, but was not sent to the front because she had a toddler to care for, and instead evacuated to the Caucasus, where she worked as a surgeon's assistant. After the war, she continued working as a nurse until the age of seventy-three. She was head nurse at her hospital for forty years. We interviewed her on July 11, 2002 and May 21, 2003 in Berdichev. [AHEYM 09.010.04-F MDV 344–346]

Derbaremdiker, Motl Levi-Isaakovich (Mordke-Oyzer) was born in 1920 in Berdichev. He traces his ancestry to the Hasidic *tsadik* Levi Yitzhak of Berdichev. Motl's father was a soap maker and later became the manager of a soap and soda shop. His mother worked as a seamstress. Motl studied at a heder and then at a Yiddish school for seven years. In 1936, he moved to Kiev to study chemistry at the Institute of Leather Industry. During the war, he was evacuated to Samara (Kuibyshev). He settled in Kiev in 1945, where he studied at the Kiev Light Industry University, before working as a research engineer in a factory. We interviewed him on May 3, 2003 and June 23, 2005 in Kiev. [AHEYM 09.010.04-F MDV 507–509, 513]. In 2002, he was also interviewed by Centropa, and the interview is available at http://www.berdichev.org/mark _derbaremdiker.htm.

Feldman, Brukhe was born in 1938 or 1939 in Bershad. Her father died fighting in the war when she was three years old, and she was brought up by her mother. She spent much of her life working in a furniture factory. We interviewed her on May 14, 2008 in Bershad. [AHEYM 09–010.06-F MDV 379–380] She was also interviewed by the Shoah Foundation [VHA 37736].

Furer, Avrom (Arkadii) Samoilovich was born in Kryzhopil in 1920. Both his parents were also natives of the town. His father was a tailor. He had two brothers, one of whom was killed fighting during the Second World War. He studied in a Yiddish school for four years, before finishing his education in a Russian school. In 1940, Furer was drafted into the army, and was in Chişinău when the war broke out. He fought first in the Caucasus, and then in Stalingrad where he was injured, but continued fighting, becoming the commander of his division and serving in Crimea. Toward the end of the war, he moved with the army through Belarus, Latvia, and Lithuania, reaching Kaliningrad. He returned to Kryzhopil in 1947 and became the manager of a shop. At the age of sixty, he moved to Vinnytsya to work for the railroad company. We interviewed him on July 13, 2002 in Vinnytsya. [AHEYM 09–010.56-F MDV 757–758]

Furman, David Zelikovich was born in 1919 in Berdichev. He worked as a carpenter before the war, and was drafted into the Red Army in 1939, serving in the Far East. He lost his leg fighting at Stalingrad. He returned to Berdichev in 1945 and found that his entire family had been killed. He married a woman from Berdichev, who had been injured when the train on which she was evacuating was bombed. We interviewed him on July 11, 2002 and December 11, 2005. [AHEYM 09–010–04-F MDV 344, 348–349]

Futiran, Alexei Romanovich was born in Tomashpil in 1925, the son of a coachman. Both his parents were also born in Tomashpil. He was one of six children; two of his brothers died fighting in the Second World War. He attended a Yiddish school for four years, and then completed his education at a

Ukrainian language school. At the age of fifteen he began working as a carpenter. During the war he evacuated to the east, from where he was drafted into the army. He served in the Far East until 1950. After the war, he worked as a leatherworker, making hats. He married his first wife in 1950. After she passed away, he remarried a Ukrainian woman. He has two sons, one in Moscow and one in Israel. We interviewed him on May 28, 2007 and May 24, 2008 in Tomashpil. [AHEYM 09–010.52-F MDV 705, 707].

Gaiviker, Naum (Nekhemye) Samoilovich was born in 1912 in Khmelnytskyy (Proskurov). The son of a barber, Naum also became a barber. In 1930 he decided to move to Moscow, but had to return to Khmelnytskyy during the famine of 1932–1933. He was drafted into the Red Army in 1941 and fought on multiple fronts, including Stalingrad, until the end of the war. We interviewed him together with his wife, Sonia, on May 29, 2007 in Khmelnytskyy. They have a daughter, who was living in Israel. [AHEYM 09–010.21-F MDV 465–466]

Gammer (née Goldis), Brukhe Fayveshevna was born in Khmilnyk in 1924. Her parents were born in Khmilnyk as well. Her father worked as a tailor in the neighboring villages and her mother worked as a cashier in a shop. She studied at a Yiddish school for seven years, until her school was converted into a Russian-language school. She graduated tenth grade from the Russian-language school. During the war, she lived in evacuation in Central Asia. She returned to Khmilnyk in 1948, and worked in a bakery for thirty-seven years. Her daughter lives in Khmilnyk. We interviewed her on May 25, 2008 in Khmilnyk. [AHEYM 09–010.12-F MDV 421–422]

Geller, Binyomin (Veniamin) Iakovlevich was born in Pyatka (Velyka Pyatyhirka) in 1923. He had three siblings. Geller studied at a Ukrainian school. His father, who worked in a sugar factory, died in 1934. Two years later, Geller moved to Zhytomyr with his family. In 1941, Geller was drafted into the army, served in the cavalry, and was injured three times. He returned to Zhytomyr after the war, and married in 1949. We interviewed him on July 9, 2002; May 23, 2003; June 11, 2007; May 28, 2008; and January 4, 2009. [AHEYM 09–010.60-F MDV 451–52, 785–87,793–94, 799, and 812–13]

Geller, David (Dovid) was born in 1929 in Zhmerynka. During the war he evacuated to Central Asia, first to Tashkent and then to Shymkent. After the war, he returned to Zhmerynka, but soon moved to Kiev, where he worked in a factory. In 1950 he was drafted into the army, served for three years, and then settled in Bratslav, where his brother lived, and where he met his wife. We interviewed him on June 27, 2005 in Bratslav. [AHEYM 09–010.09-F MDV 394–396]

Geller (née Dikkerman), Sime (Sime-Leye) was born in 1929 in Bratslav. Her father worked as a coachman before the war. During the war, she evacuated to Central Asia, where she worked on a collective farm. When she returned to Bratslav after the war, she worked in the city council. She is married to Dovid Geller. She and Dovid have two daughters who live in Moscow. We interviewed her on June 27, 2005 and July 5, 2010 in Bratslav. [AHEYM 09–010.09-F MDV 394–396]

Gelman, Arkadii (Avrum) Isaakovich was born in 1921 in Kamyanets-Podilskyy. His father, also born in Kamyanets-Podilskyy, was a locksmith. His mother, who was born in Kitaygorod, was a homemaker. He had three siblings: two brothers and one sister. Before the war, he went to a Yiddish school and worked together with his father as a locksmith. He served in the Red Army during the Second World War, and fought in the Battle of Berlin. After the war, he worked as a cattle dealer. We interviewed him on May 18, 2003 in Kamyanets-Podilskyy. [AHEYM 09–010.20-F MDV 461–463]

Gingold, Manya (Mintse-Freyde) Izrailevna was born in 1927 in Tomasphil. She attended a Yiddish school for three years, and then completed her education in a Russian school. Her father was a laborer and her mother worked as a cleaning woman in the offices of the district executive committee. She had one brother and another sibling who died in infancy. She survived the war in the Tomashpil ghetto. After the war, she continued to live with her parents and her brother in Tomashpil. We interviewed her on May 27, 2007 and May 28, 2007 in Tomashpil. [AHEYM 09–010.52-F MDV 701–702]

Golfeld, Pinia Nukhimovich was born in Tulchyn in 1932. He was imprisoned in the Pechera concentration camp during the war. After the war, he trained at a technical institute and found work in a shoe factory, where he was employed for forty-nine years. He served for four years in the military. He married and has a son. We interviewed him on May 20, 2003 in Tulchyn. [AHEYM 09–010.53-F MDV 713–714] He was also interviewed by the USC Shoah Foundation Visual History Archive [31042].

Groysman, Tsolik (Tsadik) Naumovich was born in Tarashche in 1923. His parents were also born in Tarashche. His father was a watchmaker and his mother was a homemaker. He grew up with two sisters. He went to a Yiddish school for seven years and then transferred to a Ukrainian school to complete ten grades. A month after the war broke out, he was drafted into the Red Army. He was injured twice in battle, once in Rostov and once in Stalingrad. Before the war, he had studied to become a dentist, but was unable to complete his studies after the war because of his injuries. After he was released from hospital in Tarashche, he took courses to become a massage therapist and started working in the hospital. He then moved to Almaty, where his uncle lived, and started working as a watchmaker, along with his uncle and father. He married a childhood friend from Tarashche, and moved to Korsun-Shevchenkivskyy in 1952, where he worked again as a watchmaker. We interviewed him on June 25, 2005 in Korsun Shevchenkivskyy. [AHEYM 09–010.26-F MDV 548–549]

Guzman, Dora was born in Tomashpil in 1925. She attended both a Ukrainian- and a Yiddish-language school. During the famine of 1932–1933, she moved to Pishchanka to live with her aunt and uncle. Her father, born in Tomashpil, worked as a postman. Her mother was born in the Odessa region. She had one younger brother. She survived the war in the Tomashpil ghetto. After the war, she worked as an accountant and as an inspector. We interviewed her on June 28, 2005 and May 24, 2008 in Tomashpil. [AHEYM 09–010.52-F MDV 329, 699, 706–707] She was also interviewed by the Shoah Foundation [VHA 34918].

Gvinter (née Oistrakh), Khayke (Sura) Yankelevna was born in 1930 in Bershad. She is a niece of the violinist David Oistrakh. Her father, who died when she was young, was a carpenter, and her mother was a cook. During the Second World War, she was imprisoned in the Bershad ghetto and the Pechera concentration camp. She was shot by the Germans during a mass shooting outside Pechera, but survived and pulled herself out of a mass grave. She worked for the partisans briefly in the Bershad region. She returned to Bershad after the war, married, and worked as a seamstress. We interviewed her on July 18, 2002 and June 26, 2005 in Bershad. [AHEYM 09–010.06-F MDV 602, 375–376 and 09–010.54-F MDV 733] She was also interviewed by the USC Shoah Foundation Visual History Archive. [33216]

Gvinter, Nukhim Moiseevich was born in Bershad in 1936. He is Khayke Gvinter's brother. He grew up with four siblings. He survived the war in the Bershad ghetto. After the war, he worked as a carpenter in a textile factory and then as the manager of a shoe store. He also served in the military after the war. He has three children. We interviewed him on May 14, 2008 in Bershad.

[AHEYM 09–010.06-F MDV 377–378, 380] He was also interviewed by the USC Shoah Foundation Visual History Archive. [32938]

Katsman (née Chechelniker), Klara (Khaye) was born in 1931 in Tulchyn. Her father was a brushmaker and her mother was a homemaker. She has lived in Tulchyn her entire life, other than during the war when she was imprisoned in the Pechera concentration camp. After the war, she returned to Tulchyn, where she worked as a tailor. She has a son and a daughter. We interviewed her on January 8, 2009 and June 8, 2009 in Tulchyn. [AHEYM 09–010.53-F MDV 723–724, 727] She was also interviewed by the USC Shoah Foundation Visual History Archive. [31083]

Katz, Nesye Sulimanovna was born in 1916 in Brailiv and orphaned at a young age when her parents died of typhus. Her father had worked at the mill. She was raised by her uncle, a tinsmith. She served in the Red Army as a nurse during the war and then worked in a factory for thirty-six years. She has a daughter in town and a son who lives in Europe. We interviewed her on July 13, 2002 and May 22, 2008 in Vinnytsya. [AHEYM MDV 753, 765]

Kaviner, Aba Davidovich was born in 1921 in Derazhnya, where he was able to receive a Jewish education, first in a heder and then in a clandestine yeshiva. His father worked as a cooper and his mother was a homemaker. In 1939 he was drafted into a military school in Leningrad. He remained in the army until 1946, serving in the Baltics and in Moscow. After the war he returned to Derazhnya, but soon thereafter moved to Khmelnytskyy, where he eventually found work as the director of a carpentry workshop. We interviewed him on May 30, 2007; May 26, 2008; and January 5 and 6, 2009 in Khmelnytskyy. [AHEYM 09–010.21-F MDV 469–473, 478–479, 482–483]

Khaiut, Tsilia (Tsilye bas Ber) Borisovna was born in 1917 in Mohyliv-Podilskyy. Her father, also from Mohyliv-Podilskyy, was a cobbler. Her mother came from the Bessarabian region, near Mykolaiv. She attended two Yiddish schools and finished her education in 1934. She had two sisters and a brother. She has two sons. She survived the war in the Mohyliv-Podilskyy ghetto and a concentration camp in Transnistria. We interviewed her on May 19, 2003 in Mohyliv-Podilskyy. [AHEYM MDV 582-583]

Kiselman, Nisen (Mikhail) Mikhailovich was born in Tomashpil in 1927. He is a cousin of Pesia, Sasha, and Lev Kolodenker, as well as the husband of Pesia

Kolodenker. His father was a coachman, and his mother was a homemaker. His father died during the famine in 1933, leaving his mother to care for Nisen, his sister, and his four brothers. During the war, he was confined to the Tomash-pil ghetto, where his mother and sister were both killed by the Germans in a massacre. After the war, he joined the Red Army and served for seven years.

Kislinskaia, Tseytl (Tsilia) Davidovna was born in Korsun-Shevchenkivskyy in 1924. She attended a Yiddish school for seven years. Her father was a cobbler; her mother was a homemaker, and she had two brothers. After she finished school, she helped her mother, who worked in a button factory. During the war, she evacuated to the Rostov region and worked in a collective farm, before evacuating further to Shkalov, where she worked in a military factory. After the war, she returned to Korsun-Shevchenkivskyy and worked in a sugar factory. She has one daughter. We interviewed her on June 25, 2005 in Korsun-Shevchenkivskyy. [AHEYM 09–010.26-F MDV 546–548]

Kogan, Iosif (Yosl) Abramovich was born in 1927 in Bershad. His father, a soap-maker, died during the 1932–1933 famine. He was brought up by his mother, a candy-maker. He spent much of the war in the Bershad ghetto, where he wrote songs about his experiences. He served in the Red Army and participated in the liberation of Berlin. He moved to Tulchyn in 1960 and worked in a procurement office. We interviewed him on July 14, 2002; May 20, 2003; May 27, 2007; and January 8, 2009. [AHEYM 09–010.53-F MDV 351, 709–711, 717, 719–720, 725–726]

Kolodenker, Aleksandr (Sasha) Shaevich is the brother of Pesia and Lev Kolodenker. He was born in Tulchyn in 1929. During the war, he was imprisoned first in the Tulchyn ghetto and then in the Pechera concentration camp. We interviewed him on January 8 and June 8, 2009 and July 4, 2010 in Tulchyn. [AHEYM 09–010.53-F MDV 723–724, 728–729]

Kolodenker, Lev Shaevich is the brother of Pesia and Aleksandr Kolodenker and husband of Yente Kolodenker. He was born in Tulchyn in 1925. In 1941, at the age of sixteen, he was drafted into a military training institute, and joined the Red Army in 1944, where he rose to the rank of sergeant. We interviewed him on January 8, 2009 in Tulchyn. [AHEYM 09–010.53-F MDV 728–729]

Kolodenker, Pesia (Pesye) Shaevna was born in Tulchyn in 1927. She is the sister of Lev and Aleksandr Kolodenker. She survived the war in the Tulchyn ghetto and Pechera concentration camp. We interviewed her on January 8 and

June 8, 2009 and July 4, 2010 in Tulchyn. [AHEYM 09–010.53-F MDV 723–724, 728–729] She was also interviewed by the USC Shoah Foundation Visual History Archive. [34979]

Kolodenker (née Tolkovitz), Yente Usherovna was born in Tulchyn in 1927. She is the wife of Lev Kolodenker. She has one brother and a sister. She survived the war in the Pechera ghetto. She lived in Israel briefly in the 1990s, but returned to Tulchyn. Her son lives in Canada. We interviewed her on January 8 and June 8, 2009 in Tulchyn. [AHEYM 09–010.53-F MDV 723–724, 728–729]

Kozak (née Shafir), Evgeniia (Sheyndl) Abramovna was born in 1926 in Bershad. She attended a Ukrainian school for eight years. Her parents, who were cousins, were both born in Bershad. Her father was a furrier. She had a younger brother and sister. She survived the war in evacuation in the Caucasus and then in Central Asia. When she returned to Bershad after the war, in April 1944, her mother worked as a baker. She married in 1958 and has two sons. Her husband died before her second son was born, when her first son was just a todller. We interviewed her on July 17 and 18, 2002 in Bershad. [AHEYM 09–010.06-F MDV 367–370, 733, 374]

Krasner, Evgeniia (Sheyndl) Isaakovna was born in 1936 in Shpykiv. She attended a Ukrainian school before the war. Her father worked as an accountant in a sugar factory. During the war, she was imprisoned in the Pechera concentration camp. After the war she was trained at a cultural institute in Kiev, from which she graduated as a librarian. We interviewed her on July 15, 2002 in Shpykiv. [AHEYM 09–010.45-F MDV 660, 664–666]

Kupershmidt, Moyshe (Mikhail) Aronovich was born in Bratslav in 1914. His father was a coachman and his mother stayed home and looked after the children and the cow. His parents had six children, two of whom died in infancy. He attended a Yiddish school in Bratslav for four years. He served in the military in the Finnish War, and was working as a chauffeur when the Second World War began. He survived under Nazi occupation in Reichskommissariat Ukraine, and ended the war serving in the Red Army. After the war, he returned to Bratslav, where he continued working as a driver. His first wife died in 1947. He soon remarried and has a son, who lives in Israel. We interviewed him on July 14, 2002 with his wife, Rakhil Natanovna, and then again on June 25, 2005 in Bratslav. [AHEYM MDV 09–010.09-F 392–393, 396–397; 09–010.43-F MDV 657]

Kurman, Klara Lvovna was born in 1930 in Sharhorod. Her father was born in Kamyanets-Podilskyy and worked as a physician assistant. Her mother, a homemaker, was also born in Sharhorod. She grew up with two brothers and one sister. She attended a Russian-language school. She survived the war in the Sharhorod ghetto. After the war, she worked at a printing press and at a library. We interviewed her on July 15, 2002 in Sharhorod. [AHEYM 09–010.43-F MDV 659–660]

Leiderman (née Bronfman), Gisia Moiseevna was born in 1924 in Bershad. Her father, also from Bershad, was a leatherworker. She had a sister and a brother. After she graduated from school, she trained at a technical school. She survived the war in the Bershad ghetto. We interviewed her on July 18, 2002 in Bershad. [AHEYM 09–010.06-F MDV 369–370]

Litvak, Sonia (Sure) Shevelevna was born in 1925 in Novohrad-Volynskyy. She had four siblings. Her father, a leatherworker, was also born in Novohrad-Volynskyy. Her mother worked occasionally as a freelance seamstress. Sonia studied at a Yiddish school. After the war, she worked as a curricular administrator in kindergartens, as well as in a textile factory. In the 1960s, she worked in the cultural department of the Soviet consulate in Germany. We interviewed her on May 6, 2003 in Rivne. [AHEYM 09–010.42-F MDV 645–648]

Marinina (née Palatnikova), Tatiana (Taybele) Moiseevna is the sister of Sofia Palatnikova. She was born in 1921 in Teplyk. Her father was a butcher. In the 1930s, she moved to the Lunacharskii collective farm in Crimea. She completed three grades at a Yiddish school in Crimea, and then attended a Russian-language school in Simferopol. After finishing pedagogical training, she worked for two years in an ethnic German village. She survived the war in the Bershad and Raygorod camps. After the war, she worked procuring livestock and later as a German teacher at an evening school. She has a daughter and a son, who lives in Germany. We interviewed her on July 17, 2002 in Teplyk. [AHEYM 09–010.50-F MDV 684–686] She was also interviewed by the USC Shoah Foundation Visual History Archive [37775]

Murovanaia, Mire Markovna was born in 1926 in Mykolaiv. Her father, a colonel, was born in Kublich. He was positioned in Moscow and taught at a military technical school in Babushkin. Her mother was born in Haysyn and worked as president of a tailors' collective. She had a half-sister from her father's second marriage. She attended a Russian school and finished seven grades in Haysyn.

During the war, she evacuated to Central Asia. After the war, she was trained at a pharmacy and then worked as a pharmacist technician for forty-five years. She has two daughters; they live in Moscow and in Haysyn. We interviewed her on July 16, 2002 in Haysyn. [AHEYM 09–010.16-F MDV 366 and 439; and 09–010.45-F MDV 666]

Palatnikova, Sofia (Sonia) Moiseevna was born in 1927 in Teplyk. She is the sister of Tatiana Marinina. She went to a Ukrainain school for six years, but her schooling was interrupted by the war. She was brought up mostly in the Lunacharskii collective farm in Crimea, but returned with her family to Teplyk in 1940. She survived the war in Teplyk and Bershad, and in camps in Bratslav, Haysyn, and Raygorod. After the war, she worked in an industrial complex for twenty-two years. We interviewed her on July 17, 2002 and July 2, 2010 in Teplyk. [AHEYM 09–010.50-F MDV 687–689] She was also interviewed by the USC Shoah Foundation Visual History Archive [37784].

Pecherskaia (née Disyatnik), Frida (Freyde) Isaakovna was born in Bratslav in 1927. Her father worked as a coachman. She was one of five children. She survived the war in the Pechera concentration camp, where she witnessed the murder of her mother. Her older brother died fighting in the war, and her other siblings all died at young ages. After her liberation she returned to Bratslav, where she worked as a housemaid. She later worked in a brewery. She moved to Tulchyn after she married. She has a son, who lives in Tulchyn, and a daughter in Israel. We interviewed her on January 8, 2009 and June 8, 2009 in Tulchyn. [AHEYM 09–010.53-F MDV 723–724, 731–732]

Poberevskaia, Anna (Khone) Solomonovna was born in Stanislavchyk in 1914, where her father was a rabbi and her mother worked in the market. In 1921, she moved to Dzhuryn and then later to Zhmerynka. She attended a Yiddish school for seven years and finished her schooling at a Russian school. In 1930, at the age of sixteen, she started working as a secretary for the court prosecutor. She later studied in Kalinin to be a teacher, and later at a pedagogical institute in Vinnytsya. We interviewed her on July 12, 2002 in Zhmerynka. [AHEYM 09–010.58-F MDV 752, 774–775]

Preger, Esther Khananovna was born in 1921 in Tomashpil. Her parents were also born in Tomashpil; her father was a laborer and her mother a homemaker. She attended Yiddish school for seven years and then a Ukrainian school to graduate tenth grade. After she graduated, she attended the Vinnytsya Pedagogical Technical College. She survived the war in the Tomashpil ghetto. After the war, she worked as a teacher from first through fourth grade at a local school until she retired at age fifty-five. We interviewed her on June 28, 2005 in Tomashpil. [AHEYM 09–010.52-F MDV 697, 699]

Presler (née Tolba), Donia Shoilevna was born in 1929 in Tulchyn. Her father was a musician. Her mother worked as a glazier. She had two sisters. She finished four years of Yiddish school. During the war, she was imprisoned in the Pechera camp for four years. After the war she married and worked in a shoe store with her husband. One of their two children died in infancy. We interviewed her on May 19, 2003 in Tulchyn. [AHEYM 09–010.52F MDV 694 and 09–010.53-F, MDV 712, 715–716] She was also interviewed by the USC Shoah Foundation Visual History Archive [31670]

Rivelis, Feyge (Faina) Samuilovna was born in Sharhorod in 1916, the youngest of four children. Her father was a tailor. She attended a Yiddish-language school for four years. She was a Pioneer and a member of the Komsomol. She survived the war in the Sharhorod ghetto. After the war, she worked in the local municipal government for fifty years. She had lived in Germany for a year, but returned to Sharhorod. We interviewed her on July 12, 2002. [AHEYM 09–010.43-F MDV 656]

Rubin, Efim Isaakovich (Chaim ben Yitzkhak) was born in 1922 in Uman, but moved at a young age to the neighboring town of Buki. He attended a Yiddish school for four years, before finishing his education at a Ukrainian school. His father was a barber. He was drafted in 1940 and trained as an officer in Odessa. During the war, he fought at the Moscow, Leningrad, Smolensk, and Kalinin fronts. After the war, he worked as a dental technician in Uman. He was interviewed together with his cousin, Matvei Vladimirovich (Motl ben Velvl) Rubin, who was born in 1928 in Buki. We interviewed him on July 18 and 19, 2002 and June 26, 2005 in Uman. [AHEYM 09–010.54-F MDV 733–735, 739]

Rusakovskaia, Raisa (Rokhl) Isaakovna was born in 1925 in Chernobyl. Her mother was also born in Chernobyl and her father, a carpenter, was born in Ivankovtsy. She had two sisters. She went to a Yiddish school for a few years, but finished her schooling at a Ukrainian school. She spent the war in evacuation in Central Asia. After the war, she worked as an accountant in a collective. In 1967, she moved to Kiev. We interviewed her on June 22, 2005 in Kiev. [AHEYM 09–010.23-F MDV 510–512]

Sapozhnik, Klara (Khaye) Naumovna was born in 1924 in Tomashpil as one of eight children. One of her brothers moved to Israel. Her parents worked in the "Gigant" collective farm. She never received any formal schooling. She survived the war in the Tomashpil ghetto. After the war, she moved back into her parents' house and married in 1946. After her first husband died, she married again in 1960. She worked in construction and then in a furniture factory, and now earns some money selling oil from the sea-buckthorn that grows in her garden. She has one son. We interviewed her on June 28, 2005 and May 28, 2007 in Tomashpil. [AHEYM 09–010.52-F MDV 699–701]

Shames (née Goldes), Rakhil (Rukhl) Shlemovna was born in 1915 in Ivanopil (Yanushpol). Her father was a millworker, and her mother was a homemaker. She studied in a Russian school. During the war she evacuated to the Urals, where she worked in a textile factory. Her sister and her father were killed by the Germans near Khmilnyk, but she and her mother survived. After the war, she moved to Khmilnyk, where she worked as a bookkeeper in a textile factory. We interviewed her on May 25, 2008 and January 6, 2009 in Khmilnyk. [AHEYM 09–010.12-F MDV 420–421, 424]

Shor, Grigorii Iosifovich was born in Kopayhorod in 1925. His father was a butcher. He studied for seven years at a Yiddish school and finished his education in a Ukrainian school. He lived in Kopayhorod until he was drafted into the military in 1944. Her remained in the military until 1971. We interviewed him on July 11, 2002 in Vinnytsya. [AHEYM 09–010.56-F MDV 749–752]

Shor, Liudmila (Leye) Yudelevna is the wife of Grigorii Shor and was born in Kopayhorod. She attended a Ukrainian-language school. Her father owned a flower shop, but was driven out of the house and shop in the 1930s. Her family then moved to Verkhovka and her father became a barber. She has two daughters; one lives in Israel and the other in Germany. She is active in the Vinnytsya Jewish Women's Choir. We interviewed her on July 11 and 13, 2002 in Vinnytsya. [AHEYM 09–010.56-F MDV 749–753]

Shor, Naftoli (Anatolii) Petrovich (Pinhasovich) was born in Bershad in 1922. His father was the leader of a local Hasidic group in town and worked as a hatmaker. He had two brothers and a sister. He went to a Yiddish school for four years and finished his education in a Ukrainian school. He also attended a heder. We interviewed him on July 18, 2002 in Bershad. [AHEYM 09–010.06-F MDV 372–374]

Shoykhetman, Ron Davidovich was born in 1935 in Derazhnya and moved to Lutsk in 1959. His father worked as a janitor. Ron worked in a factory. We interviewed him on June 9, 2007 in Lutsk. [AHEYM 09–010.30-F MDV 580]

Shvartzbroit, Etia Kalmanova was born in Mohyliv-Podilskyy in 1928. Her grandfather was a rabbi, and her father had a textile workshop, where her mother worked as a pattern-maker. The workshop was closed in the 1920s, after which her father worked as a government purveyor until his death in 1940. Etia went to a Yiddish school for four years. In 1942, she was imprisoned together with her family in the Pechera concentration camp, where the rest of her family died. She escaped, eventually making it back to Mohyliv-Podilskyy. After the war, she settled in Lutsk. We interviewed her on May 8, 2003 in Lutsk. [AHEYM 09–010.42-F MDV 648 and 09–010.30-F MDV 575]

Shveibish, Rita (Reyzl) Davidovna was born in 1936 in Tulchyn. She grew up with two brothers. Both of her parents were born in Tulchyn. Her father delivered products for a welding shop. She survived the war in Pechera. After the war, she trained in Vinnytsya as a nurse, and worked as a nurse for fifty years in Tulchyn. Since her retirement, she has been director of the Jewish community of Tulchyn and has been active in establishing memorials for the murdered Jews of the town. We interviewed her on July 14, 2002, May 19 and 20, 2003, May 27, 2007, May 25, 2008, and January 8 and June 9, 2009 in Tulchyn. [AHEYM 09–010.53-F MDV 351, 359, 707–709, 712–713, 720–722, 725]. She was also interviewed by the USC Shoah Foundation Visual History Archive. [31019]

Skliarskii, Semen (Shloyme) Moiseevich was born in Lipovets in 1926. His father was a furniture maker. His mother died when he was three years, old and his father passed away four years later. He was brought up by his mother's sister. He began his schooling in a Yiddish school, and completed his education in a Ukrainian-language school. He survived most of the war in hiding in Reichskommissariat Ukraine. Toward the end of the war, he joined a group of partisans. After the war he worked as a bookkeeper. He married a woman from Bershad in 1951 and moved there in 1969. We interviewed him on May 14, 2008 and January 7, 2009 in Bershad. [AHEYM 09–010.06-F MDV 381–384] He was also interviewed by the USC Shoah Foundation Visual History Archive [31843].

Skoblitsky, Chaim (Efim) Gershkovich was born in 1919 in Berdichev. His father was born in Poland, near Warsaw, and worked as a metalworker. His mother raised five sons. He studied in both a Yiddish school and in a heder. During the Second World War, he served in the Red Army as the commander of a battalion of tanks. He worked in a museum and a photography studio. We interviewed him on July 10 and 11, 2002 and May 21 and 22, 2003 in Berdichev. [AHEYM 09–010.04-F MDV 342–344, 346–347]

Sobol, Maria (Molke) Iosipovna was born in Mohyliv-Podilskyy in 1915. She was raised in a family of seven children. Her father worked in a factory, and her mother cared for the children. She attended Yiddish and Russian language schools, and worked most of her life as a nurse. We interviewed her in Mohyliv-Podilskyy in on December 13, 2005. [AHEYM 09–010.31-F MDV 764]

Soyfer, David (Dovid) Isaakovich was born in 1930 in Berdichev. His father, a kosher butcher, was also born in Berdichev and his mother was born in a village near Zhytomyr. He grew up with one brother. During the famine of 1932–1933, he moved in with his grandmother on a collective farm. In 1939, he returned to Berdichev to live with his father. During the war, he evacuated to the northern Caucasus, and then to Kazakhstan. In 1950, after his return to Berdichev, he was drafted into the Red Army for three and a half years. After his service, he worked as a cooper for thirty-five years. His has one daughter, who lives in Berdichev. We interviewed him on December 11, 2005 and January 9, 2009 in Berdichev. [AHEYM 09–010.04-F MDV 349, 356]

Teplitskaia, Raisa (Raye) Kirilovna was born in 1931 in Ternivke. She grew up with two sisters and one brother. Her father was a blacksmith and her mother was a homemaker and raised pigs. She went to a Ukrainian school. She survived the war in hiding in a village. After the war, she returned to Ternivke, before settling in Uman in 1952. She has three sons, one of whom lives in Germany, and a daughter. We interviewed her on June 25, 2005 in Uman. [AHEYM 09–010.54-F MDV 736–737]

Tkach, Anna Borisovna was born in 1935 in Chernivtsi (Vinnytsya Province). Her father worked as a trader. She survived the war in the Chernivtsi ghetto. In 1944, she resumed her education, finishing ten grades in a Ukrainian language school in Chernivtsi. After the war, she worked as a Ukrainian language journalist for a local newspaper for forty years. In 1962 she married, and moved to Yampil in 1965. We interviewed her on June 28, 2005 in Yampil. [AHEYM MDV 696–697] She was also interviewed by the USC Shoah Foundation Visual History Archive. [VHA 36404]

Vainer-Shpak, Nekha Froimovna was born in Vinnytsya in 1921. Her Hasidic father was born in Bratslav and her mother was born in Pryluky. Her father worked as the chief supplier in a factory. She had a brother and a sister. She graduated from a Yiddish school after eight years and then worked odd jobs in a village before training as a dentist. In 1940, she finished her training and got a job working in a sugar factory in the village of Moyivka. She survived the war by hiding out in Vinnytsya and disguising herself as a non-Jew. After the war, she worked as a dentist in Vinnytsya, and had two children. We interviewed her on May 21, 2003 in Vinnytsya. [AHEYM 09–010.56-F MDV 718, 759]

Vaisman, Abram (Abrashe) was born in 1940 in Sharhorod. His father was also born in Sharhorod and was unable to work because he lost his right hand. His mother was born in Chernivtsi and worked as a seamstress. He grew up with three siblings, and attended Ukrainian-language schools. He survived the war in the Sharhorod ghetto. Before his retirement, he worked as a photo-journalist. We interviewed him together with his wife and daughter on July 12, 2002 in Sharhorod. [AHEYM 09–010.43-F MDV 776, 654–656]

Vaisman (née Rainsdorf), Beyle (Bella) Moiseevna was born in 1925 in Berdichev. She is Isaak Vaisman's wife. Her father was born in Warsaw and worked as a chief accountant. She grew up in a relatively wealthy family. Days before the war began, she went to visit her cousin, as a result of which she was cut off from the rest of her family. She survived the war in evacuation in Uzbekistan, but her family was killed in Berdichev. She and Isaak have one daughter, who lives in America. We interviewed her on July 10, 2002, May 27, 2007, and January 9, 2009 in Berdichev. [AHEYM 09–010.04-F MDV 338–339, 342, 351, 354–355]

Vaisman, Isaak Iosifovich was born in 1925 in Berdichev. His father, who died in 1928, was also born in Berdichev and had worked as a tailor. Isaak attended a Yiddish school for seven years, before he was transferred to a Russian school to complete his education. He evacuated to Uzbekistan when the war began, from where he was drafted into the Red Army. He served from 1943 until 1946 in an intelligence unit. In Berdichev, he made a living selling soda water in the marketplace. We interviewed him on July 10 and 11, 2002, December 11, 2005, May 26 and 27, 2007, and January 9, 2009 in Berdychiv. [AHEYM 09–010.04-F MDV 761, 338–340, 342, 344, 348, 351, 354–355, 632]

Vanshelboim, Moyshe (Mikhail) Aronovich was born in Berdichev in 1928. His parents were both born in Berdichev, where his father worked as a painter. He studied at a Yiddish school for four years, before completing his education at a Russian school. His oldest brother died at the front, his younger brother, parents, and two sisters were murdered by the Germans. He escaped the mass shooting that killed his father and was aided in hiding by several non-Jews. After the war, he briefly worked in a mill before being drafted into the army in 1950. He served for four and a half years. After his service, he worked twenty-five years at a mill, and then at a factory. We interviewed him on May 26 and 27, 2007; January 9 and June 9, 2009; and July 5, 2010 in Berdichev. [AHEYM 09–010.04-F MDV 352–353, 359–361, 607, 632] He was also interviewed by the USC Shoah Foundation Visual History Archive [27225].

Vaynman, Klara (Khayke) Borisovna was born in 1939 in Vinnytsya. She moved to Lviv shortly thereafter. She evacuated to the Urals during the war. Her father was a director of a factory and her mother, born in Lubenets, was a teacher at a Yiddish technical institute. Her father was killed during the war. After the war, her mother worked in a sugar factory and then in the kindergarten in Bar. We interviewed her on June 29, 2005 in Bar. [AHEYM 09–010.02-F MDV 329–330]

Yakuta, Maria Andreevna was born in 1921 in Teplyk. She grew up with six siblings. Her parents were also born in Teplyk, and her father worked as a hatmaker. She attended a Yiddish school for seven years. Her parents and three siblings were killed in Teplyk during the war. We interviewed her on July 17, 2002 in Teplyk. [Sources: AHEYM 09–010.50-FMDV 682–684]

Yarmulnik, Sonia (Sure) Petrovna was born in 1929 in Khmelnytskyy. She studied at a Russian school. She spent the war years in evacuation in Uzbekistan. After the war, she worked as an economist and accountant for fifty-one years. She has a son. We interviewed her on May 28, 2007 in Khmelnytskyy. [AHEYM 09–010.21-F MDV 467–468]

Yatskova (née Kremer), Dora (Dvoyre) Iosifovna was born in Murafa in 1924. In 1931, she moved to Kopayhorod with her family. Her father was the director of the Yiddish school in Kopayhorod, but she attended a Ukrainian-language school. She survived in the Kopayhorod ghetto for most of the war. She has a younger brother who lives in Israel. After the war she worked as a bookkeeper and then at a community center. We interviewed her on May 24, 2008 in Kopayhorod. [AHEYM 09–010.09-F MDV 398, 770]

Yurkovetsky, Nisen Ovshiyevich was born in 1917 in Tulchyn. His parents were killed in a pogrom when he was less than two years old, and he was brought up by his grandmother. His father had been a barber. He trained as a chauffeur in Bratslav and fought in the Finnish War. He was injured fighting for the Red Army in the early days of the Second World War. After his demobilization, he ended up in the Pechera concentration camp and the Bershad ghetto. He later rejoined the Red Army. After the war, he continued his work as a chauffeur in Bratslav. He has two sons, who live in America, and a daughter, who lives in Tulchyn. We interviewed him on May 27, 2007 and January 8, 2009 in Tulchyn. [AHEYM 09–010.53-F MDV 720–721, 730–731]

Zhovtis, Mikhail was born in 1927 in Khmilnyk. During the war, he was forced to work in several forced labor battalions. He ended the war in Mohyliv-Podil-skyy. After the war, he was drafted into the army and served for seven years. When he returned from the service, he lived in Litin for two years. He then relocated to Bar, where he worked as a turner in a factory for thirty-two years. He has three children, two of whom live in Israel. We interviewed him on June 29, 2005 in Bar. [AHEYM 09–010.02-F MDV 330, 331, 690]

NOTES

INTRODUCTION

1. See, for instance, Daniel Mendelsohn, *The Lost: A Search for the Six Million* (New York: HarperCollins, 2006); Omer Bartov, *Erased: Vanishing Traces of Jewish Galicia in Present-Day Ukraine* (Princeton, N.J.: Princeton University Press, 2007); and Yaffa Eliach, *There Once Was a World: A 900-Year Chronicle of the Shtetl of Eishyshok* (Boston: Little Brown, 1998).

2. Irving Cutler, *The Jews of Chicago: From Shtetl to Suburb* (Urbana: University of Illinois Press, 2008); Sol Gittleman, *From Shtetl to Suburbia: The Family in Jewish Literary Imagination* (Boston: Beacon Press, 1978); or Shlomo Berger, ed., *From the Shtetl to the Metropolis* (Amsterdam: Menasseh Ben Israel Institute, 2012); and Antony Polonsky, ed. *From Shtetl to Socialism: Studies from Polin* (London: Littman Library of Jewish Civilization, 1993).

3. Still today studies of the shtetl have concentrated overwhelmingly on Polish or Galician examples, virtually ignoring those that existed within the Soviet Union. See Eva Hoffman, *Shtetl: The Life and Death of a Small Town and the World of Polish Jews* (Boston: Houghton Mifflin, 1997); Steven Katz, ed., *The Shtetl* (New York: NYU Press, 2006); and Yehuda Bauer, *The Death of the Shtetl* (New Haven, Conn.: Yale University Press, 2010). Ben Cion Pinchuk's *Shtetl Jews under Soviet Rule: Eastern Poland on the Eve of the Holocaust* (Oxford: Blackwell, 1991) looks only at Polish territories occupied by the Soviet Union during the war.

4. The most influential portrait of postwar Soviet Jewry was probably Elie Wiesel, *Jews of Silence: A Personal Report on Soviet Jewry* (New York: Holt, Rinehart and Winston, 1966). For a response to Wiesel see Yosef Kerler, "Di tseshterte legend vegn 'Shvaygndikn yidntum'" in *Tselfter oygust, 1952* (Jerusalem: Eygns, 1978), 157–71.

5. Natan Sharansky, *Fear No Evil* (New York: Public Affairs, 1998); Yakov Alpert, *Making Waves: Stories from My Life* (New Haven, Conn.: Yale University Press, 2000); Emil Draitser, *Shush! Growing Up Jewish under Stalin: A Memoir* (Berkeley: University of California Press, 2008); Saul Iakovlevich Borovoi, *Vospominaniia* (Moscow: Evreiskii universitet v Moskve, 1993); Iakov Lvovich Rapoport, *Na rubezhe dvukh vekov: Delo vrachei 1953 goda* (Moscow: Kniga, 1988).

6. Gennady J. Estraikh, *In Harness: Yiddish Writers' Romance with Communism* (Syracuse, N.Y.: Syracuse University Press, 2005); Anna Shternshis, *Soviet and Kosher* (Bloomington: Indiana University Press, 2006); David Shneer, *Yiddish and the Creation of Soviet Jewish Culture: 1918–1930* (Cambridge: Cambridge University Press, 2004); Jeffrey Veidlinger, *The Moscow State Yiddish Theater: Jewish Culture on the Soviet Stage* (Bloomington: Indiana University Press, 2000); and Elissa Bemporad, *Becoming Soviet Jews: The Bolshevik Experiment in Minsk* (Bloomington: Indiana University Press, 2013).

7. Yuri Slezkine, *The Jewish Century* (Princeton, N.J.: Princeton University Press, 2006).

8. Only in the last few years have scholars begun to investigate Soviet Jewish life in the shtetls of the former Pale of Jewish Settlement. See Arkadii Zeltser, *Evrei sovetskoi provintsii: Vitebsk i mestechki, 1917–1941* (Moscow: ROSSPEN, 2006); Deborah Yalen, "Red Kasrilevke: Ethnographies of Economic Transformation in the Soviet Shtetl, 1917–1939" (Ph.D. diss., University of California, Berkeley, 2007); Andrew Jay Sloin, "Pale Fire: Jews in Revolutionary Belorussia, 1917–1929" (Ph.D. diss., University of Chicago, 2009); Dmitry Tartakovsky, "Parallel Ruptures: Jews of Bessarabia and Transnistria between Romanian Nationalism and Soviet Communism, 1918–1940" (Ph.D. diss., University of Illinois at Urbana-Champaign, 2009); Elina Chklonikova, "The Transformation of the 'Shtetl' in the USSR in the 1930s," *Jews in Russia and Eastern Europe* 52, no. 1 (2004): 91–129; and Gennady Estraikh, "The Soviet Shtetl in the 1920s," *Polin: Studies in Polish Jewry* 17 (2004): 197–212.

9. Timothy Snyder, *Bloodlands: Europe between Hitler and Stalin* (New York: Basic Books, 2010), 26–27.

10. Hiroaki Kuromiya, *The Voices of the Dead: Stalin's Great Terror in the 1930s* (New Haven, Conn.: Yale University Press, 2007), 13. Kuromiya gives the figure of 123,421 people sentenced to be shot in 1937–1938. Timothy Snyder provides the figure of 70,868 inhabitants of Ukraine shot by NKVD men in 1937–1938. See Snyder, *Bloodlands*, 84.

11. Amir Weiner, *Making Sense of War: The Second World War and the Fate of the Bolshevik Revolution* (Princeton, N.J.: Princeton University Press, 2001), 9.

12. Between the consolidation of Soviet Ukraine at the end of the Russian Civil War (1918–1921) and 1932 these towns were subdivided into districts (*okrugi*): Bershad, Bratslav, Tomashpil, and Tulchyn were part of the Tulchyn District; Sharhorod and Mohyliv-Podilskyy were located in Mogilev District; Teplyk could be found in Uman District; and Vinnytsya was part of Vinnytsya District.

13. Snyder, *Bloodlands*.

14. Weiner, 9.

15. For a historical guidebook to Jewish Podolia see V. M. Lukin, A. V. Sokolova, and B. N. Khaymovich, *100 evreiskikh mestechek Ukrainy: istoricheskii putevoditel' Podolia*, 2 vols. (Jerusalem: Jerusalem Center for Documentation of the Diaspora Heritage; St. Petersburg: Institute for Investigation of the Jewish Diaspora, 1997–2000).

16. For a recent biography of An-sky see Gabriella Safran, *Wandering Soul: The Dybbuk's Creator, S. An-sky* (Cambridge, Mass.: Harvard University Press, 2010). For an annotated translation of his ethnographic program see Nathaniel Deutsch, *The Jewish Dark Continent: Life and Death in the Russian Pale of Settlement* (Cambridge, Mass.: Harvard University Press, 2011). Pictures from his expedition can be found in Eugene M. Avrutin et al., *Photographing the Jewish Nation: Pictures from S. An-sky's Ethnographic Expeditions* (Waltham, Mass.: Brandeis University Press, 2009). For different aspects of An-sky's life see Gabriella Safran and Steven J. Zipperstein, eds., *The Worlds of S. An-sky: A Russian Jewish Intellectual at the Turn of the Century* (Stanford, Calif.: Stanford University Press, 2006).

17. For the early rise and spread of Hasidism see Gershon David Hundert, *Jews in Poland-Lithuania in the Eighteenth-Century: A Genealogy of Modernity* (Berkeley: University of California Press, 2006).

18. The migrations and wanderings of those who originated in the communities under discussion are a fascinating topic, meriting its own study, but is not the focus of this book. For some excellent studies along these lines see Rebecca Kobrin, *Jewish Bialystok and Its Diaspora* (Bloomington: Indiana University Press, 2010) and Anna Lipphardt, *Vilne: Die Juden aus Vilnius nach dem Holocaust. Eine transnationale Beziehungsgeschichte* (Paderborn, Germany: Schöningh, 2010).

19. In the words of Catherine Evtuhov, the best provincial studies study the province "not for its own sake (the pursuit of *kraevedenie* or local history) but as an integral and indispensable part of a larger historical narrative." Catherine Evtuhov, *Portrait of a Russian Province: Economy, Society, and Civilization in Nineteenth-Century Nizhnii Novgorod* (Pittsburgh: University of Pittsburgh Press, 2011), 9.

20. Pierre Nora, *Realms of Memory: Rethinking the French Past,* edited by Lawrence D. Kritzman, translated by Arthur Goldhammer (New York: Columbia University Press, 1996–1998), vol. 1, 1.

21. I have taken the term *testimonial object* from Marianne Hirsch and Leo Spitzer in "Testimonial Objects: Memory, Gender, and Transmission," *Poetics Today* 27, no. 2 (Summer 2006): 353–83.

22. Valerii Dymshits, "Idish v byvshikh shtetlakh Podolii: po materialam polevykh issledovanii 2004–2006," in L. Katsis, M. Kaspina, and D. Fishman, eds., *Idish: iazyk i kultura v sovetskom soiuze* (Moscow: RGGU, 2009), 347–55.

23. Rakhmiel Peltz used similar reasoning in his *From Immigrant to Ethnic Culture: American Yiddish in South Philadelphia* (Stanford, Calif.: Stanford University Press, 1997).

24. On language as an activating event in Holocaust testimony see Alan Cohen, *The Wonder of Their Voices: The 1946 Holocaust Interviews of David Boder* (Oxford: Oxford University Press, 2010), 202–225. For other activating events in Holocaust testimony see Robert N. Kraft, "Archival Memory: Representations

of the Holocaust in Oral Testimony," *Poetics Today* 27, no. 2 (Summer 2006): 320–21.

25. Joshua Fishman, *In Praise of the Beloved Language: A Comparative View of Positive Ethnolinguistic Consciousness* (Berlin and New York: Mouton de Gruyter, 1997).

26. For a sample of important works on oral history see Leslie Roy Ballard et al., *History of Oral History: Foundations and Methodologies* (New York: Altamira Press, 2007); Alessandro Portelli, *The Death of Luigi Trastulli and Other Stories: Form and Meaning in Oral History* (Albany, N.Y.: SUNY University Press, 1990); Paul Thompson, *The Voice of the Past: Oral History* (New York: Oxford University Press, 2000); Ronald Grele, *Envelopes of Sound: The Art of Oral History, Revised and Enlarged* (New York: Praeger, 1991); and David Thelen, "Memory and American History," *Journal of American History* 75, no. 4 (March 1989): 1117–29.

27. Maurice Halbwachs, *On Collective Memory*, translated by Lewis A. Coser (Chicago: University of Chicago Press, 1992). The literature on collective memory is immense. For some examples see Jeffrey K. Olick, Vered Vinitzky-Seroussi, and Daniel Levy, eds., *The Collective Memory Reader* (New York and Oxford: Oxford University Press, 2011); Paul Connerton, *How Societies Remember* (Cambridge: Cambridge University Press, 1989); and Paul Ricoeur, *Memory, History, Forgetting*, translated by Kathleen Blarney and David Pellauer (Chicago: University of Chicago Press, 2006). Much scholarship on collective memory in general owes its origins to works on the memory of the Holocaust, of which some formative examples are James E. Young, *The Texture of Memory: Holocaust Memorials and Meaning* (New Haven, Conn.: Yale University Press, 1994); Lawrence L. Langer, *Holocaust Testimonies: The Ruins of Memory* (New Haven, Conn.: Yale University Press, 1991); and Geoffrey Hartman, ed., *Holocaust Remembrance: The Shapes of Memory* (Oxford: Wiley Blackwell, 1994).

28. For some studies that have focused on eyewitness accounts of traumatic memory, in particular see Hans F. M. Crombag, Willem A. Wagenaar, and Peter K. Van Koppen, "Crashing Memories and the Problem of 'Source Monitoring,'" *Applied Cognitive Psychology* 10, no. 2 (April 1996): 95–104; Veronika Nourkova, Daniel M. Bernstein, and Elizabeth F. Loftus, "Altering Traumatic Memory," *Cognition and Emotion* 18, no. 4 (2004), 575–85; and Gillian Cohen, *Memory in the Real World* (Hillsdale N. J.: Lawrence Erlbaum, 1989).

29. Elizabeth Tonkin, *Narrating Our Pasts: The Social Construction of Oral History* (Cambridge: Cambridge University Press, 1992).

30. Zhang Xinxin and Sang Ye; *Chinese Lives: an Oral History of Contemporary China*, edited by W. J. F. Jenner and Delia Davin (New York: Pantheon, 1987); Jeffrey Gould and Aldo Lauria-Santiago, *To Rise in Darkness: Revolution, Repression, and Memory in El Salvador, 1920–1932* (Durham, N.C.: Duke University Press, 2008); Daniel James, *Doña María's Story: Life History, Memory, and Political Identity* (Durham, N.C.: Duke University Press, 2001); and Gary Bruce,

The Firm: The Inside Story of the Stasi (Oxford and New York: Oxford University Press, 2010).

31. In his critique of histories that have relied overwhelmingly on official and political sources, Alon Confino has urged historians to utilize oral history as a means of approaching the private memories that public memorials obscure. Alon Confino, "Collective Memory and Cultural History: Problems of Method," *American Historical Review* 102, no. 5 (December 1997): 1395.

32. For some examples see Sheila Fitzpatrick, *Everyday Stalinism: Ordinary Life in Extraordinary Times: Soviet Russia in the 1930s* (Oxford: Oxford University Press, 2000); Catriona Kelly, "Ordinary Life in Extraordinary Times: Chronicles of the Quotidian in Russia and the Soviet Union," *Kritika: Explorations in Russian and Eurasian History* 3, no. 4 (Fall 2002): 631–51; Stephen Kotkin, *Magnetic Mountain: Stalinism as a Civilization* (Berkeley: University of California Press, 1997); Sarah Davies, *Popular Opinion in Stalin's Russia: Terror, Propaganda and Dissent, 1934–1941* (Cambridge: Cambridge University Press, 1997); Jochen Hellbeck, *Revolution on My Mind: Writing a Diary under Stalin* (Cambridge, Mass.: Harvard University Press, 2006); and Oleg Kharkhordin, *The Collective and the Individual in Russia: A Study of Practices* (Berkeley: University of California Press, 1999). For a survey of memoir literature see Irina Paperno, "Personal Accounts of the Soviet Experience," *Kritika: Explorations in Russian and Eurasian History* 3, no. 4 (Fall 2002): 577–610. For studies of "everyday life" see Nataliia Borisovna Lebina, *Povsednevnaia zhizn sovetskogo goroda: Normy i anomalii, 1920-e-1930-e gody* (St. Petersburg: Zhurnal Neva and Letnii sad, 1999); Timo Vikhavainen, ed., *Normy i tsennosti povsednevnoi zhizni: Stanovlenie sotsialisticheskogo obraza zhizni v Rossii, 1920–1030-e- gody* (St. Petersburg: Zhurnal Neva, 2000); David Crowley and Susan E. Reid, eds., *Pleasures in Socialism: Leisure and Luxury in the Eastern Bloc* (Evanston, Ill.: Northwestern University Press, 2010); and David Crowley and Susan E. Reid, eds., *Socialist Spaces: Sites of Everyday Life in the Eastern Bloc* (New York: Oxford University Press, 2002). Most of these studies have focused on the major cities, although there has been some recent scholarship on everyday life in the provinces. See, for instance, David Ransel, *Village Mothers: Three Generations of Change in Russia and Tataria* (Bloomington: Indiana University Press, 2000); Sheila Fitzpatrick, *Stalin's Peasants: Resistance and Survival in the Russian Village after Collectivization* (New York: Oxford University Press, 1994); and Oleg Leibovich, *V gorode M: Ocherki sotsialnoi povsednevnosti sovetskoi provintsii v 40-50-kh gg* (Perm: Iuil'media, 2009).

33. See, for example, Alexei Yurchak, *Everything Was Forever, Until It Was No More: The Last Soviet Generation* (Princeton, N.J.: Princeton University Press, 2005); Catherine Merridale, *Ivan's War: Life and Death in the Red Army, 1939–1945* (New York: Metropolitan Books, 2006); Catherine Merridale, *Night of Stone: Death and Memory in Twentieth-Century Russia* (New York: Viking, 2001); Donald J. Raleigh, *Russia's Sputnik Generation: Soviet Baby Boomers Talk about*

Their Lives (Bloomington: Indiana University Press, 2006); Shternshis, *Soviet and Kosher;* Orlando Figes, *The Whisperers: Private Life in Stalin's Russia* (New York: Metropolitan Books, 2007); Donald Raleigh, *Soviet Baby Boomers: An Oral History of Russia's Cold War Generation* (Oxford; New York: Oxford University Press, 2012); and Paola Messana, *Soviet Communal Living: An Oral History of the Kommunalka* (New York: Palgrave Macmillan, 2011). Even studies of Gulag survivors have tended to focus on the more privileged strata within the Gulag. See Jehanne M. Gheith and Katherine R. Jolluck, *Gulag Voices: Oral Histories of Soviet Incarceration and Exile* (New York: Palgrave Macmillan, 2011).

     34. See, for instance, the anthology by Alexander Laban Hinton and Kevin Lewis O'Neill, eds., *Genocide: Truth, Memory and Representation* (Durham, N.C.: Duke University Press, 2009); Pamela Ballinger, *History in Exile: Memory and Identity at the Borders of the Balkans* (Princeton, N.J.: Princeton University Press, 2002); and Greta Lynn Uehling, *Beyond Memory: The Crimean Tatars' Deportation and Return* (New York: Palgrave Macmillan, 2004).

     35. Among the most important Holocaust oral history projects are the Fortunoff Video Archive for Holocaust Testimonies at Yale University and the University of Southern California's Shoah Foundation Institute, established by Steven Spielberg. Both Yad Vashem in Jerusalem and the United States Holocaust Memorial Museum in Washington, D.C. also maintain oral history collections. There is a large amount of scholarship theorizing the use of Holocaust testimonies. For some examples see the special issue of *Poetics Today* (vol. 27, no. 2) on "The Humanities of Testimony." See also Langer, *Holocaust Testimonies,* and Geoffrey Hartman, *The Longest Shadow: In the Aftermath of the Holocaust* (Bloomington: Indiana University Press, 1996), especially 133–73.

     36. Christopher Browning, *Remembering Survival: Inside a Nazi Slave-Labor Camp* (New York and London: W.W. Norton & Company, 2010); Jan Tomasz Gross, *Neighbors: The Destruction of the Jewish Community in Jedwabne, Poland* (New York: Penguin, 2002). See also Rosa Lehmann, *Symbiosis and Ambivalence: Poles and Jews in a Small Galician Town* (New York; Oxford: Berghahn Books, 2001). For a sophisticated analysis of the processes of personal memory in Holocaust narrative see Mark Roseman *A Past in Hiding: Memory and Survival in Nazi Germany* (New York: Metropolitan Books, 2001).

     37. The seminal article on flashbulb memories remains R. Brown and J. Kulik, "Flashbulb Memories," *Cognition* 5 (1977): 73–99, which studied people's memories of the Kennedy Assassination thirteen years after the event. See also Lia Kvavilashvili, Jennifer Mirani, Simone Schlagman, and Diana E. Kornbrot, "Comparing Flashbulb Memories of September 11 and the Death of Princess Diana: Effects of Time Delays and Nationality," *Applied Cognitive Psychology* 17 (2003): 1017–31.

     38. On the other hand, for studies that have looked at memory distortion of traumatic events over time see U. Neisser and N. Harrsh, "Phantom Flashbulbs: False Recollections of Hearing the News about Challenger," in E. Winograd and

U. Neisser, eds., *Affect and Accuracy in Recall: Studies of "Flashbulb Memories"* (Cambridge: Cambridge University Press, 1992), 9–31; and H. Schmolck, E. A. Buffalo, and L. R. Squire, "Memory Distortions Develop over Time: Recollections of the O. J. Simpson Trial Verdict after 15 and 32 Months," *Psychological Science* 11 (2000): 39–45. These studies, however, have focused on variations in memory over significantly shorter periods of time than those dealt with here.

39. Robert N. Kraft, "Archival Memory: Representations of the Holocaust in Oral Testimony," *Poetics Today* 27, no. 2 (Summer 2006): 315. See also Robert Kraft, *Memory Perceived: Recalling the Holocaust* (Westport, Conn.: Praeger, 2002).

40. Browning, *Remembering Survival.*

41. Connerton, *How Societies Remember.*

42. Alessandro Portelli, *The Say in Harlan County: An Oral History* (New York and Oxford: Oxford University Press, 2010), 11.

43. For more on the differences between oral testimonies and written memoirs see Aleida Assman, "History, Memory, and the Genre of Testimony," *Poetics Today* 27, no. 2 (Summer 2006): 261–73.

44. For a discussion about some of the ethical issues involved in oral history see the publications of the Oral History Association, particularly Linda Shopes, "Human Subjects and IRB Review," http://www.oralhistory.org/about/do-oral -history/oral-history-and-irb-review/. See also the Oral History Association Evaluation Guidelines, which sanction anonymous interviews only in "extremely sensitive" circumstances. See http://www.oralhistory.org/wiki/index.php /Evaluation_Guide.

1. THE SHTETL

1. Maurice Samuel, *Little Did I Know: Recollections and Reflections* (New York: Alfred A. Knopf, 1963), 137–38.

2. Natalie F. Joffe, "The Dynamics of Benefice among East European Jews," *Social Forces* 27, no. 3 (March 1949): 238.

3. Elie Wiesel, "The World of the Shtetl," in Steven T. Katz, ed. *The Shtetl: New Evaluations* (New York: New York University Press, 2007), 290.

4. Ibid., 293.

5. Ben-Cion Pinchuk writes of "a composite-collective portrait of a *shtetl* in the nineteenth-century Pale." Ben-Cion Pinchuk, "The East European Shtetl and Its Place in Jewish History," *Revue des études juives* 164, nos. 1–2 (January–June 2005): 205. Pinchuk's article does not contain the name of a single individual shtetl, treating all shtetls as a collective entity.

6. Wiesel, 292.

7. See Dan Miron, *The Image of the Shtetl and Other Studies of Modern Jewish Literary Imagination* (Syracuse, N.Y.: Syracuse University Press, 2000); David G. Roskies, *The Jewish Search for a Usable Past* (Bloomington: Indiana University Press, 1999), 41–66; and Steven J. Zipperstein, *Imagining Russian Jewry: Memory,*

History, Identity (Seattle: University of Washington Press, 1999), 15–40. See also Mikhail Krutikov, *Yiddish Fiction and the Crisis of Modernity, 1905–1914* (Stanford, Calif.: Stanford University Press, 2001), especially 26–38.

8. For more on the fascinating story of Zborowski and his involvement with the Research in Contemporary Cultures project see Steven J. Zipperstein, "Underground Man: The Curious Case of Mark Zborowski and the Writing of a Modern Jewish Classic," in *Jewish Review of Books* 2 (Summer 2010): 38–42.

9. Mark Zborowski with Elizabeth Herzog. *Life Is with People: The Culture of the Shtetl* (New York: Schocken Books, 1952), 29.

10. Ibid., 306.

11. For some examples see the Hershl Polyanker, *Geven amol a shtetl: roman in dray teyln* (Moscow: Sovetski pisatel, 1991); Itsik Kipnis, *Di shtub un untervegns* (Tel Aviv: I. L. Peretz, 1977); and Itsik Kipnis, *Mayn shtetele Sloveshne*, 2 vols., (Tel Aviv: I. L. Peretz, 1971). For an analysis of some of these works see Harriet Murav, *Music from a Speeding Train: Jewish Literature in Post-Revolution Russia* (Stanford, Calif.: Stanford University Press, 2011), 245–84.

12. Shmuel Gordon, "Shtetls. (Rayze-bilder)," *Sovetishe heymland* (February 1966): 104–115. See also Shmuel Gordon, "Shtetl un shtetls. (Rayze-bilder)," *Sovetishe heymland* (June 1969): 107–128. These stories were subsequently collected in Shmuel Gordon, *Di fayl un der boygn* (Moscow: Sovetski pisatel, 1985).

13. Arnold J. Band, "Agnon's Synthetic Shtetl," in Katz, ed., 234.

14. Israel Bartal, "Imagined Geography: The Shtetl, Myth and Reality," in Katz, ed., *The Shtetl*, 183.

15. Pinchuk, "The East European Shtetl." 187.

16. Ibid., 189.

17. Ben-Cion Pinchuk, "How Jewish Was the Shtetl?" in *Polin: Studies in Polish Jewry* 17 (2004): 118.

18. See John D. Klier, "What Exactly Was a Shtetl?" in Gennady Estraikh and Mikhail Krutikov, eds., *The Shtetl: Image and Reality* (Oxford: Legenda, 2000), 23–35.

19. Samuel Kassow, "The Shtetl in Interwar Poland" in Katz, ed., 125.

20. Adam Teller, "The Shtetl as an Arena for Integration in the Eighteenth Century," *Polin: Studies in Polish Jewry* 17, "The Shtetl: Myth and Reality," 39.

21. For more on the Soviet classification of the shtetl see Motl Kiper, *Dos yidishe shtetl in Ukraine* (Kharkov: Melukhe farlag fun Ukraine, 1929).

22. Pinchuk, "The East European Shtetl," 199.

23. Ibid., 205.

24. Gershon David Hundert, *Jews in Poland-Lithuania in the Eighteenth-Century: A Genealogy of Modernity* (Berkeley: University of California Press, 2006).

25. Pinchuk, "The East European Shtetl," 210.

26. Klier, 26.

27. For some examples of studies of specific shtetls and regions see Konrad Zieliński, "The Changing Shtetl in the Kingdom of Poland during the First

World War," in *Polin: Studies in Polish Jewry* 17 (2004): 119–31; and Shimon Redlich, *Together and Apart in Brzezany: Poles, Jews, and Ukrainians, 1918–1945* (Bloomington: Indiana University Press, 2002). Other works of nonfiction have explored personal journeys to individual shtetls: Theo Richmond, *Konin: One Man's Quest for a Vanished Jewish Community* (New York: Vintage, 1996); Yaffa Eliach, *There Once Was a World: A 900-Year Chronicle of the Shtetl of Eishyshok* (Boston: Back Bay Books, 1998). Some *Yizker Bikher* (Memorial Books) also have a scholarly bent to them and could be classified as studies of individual shtetls. For on-line versions of hundreds of *yizker bikher* see the New York Public Library's on-line collection at http://legacy.www.nypl.org/research/chss/jws /yizkorbooks_intro.cfm. Short segments of some *yizker bikher* have also been published in English translation by the JewishGen website at http://www .jewishgen.org/yizkor/. For professionally edited translations with annotation of some *yizker bikher* selections see Jack Kugelmass and Jonathan Boyarin, eds., *From a Ruined Garden: The Memorial Books of Polish Jewry* (New York: Schocken Books, 1985).

28. Moyshe Olgin, *Mayn shtedtel in Ukraine* (New York: M. Gurevitsh'es farlag, 1921), 5.

29. Both quotations are cited in Bartal, 181–81.

30. Valentine Tshernovetski, *Teplik, mayn shtetele* (Buenos Aires: Argentiner magazin, 1946–1950), vol. 1, 82.

31. Olgin, 5–6.

32. For a detailed description of a typical home in early twentieth-century Teplyk see Tshernovetski, 82–95. For architectural studies of the Podolian shtetl see Alla Sokolova, "Arkhitektura shtetla v kontekste traditsionnoi kul'tury," in V. M. Lukin, A. V. Sokolova, and B. N. Khaymovich, *100 evreiskikh mestechek Ukrainyi: istoricheskii putevoditel'* (Jerusalem: Jerusalem Center for Documentation of the Diaspora Heritage; St. Petersburg: Institute for Investigation of the Jewish Diaspora, 1997–2000), vol. 2, 53–84; Alla Sokolova, "Evreiskie mestechk pamiati: lokalizatsia shtetla," in V. A. Dymshits, A. L. Lov, and A. V. Sokolova, eds., *Shtetl, XXI vek: Polevyie issledovaniia* (St. Petersburg: Jewish University Press, 2008); Alla Sokolova, "The Podolian Shtetl as Architectural Phenomenon," in Gennady Estraikh and Mikhail Krutikov, eds., *The Shtetl: Image and Reality: Papers of the Second Mendel Friedman International Conference on Yiddish* (Oxford: Legenda, 2000), 36–79.

33. Lukin, vol. 2, 154.

34. For a recent exploration of the "encounter" between Nahman and Kafka see Rodger Kamenetz, *Burnt Books: Rabbi Nachman of Bratslav and Franz Kafka* (New York: Schocken: 2010).

35. Lukin, vol. 2, 177.

36. For more on the demarcation of public space in the shtetl see Annamaria Orla-Bukowska, "Maintaining Borders, Crossing Borders: Social Relationship in the Shtetl," in *Polin: Studies in Polish Jewry* 17 "The Shtetl: Myth and Reality,"

171–95; and Alla Sokolova, "House-Building Tradition of the Shtetl in Memorials and Memories (Based on Materials of Field Studies in Podolia)," *East European Jewish Affairs* 41, no. 3 (December 2011): 111–35.

37. See "Bershad" entry in *Evreiskaia entsiklopediia*, vol. 4, 347.

38. http://www.benyehuda.org/gottlober/zixronot_umasaot.html.

39. Mi. B[erdichevsky], "Ma yifel Yisrael," *Hatsefirah*, December 27, 1887.

40. *Der emes*, October 23, 1925. Cited in Lukin, vol. 2, 135.

41. Tshernovetski, 17–18.

42. Ibid., 35.

43. Ibid., 58.

44. Ibid., 69–76.

45. Vladimir Bonch-Bruyevich, "New Pogroms," *Soviet Russia: Official Organ of the Soviet Russia Government Bureau* 2, no. 5 (January 31, 1920), 97–98.

46. Altschuler, *Soviet Jewry on the Eve of the Holocaust: A Social and Demographic Profile* (Jerusalem: Hebrew University of Jerusalem; Yad Vashem, 1998), 224.

47. Lukin, 321–22.

48. Figures provided by Rita Shveibish, the head of the Jewish community of Tulchyn.

49. Mordechai Kuper, *Di yidn fun mayn benkshaft: zikhroynes fun mayn heymshtot Sharhorod* (Buenos Aires: Poalei tsiyon, 1968), 187.

50. Lukin, vol. 2, 412.

51. Cited in ibid., 413.

52. Lukin, vol. 2, 430.

53. For the history of Sharhorod see ibid., 399–433; Charles Hoffman, *Red Shtetl: The Survival of a Jewish Town under Soviet Communism* (New York: American Jewish Joint Distribution Committee, 2002), 25–50; and Kuper.

2. THE SCARS OF REVOLUTION

1. For some surveys of this period in Ukrainian history see Paul Robert Magocsi, *A History of Ukraine: The Land and Its Peoples,* 2nd ed. (Toronto: University of Toronto Press, 2010) and Serhy Yekelchyk, *Ukraine: Birth of a Modern Nation* (Oxford; New York: Oxford University Press, 2007).

2. For more on the treatment of Jews in Russia during the First World War see Eric Lohr, *Nationalizing the Russsian Empire: The Campaign against Enemy Aliens during World War I* (Cambridge, Mass.: Harvard University Press, 2003), 129–50; Jonathan Frankel, ed., *Studies in Contemporary Jewry: An Annual,* 4, "The Jews and the European Crisis, 1914–1921" (Bloomington: Indiana University Press, 1988); and Peter Gatrell, *A Whole Empire Walking: Refugees in Russia during World War I* (Bloomington: Indiana University Press, 1999).

3. For the fate of Jews during the Civil War see Oleg Budnitskii, *Russian Jews between the Reds and the Whites, 1917–1920* (Philadelphia: University of Pennsylvania Press, 2011) and Henry Abramson, *A Prayer for the Government:*

Ukrainians and Jews in Revolutionary Times, 1917–1920 (Cambridge, Mass.: Harvard University Research Institute and Center for Jewish Studies, 1999).

4. For more on the pogroms of the Civil War see L. B. Miliakov, I. A. Ziuzina et. al, eds., *Kniga pogromov: pogromy na Ukraine, v Belorussii i evropeiskoi chasti Rossii v period grazhdanskoi voiny, 1918–1922. Sbornik dokumentov* (Moscow: ROSSPEN, 2007); Elias Heifetz, *The Slaughter of the Jews in the Ukraine in 1919* (New York: T. Seltzer, 1921); I. M. Cherikover, *Antisemitizm un pogromen in Ukrayne, 1917–1918* (Berlin: Mizreh Yidishn historishn arkhiv, 1923); Nahum Stiff, *Pogromen in Ukrayne* (Berlin: Vostok, 1923); Leon Chasanowitch, *Der yidisher khurbn in Ukrayne* (Berlin: Yehuda, 1920); and S. An-sky, *Der yidisher khurbn fun Poylin, Galitsye un Bukovine* (Wilno: Farlag An-ski, 1921).

5. See "Anketa Odesskoi rainnoi komissii Evobshchestkooma o pogromakh i polozhenii v g. Tul'chine Bratslavskogo uezda Podol'skoi gib. Letom 1921 g.," in *Kniga pogromov: pogrom na Ukraine, v Belorussii i evropeiskoi chasti Rossii v period grazhdanskoi voiny, 1918–1922. Sbornik dokumentov,* 516–18. Chasanowitch estimates the number of victims in Tulchyn at five hundred. Heifetz also mentions the summer 1919 pogrom in Tulchyn, but he gives the date of July 14th, rather than June 14th. See Heifetz, 78.

6. L. G. Zinger, *Dos banayte folk (tsifern un faktn vegn di yudn in FSSR)* Moscow: Der emes, 1941), 41.

7. The Commissariat for Nationality Affairs, which conducted an investigation of the pogroms in March 1922, estimated the death toll in Ukraine to be 100,194 based on documented evidence for 33,398 deaths, which it presumed to be one-third of all deaths. Bogoraz likely overstated the number of victims when he counted 1,520 pogroms in 911 distinct locales with a total of 200,000 murders and toward a million refugees, even if we allow that he may have included the pogroms of 1905–1907 in his calculation. See V. G. Bogoraz, *Evreiskoe mestechko v revoliutsii. Ocherki* (Leningrad: Gosudarstvennoe izdatel'stvo, 1926), 11. See also *Kniga pogromov,* xiii. Chasanowitch, *Khurbn Ukrayne;* Stiff, *Pogromen Ukrayne;* Oleg Budnitskii, "Jews, Pogroms, and the White Movement: A Historiographical Critique," in *Kritika: Explorations in Russian and Eurasian History* 2, no. 4 (2001): 751–72. Chasanowitch counted 353 locations affected by pogroms, with many of them attacked on multiple occasions, and a death toll estimated at 30,500. His figures, however, excluded large territories, including Western Podolia and Volhynia and also included only those pogroms that preceded Denikin (Chasanowitch, 89–92). Stiff collected information on 105 locales. In the 520 for which some detailed information is available, there were some 1,200 separate pogroms. During these pogroms, approximately two-thirds of all Jewish houses and 55 percent of all Jewish businesses were either burned or otherwise damaged. Hundreds of thousands of Jews were displaced, forced to flee their homes, often over the border never to return. M. Kiper states that the number of pogroms in Ukraine approached 2,000 in more than 500 locales. See M. Kiper, *Dos yidishe shtetl in Ukraine,* 22. Elias Heifetz, who chaired the All-Ukrainian Relief

Committee for the Victims of Pogroms under the auspices of the Red Cross, followed the estimate of 120,000 dead in Ukraine in his *The Slaughter of the Jews in Ukraine*, 180.

8. For more on the Proskurov pogrom see Heifetz, 202–234.

9. See, for instance, A. Sokolova, "Arkhitektura shtetla v kontekste traditsionnoi kul'tury," in V. A. Lukin, A. V. Sokolova, and B. Khaimovich, eds., *100 evreiskikh mestechek Ukrainyi: istoricheskii putevoditel*, vol. 2 (Jerusalem: Jerusalem Center for Documentation of the Diaspora Heritage; St. Petersburg: Institute for Investigation of the Jewish Diaspora, 1997–2000), 68.

10. Bogoraz, 50.

11. Jacob Lestchinsky, *Dos sovetishe idntum: zany fargangenhayt un kegnvart* (New York: Yiddisher kemfer, 1941), 96.

12. DAVO f. P-29, op.1, d. 196, ll. 45–7. Accessed at CAHJP CD 20.

13. *Vsesoiuznaia perepis naseleniia 1926 goda*, vol. 46, (Moscow: TsSU Soiuza SSR, 1928–1933), 24–53.

14. Zvi Gitelman, *Jewish Nationality and Soviet Politics: The Jewish Sections of the CPSU, 1917–1930* (Princeton, N.J.: Princeton University Press, 1972), 354.

15. See Alan M. Ball, *Russia's Last Capitalists: The Nepmen, 1921–1929* (Berkeley: University of California Press, 1987), 100.

16. Cited in Lestchinksy, 107.

17. DAVO f. P-29, op.1, d. 196, ll. 45–7. Accessed at CAHJP CD 20.

18. Ibid.

19. DAVO f. P-29, op.1, d. 196, ll. 50. Accessed at CAHJP CD 20.

20. For more on the geography of the Podolian shtetl see Sokolova. For the 1927 inspector report see DAVO f. P-29 op. 1, d. 353, ll. 146–147. Accessed at CAHJP CD 20.

21. *Vsesoiuznaia perepis naseleniia 1926 goda*, vol. 53, 260.

22. A total of 55 percent of houses in Ilnytsya and 84 percent of houses in Lypovets were built before 1900. DAVO f. P-29 op. 1, d. 353, ll. 146–147. Accessed at CAHJP CD 20.

23. Olgin, 22.

24. Lynne Viola, Denis Kozlov, and V. P. Danilov, eds., *The War against the Peasantry, 1927–1930* (New Haven, Conn.: Yale University Press, 2005), 215.

25. Ibid., 216.

26. Ibid., 320.

27. See E. A. Osokina, Kate S. Transchel, and Greta Bucher, *Our Daily Bread: Socialist Distributions and the Art of Survival in Stalin's Russia, 1927–1941* (Armonk, N.Y.: M.E. Sharpe, 2001).

28. Nahman Huberman, *Bershad: Be-tsel ayara* (Jerusalem: Entsiklopedyah shel galuyot, 1956), 239.

29. Mendl Osherowitch, *Vi menshen leben in sovet Rusland* (New York: M. Osherowitch, 1933), 359.

30. Ibid., 363.

31. For more on the Torgsin stores see Osokina, Transchel, and Bucher. For Jews receiving aid from abroad see David Meckler, *Mentsh un mashin in Sovyetn-land* (Warsaw: J. Zyman, 1936), 56–66.

32. See Miron Dolot, *Execution by Hunter: The Hidden Holocaust* (New York: W.W. Norton, 1987) and the 1985 film *Harvest of Despair: The Unknown Holocaust,* directed by Slavko Nowytski.

33. See John Paul Himka, "How Many Perished in the Famine and Why Does It Matter," Brama: News and Community Press, 2 February 2008. Accessed at http://ualberta.academia.edu/JohnPaulHimka/Papers/495038/How_Many_Perished_in_the_Famine_and_Why_Does_It_Matter.

34. Dolot, 82.

35. See John Paul Himka, "The Holodomor in the Ukrainian–Jewish Encounter Initiative" accessed at http://ualberta.academia.edu/JohnPaulHimka/Papers/492282/The_Holodomor_in_the_Ukrainian-Jewish_Encounter_Initiative.

3. SOCIAL STRUCTURE OF THE SOVIET SHTETL

1. V. G. Bogoraz, ed., *Evreiskoe mestechko v revoliutsii. Ocherki* (Leningrad: Gosudarstvennoe izdatel'stvo, 1926), 8. For more on this work and the expeditions from which it emerged see Deborah Yalen, "Documenting the New Red Kasrilevke," *East European Jewish Affairs* 37, no. 3 (2007): 353–75.

2. For more on the aspirations of Jewish youth in the immediate prerevolutionary era see Jeffrey Veidlinger, *Jewish Public Culture in the Late Russian Empire* (Bloomington: Indiana University Press, 2009).

3. For more on memories of traditional handicrafts in the Soviet shtetl see Marina Khakkarainen, "Mestechko vspominaet o proshlom: rasskazy o evreiskikh remeslennikakh i remeslakh," in V. A. Dymshits, A. L. Lvov, and A. V. Sokolova, eds., *Shtetl xxi vek: polevye issledovaniia* (St. Petersburg: Izd-vo evreiskogo universiteta v Sankt-Peterburga, 2008), 159–76.

4. *Vsesoiuznaia perepis naseleniia 1926 goda* (Moscow: TSSU Soiuza SSSR, 1928–1933), vol. 29, 7, 12.

5. Motl Kiper, *Dos yidishe shtetl in Ukrayne* (Kharkov: Melukhe farlag fun Ukraine, 1929), 36, 46.

6. *Vsesoiuznaia perepis naseleniia 1926 goda,* vol. 29, 7, 12.

7. Ibid., 170–81.

8. For a discussion of the occupational distribution of Jews in Eastern Europe see Yuri Slezkine, *The Jewish Century* (Princeton, N.J.: Princeton University Press, 2006).

9. For more on social hierarchies in the shtetl environment see Khakkarainen, as well as Celia Stopnicka Rosenthal, "Social Stratification of the Jewish Community in a Small Polish Town," *American Journal of Sociology* 59, no. 1 (July 1953): 1–10. In his study of post-Soviet Russian urban centers, Michael Paul Sacks demonstrates that Jews largely abandoned handicrafts in favor of

white-collar occupations, a phenomenon not replicated in our sample. See Michael Paul Sacks, "Privilege and Prejudice: The Occupations of Jews in Russia in 1989," *Slavic Review* 57, no. 2 (Summer 1998): 247–66.

10. For more on the role that Jews played in the nascent photography profession see David Shneer, *Through Soviet Jewish Eyes: Photography, War and the Holocaust* (New Brunswick, N.J.: Rutgers University Press, 2011).

11. B. Z. Goldberg, *The Jewish Problem in the Soviet Union: An Analysis and Solution* (New York: Crown Publishers, 1961), 34.

12. *Vsesoiuznaia perepis naseleniia 1926 goda*, vol. 29, 170–79.

13. Jacob Lestchinsky, *Dos sovetishe idntum: zany fargangenhayt un kegnvart* (New York: Yiddisher kemfer, 1941), 110.

14. Elina Chkolnikova, "The Transformation of the 'Shtetl' in the USSR in the 1930s," *Jews in Russia and Eastern Europe* 52, no. 1 (2004): 91–129.

15. Khakkarainen, 171–72.

16. Ibid., 171.

17. Lewis H. Siegelbaum, *Cars for Comrades: The Life of the Soviet Automobile* (Ithaca, N.Y.: Cornell University Press, 2008), 134, 195–96.

18. For more on the prestige of handicrafts see Khakkarainen.

19. Lestchinsky, 118–23.

20. For more on Jewish agriculture in the Soviet Union see Jonathan L. Dekel-Chen, *Farming the Red Land: Jewish Agricultural Colonization and Local Soviet Power, 1924–1941* (New Haven, Conn.: Yale University Press, 2005).

21. Kiper, 39.

22. See Chkolnikova, 9.

23. Zvi Y. Gitelman, *Jewish Nationality and Soviet Policies: The Jewish Sections of the CPSU, 1917–1930* (Princeton, N.J.: Princeton University Press, 1972).

24. See various documents in DAVO f. P-29, op.1, d. 196, such as l. 49 CAHJP CD 20).

25. DAVO f. P-29, op.1, d. 196, l. 84. Accessed at CAHJP CD 20.

26. Mendl Osherowitch, *Vi menshen leben in sovet Rusland* (New York, M. Osherowitch, 1933), 355.

27. Lestchinksy, 80.

28. L. G. Zinger, *Dos banayte folk (tsifern un faktn vegn di yudn in FSSR)* (Moscow: Der emes, 1941), 39.

29. *Vsesoiuznaia perepis naseleniia 1926 goda*, vol. 12, 203–213.

30. Bogoraz, 101.

31. *Vsesoiuznaia perepis naseleniia 1926 goda*, vol. 29, 170–79.

32. *Vsesoiuznaia perepis naseleniia 1926 goda*, vol. 46, 7.

33. Zinger, 42.

34. For collectivization see Lynne Viola and Denis Danilov, *War against the Peasantry, 1927–1930*, vol. 1: *The Tragedy of the Soviet Countryside* (New Haven, Conn.: Yale University Press, 2005); R. W. Davies, *The Socialist Offensive: The Collectivization of Soviet Agriculture, 1928–1930* (Cambridge, Mass.: Harvard

University Press, 1980); Lynne Viola, *Peasant Rebels under Stalin: Collectiviza-tion and the Culture of Peasant Resistance* (New York: Oxford University Press, 1996); Moshe Lewin, *The Making of the Soviet System* (New York: Pantheon, 1985); and Moshe Lewin, *Russian Peasants and Soviet Power: A Study of Collec-tivization* (New York: W.W. Norton, 1968).

35. Kiper, 47–50.

36. Chkolnikova, "The Transformation of the Jewish Shtetl."

37. For the Great Terror and the Polish campaign see Timothy Snyder, *Blood-lands: Europe between Hitler and Stalin* (New York: Basic Books, 2010), 89–109.

38. Mordechai Altshuler, *Soviet Jewry on the Eve of the Holocaust: A Social and Demographic Profile* (Jerusalem: Hebrew University of Jerusalem; Yad Vashem, 1998), 226.

39. Lestchinksy, 82.

40. Zinger, 40.

41. Lestchinksy, 85.

42. Zinger, 114.

43. Ibid., 45.

44. Ibid., 115–19.

45. Zinger demonstrates that in many artels, Jews constituted significant seg-ments of the artel membership, but it is impossible to discern from the statistics he provides what percentage of Jewish artisans as a whole were members of artels. His statistics are also based on a relatively small number of artels, few of which were located in small towns. Zinger, 71–84.

46. Based on newly available data from the 1939 census, Mordechai Altshuler concludes that "the social stratification of the Jews was radically different from that of the urban population as a whole" in that Jews were about twice as likely to be among the elite and intermediate strata than their urban counterparts, where-as the laboring Jewish class was about a third the proportional size of their urban counterparts. Both Zinger and Altshuler's figures are for the entire Soviet Union; in the shtetls and cities of Podolia, the proportion of Jewish elites was lower. See Altshuler, 182. Even the statistics on which Zinger bases his conclusions changed mysteriously over the course of his writings. See Solomon M. Schwarz, *The Jews in the Soviet Union* (Syracuse, N.Y.: Syracuse University Press, 1951), 23.

4. GROWING UP IN YIDDISH

1. For more on Soviet Yiddish schooling see Anna Shternshis, *Soviet and Kosher: Jewish Popular Culture in the Soviet Union, 1923–1939* (Bloomington: Indiana University Press, 2006), 14–20; Elias Schulman, "The Yiddish School in the Soviet Union, 1918–1948" (Ph.D. diss., Dropsie College, 1965); Harry Lipset, "Jewish Schools in the Soviet Union, 1917–1941: An Aspect of Soviet Minorities Policy" (Ph.D. diss., Columbia University, 1965); and Arkadii Zeltser, "Shkola na idishe i samoidentifikatsiia belorusskikh evreev," in L. Katsis, M. Kaspina, and

D. Fishman, eds., *Idish: iazik i kultura v sovetskom soiuze* (Moscow: RGU, 2009), 218–28.

2. Jacob Lestchinsky, *Dos sovetishe idntum: zany fargangenhayt un kegnvart* (New York: Yiddisher kemfer, 1941), 329; Schulman, 152.

3. Motl Kiper, *Dos yidishe shtetl in Ukrayne* (Kharkov: Melukhe farlag fun Ukraine, 1929), 125. Until 1945, Soviet primary education consisted of four grades, which began when the child turned eight years of age. Three additional grades could be added onto the child's education for a seven-year education. For more on Soviet educational policy see A. A. Abakumov et al., *Narodnoe obrazovanie v SSSR: obshchesobrazovat shkola. Sbornik doikumentov, 1917–1973 gg.* (Moscow: Pedagogica, 1974).

4. V. M. Lukin, A. V. Sokolova, and B. N. Khaymovich. *100 evreiskikh mestechek Ukrainy: istoricheskii putevoditel'* (Jerusalem: Jerusalem Center for Documentation of the Diaspora Heritage; St. Petersburg: Institute for Investigation of the Jewish Diaspora, 1997–2000), vol. 2, 135.

5. DAVO f. P-29, op. 1, d 353, l. 17. Accessed at CAHJP CD 20.

6. See George O. Liber, *Soviet Nationality Policy, Urban Growth, and Identity Change in the Ukrainian SSR, 1923–1934* (Cambridge: Cambridge University Press, 2002) and Terry Martin, *The Affirmative Action Empire: Nations and Nationalism in the Soviet Union, 1923–1939* (Ithaca, N.Y.: Cornell University Press, 2001).

7. For more on Soviet schooling see Larry E. Holmes, *The Kremlin and the Schoolhouse: Reforming Education in Soviet Russia, 1917–1931* (Bloomington: Indiana University Press, 1991).

8. Cited in Schulman, 116.

9. David Meckler, *Mentsh un mashin in Sovyetn-land* (Warsaw: J. Zyman, 1936), 330–342.

10. Minna Varshavskay. Interview 24165. *Visual History Archive.* USC Shoah Foundation.

11. See E. M. Balashov, *Shkola v rossiiskom obshchestve, 1917–1927 gg.* (St. Petersburg: Dmitrii Bulanin, 2003), 143–51.

12. Lestchinsky, 324. Schulman estimates that about 60 percent of Jewish children in Ukraine attended a Yiddish school; see Schulman, vii.

13. DAVO f. P-29 op. 1, d. 353, l. 85. Accessed at CAHJP CD 20.

14. *Vsesoiuznaia perepis naseleniia 1926 goda* vol. 11, 8–9, 61 and vol. 12, 19, 35. Notably, 96 percent of those Jews who reported a mother tongue other than Yiddish listed Russian, with only 4 percent choosing to cite Ukrainian as their mother tongue.

15. DAVO f. P-29, op. 1, d 353, l. 17. Accessed at CAHJP CD 20.

16. DAVO f. P- 29, op. 1, d 353, l. 18. Accessed at CAHJP CD 20.

17. DAVO f. P-29, op. 1, d 353, l. 17. Accessed at CAHJP CD 20. See also *Der Emes,* November 15, 1935. According to figures compiled by Harry Lipset, however, student–teacher ratios were better for Yiddish schools in Ukraine as a whole.

In 1925, he finds that the teacher–student ratio was 1:29 for Yiddish schools, compared with a teacher–student ratio of 1:40 for all schools in Ukraine; see Lipset, 222.

18. Lestchinsky, 335–36. See also examples from DAVO f. P-29, op.1, d. 196, l. 45–47. Accessed at CAHJP CD 20.

19. On the closing of Yiddish schools see Lipset, 250–57.

20. Jacob Lestchinsky writes that there were 50,000 students in Yiddish schools in Ukraine in 1940, but these figures are disputed by Harry Lipset, who instead cites the *Bolshaia Sovetskaia entsiklopediia*, which counts only nineteen Yiddish schools in all of Ukraine in 1939. See Lipset, 250–51 and Letschinsky, 342.

21. *Vsesoiuznaia perepis naseleniia 1926 goda*, vol. 11, 20–21.

22. Zvi Y. Gitelman, *Jewish Nationality and Soviet Politics: The Jewish Sections of the CPSU, 1917–1930* (Princeton, N.J.: Princeton University Press, 1972).

23. Semen Markovich Dimanshtein, *Yidn in F.S.S.R* (Moscow: Der emes, 1935), 81.

24. H. Sh. Kazdan, *Fun kheyder un shkoles biz Tsisho. Dos ruslendishe yidntum in gerangel far shul, shprakh, kultur* (Mexico City: Shlomo Mendelson fond bay der gezelshaft far kultur un hilf, 1956), 135.

25. Ibid., 139–54.

26. See Eliyana Adler, *In Her Hands: The Education of Jewish Girls in Tsarist Russia* (Detroit: Wayne State University Press, 2010).

27. Cited in Schulman, 99.

28. "Bershad un Tulchin," *Der emes*, October 23, 1925. For a similar article on Mohyliv-Podilskyy see *Der emes*, May 22, 1937.

29. For a slightly different version of this rhyme see Ruth Rubin, "Nineteenth-Century Yiddish Folksongs of Children in Eastern Europe," *Journal of American Folklore* 65, no. 257 (July–September 1952), 231–32.

30. Translation from http://www.ou.org/yerushalayim/yizkor/emman.htm.

31. A. Gershuni points out that many Soviet Jews utilized both the Soviet Yiddish school system and private Jewish education, some of whom received daily Jewish educations in the home to supplement their state schooling, some of whom stayed home from school on the Sabbath to receive weekly Jewish instruction, and some of whom abstained from the state school system altogether in violation of state law. See A. A. Gershuni, *Yehudim ve-yahadut bi-verit ha-mo'atsot*, 138–40.

32. V. G. Bogoraz, ed., *Evreiskoe mestechko v revoliutsii. Ocherki* (Leningrad: Gosudarstvennoe izdatel'stvo, 1926), 24.

33. DAVO f. P-29, op.1, d. 196, l. 50. Accessed at CAHJP CD 20.

34. Ibid.

35. Olga Bertelsen, "New Archival Documentation on Soviet Jewish Policy in Interwar Ukraine. Part One: GPU Repression of Zionist Parties and Groups in the 1920," *On the Jewish Street: A Journal of Russian-Jewish History and Culture* 1,

no. 1 (2011), 75–76. See also DAVO f. P-29, op.1, d. 196, l. 61. Access at CAHJP CD 20 for other examples.

36. DAVO f. P-29, op.1, d. 196, l. 61. Accessed at CAHJP CD 20.

37. Valentine Tshernovetski, *Teplik, mayn shtetele* (Buenos Aires: Argentiner magazin, 1946–1950).

38. Kuper, *Di yidn fun mayn benkshaft: zikhroynes fun mayn heymshtot Shargorod* (Buenos Aires: Poalei tsiyon, 1968), 44.

39. Ibid., 126.

40. L. Feldblium, "Dos shtetl Teplyk," *Der emes,* June 21, 1938.

5. THE SANCTUARY OF THE SYNAGOGUE

1. The song was recorded by the Yiddish theater actor and singer, Aaron Lebedeff (1873–1960), in 1947.

2. For more on Soviet religious policies in the provinces see Glennys Young, *Power and the Sacred in Revolutionary Russia: Religious Activists in the Village* (University Park: Pennsylvania State University Press, 1997) and Iu. N. Bakaev, *Vlast' i religiia: istoriia otnoshenii, 1917–1941* (Khabarovsk: Izd-vo KhGTU, 2002).

3. For more on Soviet religious policy in the interwar period see Philip Walters, "A Survey of Soviet Religious Policy," in Sabrina Petra Ramet, ed., *Religious Policy in the Soviet Union* (Cambridge: Cambridge University Press, 1993), 3–30.

4. For more on the antireligious campaigns see Zvi Y. Gitelman, *Jewish Nationality and Soviet Politics: The Jewish Sections of the CPSU, 1917–1930* (Princeton, N.J.: Princeton University Press, 1972). For Soviet policies on Jewish religious practice see Joshua Rothenberg, *The Jewish Religion in the Soviet Union* (New York: Ktav, 1972); A. A. Gershuni, *Yehudim ve-Yahadut bi-Verit ha-moatsot; Yahadut Rusyah mi-tekufat Stalin ve'ad ha-zeman ha-aharon* (Jerusalem: Feldheim, 1970); and A. A. Gershuni, *Yahadut ba-Rusyah ha-Sovyetit* (Jerusalem, Mosad ha-Rav Kuk, 1960).

5. DAVO f. P-29, op. 1, d. 196, l. 71. Accessed at CAHJP CD 20.02.

6. See, for instance, Anna Shternshis, "May Day, Tractors, and Piglets:Yiddish Songs for Little Communists," in Barbara Kirshenblatt-Gimblett and Jonathan Karp, eds., *The Art of Being Jewish in Modern Times* (Philadelphia: University of Pennsylvania Press, 2008), 83–97.

7. Daniel Peris notes a similar pattern of mixed results from the parallel propaganda aimed at Orthodox Christians by the Soviet League of the Militant Godless. See Daniel Peris, *Storming the Heavens: The Soviet League of the Militant Godless* (Ithaca, N.Y. and London: Cornell University Press, 1998).

8. Cited in Elias Schulman, "The Yiddish School in the Soviet Union, 1918–1948." Ph.D. diss., Dropsie College, 1965, 215.

9. DAVO f. P-29, op. 1, d. 196, l. 42. Accessed at CAHJP CD 20.02.

10. DAVO f. P-29, op.1, d. 196, l. 41. Accessed at CAHJP CD 20.

11. Young, 92–100; Elizabeth A. Wood, *Performing Justice: Agitation Trials in Early Soviet Russia* (Ithaca, N.Y.: Cornell University Press, 2005). For trials

against the Jewish religion see Anna Shternshis, *Soviet and Kosher: Jewish Popular Culture in the Soviet Union, 1923–1939* (Bloomington: Indiana University Press, 2006), 93–97.

12. V. M. Lukin, A. V. Sokolova, and B. N. Khaymovich, *100 evreiskikh mestechek Ukrainy: istoricheskii putevoditel'* (Jerusalem: Jerusalem Center for Documentation of the Diaspora Heritage; St. Petersburg: Institute for Investigation of the Jewish Diaspora, 1997–2000), vol. 2, 135.

13. "Bershad un Tulchin," *Der emes*, October 23, 1925.

14. Nahman Huberman, *Bershad: Be-tsel ayara* (Jerusalem: Entsiklopedyah shel galuyot, 1956), 237.

15. Benjamin Pinkus, *Jews of the Soviet Union: The History of a National Minority* (Cambridge and New York: Cambridge University Press, 1988), 104. He states that 1,034 synagogues still existed in Ukraine alone, with 830 rabbis.

16. DAVO f. 595, op. 1, d. 950, ll. 6–8, Accessed at CAHJP HM2–9671.2. For Orthodoxy, see Peris, *Storming the Heavens*.

17. Pinkus, 104.

18. For more on the arrest of rabbis and the closure of the synagogues see Gershuni, *Yehudim ve-yahadut*, 75–82; 96–104.

19. TsDAGOU f. 1, op. 6, d. 538, l. 226 CAHJP RU 1938.

20. TsDAGOU f. 1, op. 6, d. 621, l. 236 CAHJP RU 1938.

21. TsDAGOU f. 1, op. 6, d. 621, ll. 236–37 CAHJP RU 1938.

22. For more on the attitudes of Soviet Jews regarding the closure of synagogues see Shternshis, *Soviet and Kosher*, 7–14. For more on the secret minyans see Gershuni, *Yehudim ve-yahadut*, 98.

23. See William C. Fletcher, *The Russian Orthodox Church Underground, 1917–1970* (New York and Oxford: Oxford University Press, 1971). For another example of Jews using private homes to circumvent prohibitions on prayer, in this case in Morocco, see Emily Gottreich, *The Mellah of Marrakesh: Jewish and Muslim Space in Morocco's Red City* (Bloomington: Indiana University Press, 2007).

24. See Robin Judd, "Circumcision and Modern Jewish Life: A German Case Study, 1843–1914," in Elizabeth Wynder Mark, ed., *The Covenant of Circumcision: New Perspectives on an Ancient Jewish Rite* (Hanover, N.H. and London: Brandeis University Press, 2003): 142–55.

25. David Meckler, *Mentsh un mashin in Sovyetn-land* (Warsaw: J. Zyman, 1936), 297–300.

26. Elissa Bemporad, "Behavior Unbecoming a Communist: Jewish Religious Practice in Soviet Minsk," *Jewish Social Studies* 14, no. 2 (2008): 1–31. See also A. A. Gershuni, *Yehudim ve-yahadut*, 93–95.

27. The term *krishmeleyenen* literally refers to the reading of the *Shema* prayer, but had come to be associated with the reading of the prayer at ceremonies surrounding the birth of a child. The term retained its usage for these ceremonies even when the prayer itself was not recited.

28. This custom is also attested in An-sky's questionnaire. See Nathaniel Deutsch, *The Jewish Dark Continent: Life and Death in the Russian Pale of Settlement* (Cambridge, Mass.: Harvard University Press, 2011), 125.

29. The role of pilgrimage in Jewish life has received relatively little scholarly attention. For some exceptions see Dimitri Ioannides and Mara Cohen Ioannides, "The Jewish Past as a 'Foreign Country': The Travel Experiences of American Jews," in Tim Edward Coles and Dallen J. Timothy, eds., *Tourism, Diasporas, and Space* (London and New York: Routledge, 2004), 95–109; and A. Levy, "To Morocco and Back: Tourism and Pilgrimage among Moroccan Born Israelis," in Eyal Ben-Ari and Yoram Bilu, eds., *Grasping Land: Space and Place in Contemporary Israeli Discourse and Experience* (Albany, N.Y.: SUNY Press, 1997).

30. See, for instance, Yoel Matveev, "Di 'toyte khsidim' praven dem 200stn geboyrn-tog" *Forverts,* August 12–18, 2011, p. 11.

31. For more on Marchak, see Lukin, vol. 2, 135.

32. For further evidence of continued clandestine meetings of Breslov Hasids see Gershuni, *Yehudim ve-yahadut,* 129–34, which includes several letters sent from members of the Breslov Hasidic circles in Tulchyn and Teplyk to Breslov circles in America between 1931 and 1935, some of which include evidence that the American group was providing financial assistance to their coreligionists in order to support the distribution of food for the pilgrimage and restoration of the gravesite. In February 1938, the remaining Breslov Hasids in Uman were accused of belonging to an international Trotskyite conspiracy and were arrested and tortured, after which they either died in prison in Uman or were sent to camps in Siberia. See Gershuni, *Yehudim ve-yahadut,* 134.

33. Olga Bertelsen, "New Archival Documentation on Soviet Jewish Policy in Interwar Ukraine. Part Two: GPU Repression of Jews and Jewish Groups in 1937–1940," *On the Jewish Street: A Journal of Russian-Jewish History and Culture* 1, no. 2 (2011): 172.

34. Jewish law requires women to observe strict laws of purity, including regular immersion in a ritual bath (*mikveh*). Although there are reports of clandestine *mikveh*s existing in Tulchyn and other towns in the 1930s, we encountered no testimony about their existence, perhaps owing to the modesty of the women we interviewed, who chose not to address this topic with male interviewers. See Gershuni, *Yehudim ve-yahadut,* 105–106.

35. For more on *tkhines* see Chava Weissler, *Voices of the Matriarchs: Listening to the Prayers of Early Modern Jewish Women* (Boston: Beacon Press, 1998).

36. Susan Starr Sered has noticed a similar phenomenon among the Middle Eastern Jewish women she studied in a Jerusalem day center, and argues that this is a component of domestic religion. She argues that the key component of domestic religion is that the ultimate concerns of the worshipper are personalized, and that "domestic religion has to do with the lives, sufferings, and deaths of *particular,* usually well-loved, individuals" rather than abstract concepts. See

Susan Starr Sered, *Women as Ritual Experts: The Religious Lives of Elderly Jewish Women in Jerusalem* (New York and Oxford: Oxford University Press, 1992), 32.

37. For other examples see the videos collected by Maria Kaspina at http://www.youtube.com/watch?v=q3j4-H6ms2U&list=PL5C664C122D2B99BD&index=8&feature=plpp_video and http://www.youtube.com/watch?v=g2fERn_KsC4&feature=relmfu.

38. Arkadii Zeltser, *Evrei sovetskoi provintsii: Vitebsk i mestechki, 1917–1941* (ROSSPEN, 2006); Elissa Bemporad, "Red Star on the Jewish Street: The Reshaping of Jewish Life in Soviet Minsk, 1917–1939" (Ph.D. diss., Stanford University, 2006); Elissa Bemporad, "Behavior Unbecoming a Communist: Jewish Religious Practice in Soviet Minsk," *Jewish Social Studies* 14, no. 2 (2008): 1–31; Jonathan L. Dekel-Chen, *Farming the Red Land: Jewish Agricultural Colonization and Local Soviet Power, 1924–1941* (New Haven, Conn.: Yale University Press, 2005), especially 155–58. See also Frank Grüner, "Jüdischer Glaube und religiöse Praxis unter dem stalinistischen Regime in der Sowjetunion während der Kriegs- und Nachkriegsjahre," *Jahrbücher für Geschichte Osteuropas* 52, no. 4 (2004): 534–56.

39. See Aryeh Yodfat, "Jewish Religious Communities in the USSR," *Soviet Jewish Affairs* 2 (1971): 61–67; Aryeh Yodfat, "The Closure of Synagogues in the Soviet Union," *Soviet Jewish Affairs* 3 (1973): 48–56; Avraham Greenbaum, "The Jewish Religion in the Soviet Union in the 1930s," *Shvut* 1–2 [17–18] (1995): 146–60; 39–46; Mordechai Altshuler, "Religion in the Soviet Union in the Late 1930s in the Light of Statistics," *Jews and Jewish Topics in the Soviet Union and Eastern Europe* 14 (1991): 23–26; David Eliahu Fishman, "Preserving Tradition in the Land of Revolution: The Religious Leadership of Soviet Jewry, 1917–1930," in Jack Wertheimer, ed., *The Uses of Tradition: Jewish Continuity in the Modern Era* (New York: JTS, 1992), 85–118; Gershon Swet, "Jewish Religion in Soviet Russia," in Gregor Aronson et al., *Russian Jewry 1917–1967* (New York: Thomas Yoseloff, 1969), 209–222; and Gershuni, *Yehudim ve-Yahadut.*

40. Bertelsen, 195.

41. See analysis in Mordechai Altshuler, "Religion in the Late 1930s" and Mordechai Altshuler, *Soviet Jewry on the Eve of the Holocaust: A Social and Demographic Profile* (Jerusalem: Hebrew University of Jerusalem; Yad Vashem, 1998), 98–102.

42. Natan Meir makes a similar argument about the ambiguities of Jewish religious practice and belief among migrants to the city of Kiev in the late imperial period. See his "From Prok to 'Kapores:' Transformations in Religious Practice among the Jews of Late Imperial Kiev," *Jewish Quarterly Review* 97, no. 4 (2007): 616–45. Anna Shternshis's oral history project as described in *Soviet and Kosher* also points to similar ambiguities. See especially 35–43.

6. RELIGION OF THE HOME

1. Mendl Osherowitch, *Shtet un shtetlekh in Ukrayne* (New York: M. Osherowitch Jubilee Committee, 1948), 117–18.

2. The notion of the "Great Tradition" was popularized by Milton Singer and Robert Redfield as part of the Comparative Civilizations Project that Redfield led at the University of Chicago in the 1950s and 1960s. Redfield and Singer distinguished the village culture that they sought to study in India from what they termed the "Great Tradition," the written and canonized tradition that is consciously cultivated by predominantly urban and modernized intellectuals. Village culture, they believed, developed organically from below and therefore best encapsulated the beliefs of the common folk. Such stark dichotomies between popular religiosity and institutionalized religious observance rarely exist in actual religious expression, but as a heuristic tool, this terminology can help us think about the various aspects of religious observance in multifaceted ways. Anthropologists and scholars of religion have demonstrated that these two phenomena often coexisted, but the distinction is still a useful one.

3. For a discussion of the role food can play in traversing the private and public spheres, particularly in regards to memorialization see Jon D. Holtzman, "Food and Memory," *Annual Review of Anthropology* 35 (October 2006): 361–78. For the particular case of Russian Jewish cuisine see Alice Nakhimovsky, "You Are What They Ate: Russian Jews Reclaim Their Foodways," *Shofar: An Interdisciplinary Journal of Jewish Studies* 25, no. 1 (2006): 63–77.

4. For some anthropological and historical studies of food and memory see David E. Sutton, *Remembrance of Repasts: An Anthropology of Food and Memory* (Oxford and New York: Berg, 2001); Joelle Bahloul, *The Architecture of Memory: A Jewish-Muslim Household in Colonial Algeria, 1937–1962* (Cambridge: Cambridge University Press, 1996); and Hasia R. Diner, *Hungering for America: Italian, Irish, and Jewish Foodways in the Age of Migration* (Cambridge, Mass.: Harvard University Press, 2003).

5. For more on remembrance of food and hunger see Diner, and Sutton, 73–103.

6. As Susan Starr Sered notes of Middle Eastern elderly women in Jerusalem, "Food is the central symbol of each holiday, and food preparation is the most important ritual activity that they as women perform." Susan Starr Sered, *Women as Ritual Experts: The Religious Lives of Elderly Jewish Women in Jerusalem* (New York and Oxford: Oxford University Press, 1992), 80.

7. These words were also used by Barbara Myerhoff's informant in Venice, California, who also insisted "that's just how things are supposed to be." See Myerhoff, *Number Our Days* (New York: Simon & Schuster, 1978), 234.

8. For the norms of religious behavior in Soviet cities of the 1930s see Nataliia Borisovna Lebina, *Povsednevnaia zhizn' sovetskogo goroda: Normy i anomalii, 1920-e-1930-e gody* (St. Petersburg: Zhurnal Neva and Letnii sad, 1999), 119–58.

9. A. A. Gershuni, *Yehudim ve-Yahadut bi-Verit ha-moatsot; Yahadut Rusyah mi-tekufat Stalin ve'ad ha-zeman ha-aharon*, (Jerusalem: Feldheim, 1970), 86–87.

10. Anna Shternshis, *Soviet and Kosher: Jewish Popular Culture in the Soviet Union, 1923–1939* (Bloomington: Indiana University Press, 2006).

11. For analyses of Passover in the Soviet Union see Yaacov Ro'i, "Ha-pesakh mul ha-mishtar ha-sovyeti," *Bar Ilan* 24/25 (1989): 173–95; Anna Shternshis, "Passover in the Soviet Union, 1917–1941," *East European Jewish Affairs* 31, no. 1 (2001): 61–76; and Gershuni, 110–12.

12. Alice Nakhimovsky has observed a similar phenomenon among urban assimilated Jews in the Soviet Union, who divorce food from its association with the ritual calendar and instead utilize it as a general signifier of intimacy and symbol of Jewish life. See Nakhimovsky, "You Are What They Ate."

13. Gershuni, 110.

14. Ro'i, 173–95.

15. Nahman Huberman, *Bershad: Be-tsel ayara* (Jerusalem: Entsiklopedyah shel galuyot, 1956), 240.

16. A. Sokolova, "Arkhitektura shtetla v kontekste traditsionnoi kul'tury," in V. M. Lukin, A. V. Sokolova, and B. N. Khaymovich, eds., *100 evreiskikh mestechek Ukrainy: istoricheskii putevoditel'.* 2 vols. . Jerusalem: Jerusalem Center for Documentation of the Diaspora Heritage; St. Petersburg: Institute for Investigation of the Jewish Diaspora, 1997–2000), vol. 2, 81–82.

17. For more on the custom of throwing burrs during Tishah b'Av see Norman Salsitz and Richard Skolnik, *A Jewish Boyhood in Poland: Remembering Kolbuszowa* (Syracuse, N.Y.: Syracuse University Press, 1999), 65.

18. Cited in Genadi Estraikh, "Di metamorfozn fun Khanuke," *Forverts*, December 17–23, 2010, 11.

19. See Zvi Y. Gitelman, "Thinking about Being Jewish in Russia and Ukraine," in Zvi Y. Gitelman with Musya Glants and Marshall I. Goldman, eds., *Jewish Life after the USSR* (Bloomington: Indiana University Press, 2003), 49–60. See also Zvi Y. Gitelman, *Jewish Identity in Postcommunist Russia and Ukraine: An Uncertain Ethnicity* (Cambridge: Cambridge University Press, 2012).

20. Barbara Myerhoff originally adapted the term *domestic religion* from a female informant of hers in a Jewish senior citizens' center in Venice, California, who explained that whereas Jewish men were taught religious precepts in the heder, they often understood these precepts only abstractly and rationally, but failed to feel them spiritually. Men, Myerhoff's informant continued, were required to think about their observance, and thus could come to doubt the faith. Women, on the other hand, "were more superficial. We couldn't question things. 'That's just how things are supposed to be.' God said it. We girls had what you could call domestic religion, that means it comes into you through the rituals." Following Myerhoff's informant, much of the scholarship that has emerged around the concept of domestic religion highlights the religious lives of women, whose piety was more commonly expressed in the home than in public venues. See Barbara Myerhoff, *Number Our Days* (New York: Simon & Schuster, 1978), 234. For more on domestic religion see Sered.

21. See, for instance, Moshe Lewin, *The Making of the Soviet System: Essays in the Social History of Interwar Russia* (London: Methuen, 1985), 57–71; and

Glennys Young, *Power and the Sacred in Revolutionary Russia: Religious Activists in the Village* (University Park: Pennsylvania State University Press, 1997).

22. Young, 133.

7. LIFE AND DEATH IN REICHSKOMMISSARIAT UKRAINE

1. Alexander Werth, *Russia at War, 1941–1945* (London: Pan, 1965), 170.

2. For the massacres in Sokal see Yitzhak Arad et al., eds. *The Einsatzgruppen Reports: Selections from the Dispatches of the Nazi Death Squads' Campaign Against the Jews July 1941–January 1943* (New York, N.Y: Holocaust Library, 1989), 31.

3. For some studies of the Holocaust in the Soviet Union in general, and Ukraine in particular, see Martin Dean, *Collaboration in the Holocaust: Crimes of the Local Police in Belorussia and Ukraine, 1941–44* (New York: St. Martin's Press, 2000); Wendy Lower, *Nazi Empire-Building and the Holocaust in Ukraine* (Chapel Hill: University of North Carolina Press, 2005); Omer Bartov, *The Eastern Front, 1941–45: German Troops and the Barbarisation of Warfare* (Basingstoke, Hampshire: Macmillan in association with St. Antony's College, Oxford, 1985); Patrick Desbois, *The Holocaust by Bullets: A Priest's Journey to Uncover the Truth behind the Murder of 1.5 Million Jews* (New York: Palgrave Macmillan, 2008); Yitzhak Arad, *The Holocaust in the Soviet Union* (Lincoln: University of Nebraska Press, 2009); Center for Advanced Holocaust Studies and United States Holocaust Memorial Museum, *The Holocaust in the Soviet Union: Symposium Presentations* (Washington, D.C.: Center for Advanced Holocaust Studies, United States Holocaust Memorial Museum, 2005); Ray Brandon and Wendy Lower, eds., *The Shoah in Ukraine: History, Testimony, Memorialization* (Bloomington: Indiana University Press, 2008); and Joshua Rubenstein et al., *The Unknown Black Book: The Holocaust in the German-Occupied Soviet Territories* (Bloomington: Indiana University Press, 2007).

4. Estimates vary on the exact number: the 1939 census counted 2,100,000 Jews in the territories that would be conquered by the Germans. Yitzhak Arad estimates that approximately 1,700,000 Jews were living in the territories annexed by the Soviet Union in 1939–1940. Thus, on June 22, 1941, there were approximately 3,800,000 Jews in the territories that would be conquered by the Germans. Of these approximately 1,150,000 fled or were drafted, leaving approximately 2,650,000 Jews under occupation, 950,000 of whom lived in the pre-1939 borders of the Soviet Union. See Yitzhak Arad, *In the Shadow of the Red Banner: Soviet Jews in the War against Nazi Germany* (Jerusalem: Yad Vashem, 2010), 160–61. Alexander Kruglov estimates that some 2.47 million Jews lived in Soviet Ukraine in June 1941, of whom more than 900,000 escaped into evacuation, leaving approximately 1.6 million Jews in Ukraine under German and Romanian rule. See Alexander Kruglov, "Jewish Losses in Ukraine," in Ray Brandon and Wendy Lower, eds., *The Shoah in Ukraine*, 273.

5. Aleksandr Iosifovich Kruglov, *Poteri evreev ukrainy v 1941–1944 gg* (Kharkov: Tarbut laam, 2005), especially 359–62.

6. For Soviet policies and experiences of evacuation see Rebecca Manley, *To the Tashkent Station: Evacuation and Survival in the Soviet Union at War* (Ithaca, N.Y.: Cornell University Press, 2009), especially 24–47. For studies demonstrating the absence of any specific policies relating to the evacuation of Jewish civilians see Ben-Cion Pinchuk, "Was there a Soviet Policy for Evacuating the Jews? The Case of the Annexed Territories," *Slavic Review* 39, no. 1 (1980): 44–55; Mordechai Altshuler, "Escape and Evacuation of Soviet Jews at the Time of the Nazi Invasion: Policies and Realities," in Lucjan Dobroszycki and Jeffrey S. Gurock, eds., *The Holocaust in the Soviet Union* (Armonk, N.Y.: M. E. Sharpe, 1993), 77–104; and Vadim Dubson,"On the Problem of the Evacuation of Soviet Jews in 1941 (New Archival Sources)," *Jews in Eastern Europe* 3, no. 40 (1999): 37–56.

7. Geoffrey P. Megargee, *USHMM Encyclopedia of Camps and Ghettos, 1933–1945* (Bloomington: Indiana University Press, 2009), 1571.

8. In addition to the testimony that Palatnikova gave for AHEYM, she has also given testimony for the USC Shoah Foundation and in Boris Zabarko's *The Holocaust in Ukraine* (London and Portland: Vallentine Mitchell, 2005), 192–94.

9. For more on Todt and the role of Jewish slave labor in the construction of roads in Ukraine see Andrej Angrick, "Annihilation and Labor: Jews and Thoroughfare IV in Central Ukraine" in Brandon and Lower, *Shoah in Ukraine*, 190–223.

10. For details on the Sobolivka massacre see Megargee, vol. 2, 1569.

11. Kruglov, 17.

12. Ibid.

13. In accordance with a July 17, 1941 directive issued by Heydrich, Jews captured as prisoners of war were to be singled out together with political commissars in the Red Army and high-level state and party functionaries, and executed. For more on Jewish prisoners of war see Arad, *In the Shadow*, 249.

14. Yitzhak Arad, ed., *Unichtozhenie Evreev SSSR v gody nemetskoi okkupatsii, 1941–1944: sbornik dokumentov i materialov* (Jerusalem: Yad Vashem, 1991), 302.

15. Yitzhak Arad et al., eds., *The Einsatzgruppen Reports: Selections from the Dispatches of the Nazi Death Squads' Campaign against the Jews July 1941–January 1943* (New York: Holocaust Library, 1989), 252.

16. Ibid., 229. For more on the Nemyriv ghetto see USHMM/ACC 2000.214 and Megargee, 1550–51.

17. Nahman Huberman, *Bershad: Be-tsel ayara* (Jerusalem: Entsiklopedyah shel galuyot, 1956), 20–21.

18. Kupershmidt told of about two hundred Jewish children being thrown into the river. The Soviet Extraordinary Commission that, in 1944, investigated German atrocities in Bratslav reported on a February 1942 incident in which an unspecified number of people, including children, were drowned in

the Southern Bug. Thirteen names of known victims are listed. See USHMM/ RG22.002M/1241/14. It is possible that this is the incident to which Kupershmidt is referring. Other witnesses we have interviewed outside of Bratslav also tell of shootings into the Southern Bug, so it is also possible that Kupershmidt was referring to an altogether different episode.

19. Megargee, 1581.

20. Kruglov provides the figure of thirteen Jews executed in Zhornishche in Kruglov, *Poteri evreev ukrainy*, 16. This figure is derived from the testimony of Boris Yavorsky in Zabarko, 385, and is repeated in the entry on Zhornishche in Megargee, 1581. Skliarskii put the number at eleven in his testimony.

21. Zabarko, 385–87.

22. In April 1945 a Soviet Extraordinary Commission, established with the goal of investigating German crimes in the newly liberated territories, compiled a report taken from eyewitnesses that corroborates many of the details described by Skliarskii. In particular, the report documents the May 27, 1942 arrest and torture of "more than 800 people" who were detained in the Jewish school of Ilnytsya "after which they were all beaten and executed." GARF, f. 7021, op. 54, d. 1243, l. 99. Accessed at USHMM RG 22.002.

23. GARF, f. 7021, op. 54, d. 1243, l. 99. Accessed at USHMM RG 22.002.

24. GARF, f. 7021, op. 54, d. 1243, l. 108. Accessed at USHMM RG 22.002.

25. GARF, f. 7021, op. 54, d. 1243, l. 107. Accessed at USHMM RG 22.002. For more on the looting of Jewish property see Jan Tomasz Gross, *Golden Harvest: Events at the Periphery of the Holocaust* (New York: Oxford University Press, 2012).

26. GARF, f. 7021, op. 54, d. 1243, l. 38. Accessed at USHMM RG 22.002.

27. http://www.blavatnikarchive.org/archives/792.

28. For more on *zemlyankas* see Mark Edele, *Soviet Veterans of the Second World War: A Popular Movement in an Authoritarian Society, 1941–1991* (Oxford: Oxford University Press, 2009) and Catherine Merridale, *Ivan's War: Life and Death in the Red Army, 1939–1945* (New York: Metropolitan Books, 2006), 169.

29. Arad, *In the Shadow*, 177.

30. See ibid., 340–44.

31. For memory of the Holocaust in the Soviet Union see Zvi Y. Gitelman, *Bitter Legacy: Confronting the Holocaust in the USSR* (Bloomington: Indiana University Press, 1997); Zvi Y. Gitelman, "History, Memory and Politics: The Holocaust in the Soviet Union," *Holocaust and Genocide Studies* 5, no. 1 (1990): 23–37; Harvey Asher, "The Holocaust and the USSR," in Dagmar Herzog, ed., *Lessons and Legacies VII: The Holocaust in International Perspective* (Evanston, Ill.: Northwestern University Press, 2006), 253–68; and Bob Weinberg, "The Politics of Remembering: The Treatment of the Holocaust in the Soviet Union," in Herzog, 314–29.

32. On conditions in wartime Ukraine and the deportations see Karel C. Berkhoff, *Harvest of Despair: Life and Death in Ukraine under Nazi Rule*

(Cambridge, Mass.: Belknap Press of Harvard University Press, 2004). Viktor
Zemskov counted 1,650,343 Ukrainians repatriated to the Soviet Union as of
March 1, 1946, the vast majority of whom had been taken to Germany as laborers. See V. I. Zemskov, "K voprosy o repatriatsii sovetskikh grazhdan 1944–1951
gody," *Istoriia SSSR* 1990, no. 4, 35.

8. LIFE BEYOND THE RIVER

1. USHMM Acc.2000.214, p. 1.
2. For more on Transnistria see Jean Ancel, *Transnistria* (Bucharest: Atlas,
1998); Matatias Carp, *Cartea Neagră. Suferințele Evreilor din România, 1940–1944*
(Bucharest: Editura Diogene, 1996); Randolph L. Braham, ed., *The Destruction of
Romanian and Ukrainian Jews during the Antonescu Era* (New York: Columbia
University Press, 1997); Radu Ioanid, *The Holocaust in Romania: The Destruction of Jews and Gypsies under the Antonescu Regime, 1940–1944* (Chicago, Ill:
Ivan R. Dee, 2000); Dennis Deletant, "Transnistria and the Romanian Solution
to the 'Jewish Problem,'" in Ray Brandon and Wendy Lower, eds., *The Shoah in
Ukraine: History, Testimony, Memorialization* (Bloomington: Indiana University
Press, 2008), 156–89; Dalia Ofer, "The Holocaust in Transnistria: A Special Case
of Genocide," in Lucjan Dobroszycki and Jeffrey S. Gurock, eds., *The Holocaust
in the Soviet Union: Studies and Sources on the Destruction of the Jews in the Na-
zi-Occupied Territories of the USSR, 1941–1945* (Armonk, NY: M. E. Sharpe, 1993),
133–54; Rebecca Golbert, "Holocaust Sites in Ukraine: Pechora and the Politics of
Memorialization," *Holocaust and Genocide Studies* 18, no. 2 (Fall 2004): 205–233;
Dennis Deletant, "Ghetto Experience in Golta, Transnistria, 1942–1944," Holocaust and Genocide Studies 18, no. 1: 1–26; Avigdor Shachan, *Burning Ice: The
Ghettos of Transnistria,* translated by Dr. Shmuel Himelstein (Boulder, Colo.:
East European Monographs, 1996); Matatias Carp, *Transnistrie* (Buenos Aires:
Besaraber landslayt-farayn in Argentine, 1950); and Dennis Deletant, "Lebens-
bingungen in den Ghettos und Arbeitslagern in Transnistrien 1942–1944: Der
Fall Golta," in Wolfgang Benz and Brigitte Mihok, eds., *Holocaust an der Periph-
erie: Judenpolitik und Judenmord in Rumanien und Transnistrien 1940–1944* (Ber-
lin: Metropol, 2009), 45–70. For some memoirs and specialized studies see Ruth
Glasberg Gold, *Ruth's Journey: A Survivor's Memoir* (Gainesville: University
Press of Florida, 1996); Siegfried Jagendorf, *Jagendorf's Foundry: Memoir of the
Romanian Holocaust, 1941–1944,* 1st ed. (New York: HarperCollins Publishers,
1991); and S. Ia. Borovoi, "Gibel' evreiskogo naseleniia Odessy vo vremia rumynskoi okkupatsii," in *Katastrofa i opir ukrain'skogo evreistva* (Kiev: National'na
Akademiia nauk Ukraini, 1999).
3. Yitzchak Arad gives the figures of 320,000 in the areas that became Transnistria with 200,000 in Odessa. See Arad, *In the Shadow of the Red Banner: Soviet Jews in the War against Nazi Germany* (Jerusalem: Yad Vashem, 2010), 163.
4. The figure of 147,000 was calculated by Dennis Deletant in "Transnistria
and the Romanian Solution to the 'Jewish Problem'" in Ray Brandon and Wendy

Lower, eds., *The Shoah in Ukraine History: Testimony, Memorialization* (Bloomington: Indiana University Press, 2008). Yitzchak Arad provides the figure of 120,000 deported between September and October 1941. See Arad, *In the Shadow*, 163.

5. See Shachan, 146.

6. Shachan, for instance, writes that "the local Jews of Transnistria were almost all killed immediately after the invasion," Shachan, 168, and estimates that 310,000 of the 330,000 Jews living in the region in 1940 were killed.

7. USHMM Acc.2000.214, p. 6.

8. Cited in V. M. Lukin, A. V. Sokolova, and B. N. Khaymovich, eds., *100 evreiskikh mestechek Ukrainy: istoricheskii putevoditel'* (Jerusalem: Jerusalem Center for Documentation of the Diaspora Heritage; St. Petersburg: Institute for Investigation of the Jewish Diaspora, 1997–2000), vol. 2, 334–35.

9. USHMM Acc.2000.214, p. 3.

10. This is perhaps a reference to Acts 2:32 of the New Testament, in which Peter affirms to the public: "God has raised this Jesus to life, and we are all witnesses to this fact." It may also be a reference to the *she'erit hapletah* (the surviving remnant) from Ezra 9, a term that was broadly adapted to refer to Jewish Displaced Persons after the Holocaust.

11. Guy Miron, ed., *The Yad Vashem Encyclopedia of the Ghettos during the Holocaust* (Jerusalem: Yad Vashem, 2009), 41.

12. According to testimony taken in 1944 by a Soviet Extraordinary State Commission for the Determination and Investigation of Nazi and their Collaborators' Atrocities in the USSR, 150 people were murdered on August 11, 1941. The Commission was able to obtain the names or other identifying information of 103 victims. The Commission also noted another massacre of six individuals that took place on July 25, 1941. See GARF f. 7021, op. 54, d. 1235. Accessed at USHMM RG22.002M 1235. See also Kruglov, *Poteri evreev ukrainy v 1941–1944 gg.* (Kharkov: Tarbut laam, 2005), 247.

13. Kruglov, 242–43 and 13.

14. USHMM Acc.2000.214, p. 8.

15. For more on the problematization of the terminology of *ghetto* see Dan Michman, *The Emergence of Jewish Ghettos during the Holocaust* (Cambridge: Cambridge University Press, 2011).

16. Deletant, "Ghetto Experience," 6.

17. Kruglov, 21, 248.

18. DAVO f. 1417-3c-1. Accessed at USHMM RG-31.011M.

19. Miron, 851.

20. Kruglov, 21.

21. Grinberg, Clara. Interview 8412. *Visual History Archive*. USC Shoah Foundation.

22. Miron, 42.

23. See Irene Heskes, *Yiddish American Popular Songs 1895–1950* (Washington, D.C.: Library of Congress, 1992), 140, 174.

24. See Szmerke Kaczerginski, *Lider fun di getos un lagern* (New York: Tsiko, 1948), 244–45. I owe a particular thanks to Dov-Ber Kerler for this reference as well as for assistance in deciphering and interpreting Yosl Kogan's songs.

25. Shachan, 187.

26. Meir Teich, "The Jewish Self-Administration in Ghetto Sharhorod (Transnistria)," *Yad Vashem Studies* 2, no. 1 (1958): 232.

27. Miron, 700.

28. Teich, 238.

29. Kruglov, 21.

30. See Teich.

31. Kruglov, 21.

32. Deletant, "Ghetto Experience." See also Vladimir Solonari, *Purifying the Nation: Population Exchange and Ethnic Cleansing in Nazi-Allied Romania* (Baltimore: Johns Hopkins University Press, 2009).

33. There is some debate over the exact date. Several witnesses recall the date being December 7th, but others have given December 5th as the date. Lukin, basing his choice on Kruglov, gives the date of December 13th.

34. Lukin, vol. 2, 336.

35. Kruglov, 20.

36. See Golbert, 219.

37. Lukin, vol. 2, 336; Miron, 851.

38. In all likelihood Schreiber is mistaken here; the majority of the population had been deported to Pechera, not killed by the Germans.

39. Leo Baeck Institute archive, ME 1416.MM III 14, p. 29. Memoir of Gerhard Schreiber.

40. Ibid.

41. Kruglov, 21.

42. Rita Shveibish also singles out Mukha as one of the more notorious police.

43. USHMM Acc.2000.214, p. 12.

44. "Personal Testimonies: Dr. Felicia Carmelly (Steigman)," http://www.nizkor.org/hweb/people/c/carmelly-felicia/carmelly-felicia.html.

45. There are several testimonies regarding the level of organization and kindness of the Jews of the Chechelnyk ghetto. This ghetto had a council of Jews who managed to bribe the Romanian gendarmes in order to alleviate their situation. They also managed to set up a system that allowed them to provide aid to new deportees who arrived in the town. See Shacham, 240–41, 273.

46. Jean Ancel, "The Romanian Campaigns of Mass Murder in Transnistria, 1941–1942," in Randoph L. Braham, ed., *The Destruction of Romanian and Ukrainian Jews during the Antonescu Era* (New York: Rosenthal Institute for Holocaust Studies, 1997), 87–133.

47. Kruglov, 19-21. For more on the construction of the thoroughfare, see Andrej Angrick, "Annihilation and Labor: Jews and Thoroughfare IV in Central Ukraine," in Brandon and Lower, 190-223.

48. Kruglov, 21.

49. For more on the history of the song see Itzik Gottesman's March 17, 2011 post on the blog "Yiddish Song of the Week," "'Eykho' Performed by Clara Crasner" at *http://yiddishsong.wordpress.com/2011/03/17/eykho-performed-by-clara-krasner/*. See also Kaczerginski, 14-15.

50. See also Shachan, 360-62, citing the Yad Vashem interviews with Berta Morgenstern, Anna Cohen, and Malik Trude. Kruglov gives the dates of execution as February 11th and March 11th.

51. It is difficult to determine the exact number of people in the ghetto. Kruglov writes that 11,129 people were counted at the time of liberation, based on Russian archival documents (GARF 7021, op. 54, d. 1241). January 1943 figures from the Central Bureau of Romanian Jews, on the other hand, counted 9,200 Jews in the ghetto, of whom 6,950 were Romanian deportees and 2,250 were locals. Both figures are cited in Kruglov, 21. See also Miron, 43.

52. Nina Tumarkin, *The Living and the Dead: The Rise and Fall of the Cult of World War II in Russia* (New York: Basic Books, 1994), 134. See also Mark von Hagen, "From 'Great Fatherland War' to the Second World War," in Ian Kershaw and Moshe Lewin, eds., *Stalinism and Nazism: Dictatorships in Comparison* (Cambridge: Cambridge University Press, 1997), 238; and Amir Weiner, *Making Sense of War: The Second World War and the Fate of the Bolshevik Revolution* (Princeton, N.J.: Princeton University Press, 2001).

53. Gennadii Kostyrchenko, *Tainaia politka Stalina: Vlast' i antisemitism* (Moscow: Mezdunarodnye otnosheniia, 2001).

9. A KIND OF VICTORY

1. Yitzchak Arad, *In the Shadow of the Red Banner: Soviet Jews in the War against Nazi Germany* (Jerusalem: Yad Vashem, 2010), 167.

2. Arad, who brings attention to this point, also writes that "It can be stated with some certainty that overt discrimination of the Jews as a policy of the upper echelons in the Soviet government did not exist during the war, but did exist as an undercurrent," 115. He notes that promotion rates as a whole were lower for Jews than their proportion of the general population, but they were promoted to senior officer at a higher rate. Jews were discriminated against by being denied public recognition of Jewish heroism. Although Jews received medals and orders in disproportionately high rates, those figures were often left out of official reports. For instance, 5,163 Jews had been awarded medals by October 1942 and 11,908 by June 1943—far more than Armenians, Georgians, Azeris, or Uzbeks—yet official publications neglected to mention Jews among those nations who had distinguished themselves in the war. Arad sees antisemitic motivations in the dismissal of David Ortenberg as editor in chief of *Red Star* in July 1943.

Ortenberg's high profile position until that point, though, is indicative of a toler-ance for high-level Jewish voices. See Arad, 115–17. See also Gennadii Kostyrch-enko, *Tainaia politika Stalina: Vlast' i antisemitizm* (Moscow: Mezdunarodnye otnosheniia, 2001), 242–49. The Blavatnik Archive Foundation has also been col-lecting testimonies of Soviet Jewish war veterans. Typical of their recollections is the testimony of Arkady Dayel, who claimed "we had normal relationships of friendship. I didn't feel antisemitism or anything like that . . . I didn't feel it, though everyone knew I was a Jewish boy." Cited in Julie Chervinsky, ed., *Lives of the Great Patriotic War: The Untold Stories of Soviet Jewish Soldiers in the Red Army during WWII* (New York: Blavatnik Archive Foundation, 2011), 73.

3. Chervinsky, 84.

4. Cited in Joshua Rubenstein et al., *The Unknown Black Book:The Holocaust in the German-Occupied Soviet Territories* (Bloomington: Indiana University Press, 2007), 26. See also Dov-Ber Kerler, "The Soviet Yiddish Press: *Eynikayt* during the War, 1942–1945," in Robert Moses Shapiro, ed., *Why Didn't the Press Shout? American and International Journalism during the Holocaust* (Hoboken, N.J.: Yeshiva University Press, 2003), 221–49.

5. See Mark Edele, *Soviet Veterans of the Second World War: A Popular Movement in an Authoritarian Society, 1941–1991.* Oxford: Oxford University Press, 2009.

6. See ibid, 136–37. Edele shows that Jews continued to be overrepresented in military Party organizations and were more likely than other nationalities to make a career in the army after the war.

7. Arad, 126. For more on the experience of Soviet soldiers during the war see Catherine Merridale, *Ivan's War: Life and Death in the Red Army, 1939–1945* (New York: Metropolitan Books, 2006).

8. Mordechai Altshuler, *Soviet Jewry since the Second World War: Population and Social Structure* (New York: Greenwood Press, 1987), 93.

9. On the return of demobilized soldiers see Edele, 21–38. On the return of evacuees see Rebecca Manley, *To the Tashkent Station: Evacuation and Survival in the Soviet Union at War,* (Ithaca, N.Y.: Cornell University Press, 2009), 238–69.

10. For studies of ruin and reconstruction of particular cities in Ukraine see Karl Qualls, *From Ruin to Reconstruction: Urban Identity in Soviet Sevastopol after World War II* (Ithaca, N.Y.: Cornell University Press, 2009); Martin Black-well "Regime City of the First Category: The Experience of the Return of Soviet Power to Kyiv, Ukraine, 1943–1946" (Ph.D. diss., Indiana University, 2005).

11. See Manley, 246; and Blackwell, especially 112–18.

12. See Manley 249–51; Blackwell, 355–75; Mordechai Altshuler, ed. and trans., "Antisemitism in Ukraine toward the End of the Second World War," *Jews in Eastern Europe,* no. 3 (1993): 43; Kostyrchenko, 248–49.

13. For more on the problems of residency rights for returnees see Manley, 256–64.

14. Mikhail Mitsel, *Obshchiny iudeiskogo veroispovedaniia v Ukraine: Kiev, l'vov—1945–1981* (Kiev: Sfera, 1998), 56.

15. For more on the famine of 1946–1947 and the end of rationing see Zubkova, *Russia after the War: Hopes, Illusions, and Disappointments, 1945–1957* (Armonk, N.Y.: M.E. Sharpe, 1998) 40–55.

16. For more on postwar antisemitism in the postwar Soviet Union see Kostyrchenko; Yehoshua A. Gilboa, *The Black Years of Soviet Jewry, 1939–1953* (Boston: Little, Brown, 1971); Arkadii Vaksberg, *Stalin against the Jews* (New York: Knopf, 1994); Timothy Snyder, *Bloodlands: Europe between Hitler and Stalin* (New York: Basic Books, 2010), 339–77; Joshua Rubenstin and Vladimir P. Naumov, eds., *Stalin's Secret Pogrom: The Postwar Inquisition of the Jewish Anti-Fascist Committee* (New Haven, Conn.: Yale University Press, 2001), 1–64.

17. This is, in large part, Jan Gross's argument about antisemitism in postwar Poland. See Jan Tomasz Gross, *Fear: Anti-Semitism in Poland After Auschwitz* (New York: Random House, 2006). For more on postwar pillaging of Jewish property see Jan Tomasz Gross, *Golden Harvest: Events at the Periphery of the Holocaust* (New York: Oxford University Press, 2012).

18. Cited in Blackwell, 371.

19. TsDAGOU f. 1, op. 23, d. 2366, ll. 3–4, 10–11. Accessed at CAHJP.

20. Ilya Luvish, "Post World War 2 Pogroms in Eastern Europe—Kiev Pogrom" http://www.ilyaluvish.com/2008/07/10/post-world-war-2-pogroms-in-eastern-europe-kiev-pogrom/#_ftnref16.

21. See, for instance, Mordechai Altshuler, "The Jewish Anti-fascist Committee in the USSR in Light of New Documentation," in Jonathan Frankel, ed. *Studies in Contemporary Jewry* (Bloomington: Indiana University Press, 1984), 271–80; Allan L. Kagedan, "Revival, Reconstruction or Rejection: Soviet Jewry in the Postwar Years, 1944–48," in Yaacov Ro'i ed., *Jews and Jewish Life in Russia and the Soviet Union* (Portland, Ore.: Frank Cass, 1995), 189–98.

22. Khayim Melamud, "Ineynem mit di landslayt," *Eynikayt*, March 27, 1947, 3.

23. Khayim Melamud, "In a Nokhmilkhomedikn shtetl," *Eynikayt*, April 8, 1947, 2.

24. Hershl Polyanker, "Baym kval," *Eynikayt* 144, December 3, 1947, 2.

25. Sh. Zinger, "Inem shtetl Sharhorod," *Eynikayt*, June 19, 1947, 2.

26. Altshuler, *Soviet Jewry*, 57–84.

27. Ibid., 40–48.

28. For more on contemporary Jewish customs about visits to graves in Podolia see Valery Dymshits, "Evreiskoe kladbishche: mesto, kuda ne khodiat," www.jewishpetersburg.ru/modules.php?name=News&file=article&sid=6114. For other reports of prayer helping alleviate the 1947 famine see Zubkova, 70.

29. The complete document is printed in Mitsel, 20–22.

30. Lukin, vol. 2, 263.

31. Ibid., 206.

32. This notion likely is derived from the *Seyfer Khsidim,* which states that one should not wear the shoes of the deceased. See also Berachot 57b.

33. For the reconstruction of religious life after the war see Yaacov Ro'i, "The Reconstruction of Jewish Communities in the USSR, 1944–1947" in David Bankier, ed., *The Jews Are Coming Back: The Return of the Jews to Their Countries of Origins after WWII* (Jerusalem: Yad Vashem, 2005), 186–205; and Yaacov Ro'i, "The Jewish Religion in the Soviet Union after World War II," in Yaacov Ro'i, ed., *Jews and Jewish Life in Russia and the Soviet Union* (Ilford: Frank Cass, 1995), 263–89; Mordechai Altshuler, *Religion and Jewish Identity in the Soviet Union, 1941–1964* (Waltham, Mass.: Brandeis University Press, 2012); and Mitsel.

34. For newfound Soviet tolerance of the Christian religion see Philip Walters, who writes, "In the last years of Stalin's rule, then, life for ordinary religious believers and the churches settled down at a level of humdrum difficulty." Walters,"A Survey of Soviet Religious Policy," in Sabrina Petra Ramet ed., *Religious Policy in the Soviet Union* (Cambridge: Cambridge University Press, 1993), 19. See also Tatiana Chumachenko, *Church and State in Soviet Russia: Russian Orthodoxy from World War II to the Khrushchev Years* (New York: M.E. Sharpe, 2002); and Zubkova, 68–73.

35. For the role of religious organizations in reintegrating veterans see Edele, 64–71.

36. Ro'i, "Reconstruction of Jewish Communities," 189.

37. TsDAGOU f. 4648 op. 2 d, 212, l. 10. Accessed at CAHJP RU 1913.

38. TsDAGOU f. 4648 op. 2 d, 212, l. 9. Accessed at CAHJP RU 1913 See also, Mordechai Altshuler, "Synagogues and Rabbis in the Soviet Union in the Light of Statistics, 1953–1964," *Jews in Eastern Europe* 1 [35] (1998).

39. Lukin, vol. 2, 140.

40. Mitsel, 19. For more on the Council for Affairs of Religious Cults see John Anderson, "The Council for Religious Affairs and the Shaping of Soviet Religious Policy," *Soviet Studies* 43, no. 4 (1991): 689–710; and Chumachenko.

41. TsDAGOU f. 4648, op. 2, d. 212, l. 20 Accessed at CAHJP RU 1913.

42. DAVO f. P-2700, op. 7, d. 404.

43. Mitsel, 29.

44. TsDAGOU f. 4648, op. 2, d, 212, ll. 249–253. Accessed at CAHJP RU 1913.

45. Altshuler, "Synagogues and Rabbis."

46. Mitsel, 25.

47. GAVO f. P-2700, op. 7, d. 404, l. 10. Accessed at CAHJP CD-20.

48. GAVO f. P-2700, op. 7, d. 478, ll. 86–89. Accessed at CAHJP RU 1983.

49. Cited in Mitsel, 56.

50. GAVO f. P-2700, op. 7, d. 404, l. 85. Accessed at CAHJP CD-20.

51. Mitsel, 15–16.

52. GAVO f. P-2700, op. 7, d. 404, ll. 82–5. Accessed at CAHJP CD-20.

53. Ibid.

54. GAVO f. P-2700, op. 7, d. 460. Accessed at CAHJP CD-20.

CONCLUSION

1. Zvi Gitelman, *Jewish Identity in Postcommunist Russia and Ukraine: An Uncertain Ethnicity* (Cambridge: Cambridge University Press, 2012). See also Mordechai Altshuler, *Religion and Jewish Identity in the Soviet Union, 1941–1964* (Waltham, Mass.: Brandeis University Press, 2012).

2. GARF, f. 7021, op. 54, d. 1243, l. 37. Accessed at USHMM RG 22.002.

3. Notably, Luisa Passerini makes the same point about references to fascism among the Italians she interviewed in the 1970s. See her "Work Ideology and Working Class Attitudes to Fascism," in Paul Thompson with Natasha Burchardt, eds., *Our Common History: The Transformation of Europe* (Atlantic Highlands, N.J.: Humanities Press, 1982), 60–61. In our own interviews, it is worth noting that when we have conducted interviews in larger cities or even among intellectuals in medium-sized towns, however, party politics has been integrated into life stories far more consistently.

4. Arnold Dashevsky and Ira Sheskin, eds., *American Jewish Year Book 2012* (London: Springer, 2012); Arnold Dashevsky, Sergio DellaPergola, and Ira Sheskin, eds., *World Jewish Population, 2010* (Storrs, Conn.: Mandell L. Berman Institute, 2010).

5. Cnaan Liphshiz, "With 25,000 Breslaver,Chasidim Coming to Uman for Rosh Hashanah, Small Ukrainian City Braces Itself," JTA, September 11, 2012. http://www.jta.org/news/article/2012/09/11/3106681/with-25000-breslaver -chasidim-coming-to-uman-for-rosh-hashanah-small-ukrainian-city-braces -itself.

6. Sergei Belokon, "Dvatsat let evreiskoi gosudarstvennosti v Ukraine, 1918–1938" *Personal* 2 (2004): 19.

BIBLIOGRAPHY

Archives

Gosudarstvennyi arkhiv Rossiiskoi federatsii (GARF), State Archive of the Russian Federation.
(Accessed at United States Holocaust Memorial Museum)
F. 7021 Archives of the Soviet Extraordinary State Commissions (USHMM RG 22.002)
F. P-8114 Jewish Anti-Fascist Committee
Derzhavnii arkhiv Vinnytskoi oblast (DAVO), State Archive of Vinnytsya Province
(Accessed at Central Archives for the History of the Jewish People, CAHJP)
CD 20
F. P-29 Vinnytsa District Committee of the Communist Party (Bolshevik) of Ukraine
F. P-2700 Council for Affairs of Religious Cults
F. P- 595 Vinnytsa District Executive Committee of the Bureau of National Minorities
Tsentralnii derzhavnii arkhiv gromadskikh obednan Ukraini (TsDAGOU), Central State Archive of Public Organizations
(Accessed at Central Archives for the History of the Jewish People)
F. 4648 Council for Affairs of Religious Cults
United States Holocaust Memorial Museum
RG-31.011M. Vinnitsa Oblast Archive Records
Acc.2000.214 Manya Ganiyevva, "Moi vospominaniia o perezhitom v gody voiny,"
Leo Baeck Institute Archive
ME 1416.MM III 14, "Memoir of Gerhard Schreiber."
USC Shoah Foundation Visual History Archive
Elizaveta Konstantinovna Bershadskaia. Interview 37797.
Arkadii Lvovich Burshtein. Interview 46564.
Pinia Nukhimovich Golfeld. Interview 31042.
Clara Grinberg. Interview 8412.
Khayke Yankelevna Gvinter. Interview 33216.
Nukhim Moiseevich Gvinter. Interview 32938.

Klara Katsman. Interview 31083.

Pesia Shaevna Kolodenker. Interview 34979.

Tatiana Moiseevna Marinina. Interview 37775.

Sofia Moiseevna Palatnikova. Interview 37784.

Donia Shoilevna Presler. Interview 31670.

Rita Davidovna Shveibish. Interview 31019.

Solomon Moiseevich Skliarskii. Interview 31843.

Anna Borisovna Tkach. Interview 36404.

Moyshe Aronovich Vanshelboim. Interview 27225.

Minna Vashavskay. Interview 24165.

Newspapers

Der emes

Eynikayt

Books and Articles

Abakumov, A. A. et al. *Narodnoe obrazovanie v SSSR: obshchesobrazovat shkola. Sbornik doikumentov, 1917–1973 gg.* Moscow: Pedagogica, 1974.

Abramson, Henry. *A Prayer for the Government: Ukrainians and Jews in Revolutionary Times, 1917–1920.* Cambridge, Mass.: Harvard University Research Institute and Center for Jewish Studies, 1999.

Adler, Eliyana. *In Her Hands: The Education of Jewish Girls in Tsarist Russia.* Detroit: Wayne State University Press, 2010.

Alpert, Yakov. *Making Waves: Stories from My Life.* New Haven, Conn.: Yale University Press, 2000.

Altshuler, Mordechai. "Escape and Evacuation of Soviet Jews at the Time of the Nazi Invasion: Policies and Realities." In *The Holocaust in the Soviet Union,* edited by Lucjan Dobroszycki and Jeffrey S. Gurock, 77–104. Armonk, N.Y.: M.E. Sharpe, 1993.

———. "The Jewish Anti-fascist Committee in the USSR in Light of New Documentation." In *Studies in Contemporary Jewry,* edited by Jonathan Frankel, 271–80. Bloomington: Indiana University Press, 1984.

———. *Religion and Jewish Identity in the Soviet Union, 1941–1964.* Waltham, Mass.: Brandeis University Press, 2012.

———. "Religion in the Soviet Union in the late 1930s in the Light of Statistics." *Jews and Jewish Topics in the Soviet Union and Eastern Europe* 14 (1991): 23–26.

———. *Soviet Jewry on the Eve of the Holocaust: A Social and Demographic Profile.* Jerusalem: Hebrew University of Jerusalem; Yad Vashem, 1998.

———. *Soviet Jewry since the Second World War: Population and Social Structure.* New York: Greenwood Press, 1987.

———. "Synagogues and Rabbis in the Soviet Union in the Light of Statistics, 1953–1964." *Jews in Eastern Europe* 35, no. 1 (1998), 39–46.

Altschuler, Mordechai, ed. and trans. "Antisemitism in Ukraine toward the End of the Second World War." *Jews in Eastern Europe* 22, no. 3 (1993): 40–81.

Altskan, Vadim, "On the Other Side of the River: Dr. Adolph Herschmann and the Zhmerinka Ghetto, 1941–1944." *Holocaust and Genocide Studies* 26, no. 1 (Spring 2012): 2–28.

Ancel, Jean. *Transnistria*. Bucharest: Atlas, 1998.

———. "The Romanian Campaigns of Mass Murder in Transnistria, 1941–1942." In *The Destruction of Romanian and Ukrainian Jews during the Antonescu Era*, edited by Randoph L. Braham, 87–133. New York: Rosenthal Institute for Holocaust Studies, 1997.

Anderson, John. "The Council for Religious Affairs and the Shaping of Soviet Religious Policy." *Soviet Studies* 43, no. 4 (1991): 689–710.

Angrick, Andrej. "Annihilation and Labor: Jews and Thoroughfare IV in Central Ukraine." In *Shoah in Ukraine: History, Testimony, Memorialization*, edited by Ray Brandon and Wendy Lower, 190–223. Bloomington: Indiana University Press, 2008.

An-sky, S. *Der yidisher khurbn fun Poyln, Galitsye un Bukovine*. Wilno: Farlag An-ski, 1921.

Arad, Yitzhak, ed. *Unichtozhenie evreev SSSR v gody nemetskoi okkupatsii, 1941–1944: sbornik dokumentov i materialov*. Jerusalem: Yad Vashem, 1991.

Arad, Yitzhak. *In the Shadow of the Red Banner: Soviet Jews in the War against Nazi Germany*. Jerusalem: Yad Vashem, 2010.

———. *The Holocaust in the Soviet Union*. Lincoln: University of Nebraska Press, 2009.

Arad, Yitzhak et al., eds. *The Einsatzgruppen Reports: Selections from the Dispatches of the Nazi Death Squads' Campaign against the Jews July 1941–January 1943*. New York: Holocaust Library, 1989.

Asher, Harvey. "The Holocaust and the USSR." In *Lessons and Legacies VII: The Holocaust in International Perspective*, edited by Dagmar Herzog, 253–68. Evanston, Ill.: Northwestern University Press, 2006.

Assman, Aleida. "History, Memory, and the Genre of Testimony." In *Poetics Today* 27, no. 2 (Summer 2006): 261–73.

Avrutin, Eugene M., Valerii Dymshits et al. *Photographing the Jewish Nation: Pictures from S. An-sky's Ethnographic Expeditions*. Waltham, Mass.: Brandeis University Press, 2009.

Bahloul, Joelle. *The Architecture of Memory: A Jewish-Muslim Household in Colonial Algeria, 1937–1962*. Cambridge: Cambridge University Press, 1996.

Bakaev, Iu. N. *Vlast' i religiia: istoriia otnoshenii, 1917–1941*. Khabarovsk: Izd-vo KhGTU, 2002.

Balashov, E. M. *Shkola v rossiiskom obshchestve, 1917–1927 gg*. St. Petersburg: Dmitrii Bulanin, 2003.

Ball, Alan M. *Russia's Last Capitalists: The Nepmen, 1921–1929*. Berkeley: University of California Press, 1987.

Ballard, Leslie Roy et al., *History of Oral History: Foundations and Methodologies*. New York: Altamira Press, 2007.

Ballinger, Pamela. *History in Exile: Memory and Identity at the Borders of the Balkans*. Princeton, N.J.: Princeton University Press, 2002.

Band, Arnold J. "Agnon's Synthetic Shtetl." In *The Shtetl: New Evaluations*, edited by Steven T. Katz, 233–43. New York: New York University Press, 2007.

Bartal, Israel. "Imagined Geography: The Shtetl, Myth, and Reality." In *The Shtetl: New Evaluations*, edited by Steven T. Katz, 179–92, New York: New York University Press, 2007.

Bartov, Omer. *The Eastern Front, 1941–45: German Troops and the Barbarisation of Warfare*. Basingstoke, Hampshire: Macmillan in association with St. Antony's College, Oxford, 1985.

———. *Erased: Vanishing Traces of Jewish Galicia in Present-Day Ukraine*. Princeton, N.J.: Princeton University Press, 2007.

Bauer, Yehuda. *The Death of the Shtetl*. New Haven, Conn.: Yale University Press, 2010.

Belokon, Sergei. "Dvatsat let evreiskoi gosudarstvennosti v Ukraine, 1918–1938." *Personal* 2 (2004): 19.

Bemporad, Elissa. *Becoming Soviet Jews: The Bolshevik Experiment in Minsk*. Bloomington: Indiana University Press, 2013.

———. "Behavior Unbecoming a Communist: Jewish Religious Practice in Soviet Minsk." *Jewish Social Studies* 14, no. 2 (2008): 1–31.

———. "Red Star on the Jewish Street: The Reshaping of Jewish life in Soviet Minsk, 1917–1939." Ph.D. diss., Stanford University, 2006.

Benz, Wolfgang, and Brigitte Mihok, eds. *Holocaust an der Peripherie: Juden und Judenmord in Rumänien und Transnistrien 1940–1944*. Berlin: Metropol, 2009.

Berger, Shlomo, ed. *From the Shtetl to the Metropolis*. Amsterdam: Menasseh Ben Israel Institute, 2012.

Berkhoff, Karel C. *Harvest of Despair: Life and Death in Ukraine under Nazi Rule* (Cambridge, Mass.: Belknap Press of Harvard University Press, 2004).

Bertelsen, Olga. "New Archival Documentation on Soviet Jewish Policy in Interwar Ukraine. Part One: GPU Repression of Zionist Parties and Groups in the 1920." *On the Jewish Street: A Journal of Russian-Jewish History and Culture* 1, no. 1 (2011): 75–76.

———. "New Archival Documentation on Soviet Jewish Policy in Interwar Ukraine. Part Two: GPU Repression of Jews and Jewish Groups in 1937–1940." *On the Jewish Street: A Journal of Russian-Jewish History and Culture* 1, no. 2 (2011): 172.

Blackwell, Martin. "Regime City of the First Category: The Experience of the Return of Soviet Power to Kyiv, Ukraine, 1943–1946." Ph.D. diss., Indiana University, 2005.

Bogoraz, V. G., ed. *Evreiskoe mestechko v revoliutsii. Ocherki*. Leningrad: Gosudarstvennoe izdatel'stvo, 1926.

Bonch-Bruyevich, Vladimir. "New Pogroms." *Soviet Russia: Official Organ of the Soviet Russia Government Bureau* 2, no. 5 (January 31, 1920): 97–98.

Borovoi, S. Ia. "Gibel' evreiskogo naseleniia Odessy vo vremia rumynskoi okkupatsii." In *Katastrofa i opir ukrain'skogo evreistva*. Kiev: National'na akademiia nauk Ukraini, 1999.

———. *Vospominaniia*. Moscow: Evreiskii universitet v Moskve, 1993.

Braham, Randolph L., ed. *The Destruction of Romanian and Ukrainian Jews during the Antonescu Era*. New York: Columbia University Press, 1997.

Brandon, Ray, and Wendy Lower, eds. *The Shoah in Ukraine: History, Testimony, Memorialization*. Bloomington: Indiana University Press, 2008.

Brown, R., and J. Kulik. "Flashbulb Memories." *Cognition* 5 (1977): 73–99.

Browning, Christopher. *Remembering Survival: Inside a Nazi Slave-Labor Camp*. New York and London: W.W. Norton & Company, 2010.

Bruce, Gary. *The Firm: The Inside Story of the Stasi*. Oxford; New York: Oxford University Press, 2010.

Budnitskii, Oleg. "Jews, Pogroms, and the White Movement: A Historiographical Critique." *Kritika: Explorations in Russian and Eurasian History* 2, no. 4 (2001): 751–72.

———. *Russian Jews between the Reds and the Whites, 1917–1920*. Philadelphia: University of Pennsylvania Press, 2011.

Carp, Matatias. *Transnistrie*. Buenos Aires: Besaraber landslayt-farayn in Argentine, 1950.

Center for Advanced Holocaust Studies and United States Holocaust Memorial Museum. *The Holocaust in the Soviet Union: Symposium Presentations*. Washington, D.C: Center for Advanced Holocaust Studies, United States Holocaust Memorial Museum, 2005.

Chasanowitch, Leon. *Der yidisher khurbn in Ukrayne*. Berlin: Yehuda, 1920.

Cherikover, I. M. *Antisemitizm un pogromen in Ukrayne, 1917–1918*. Berlin: Mizrekh yidisher historisher arkhiv, 1923.

Chervinsky, Julie, ed. *Lives of the Great Patriotic War: The Untold Stories of Soviet Jewish Soldiers in the Red Army during WWII*. New York: Blavatnik Archive Foundation, 2011.

Chklonikova, Elina. "The Transformation of the 'Shtetl' in the USSR in the 1930s." *Jews in Russia and Eastern Europe* 52, no. 1 (2004): 91–129.

Chumachenko, Tatiana. *Church and State in Soviet Russia: Russian Orthodoxy from World War II to the Khrushchev Years*, translated by Edward E. Roslof. New York: M.E. Sharpe, 2002.

Cohen, Gillian. *Memory in the Real World*. Hillsdale N. J.: Lawrence Erlbaum, 1989.

Confino, Alon. "Collective Memory and Cultural History: Problems of Method." *American Historical Review* 102, no. 5 (December 1997): 1386–1403.

Connerton, Paul. *How Societies Remember*. Cambridge: Cambridge University Press, 1989.

Crombag, Hans F. M., Willem A. Wagenaar, and Peter K. Van Koppen. "Crashing Memories and the Problem of 'Source Monitoring.'" *Applied Cognitive Psychology* 10, no 2 (April 1996): 95–104.

Crowley, David, and Susan E. Reid, eds. *Pleasures in Socialism: Leisure and Luxury in the Eastern Bloc*. Evanston, Ill.: Northwestern University Press, 2010.

Crowley, David, and Susan E. Reid, eds. *Socialist Spaces: Sites of Everyday Life in the Eastern Bloc*. New York: Oxford University Press, 2002.

Cutler, Irving. *The Jews of Chicago: From Shtetl to Suburb*. Urbana: University of Illinois Press, 2008.

Dashevsky, Arnold, and Ira Sheskin, eds., *American Jewish Year Book 2012*. London: Springer, 2012.

Dashevsky, Arnold, Sergio DellaPergola, and Ira Sheskin, eds., *World Jewish Population, 2010*. Storrs, Conn.: Mandell L. Berman Institute, 2010.

Davies, R. W. *The Socialist Offensive: The Collectivization of Soviet Agriculture, 1928–1930*. Cambridge, Mass.: Harvard University Press, 1980.

Davies, Sarah. *Popular Opinion in Stalin's Russia: Terror, Propaganda and Dissent, 1934–1941*. Cambridge: Cambridge University Press, 1997.

Dean, Martin. *Collaboration in the Holocaust: Crimes of the Local Police in Belorussia and Ukraine, 1941–44*. New York: St. Martin's Press, 2000.

Dekel-Chen, Jonathan L. *Farming the Red Land: Jewish Agricultural Colonization and Local Soviet Power, 1924–1941*. New Haven, Conn.: Yale University Press, 2005.

Deletant, Dennis. "Ghetto Experience in Golta, Transnistria, 1942–1944." *Holocaust and Genocide Studies* 18, no. 1 (Spring 2004): 1–26.

———. "Lebensbedingungen in den Ghettos und Arbeitslagern in Transnistrien 1942–1944: Der Fall Golta." In *Holocaust an der Peripherie: Judenpolitik und Judenmord in Rumänien und Transnistrien 1940–1944*, edited by Wolfgang Benz and Brigitte Mihok, 45–70. Berlin: Metropol, 2009.

———. "Transnistria and the Romanian Solution to the 'Jewish Problem.'" In *The Shoah in Ukraine History: Testimony, Memorialization*, edited by Ray Brandon and Wendy Lower, 156–89. Bloomington: Indiana University Press, 2008.

Desbois, Patrick. *The Holocaust by Bullets: A Priest's Journey to Uncover the Truth Behind the Murder of 1.5 Million Jews*. New York: Palgrave Macmillan, 2008.

Deutsch, Nathaniel. *The Jewish Dark Continent: Life and Death in the Russian Pale of Settlement*. Cambridge, Mass.: Harvard University Press, 2011.

Dimanshtein, Semen Markovich. *Yidn in F.S.S.R.* Moscow: Der emes, 1935.

Diner, Hasia. *Hungering for America: Italian, Irish, and Jewish Foodways in the Age of Migration*. Cambridge, Mass.: Harvard University Press, 2003.

Dolot, Miron. *Execution by Hunger: The Hidden Holocaust*. New York: W.W. Norton, 1987.

Draitser, Emil. *Shush! Growing Up Jewish under Stalin: A Memoir*. Berkeley: University of California Press, 2008.

Dubson, Vadim. "On the Problem of the Evacuation of Soviet Jews in 1941 (New Archival Sources)." In *Jews in Eastern Europe* 3, no. 40 (1999): 37–56.

Dymshits, V. A. "Evreiskoe kladbishche: mesto, kuda ne khodiat." www .jewishpetersburg.ru/modules.php?name=News&file=article&sid=6114.

———. "Idish v byvshikh shtetlakh Podolii: po materialam polevykh issledovanii 2004–2006." In *Idish: iazyk i kultura v sovetskom soiuze*, edited by L. Katsis, M. Kaspina, and D. Fishman, 347–55. Moscow: RGU, 2009.

Dymshits, V. A., A. L. Lvov, and A. V. Sokolova. *Shtetl xxi vek: polevye issledovaniia.* St. Petersburg: Izd-vo Evreiskogo universiteta v Sankt-Peterburga, 2008.

Edele, Mark. *Soviet Veterans of the Second World War: A Popular Movement in an Authoritarian Society, 1941–1991.* Oxford: Oxford University Press, 2009.

Eliach, Yaffa. *There Once Was a World: A 900-Year Chronicle of the Shtetl of Eishyshok.* Boston: Little, Brown, 1998.

Estraikh, Gennady. "Di metamorfozn fun Khanuke," *Forverts*, December 17–23, 2010, p. 11.

———. *Soviet Yiddish: Language Planning and Linguistic Development.* New York: Clarendon Press, 1999.

———. "The Soviet Shtetl in the 1920s." *Polin: Studies in Polish Jewry* 17 (2004): 197–212.

———. *In Harness: Yiddish Writers' Romance With Communism.* Syracuse, N.Y.: Syracuse University Press, 2005.

Estraikh, Gennady, and Mikhail Krutikov, eds. *The Shtetl: Image and Reality: Papers of the Second Mendel Friedman International Conference on Yiddish.* Oxford: Legenda, 2000.

Evtuhov, Catherine. *Portrait of a Russian Province: Economy, Society, and Civilization in Nineteenth-Century Nizhnii Novgorod.* Pittsburgh: University of Pittsburgh Press, 2011.

Figes, Orlando. *The Whisperers: Private Life in Stalin's Russia.* New York: Metropolitan Books, 2007.

Fishman, David Eliahu. "Preserving Tradition in the Land of Revolution: The Religious Leadership of Soviet Jewry, 1917–1930." In *The Uses of Tradition: Jewish Continuity in the Modern Era*, edited by Jack Wertheimer, 85–118. New York: JTS, 1992.

Fishman, Joshua. *In Praise of the Beloved Language: A Comparative View of Positive Ethnolinguistic Consciousness.* Berlin; New York: Mouton de Gruyter, 1997.

Fitzpatrick, Sheila. *Everyday Stalinism: Ordinary Life in Extraordinary Times: Soviet Russia in the 1930s.* New York: Oxford University Press, 1999.

———. *Stalin's Peasants: Resistance and Survival in the Russian Village after Collectivization.* New York: Oxford University Press, 1994.

Fletcher, William C. *The Russian Orthodox Church Underground, 1917–1970.* New York and Oxford: Oxford University Press, 1971.

Frankel, Jonathan, ed. *Studies in Contemporary Jewry: An Annual. 4, The Jews and the European Crisis, 1914–1921.* Bloomington: Indiana University Press, 1988.

Garros, Veronique et al. *Intimacy and Terror.* New York: New Press, 1997.

Gatrell, Peter. *A Whole Empire Walking: Refugees in Russia during World War I.* Bloomington: Indiana University Press, 1999.

Gershuni, A. A. *Yahadut ba-Rusyah ha-Sovyetit.* Jerusalem: Mosad ha-Rav Kuk, 1960.

———. *Yehudim ve-Yahadut bi-Verit ha-moatsot; Yahadut Rusyah mi-tekufat Stalin ve'ad ha-zeman ha-aharon.* Jerusalem: Feldheim, 1970.

Gheith, Jehanne M., and Katherine R. Jolluck. *Gulag Voices: Oral Histories of Soviet Incarceration and Exile.* New York: Palgrave Macmillan, 2011.

Gilboa, Yehoshua A. *The Black Years of Soviet Jewry, 1939–1953.* Boston: Little Brown, 1971.

Gitelman, Zvi Y. *Bitter Legacy: Confronting the Holocaust in the USSR.* Bloomington: Indiana University Press, 1997.

———. "History, Memory and Politics: The Holocaust in the Soviet Union." *Holocaust and Genocide Studies* 5, no. 1 (1990): 23–37.

———. *Jewish Identity in Postcommunist Russia and Ukraine: An Uncertain Ethnicity.* Cambridge: Cambridge University Press, 2012.

———. *Jewish Nationality and Soviet Politics: The Jewish Sections of the CPSU, 1917–1930.* Princeton, N.J.: Princeton University Press, 1972.

———. "Thinking about Being Jewish in Russia and Ukraine." In *Jewish Life after the USSR,* edited by Zvi Y. Gitelman, Musya Glants, and Marshall I. Goldman, 49–60. Bloomington: Indiana University Press, 2003.

Gittleman, Sol. *From Shtetl to Suburbia: The Family in Jewish Literary Imagination.* Boston: Beacon Press, 1978.

Golbert, Rebecca. "Holocaust Sites in Ukraine: Pechora and the Politics of Memorialization." *Holocaust and Genocide Studies* 18, no. 2 (Fall 2004): 205–233.

Gold, Ruth Glasberg, *Ruth's Journey: A Survivor's Memoir.* Gainesville: University Press of Florida, 1996.

Goldberg, B. Z. *The Jewish Problem in the Soviet Union: An Analysis and Solution.* New York: Crown Publishers, 1961.

Gordon, Shmuel. *Di fayl un der boygn.* Moscow: Sovetski pisatel, 1985.

Gorsuch, Anne. *Youth in Revolutionary Russia: Enthusiasts, Bohemians, Delinquents.* Bloomington: Indiana University Press, 2000.

Gottreich, Emily. *The Mellah of Marrakesh: Jewish and Muslim Space in Morocco's Red City.* Bloomington: Indiana University Press, 2007.

Gould, Jeffrey, and Aldo Lauria-Santiago. *To Rise in Darkness: Revolution, Repression, and Memory in El Salvador, 1920–1932.* Durham, N.C.: Duke University Press, 2008.

Greenbaum, Avraham. "The Jewish Religion in the Soviet Union in the 1930s." *Shvut* 1–2 [17–18] (1995): 146–60.

Grele, Ronald. *Envelopes of Sound: The Art of Oral History, Revised and Enlarged.* New York: Praeger, 1991.

Gross, Jan Tomasz. *Fear: Anti-Semitism in Poland after Auschwitz.* New York: Random House, 2006.

———. *Golden Harvest: Events at the Periphery of the Holocaust.* New York: Oxford University Press, 2012.

———. *Neighbors: The Destruction of the Jewish Community in Jedwabne, Poland.* New York: Penguin, 2002.

Grüner, Frank. "Jüdischer Glaube und religiöse Praxis unter dem stalinistischen Regime in der Sowjetunion während der Kriegs- und Nachkriegsjahre." *Jahrbücher für Geschichte Osteuropas* 52, no. 4 (2004): 534–56.

Hagen, Mark von. "From 'Great Fatherland War' to the Second World War: New Perspectives and Future Prospects." In *Stalinism and Nazism: Dictatorships in Comparison,* edited by Ian Kershaw and Moshe Lewin, 238–50. Cambridge: Cambridge University Press, 1997.

Halbwachs, Maurice. *On Collective Memory,* translated by Lewis A. Coser. Chicago: University of Chicago Press, 1992.

Hartman, Geoffrey. *Holocaust Remembrance: The Shapes of Memory.* Oxford: Wiley Blackwell, 1993.

Heifetz, Elias. *The Slaughter of the Jews in the Ukraine in 1919.* New York: T. Seltzer, 1921.

Hellbeck, Jochen. *Revolution on My Mind: Writing a Diary under Stalin.* Cambridge, Mass.: Harvard University Press, 2006.

Heskes, Irene. *Yiddish American Popular Songs 1895–1950.* Washington: Library of Congress, 1992.

Himka, John Paul. "The Holodomor in the Ukrainian-Jewish Encounter Initiative." Accessed at http://ualberta.academia.edu/JohnPaulHimka/Papers /492282/The_Holodomor_in_the_Ukrainian-Jewish_Encounter_Initiative.

———. "How Many Perished in the Famine and Why Does It Matter." *Brama: News and Community Press,* February 2, 2008. Accessed at http://ualberta.academia.edu/JohnPaulHimka/Papers/495038/ How_Many_Perished_in_the_Famine_and_Why_Does_It_Matter.

Hirsch, Marianne, and Leo Spitzer. *Ghosts of Home: The Afterlife of Czernowitz in Jewish Memory.* Berkeley: University of California Press, 2010.

———. "Testimonial Objects: Memory, Gender, and Transmission." *Poetics Today* 27, no. 2 (Summer 2006): 353–83.

Hoffman, Charles. *Red Shtetl: The Survival of a Jewish Town under Soviet Communism.* New York: American Jewish Joint Distribution Committee, 2002.

Hoffman, Eva. *Shtetl: The Life and Death of a Small Town and the World of Polish Jews.* Boston: Houghton Mifflin, 1997.

Holmes, Larry E. *The Kremlin and the Schoolhouse: Reforming Education in Soviet Russia, 1917–1931.* Bloomington: Indiana University Press, 1991.

Holtzman, Jon D. "Food and Memory." *Annual Review of Anthropology* 35 (October 2006): 361–78.

Huberman, Nahman. *Bershad: Be-tsel ayara.* Jerusalem: Entsiklopedyah shel galuyot, 1956.

Hundert, Gershon David. *Jews in Poland-Lithuania in the Eighteenth-Century: A Genealogy of Modernity.* Berkeley: University of California Press, 2006.

Ioanid, Radu. *The Holocaust in Romania: The Destruction of Jews and Gypsies under the Antonescu Regime, 1940–1944.* Chicago: Ivan R. Dee, 2000.

Ioannides, Dimitri, and Mara Cohen Ioannides. "The Jewish Past as a 'Foreign Country': The Travel Experiences of American Jews." In *Tourism, Diasporas, and Space,* edited by Tim Edward Coles and Dallen J. Timothy, 95–109. London and New York: Routledge, 2004.

Jagendorf, Siegfried. *Jagendorf's Foundry: Memoir of the Romanian Holocaust, 1941–1944.* New York: HarperCollins Publishers, 1991.

James, Daniel. *Doña María's Story: Life History, Memory, and Political Identity.* Durham, N.C.: Duke University Press, 2001.

Joffe, Natalie F. "The Dynamics of Benefice among East European Jews." *Social Forces* 27, no. 3 (March 1949): 238.

Judd, Robin. "Circumcision and Modern Jewish Life: A German Case Study, 1843–1914." In *The Covenant of Circumcision: New Perspectives on an Ancient Jewish Rite,* edited by Elizabeth Wynder Mark, 142–55. Hanover, N.H. and London: Brandeis University Press, 2003.

Kaczerginski, Szmerke. *Lider fun di getos un lagern.* New York: Tsiko, 1948.

Kagedan, Allan L. "Revival, Reconstruction or Rejection: Soviet Jewry in the Postwar Years, 1944–48." In *Jews and Jewish Life in Russia and the Soviet Union,* edited by Yaacov Ro'i, 189–98. Portland, Ore.: Frank Cass, 1995.

Kamenetz, Rodger. *Burnt Books: Rabbi Nachman of Bratslav and Franz Kafka.* New York: Schocken: 2010.

Kassow, Samuel. "The Shtetl in Interwar Poland." In *The Shtetl: New Evaluations,* edited by Steven T. Katz, 121–39. New York: NYU Press, 2007.

Katz, Dovid. *Words on Fire: The Unfinished Story of Yiddish.* New York: Basic Books, 2004.

Katz, Steven, ed. *The Shtetl.* New York: NYU Press, 2006.

Kazdan, H. Sh. *Fun kheyder un shkoles biz Tsisho. Dos ruslendishe yidntum in gerangl far shul, shprakh, kultur.* Mexico City: Shlomo Mendelson fond bay der gezelshaft far kultur un hilf, 1956.

Kelly, Catriona. *Children's World: Growing Up in Russia, 1890–1991.* New Haven, Conn.: Yale University Press, 2008.

———. "Ordinary Life in Extraordinary Times: Chronicles of the Quotidian in Russia and the Soviet Union." In *Kritika: Explorations in Russian and Eurasian History* 3, no. 4 (Fall 2002): 631–51.

Kerler, Dov-Ber. "The Soviet Yiddish Press: *Eynikayt* during the War, 1942–1945." In *Why Didn't the Press Shout? American and International Journalism during the Holocaust,* edited by Robert Moses Shapiro, 221–49. Hoboken, N.J.: Yeshiva University Press, 2003.

Khakkarainen, Marina. "Mestechko vspominaet o proshlom: rasskazy o evreiskikh remeslennikakh i remeslakh." In *Shtetl xxi vek: polevye issledovaniia*, edited by V. A. Dymshits, A. L. Lvov, and A. V. Sokolova, 159–76. St. Petersburg: Izd-vo evreiskogo universiteta v Sankt-Peterburga, 2008.

Kharkhordin, Oleg. *The Collective and the Individual in Russia: A Study of Practices*. Berkeley: University of California Press, 1999.

Kiper, Motl. *Dos yidishe shtetl in Ukrayne*. Kharkov: Melukhe farlag fun Ukraine, 1929.

Kipnis, Itsik. *Di shtub un untervegns*. Tel Aviv: I. L. Peretz, 1977.

———. *Mayn shtetele Sloveshne*, 2 vols. Tel Aviv: I. L. Peretz, 1971.

Kirschenbaum, Lisa A. *Small Comrades: Revolutionizing Childhood in Soviet Russia, 1917–1932*. New York: Routledge, 2000.

Klier, John D. "What Exactly Was a Shtetl?" In *The Shtetl: Image and Reality: Papers of the Second Mendel Friedman International Conference on Yiddish*, edited by Gennady Estraikh and Mikhail Krutikov, 23–35. Oxford: Legenda, 2000.

Kobrin, Rebecca. *Jewish Bialystok and Its Diaspora*. Bloomington: Indiana University Press, 2010.

Kostyrchenko, Gennadii. *Tainaia politika Stalina: Vlast' i antisemitism*. Moscow: Mezdunarodnye otnosheniia, 2001.

Kotkin, Stephen. *Magnetic Mountain: Stalinism as a Civilization*. Berkeley: University of California Press, 1995.

Kruglov, Aleksandr Iosifovich. *Poteri evreev ukrainy v 1941–1944 gg*. Kharkov: Tarbut laam, 2005.

Krutikov, Mikhail. *Yiddish Fiction and the Crisis of Modernity, 1905–1914*. Stanford, Calif.: Stanford University Press, 2001.

Kugelmass, Jack, and Jonathan Boyarin, eds. *From a Ruined Garden: The Memorial Books of Polish Jewry*. New York: Schocken Books, 1985.

Kuper, Mordechai. *Di yidn fun mayn benkshaft: zikhroynes fun mayn heymshtot Shargorod*. Buenos Aires: Poalei tsiyon, 1968.

Kuromiya, Hiroaki. *The Voices of the Dead: Stalin's Great Terror in the 1930s*. New Haven, Conn.: Yale University Press, 2007.

Kvavilashvili, Lia, Jennifer Mirani, Simone Schlagman, and Diana E. Kornbrot. "Comparing Flashbulb Memories of September 11 and the Death of Princess Diana: Effects of Time Delays and Nationality." *Applied Cognitive Psychology* 17 (2003): 1017–31.

Laban Hinton, Alexander, and Kevin Lewis O'Neill, eds. *Genocide: Truth, Memory and Representation*. Durham, N.C.: Duke University Press, 2009.

Langer, Lawrence L. *Holocaust Testimonies: The Ruins of Memory*. New Haven, Conn.: Yale University Press, 1993.

Lebina, Nataliia Borisovna. *Povsednevnaia zhizn' sovetskogo goroda: Normy i anomalii, 1920-e-1930 gody*. St. Petersburg: Zhurnal Neva and Letnii sad, 1999.

Lehmann, Rosa. *Symbiosis and Ambivalence: Poles and Jews in a Small Galician Town*. New York; Oxford: Berghahn Books, 2001.

Leibovich, Oleg. *V gorode M: Ocherki sotsialnoi povsednevnosti sovetskoi provintsii v 40–50-kh gg*. Perm: Iuil'media, 2009.

Lestschinsky, Jacob. *Dos sovetishe yidntum: zayn fargangenhayt un kegnvart*. New York: Yiddisher kemfer, 1941.

Levy, André. "To Morocco and Back: Tourism and Pilgrimage among Moroccan-Born Israelis." In *Grasping Land: Space and Place in Contemporary Israeli Discourse and Experience*, edited by Eyal Ben-Ari and Yoram Bilu, 25–46. Albany, N.Y.: SUNY Press, 1997.

Lewin, Moshe. *The Making of the Soviet System: Essays in the Social History of Interwar Russia*. London: Methuen; New York: Pantheon, 1985.

———. *Russian Peasants and Soviet Power: A Study of Collectivization*. New York: Norton, 1968.

Liber, George O. *Soviet Nationality Policy, Urban Growth, and Identity Change in the Ukrainian SSR, 1923–1934*. Cambridge: Cambridge University Press, 2002.

Liphshiz, Cnaan. "With 25,000 Breslaver,Chasidim Coming to Uman for Rosh Hashanah, Small Ukrainian City Braces Itself." JTA, September 11, 2012. http://www.jta.org/news/article/2012/09/11/3106681/with-25000-breslaver-chasidim-coming-to-uman-for-rosh-hashanah-small-ukrainian-city-braces-itself.

Lipphardt, Anna. *Vilne. Die Juden aus Vilnius nach dem Holocaust. Eine Transnationale Beziehungsgeschichte*. Paderborn, Germany: Schöningh, 2010.

Lipset, Harry. "Jewish Schools in the Soviet Union, 1917–1941: An Aspect of Soviet Minorities Policy." Ph.D. diss., Columbia University, 1965.

Lohr, Eric. *Nationalizing the Russian Empire: The Campaign against Enemy Aliens during World War I*. Cambridge, Mass.: Harvard University Press, 2003.

Lower, Wendy. *Nazi Empire-Building and the Holocaust in Ukraine*. Chapel Hill: University of North Carolina Press, 2005.

Lukin, V. M., A. V. Sokolova, and B. N. Khaymovich. *100 evreiskikh mestechek Ukrainy: istoricheskii putevoditel'*. 2 vols. Jerusalem: Jerusalem Center for Documentation of the Diaspora Heritage; St. Petersburg: Institute for Investigation of the Jewish Diaspora, 1997–2000.

Lukin, V. M., B. N. Khaimovich, and V. A. Dymshits, *Trudy po iudaike: istoriia evreev na Ukraine i v Belorussii: ekspeditsii. pamiatniki. nakhodki*. St. Petersburg, Peterburskii evreiskii universitet, 1994.

Luvish, Ilya. "Post World War 2 Pogroms in Eastern Europe—Kiev Pogrom." http://www.ilyaluvish.com/2008/07/10/post-world-war-2-pogroms-in-eastern-europe-kiev-pogrom/#_ftnref16.

Magocsi, Paul Robert. *A History of Ukraine: The Land and Its Peoples*. 2nd ed. Toronto: University of Toronto Press, 2010.

Manley, Rebecca. *To the Tashkent Station: Evacuation and Survival in the Soviet Union at War*. Ithaca, N.Y.: Cornell University Press, 2009.

Martin, Terry. *The Affirmative Action Empire: Nations and Nationalism in the Soviet Union, 1923–1939*. Ithaca, N.Y.: Cornell University Press, 2001.

Matveev, Yoel. "Di 'toyte khsidim' praven dem 200stn geboyrn-tog." *Forverts* August 12–18, 2011, p. 11.

McDannell, Colleen. *The Christian Home in Victorian America 1840–1900.* Bloomington: Indiana University Press, 1986.

Meckler, David. *Mentsh un mashin in Sovyetn-land.* Warsaw: J. Zyman, 1936.

Megargee, Geoffrey P. *USHMM Encyclopedia of Camps and Ghettos, 1933–1945.* Bloomington: Indiana University Press, 2009.

Meir, Natan. "From Pork to 'Kapores': Transformations in Religious Practice among the Jews of Late Imperial Kiev." *Jewish Quarterly Review* 97, no. 4 (2007): 616–45.

Melamud, Khayim. "In a Nokhmilkhomedikn shtetl." *Eynikayt,* April 8, 1947, p. 2.

———. "Ineynem mit di landslayt." *Eynikayt,* March 27, 1947, p. 3.

Mendelsohn, Daniel. *The Lost: A Search for the Six Million.* New York: Harper-Collins, 2006.

Merridale, Catherine. *Ivan's War: Life and Death in the Red Army, 1939–1945.* New York: Metropolitan Books, 2006.

———. *Night of Stone: Death and Memory in Twentieth-Century Russia.* New York: Penguin, 2002.

Messana, Paola. *Soviet Communal Living: An Oral History of the Kommunalka.* New York: Palgrave Macmillan, 2011.

Michman, Dan. *The Emergence of Jewish Ghettos during the Holocaust.* Cambridge: Cambridge University Press, 2011.

Miliakov, L. B., I. A. Ziuzina et al., eds. *Kniga pogromov: pogromy na Ukraine, v Belorussii i evropeiskoi chasti Rossii v period grazhdanskoi voiny, 1918–1922.* Sbornik dokumentov. Moscow: ROSSPEN, 2007.

Miron, Dan. *The Image of the Shtetl and Other Studies of Modern Jewish Literary Imagination.* Syracuse, N.Y.: Syracuse University Press, 2000.

Miron, Guy, ed. *The Yad Vashem Encyclopedia of the Ghettos during the Holocaust.* Jerusalem: Yad Vashem, 2009.

Mitsel, Mikhail. *Obshchiny iudeiskogo veroispovedaniia v Ukraine: Kiev, l'vov, 1945–1981.* Kiev: Sfera, 1998.

Moore, Deborah Dash. *GI Jews: How World War II Changed a Generation.* Cambridge, Mass.: Belknap Press of Harvard University Press, 2004.

Murav, Harriet. *Music from a Speeding Train: Jewish Literature in Post-Revolution Russia.* Stanford, Calif.: Stanford University Press, 2011.

Myerhoff, Barbara. *Number Our Days.* New York: Simon & Schuster, 1978.

Nakhimovsky, Alice. "You Are What They Ate: Russian Jews Reclaim Their Foodways." *Shofar: An Interdisciplinary Journal of Jewish Studies* 25, no. 1 (2006): 63–77.

Neisser, U., and N. Harrsh. "Phantom Flashbulbs: False Recollections of Hearing the News about Challenger." In *Affect and Accuracy in Recall: Studies of 'Flashbulb Memories,* edited by E. Winograd and U. Neisser, 9–31. Cambridge: Cambridge University Press, 1992.

Nora, Pierre. *Realms of Memory: Rethinking the French Past,* edited by Lawrence D. Kritzman, translated by Arthur Goldhammer. New York: Columbia University Press, 1996–98.

Nourkova, Veronika, Daniel M. Bernstein, and Elizabeth F. Loftus. "Altering Traumatic Memory." *Cognition and Emotion* 18, no. 4 (2004): 575–85.

Ofer, Dalia. "The Holocaust in Transnistria: A Special Case of Genocide." In *The Holocaust in the Soviet Union: Studies and Sources on the Destruction of the Jews in the Nazi-Occupied Territories of the USSR, 1941–1945,* edited by Lucjan Dobroszycki and Jeffrey S. Gurock, 133–54. Armonk, N.Y.: M. E. Sharpe, 1993.

Olgin, Moyshe. *Mayn shtetl in Ukrayne.* New York: M. Gurevitsh'es farlag, 1921.

Olick, Jeffrey K., Vered Vinitzky-Seroussi, and Daniel Levy, eds. *The Collective Memory Reader.* New York and Oxford: Oxford University Press, 2011.

Orla-Bukowska, Annamaria. "Maintaining Borders, Crossing Borders: Social Relationship in the Shtetl." In *Polin: Studies in Polish Jewry* 17 (2004): 171–95.

Osherowitch, Mendl. *Shtet un shtetlekh in Ukrayne.* New York: M. Osherowitch Jubilee Committee, 1948.

———. *Vi mentshn lebn in Sovet Rusland.* New York: M. Osherowitch, 1933.

Osokina, E. A., Kate S. Transchel, and Greta Bucher. *Our Daily Bread: Socialist Distributions and the Art of Survival in Stalin's Russia, 1927–1941.* Armonk, N.Y.: M.E. Sharpe, 2001.

Paperno, Irina. "Personal Accounts of the Soviet Experience." *Kritika: Explorations in Russian and Eurasian History* 3, no. 4 (Fall 2002): 577–610.

Passerini, Luisa. "Work Ideology and Working-Class Attitudes to Fascism." In *Our Common History: The Transformation of Europe,* edited by Paul Thompson with Natasha Burchardt, 54–78. Atlantic Highlands, N.J.: Humanities Press.

Peltz, Rakhmiel. *From Immigrant to Ethnic Culture: American Yiddish in South Philadelphia.* Stanford, Calif.: Stanford University Press, 1997.

Peris, Daniel. *Storming the Heavens: The Soviet League of the Militant Godless.* Ithaca, N.Y.: Cornell University Press, 1998.

Pinchuk, Ben-Cion. "The East European Shtetl and Its Place in Jewish History." In *Revue des études juives* 164, nos. 1–2 (January–June 2005): 187–212.

———. "How Jewish Was the Shtetl?" In *Polin: Studies in Polish Jewry* 17 (2004): 109–118.

———. *Shtetl Jews under Soviet Rule: Eastern Poland on the Eve of the Holocaust.* Oxford: Blackwell, 1991.

———. "Was There a Soviet Policy for Evacuating the Jews? The Case of the Annexed Territories." *Slavic Review* 39, no. 1 (1980): 44–55.

Pinkus, Benjamin. *Jews of the Soviet Union: The History of a National Minority.* Cambridge and New York: Cambridge University Press, 1988.

Polonsky, Antony, ed. *From Shtetl to Socialism: Studies from Polin.* Washington, D.C.: Littman Library of Jewish Civilization, 1993.

Polyanker, Hershl. *Geven amol a shtetl: roman in dray teyln.* Moscow: Sovetski pisatel, 1991.

Portelli, Alessandro. *The Death of Luigi Trastulli and Other Stories: From and Meaning in Oral History.* Albany, N.Y.: SUNY University Press, 1990.

———. *They Say in Harlan County: An Oral History.* New York and Oxford: Oxford University Press, 2010.

Qualls, Karl. *From Ruin to Reconstruction: Urban Identity in Soviet Sevastopol after World War II.* Ithaca, N.Y.: Cornell University Press, 2009.

Raleigh, Donald J. *Russia's Sputnik Generation: Soviet Baby Boomers Talk about Their Lives.* Bloomington: Indiana University Press, 2006.

———. *Soviet Baby Boomers: An Oral History of Russia's Cold War Generation.* Oxford; New York: Oxford University Press, 2012.

Ransel, David. *Village Mothers: Three Generations of Change in Russia and Tataria.* Bloomington: Indiana University Press, 2000.

Rapoport, Iakov Lvovich. *Na rubezhe dvukh vekov: Delo vrachei 1953 goda.* Moscow: Kniga, 1988.

Redlich, Shimon. *Together and Apart in Brzezany: Poles, Jews, and Ukrainians, 1918–1945.* Bloomington: Indiana University Press, 2002.

Richmond, Theo. *Konin: One Man's Quest for a Vanished Jewish Community.* New York: Vintage, 1996.

Ricoeur, Paul. *Memory, History, Forgetting,* translated by Kathleen Blarney and David Pellauer. Chicago: University of Chicago Press, 2006.

Ro'i, Yaacov. "Ha-pesakh mul ha-mishtar ha-sovyeti." *Bar Ilan* 24/25 (1989): 173–95.

———. "The Jewish Religion in the Soviet Union After World War II." In *Jews and Jewish Life in Russia and the Soviet Union,* edited by Yaacov Ro'i, 263–89. Ilford: Frank Cass, 1995.

———. "The Reconstruction of Jewish Communities in the USSR, 1944–1947." In *The Jews Are Coming Back: The Return of the Jews to Their Countries of Origins after WWII,* edited by David Bankier, 186–205. Jerusalem: Yad Vashem, 2005.

Roseman, Mark. *A Past in Hiding: Memory and Survival in Nazi Germany.* New York: Metropolitan Books, 2001.

Rosen, Alan. *The Wonder of Their Voices: The 1946 Holocaust Interviews of David Boder.* Oxford: Oxford University Press, 2010.

Rosenthal Stopnicka, Celia. "Social Stratification of the Jewish Community in a Small Polish Town." *American Journal of Sociology* 59, no. 1 (July 1953): 1–10.

Roskies, David G. *The Jewish Search for a Usable Past.* Bloomington: Indiana University Press, 1999.

Rothenberg, Joshua. *The Jewish Religion in the Soviet Union.* New York: Ktav, 1972.

Rubenstein, Joshua et. al., *The Unknown Black Book: The Holocaust in the German-Occupied Soviet Territories.* Bloomington: Indiana University Press, 2007.

Rubenstein, Joshua, and Vladimir P. Naumov, eds. *Stalin's Secret Pogrom: The Postwar Inquisition of the Jewish Anti-Fascist Committee.* New Haven, Conn.: Yale University Press, 2001.

Rubin, Ruth. "Nineteenth-Century Yiddish Folksongs of Children in Eastern Europe." *Journal of American Folklore* 65, no. 257 (July–September 1952): 231–32.

Sacks, Michael Paul. "Privilege and Prejudice: The Occupations of Jews in Russia in 1989." *Slavic Review* 57, no. 2 (Summer 1998): 247–66.

Safran, Gabriella. *Wandering Soul: The Dybbuk's Creator, S. An-sky.* Cambridge, Mass.: Harvard University Press, 2010.

Safran, Gabriella, and Steven J. Zipperstein, eds. *The Worlds of S. An-sky: A Russian Jewish Intellectual at the Turn of the Century.* Stanford, Calif.: Stanford University Press, 2006.

Salsitz, Norman, and Richard Skolnik. *A Jewish Boyhood in Poland: Remembering Kolbuszowa.* Syracuse, N.Y.: Syracuse University Press, 1999.

Samuel, Maurice. *Little Did I Know: Recollections and Reflections.* New York: Alfred A. Knopf, 1963.

Schmolck, H., E. A. Buffalo, and L. R. Squire. "Memory Distortions Develop over Time: Recollections of the O. J. Simpson Trial Verdict after 15 and 32 Months." *Psychological Science* 11 (2000): 39–45.

Schulman, Elias. "The Yiddish School in the Soviet Union, 1918–1948." Ph.D. diss., Dropsie College, 1965.

Schwarz, Solomon M. *The Jews in the Soviet Union.* Syracuse, N.Y.: Syracuse University Press, 1951.

Shachan, Avigdor. *Burning Ice: The Ghettos of Transnistria,* translated by Shmuel Himelstein. Boulder, Colo.: East European Monographs, 1996.

Sharansky, Natan. *Fear No Evil.* New York: Public Affairs, 1998.

Shneer, David. *Through Soviet Jewish Eyes: Photography, War and the Holocaust.* New Brunswick, N.J.: Rutgers University Press, 2011.

———. *Yiddish and the Creation of Soviet Jewish Culture: 1918–1930.* Cambridge: Cambridge University Press, 2004.

Shopes, Linda. "Human Subjects and IRB Review." http://www.oralhistory.org /about/do-oral-history/oral-history-and-irb-review.

Shternshis, Anna. "May Day, Tractors, and Piglets: Yiddish Songs for Little Communists." In *The Art of Being Jewish in Modern Times,* edited by Barbara Kirshenblatt-Gimblett and Jonathan Karp, 83–97. Philadelphia: University of Pennsylvania Press, 2008.

———. "Passover in the Soviet Union, 1917–1941." In *East European Jewish Affairs* 31, no. 1 (2001): 61–76.

———. *Soviet and Kosher: Jewish Popular Culture in the Soviet Union, 1923–1939.* Bloomington: Indiana University Press, 2006.

Siegelbaum, Lewis H. *Cars for Comrades: The Life of the Soviet Automobile.* Ithaca, N.Y.: Cornell University Press, 2008.

Slezkine, Yuri. *The Jewish Century*. Princeton, N.J.: Princeton University Press, 2006.

Sloin, Andrew Jay. "Pale Fire: Jews in Revolutionary Belorussia, 1917–1929." Ph.D. diss., University of Chicago, 2009.

Snyder, Timothy. *Bloodlands: Europe between Hitler and Stalin*. New York: Basic Books, 2010.

Sokolova, Alla. "Arkhitektura shtetla v kontekste traditsionnoi kul'tury." In *100 evreiskikh mestechek Ukrainyi: istoricheskii putevoditel*, edited by V. A. Lukin, A. V. Sokolova, and B. Khaimovich, vol. 2, 53–84. Jerusalem: Jerusalem Center for Documentation of the Diaspora Heritage; St. Petersburg: Institute for Investigation of the Jewish Diaspora, 1997–2000.

——. "Evreiskie mestechki pamiati: lokalizatsia shtetla." In *Shtetl, XXI vek: Polevyie issledovaniia*, edited by V. A. Dymshits, A. L. Lvov, and A. V. Sokolova. St. Petersburg: Jewish University Press, 2008, 29–64.

——. "House-Building Tradition of the Shtetl in Memorials and Memories (Based on Materials of Field Studies in Podolia)." *East European Jewish Affairs* 41, no. 3 (December 2011): 111–35.

——. "The Podolian Shtetl as Architectural Phenomenon." In *The Shtetl: Image and Reality: Papers of the Second Mendel Friedman International Conference on Yiddish*, edited by Gennady Estraikh and Mikhail Krutikov, 36–79. Oxford: Legenda, 2000.

Solonari, Vladimir. *Purifying the Nation: Population Exchange and Ethnic Cleansing in Nazi-Allied Romania*. Baltimore: Johns Hopkins University Press, 2009.

Starr Sered, Susan. *Women as Ritual Experts: The Religious Lives of Elderly Jewish Women in Jerusalem*. New York and Oxford: Oxford University Press, 1992.

Stiff, Nahum. *Pogromen in Ukrayne*. Berlin: Vostok, 1923.

Sutton, David E. *Remembrance of Repasts: An Anthropology of Food and Memory*. Oxford and New York: Berg, 2001.

Swet, Gershon. "Jewish Religion in Soviet Russia." In *Russian Jewry 1917–1967*, edited by Gregor Aronson et al. 209–222. New York: Thomas Yoseloff, 1969.

Tartakovsky, Dmitry, "Parallel Ruptures: Jews of Bessarabia and Transnistria Between Romanian Nationalism and Soviet Communism, 1918–1940." Ph.D. diss., University of Illinois at Urbana-Champaign, 2009.

Teich, Meir. "The Jewish Self-Administration in Ghetto Shargorod (Transnistria)." In *Yad Vashem Studies* 2, no. 1 (1958): 219–54.

Teller, Adam. "The Shtetl as an Arena for Integration in the Eighteenth Century." In *Polin. Studies in Polish Jewry* 17 (2004): 25–40.

Thelen, David. "Memory and American History." *Journal of American History* 75, no. 4 (March 1989): 1117–29.

Thompson, Paul. *The Voice of the Past: Oral History*. New York: Oxford University Press, 2000.

Timo Vikhavainen, ed. *Normy i tsennosti povsednevnoi zhizni: Stanovlenie sotsi-alisticheskogo obraza zhizni v Rossii, 1920–1030-e- gody*. St. Petersburg: Zhurnal Neva, 2000.

Tonkin, Elizabeth. *Narrating Our Pasts: The Social Construction of Oral History*. Cambridge: Cambridge University Press, 1992.

Tshernovetski, Valentine. *Teplik, mayn shtetele*. Buenos Aires: Argentiner magazin, 1946–1950.

Tumarkin, Nina. *The Living and the Dead: The Rise and Fall of the Cult of World War II in Russia*. New York: Basic Books, 1994.

Uehling, Greta Lynn. *Beyond Memory: The Crimean Tatars' Deportation and Return*. New York: Palgrave Macmillan, 2004.

Vaksberg, Arkadii. *Stalin against the Jews*. New York: Knopf, 1994.

Veidlinger, Jeffrey. *Jewish Public Culture in the Late Russian Empire*. Bloomington: Indiana University Press, 2009.

———. *The Moscow State Yiddish Theater: Jewish Culture on the Soviet Stage*. Bloomington: Indiana University Press, 2000.

Viola, Lynne. *Peasant Rebels under Stalin: Collectivization and the Culture of Peasant Resistance*. New York: Oxford University Press, 1996.

Viola, Lynne, and Denis Danilov. *War against the Peasantry, 1927–1930*, vol. 1: *The Tragedy of the Soviet Countryside*. New Haven, Conn.: Yale University Press, 2005.

Viola, Lynne, Denis Kozlov, and V. P. Danilov, eds. *The War against the Peasantry, 1927–1930*. New Haven, Conn.: Yale University Press, 2005.

Vsesoiuznaia perepis naseleniia 1926 goda. Moscow: TSSU Soiuza SSSR, 1928–1933. 56 volumes.

Walters, Philip. "A Survey of Soviet Religious Policy." In *Religious Policy in the Soviet Union*, edited by Sabrina Petra Ramet, 3–30. Cambridge: Cambridge University Press, 1993.

Weinberg, Bob. "The Politics of Remembering: The Treatment of the Holocaust in the Soviet Union." In *Lessons and Legacies VII: The Holocaust in International Perspective*, edited by Dagmar Herzog, 314–29. Evanston, Ill.: Northwestern University Press, 2006.

Weiner, Amir. *Making Sense of War: The Second World War and the Fate of the Bolshevik Revolution*. Princeton, N.J.: Princeton University Press, 2001.

Weissler, Chava. *Voices of the Matriarchs: Listening to the Prayers of Early Modern Jewish Women*. Boston, Mass: Beacon Press, 1998.

Werth, Alexander. *Russia at War, 1941–1945*. London: Pan, 1965.

Wiesel, Elie. *Jews of Silence: A Personal Report on Soviet Jewry*. New York: Holt, Rinehart and Winston, 1966.

———. "The World of the Shtetl." In *The Shtetl: New Evaluations*, edited by Steven T. Katz, 290–306. New York: NYU Press, 2007.

Wood, Elizabeth A. *Performing Justice: Agitation Trials in Early Soviet Russia*. Ithaca, N.Y.: Cornell University Press, 2005.

Xinxin Zhang, and Sang Ye. *Chinese Lives, an Oral History of Contemporary China,* edited by W. J. F. Jenner and Delia Davin. New York: Pantheon, 1987.

Yalen, Deborah. "Documenting the New Red Kasrilevke." In *East European Jewish Affairs* 37, no. 3 (2007): 353–75.

———. "Red Kasrilevke: Ethnographies of Economic Transformation in the Soviet Shtetl, 1917–1939." Ph.D. diss., University of California, Berkeley, 2007.

Yekelchyk, Serhy. *Ukraine: Birth of a Modern Nation.* Oxford; New York: Oxford University Press, 2007.

Yodfat, Aryeh. "The Closure of Synagogues in the Soviet Union." *Soviet Jewish Affairs* 3 (1973): 48–56.

———. "Jewish Religious Communities in the USSR." *Soviet Jewish Affairs* 2 (1971): 61–67.

Young, Glennys. *Power and the Sacred in Revolutionary Russia: Religious Activists in the Village.* University Park: Pennsylvania State University Press, 1997.

Young, James E. *The Texture of Memory: Holocaust Memorials and Meaning.* New Haven, Conn.: Yale University Press, 1994.

Yurchak, Alexei. *Everything Was Forever, Until It Was No More: The Last Soviet Generation.* Princeton, N.J.: Princeton University Press, 2005.

Zabarko, Boris, ed. *The Holocaust in Ukraine.* London and Portland: Vallentine Mitchell, 2005.

Zborowski, Mark, with Elizabeth Herzog. *Life Is with People: The Culture of the Shtetl.* New York: Schocken Books, 1952.

Zeltser, Arkadii. *Evrei Sovetskoi provintsii: Vitebsk i mestechki, 1917–1941.* Moscow: ROSSPEN, 2006.

———. "Shkola na idishe i samoidentifikatsiia belorusskikh evreev." In *Idish: iazik i kultura v sovetskom soiuze,* edited by L. Katsis, M. Kaspina, and D. Fishman, 218–28. Moscow: RGU, 2009.

Zemskov, V. I. "K voprosy o repatriatsii sovetskikh grazhdan 1944–1951 gody." *Istoriia SSSR* 1990, no. 4.

Zieliński, Konrad. "The Changing Shtetl in the Kingdom of Poland during the First World War." In *Polin. Studies in Polish Jewry* 17 (2004): 119–31.

Zinger, L. G. *Dos banayte folk (tsifern un faktn vegn di yidn in FSSR).* Moscow: Der emes, 1941.

Zinger, Sh. "Inem shtetl Sharhorod." *Eynikayt,* June 19, 1947, p. 2.

Zipperstein, Steven J. *Imagining Russian Jewry: Memory, History, Identity.* Seattle: University of Washington Press, 1999.

———. "Underground Man: The Curious Case of Mark Zborowski and the Writing of a Modern Jewish Classic." *Jewish Review of Books* 2 (Summer 2010): 38–42.

Zubkova, Elena Iur'evna. *Russia after the War: Hopes, Illusions, and Disappointments, 1945–1957.* Armonk, N.Y.: M.E. Sharpe, 1998.

ACKNOWLEDGMENTS

This book is the product of a collective effort. I am grateful to all those people throughout Ukraine who allowed us to interview them, often on multiple occasions. I recognize that it is sometimes difficult to speak about the past on camera to strangers, and I hope that all those who chose to engage with us came out of the process gratified with the experience. I hope as well that they feel this book has done them justice.

The initial idea to interview Yiddish-speakers in Eastern Europe came from Dovid Katz, and I am grateful to him for joining us on several of our early expeditions, and for generously sharing with us his expertise. Dov-Ber Kerler extended Dovid's project into Ukraine, and conducted most of the interviews: his enthusiasm, exuberance, and optimistic energy always bring out the best in people. I have seen elderly, frail, and somber people come to life when they speak with Dov-Ber, joyfully relieving their youthful vigor. I cannot thank Dov-Ber enough for inviting me along with him and for helping me with this book at every step of the way.

I appreciate the assistance we were given in Ukraine by Liudmilla Makedonskaya, who helped organize several of our trips, and by our drivers, Petr Ivanov and Yuri Shpuryk. Artur Frątczak and Pawel Figurski kept the cameras rolling for many hours and often shared with us their own distinctive viewpoints on what we were hearing. Our graduate students, Margot Valles and Anya Quilitzsch, were always helpful when they came along on expeditions. Pearl Gluck came with us in 2010, filmed every moment, and is working with us on a film about the project. I am grateful as well to Moyshe Lemster, who joined a few expeditions and lent us his humor and expertise on Bessarabia.

In Bloomington, I had the benefit of having several graduate student assistants, who helped construct summaries of the interviews and aided with translations: Sebastian Schulman, Margot Valles, Charles Bonds, and especially Anya Quilitzsch, who also compiled the Appendix and sat with me for hours pouring over video. Anya, Sebastian, and Charles also read the complete manuscript and provided helpful suggestions. I thank Amy Simon and Anthony Zannino for helping me identify and photocopy documents at the United

States Holocaust Memorial Museum in Washington D.C., and Vadim Atskan at the museum for sharing archival guides with me. I also appreciate having the opportunity to share ideas with my colleagues in Bloomington. Hiroaki Kuromiya and Dov-Ber Kerler, in particular, read the entire manuscript and gave helpful comments; Mark Roseman also read and commented on significant portions. I benefited particularly from discussions about Soviet and Ukrainian history with Ben Eklof, David Ransel, and Padraic Kenney; about oral history with Jeff Gould and John Bodnar; about Jews and Judaism with Matthias Lehmann and Shaul Magid; and about all of the above with Mark Roseman. Thanks also to those who read the entire manuscript as referees for IU Press: Anna Shternshis and a referee who remained anonymous, and to others who have read chapters or commented on presentations at various points: Zvi Gitelman, Samuel Kassow, Antony Polonsky, Jonathan Dekel-Chen, and Louis Greenspan.

The entire Archive of Historical and Ethnographic Yiddish Memories (AHEYM) was collected and preserved thanks to the generous assistance of two Preservation and Access grants from the National Endowment for the Humanities. I am grateful to the NEH for its support of the project. The NEH grants allowed us to work with the Archives of Traditional Music at Indiana University in preserving, cataloguing, and transcoding the interviews. Thanks to Alan Burdette, Suzanne Mudge, Will Cowan, Daniel Reed, and Marilyn Graf for their cooperation, and especially to graduate student assistant Anthony Guest-Scott for diligently transferring and transcoding the entire collection. I owe a special thanks to Asya Vaisman who came on as project director to oversee the archive for two years.

The title for the book was proposed by Dan O'Connell, and I thank him for working with me at an early stage in conceiving the project. Thanks to Paul and Jeannette Smedberg for designing the maps. Thanks to Indiana University Press and Janet Rabinowitch in particular, for working with me on this project from the beginning to the end. As university presses have come under increasing threat, IU Press has been stalwart in its commitment to extending the frontiers of knowledge by publishing cutting edge scholarship in high quality editions at affordable prices. I am privileged to be among those who have published multiple books with the press, and am grateful to Janet for her constant guidance and support.

Finally, I would like to thank my family—Rebecca, Naomi, and Leah Mae—for their love.

INDEX

JEFFREY VEIDLINGER is Joseph Brodsky Collegiate Professor of History and Judaic Studies at the University of Michigan. He is author of *The Moscow State Yiddish Theater* (IUP, 2006) and *Jewish Public Culture in the Late Russian Empire* (IUP, 2009).